ON COMPUTER SYSTEMS AND TELECOMMUNIC...

	PRINCIPLES OF DISTRIBUTED PROCESSING	INTRODUCTION TO TELEPROCESSING	TELEMATIC SOCIETY
OTEX	COMPUTER NETWORKS AND DISTRIBUTED PROCESSING	INTRODUCTION TO COMPUTER NETWORKS	TELE-COMMUNICATIONS AND THE COMPUTER (second edition)
GN OF MPUTER OGUES	DESIGN AND STRATEGY FOR DISTRIBUTED PROCESSING	TELEPROCESSING NETWORK ORGANIZATION	COMMUNICATIONS SATELLITE SYSTEMS
AMMING TIME R SYSTEMS	DISTRIBUTED FILE AND DATA-BASE DESIGN	SYSTEMS ANALYSIS FOR DATA TRANSMISSION	FUTURE DEVELOPMENTS IN TELE-COMMUNICATIONS (second edition)
GN OF TIME R SYSTEMS			
ks On ve Systems	Books On Distributed Processing	Books On Teleprocessing	Books On Telecommunications

**SYSTEM DESIGN
FROM PROVABLY
CORRECT CONSTRUCTS**

A *James Martin* **BOOK**

SYSTEM
FROM
CORRECT

DESIGN PROVABLY CONSTRUCTS

JAMES MARTIN

The Beginnings of True Software Engineering

PRENTICE-HALL, INC., Englewood Cliffs, New Jersey 07632

Library of Congress Cataloging in Publication Data

MARTIN, JAMES (date)
System design from provably correct constructs.

Includes bibliographies and index.
1. System design.   2. Electronic digital computers—
Programming.   3. Debugging in computer science.
I. Title.
QA76.9.S88M37 1984   001.64′25   84-16063
ISBN 0-13-881483-X

Editorial/production supervision: *Kathryn Gollin Marshak
and Linda Mihatov*
Manufacturing buyer: *Gordon Osbourne*

System Design from Provably Correct Constructs
James Martin

Printed in the United States of America

10 9 8 7 6 5 4 3 2 1

ISBN 0-13-881483-X

PRENTICE-HALL INTERNATIONAL, INC., *London*
PRENTICE-HALL OF AUSTRALIA PTY. LIMITED, *Sydney*
EDITORA PRENTICE-HALL DO BRASIL, LTDA., *Rio de Janeiro*
PRENTICE-HALL CANADA INC., *Toronto*
PRENTICE-HALL OF INDIA PRIVATE LIMITED, *New Delhi*
PRENTICE-HALL OF JAPAN, INC., *Tokyo*
PRENTICE-HALL OF SOUTHEAST ASIA PTE. LTD., *Singapore*
WHITEHALL BOOKS LIMITED, *Wellington, New Zealand*

TO CORINTHIA

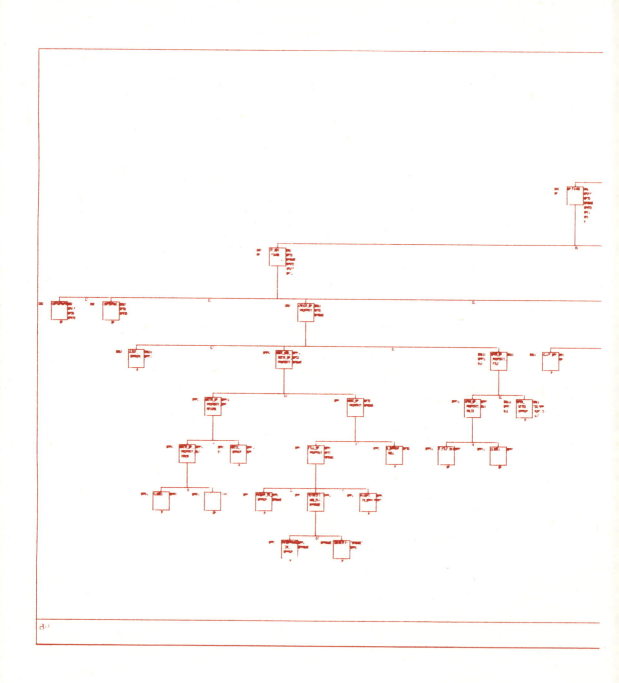

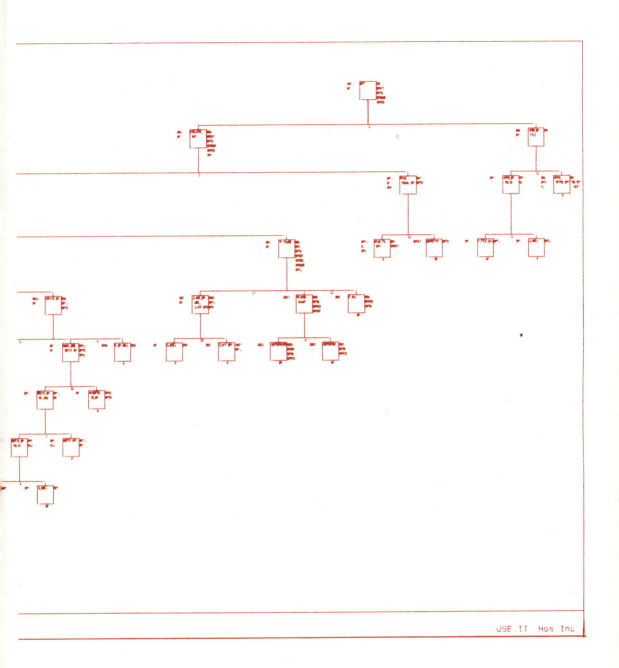

This book presents not merely a design technique but an important way of thinking about systems which ought to be understood by all DP staff members.

The technique applies from the highest level of systems conceptualization down to the lowest level of program design. It results in automatic generation of program code, without programmers. The automation can save much time and money.

*Its main importance, however, is that the logic so created is **provably** free from internal errors and inconsistencies. At last we have the capability to create specifications for complex systems which are engineered with a precise discipline to be bug-free.*

CONTENTS

15   Data Flow Diagrams   *251*

PART IV   EFFECTS

16   Errors and Verification   *269*

17   Solutions to DP's Problems   *281*

18   The Changing Development Life Cycle   *301*

PREFACE

Historians of future centuries will look back at the growth of computing as one of the most important factors in the fate of humankind. Computerizing began, they will say, with crude machines and manual techniques. But just as the industrial revolution, two centuries before, was to bootstrap itself from primitive beginnings, so also was the computer revolution.

The industrial revolution led to machines with immensely greater *physical* muscle than those of human beings; the computer revolution led to machines with immensely greater *mental* muscle than those of human beings. Awesome libraries of programmed knowledge and functions circled the earth, available everywhere via computer networks. The screens in almost every home and office became windows to logic power vastly beyond the comprehension of any one person. New social contracts had to evolve to establish people's roles in a world where cybernetic tools outstripped human brains as much as a jumbo jet outstrips a butterfly.

The steam engine introduced a new phase into the ascent of machines, giving the first power source that could be installed *anywhere*. An equivalent phase in the ascent of computers was the *automation* of the methods of systems analysis and programming.

As long as systems analysis and programming used *manual* methods, the methodologies were restricted to those with which a humble human being could cope. More powerful methodologies were suggested, but they were too tedious to be practical for our error-prone brains. The powerful methodologies needed automation. It was a shock for the early systems analysts and programmers to realize that they must automate their own jobs. But only when that was done could computing take off beyond the confines of the human sitting at a pad of paper.

It began to happen in the 1980s. Prior to that, programs were handcrafted in languages crudely designed for human beings, such as COBOL, FORTRAN, and Ada. Complex programs were undebuggable and the computer world accommodated itself to software that was not quite trustworthy. Operating systems exhibited mysterious behavior, and maintenance was a nightmare. Large numbers of analysts and programmers were trained in various "structured techniques," but these were still designed for use with pencil and paper. Corporate data bases were filled with jumbles of redundant data that often defied the extraction of information needed by management. Computer science professors lectured on mathematical techniques but applied them to programs with fewer than fifty instructions. Fred Brooks cynically compared building complex software to C. S. Lewis's summary of history:

> Great energy is expended—civilizations are built up— excellent institutions devised; but each time something goes wrong. Some fatal flaw always brings the selfish and cruel people to the top, and then it all slides back into misery and ruin. In fact, the machine conks. It seems to start up all right and runs a few yards, and then it breaks down.*

To prevent software from "conking," it needs to be based on constructs which are mathematically provably correct, and modifiable with the same techniques, so that correctness is preserved. These techniques are too tedious for pencil-and-paper design. They require computerized tools. The tools must *automatically* generate bug-free programs because we cannot expect human beings to do so.

Only with this rigorously based automation can the chain reaction occur which allows explosive growth of complex software. No doubt we shall see diverse powerful new methodologies *now that we have the capability to automate them.*

This book describes what may be the most important change in methodology of system development that we have yet seen: the beginning of automated development of systems in which complex specifications and resulting code are mathematically provably free from internal errors and inconsistencies.

* Fred Brooks, *The Mythical Man-Month* (Reading, MA: Addison-Wesley Publishing Co., Inc., 1975).

ACKNOWLEDGMENTS   The author has used freely material provided by Higher Order Software, Inc., Cambridge, Massachusetts. He has received much generous help from the brilliant creators of HOS, Margaret Hamilton and Saydean Zeldin, and from the staff of Higher Order Software Inc., Richard Smaby, Woodrow Vandever, Ron Hackler, Allen Razdow, and Steven Cushing. Richard Smaby spent much time helping to work out examples, using the HOS software. Ron Noates of Lockheed provided valuable examples of his work. Ron Hackler and Norbert Albertson spent much time on detailed checking. Pieter Mimno and his wife were extremely generous in their help and hospitality. Pieter provided many examples and insights. The author would like to express his gratitude for all the help received and pay tribute to the genius and professionalism of this group in developing the techniques described in this book.

For the data-base portions of the book, the author is grateful for help and ideas from Al Hershey and Ken Winter of Database Design Inc., Ann Arbor, Michigan, and from John Hope.

The author thanks Carma McClure for her detailed checking of the manuscript and many suggestions for its improvement.

**SYSTEM DESIGN
FROM PROVABLY
CORRECT CONSTRUCTS**

PART **I**   RATIONALE

The attempt to build a discipline of software engineering on such shoddy foundations must surely be doomed, like trying to base chemical engineering on the phlogiston theory, or astronomy on the assumption of a flat earth.

C. A. R. Hoare
Professor of Computing
Oxford University
—commenting on today's programming techniques

1 SOFTWARE MISENGINEERING

INTRODUCTION
Legend has it that in the early days of computing a certain magazine publisher's computer became stuck in a program loop. It printed the same address on mailing wrappers all afternoon. The wrappers were automatically wrapped around the magazines and automatically franked. Next day some farmer way out in the wilds of Nebraska was surprised to see a dozen large trucks rolling up filled with magazines.

True or not, it is difficult at a cocktail party to reveal that one works on computers without being regaled with stories about crazy telephone bills, a computer allocating the wrong patient to surgery, or so-and-so getting rich because some lunatic computer sent him a big check.

The Mariner I shot to Venus plunged into space and was lost forever because a programmer had an undeclared variable. Today Cruise missiles intended to carry hydrogen bombs are being programmed with a language that does not force its programmers to declare variables.

QUANTUM LEAPS
Computing hardware has progressed through a number of steps which dramatically changed its capability: the coming of magnetic tape in the 1950s, the coming of discs in the 1960s, the coming of terminals and data transmission, the spread of distributed processing, and the arrival of the microcomputer. Computer industry observers have sometimes lamented that there have not been revolutions of equivalent power in software. However, techniques *are* available today which can bring a revolutionary change in software development, equivalent in their importance to the coming of discs or terminals.

One might dread to reflect what the computer world might be like in 10 years' time if we do not have dramatic breakthroughs in software. Computing power is plunging down in cost. Big machines are becoming bigger. Small machines are springing up like mushrooms. Numerous machines are being interconnected into computer networks.

It has been commented that in a few years there will be one computer for every two white-collar workers in the United States. There cannot be one professional programmer for every two white-collar workers. Today there is one programmer for about every 200 white-collar workers.

The VHSIC program of the U.S. Department of Defense is creating a microprocessor on a chip with the power of an IBM 370 model 168. Such chips will become mass-producible like newsprint. Future computers need to be fundamentally re-architected so that they can take advantage of such microelectronics. They will have large numbers of microprocessors operating in parallel.

The Japanese have described a fifth generation of computers with which they hope to wrest computer industry dominance away from the United States. They have described a highly parallel mainframe with 10,000 processors capable of executing a combined instruction rate of 10 billion instructions per second, and operating with fundamentally different software.

Any way that we assess the future of the computer industry, computing power will vastly outstrip that of today. But the number of professional programmers will increase only slowly. Somehow or other one programmer must support a vast increase in processor power.

There is no shadow of doubt that we are going to see a spectacular quantum leap in hardware. We *must* achieve a quantum leap in software creation.

GENERATION OF PROVABLY CORRECT CODE

It is desirable to have high-level languages, unlike programming languages, with which we can express requirements and specifications. The early versions of such languages were useful documentation tools but were not *computable*. This book describes such a language which *is* computable. Its statements are successively refined until program code can be automatically generated. It is mathematically based so that it produces *bug-free and consistent logic*. The mathematics, however, must be completely hidden under the covers because most users are not mathematicians.

At last we have the ability to create specifications without internal errors and inconsistencies and to automatically produce bug-free code from these. More than that, they can be produced quickly, without manual program coding. Where the statement of specifications is inadequate (as they all are in the beginning) it is adjusted and broken into more detail until bug-free code can be generated from it.

When we build systems from provably correct constructs we do not necessarily create programs without fault. We can still tell the computer to do things which are stupid. If we create a forecasting program based on the phases of the moon and the behavior of groundhogs, no mathematics will help. Provably correct code will not improve a stockbroker's predictions. However, the majority of bugs in programs today are caused by the mechanics of programming, inconsistent data, sequence errors, and so on. These can be eliminated.

The revolution which this book describes, then, is one of replacing the ad hoc coding process, which is so vulnerable to the frailties of the human coder, with a rigorous machine-checkable process. This is how the computer world *must* progress. Program coding as we know it today *must* largely disappear. It is too error-prone, too expensive, and creates results which are too difficult to modify. It is an inhuman use of human beings because it asks them to do something beyond their capabilities—produce perfect, intricate, complex logic which can be easily understood and modified. That is a task for computers, not human beings.

Human beings can invent, conceptualize, demand improvements, and create visions. They can write music, start wars, build cities, create art, fall in love, go to the moon, and colonize the solar system, but they cannot write COBOL or Ada code which is guaranteed correct. They need automated tools that will translate their desires into computer code. And because most of their desires are not computable, the tools must help in successively refining their requests until they are computable.

As automation of programming matures, the specification languages which predominate may be different from the language described in this book, but they need to have the property that they *translate broad human thinking about requirements into a computable form and successively refine it until it is possible to automatically allocate the resources needed and generate bug-free machine code.*

The technique described in this book has been used on complex systems. Some analysts who have become expert with it have obtained results startlingly fast. The key to obtaining fast results is the interactive graphics software, which facilitates the building of the diagrams at a screen, links them to a library of data types and previously defined operations, and checks for errors so that correct program code can be generated. Partially complete programs can be executed at the screen with the missing pieces being simulated.

Because of the speed of obtaining results, the technique is a powerful productivity tool. Applications can be built by a designer who has acquired the necessary expertise in a tenth of the time required with conventional analysis and programming. The results are documented, and built in such a way that modification (maintenance) is easy.

New graduates often learn the technique and become skilled with it faster than many established programmers. This phenomenon has been observed and measured with other application generators also. The reason is that it requires a new way of thinking about systems. The established programmer or analyst has to do much *unlearning* of current thought patterns. However, because the estab-

lished programmer or analyst does have much experience that is valuable, he*
is challenged to put his knowledge to work with a methodology that will make
him far more powerful. We challenge him in reading this book to set aside his
hard-learned preconceptions about systems design and think about the future. The
techniques in this book are easier than conventional programming once familiarity
with them is built.

SPECIFICATION PROBLEMS

To obtain error-free computing, techniques that prevent logic errors are vital, but satisfactory systems need
more than that. Too often, problems lie not in the
programmers' coding but in the specifications.

Time and time again one finds stories of a system being cut over after years
of development effort and the end users saying it is not what they want, or trying
it for a while and then giving up. The requirements were not specified sufficiently
thoroughly, so that more elaborate procedures have been devised for requirements
specification, sometimes resulting in voluminous documentation. But still the
system has been unsatisfactory.

Many DP organizations have realized that their application creation process
is not working well and have taken steps to correct this. Steps are often taken to
enforce more formal procedures. Application creation, it is said, must be converted from a sloppy ad hoc operation to one that follows rules like an engineering
discipline. Unfortunately, the steps they take often make the situation worse.

FAILURES

In one large insurance company a system was developed for claim processing which would put terminals
in all branch offices. It took about three years to develop at a cost of about $4
million. To ensure that the end users were well understood, an end-user manager
was moved into a high position in the development process. When the first
terminals were cut over, to everybody's horror the users gave up using them after
a short period. They perceived the system as unsatisfactory compared with their
previous method. The system was eventually abandoned.

A Department of Defense study was conducted of 10 major automated
systems. It concluded that all 10 had *unstable and changing* requirements, indicating the need for techniques that could adapt much more quickly to such
changes.

The difficulty of writing adequate requirements specifications has resulted
in some spectacular court cases. In the early 1970s two major airlines sued
computer suppliers who were to provide application programs, after $40 million
had been spent, because the application programs were not about to work. At

* To avoid a sexist connotation, the author has not used words like "man" and "manpower."
However, avoiding the use of "he," "his," and "him" makes sentences clumsy. Please recognize
these as neuter words meaning "he or she," "his or her," and "him or her."

the time of writing a European bank is in court for a $70 million claim over application software. The U.S. Air Force spent more than $300 million in a futile attempt to automate an Advanced Logistics System (ALS) [1].

The public record is replete with examples of inadequate specifications of military systems causing enormous cost escalations, or redevelopment because systems did not work as expected [2–4].

If a software engineer has unclear or ambiguous specifications, as is often the case, he tends to fill in the gaps with his own initiative. Often he is entranced with his own invention. He creates some ingenious subsystem and the rest of the system is built around this device.

A contractor or programming manager without clear specifications often has to redo parts of systems. He can then justify time slippages, cost overruns, and system failures.

For every big failure that hits the headlines there are a thousand small ones where ordinary end users abandon their terminal or complain that it does not do what they want. This can become a disaster when it results in the inability of organizations to respond to changing economic or competitive environments.

Once developed, conventional computer programs are difficult to change, to respond to a changing external environment. We are locked in a thickening morass of maintenance complexity—a morass which is turning to concrete.

PROBLEMS WITH THE SPECIFICATION PROCESS

In most software development, specifications written for the applications that must be programmed take person-years to complete and become voluminous documents.

The specification document is extremely important in the traditional system development life cycle. It guides programmers and is supposed to answer numerous questions that arise about the system. In practice there are serious problems with it.

- It lacks precision. It cannot be converted into computer code without many assumptions and interpretations.

- It contains many ambiguities and inconsistencies.

- It is usually incomplete.

- It is often so long and boring that key managers do not read it. They read the summary.

- It is often misinterpreted by both sides. Often its readers *think* they understand it but in fact do not.

- Sometimes much trivia and motherhood is added to the document. Both sides understand this. It increases the comfort level, but has zero value.

- The specification document is not designed for successive refinement as the problems become better understood. It is intended to be a complete document which users sign.

SPECIFICATION FREEZE

It is important in the traditional development cycle to *freeze* the specifications when programming begins.

The users are coerced to sign-off on the specification document. They know that until they do the detailed design and programming will not begin.

The sign-off is invariably a moment of apprehension on both sides. The users are not sure whether it is really what they want. They often feel that their views on the system are changing as they learn and think more about it. Halfway up a learning curve the specifications are *frozen*. The data processing (DP) personnel are apprehensive because they are not sure that they understand all the users' needs. They are about to put much effort into the implementation and any imperfections in the specifications will prove expensive.

BUGS

When delivered systems do not work as intended, the problems are more often caused by the specification process than by the programming process. In one typical case a large corporation found that 64% of its bugs were in requirements analysis and design—in spite of a formal sign-off by the user departments. Even worse, *45% of these bugs were discovered after the acceptance tests for the finished applications were completed.*

This corporation had a formal development life cycle and was following its installation standards meticulously. It was using a formal method of structured analysis in creating the specifications. The bugs in the requirements specification are much more time consuming and expensive to correct than those in coding. Ninety-five percent of the cost of correcting bugs in one large bank project was for the bugs in requirements and design.

SUCCESSIVE REFINEMENT

In order to generate correct code, the specification must be rigorous. A rigorous specification cannot be created in one shot. There will be much successive refinement. Each step in this refinement needs to be rigorous.

The specification process we advocate in this book does not create a single specification document from which programmers code. Instead, it produces a succession of formal representations of the system which can steadily be broken down into more detail. Different persons are likely to be involved at different levels of detail. All use the same type of chart.

At the highest level the chart has a few blocks which represent the broad requirements of the system. At the lowest level the chart has enough detail for automatic generation of program code. Separate portions of the chart will be developed separately. The technique is designed so that they can be linked together without interface problems. When changes are made, as they often are, at a lower level in the chart, these are automatically reflected upward so that the high-level representations of the system can be checked.

A certain stage in the evolution of the specification chart may be regarded as detailed design which is handed over to a different team. This team can feed back refinements to the chart, which are then checked by the original specifiers. The traditional development life cycle goes through the steps shown in Fig. 1.1.

There is often argument about what should be in the requirements statement, what should be in the specification, and what should be in the design documents. We believe that this is an artificial distinction. Requirements, specification, and design are all the same process carried to greater levels of detail. It is possible to have one diagramming technique and language that handles all of these.

Different languages and techniques have been developed for different aspects of the development life cycle. Sometimes one language is used for the requirements statement (often English); a different language or technique is used for the specification of, for example, data flow diagrams, and yet a different one for detailed program design; and then a programming language is used for coding. As each new phase in Fig. 1.1 was recognized as being necessary in the history of computing, new techniques and languages were created for it.

The specification writers commonly misinterpret the requirements. The program designers commonly misinterpret the specifications. The coders make errors in coding from the design diagrams. There are many opportunities to introduce manual processes during and between the phases of the life cycle. At each of these points new errors arise.

It has proven difficult to make each new phase of Fig. 1.1 correspond to the previous phase. This is partly because they have been defined in different languages [6].

VERIFICATION

The traditional development life cycle leaves most of the verification and validation until after the programming. The reason has been that programming language has been the only language formal enough for computerized verification.

Program testing produces a crop of surprises. Integration testing produces worse surprises. Deployment can be even worse if the users do not like what they get. It is very expensive to deal with surprises which occur late in the cycle and which cause earlier parts of the cycle to be redone.

It is desirable to do as much verification as early as possible in the life cycle, where it is less expensive. To do this, formal computable specification techniques are needed with rigorous techniques for verifying their correctness. *One design technique* is desirable which extends from the expression of requirements to the automatic generation of program code, with rigorous vertification checks from top to bottom.

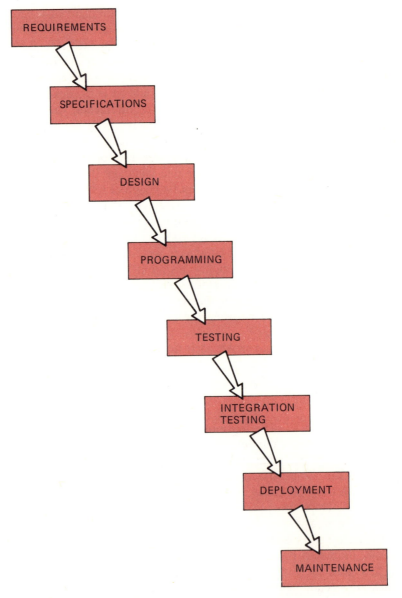

Figure 1.1   Traditional development life cycle.

SOLVING THE WRONG PROBLEM

Much of today's research into the development process is oriented toward improving the existing methods. Improve programming with the move to structured programming. Improve systems analysis with the move to structured analysis. Formalize the conventional development life cycle and provide tools within it for documentation and review. Add yet more reserved words and instruction types to COBOL. Adapt languages and compilers for better structured programming. Develop the Ada language. And so on.

In a sense these activities (although highly valuable because much conventional programming will remain) are solving the wrong problem. The important problem is how to migrate from conventional programming and the old development life cycle to development methodologies which are fast, flexible, interactive, and employ provably correct constructs; methodologies in which interactive prototyping replaces formal, voluminous specifications which must be frozen; methodologies with which end users, managers, specifiers, implementers, and maintainers can interact without mismatches.

If a hammer is not achieving much success in fixing screws, the solution is not to obtain a better hammer. The problem is that the wrong methodology is being used. More appropriate tools are now available for software development. In some cases computer executives still want to use the old development life cycle even with the new tools. This is rather like the old hammer enthusiasts driving in screws by hitting them hard with the handle of the screwdriver.

RESISTANCE TO CHANGE

Fundamental changes in methodology meet great emotional resistance. Napoleon refused to believe in steamships 20 years after the first one was working, even though he could have left Nelson's fleet standing on a windless day. Steam engine designers kept on building more elaborately tuned and complex mechanisms 30 years after the electric motor was in common use.

The methodology in this book is a quantum leap from conventional programming, but it will encounter resistance. Many programmers will reject it because it seems alien to the God-given order. Many executives will be unaware of it because they are too busy putting out fires caused by the use of inadequate methodologies. Computer professionals who have done so much to automate other people's jobs are remarkably reluctant to have their own job automated.

A major reason for resistance is that DP organizations have struggled to achieve discipline in the DP development process. This process used to be an unruly free-for-all until standards and guidelines were established relatively recently. The standards and methods have assumed the force of law, have been taught to all DP staff in an organization, and are regarded as a vital necessity in the crusade against unmet requirements, unmaintainable code, and nonportable programs. The installation standards, religiously adhered to, have frozen the

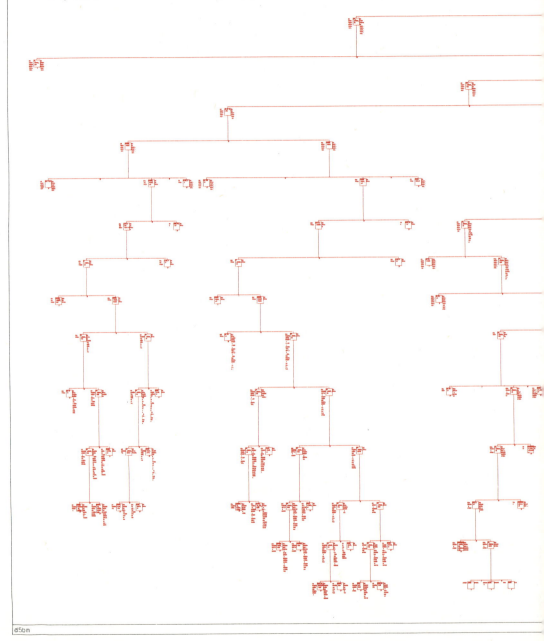

The HOS technique successively decomposes a high-level functional description into lower level operations. The decomposition proceeds until it reaches blocks for which correct code can be generated. Each step in the decomposition must obey mathematical axioms which rigorously enforce its correctness.

d5bm

By designing systems with mathematically provable constructs complex specifications can be made consistent, unambiguous, and internally error-free and correct. The internal clockwork can be made to mesh correctly. Correctly meshing clockwork does not mean that the *concepts* of the system are complete and valid. (Photograph courtesy of the Science Museum, London.)

methodologies of large installations at a time when the technology is plunging into new forms.

One typical corporation with many computer installations in many countries spent much effort in the 1970s perfecting a project management system. This incorporates installation standards, guidelines, and some software for project control. It is referred to as the installation "Bible." No DP manager will admit that he does not use it; to do so would be detrimental to his career.

If the Bible is followed literally, it prevents DP managers and analysts from using most of the methods we advocate in this book. It insists that specifications for all applications be created with techniques that are entirely nonrigorous. These specifications are typically 1 inch thick or more, are usually difficult to read, impossible to verify, and full of ambiguities, inconsistencies, errors, and omissions.

One methodology sold and used in many installations consists of thirty-two 2-inch-thick binders which spell out in detail how to create requirements and specifications. They expand the methods of the 1970s, which have proven to be so inadequate, into a bureaucracy that is immensely time consuming, entirely nonrigorous, prevents automation of code generation, and is unchangeable.

Many government departments are still issuing application development directives which lock their vast organizations into conventional procedural techniques which *prevent* productivity, nonprocedural languages, and rigorous methods. Most of this bureaucratization of inadequate techniques is accompanied by high-sounding phrases. A paper about the Department of Defense programming directives states, typically: "The theme pervading all of these steps is to elevate software policy, practices, procedure and technology from an artistic discipline to a true engineering discipline." The directives referred to prevent the use of engineering-like methods.

ON ENGINEERING   C. A. R. Hoare, Professor of Computing at Oxford, describes the term "engineering" in connection with such practices as a startling contradiction: *"The attempt to build a discipline of software engineering on such shoddy foundations must surely be doomed, like trying to base chemical engineering on the phlogiston theory, or astronomy on the assumption of a flat earth"* [7]. He compares the characteristics of engineering as a profession with "software engineering" as currently practiced.

An engineer has a range of trusted and proven techniques which give a precise result at minimum cost. He recommends these to his customers and insists that only proven techniques be used. He often understands the true needs of his client better than the client himself. A "software engineer" more often concocts his own programs. "How many of them are ignorant of, or prefer to ignore, the known techniques used successfully by others, and embark on some spatchcocked implementation of their own defective invention" [7].

Second, an engineer is vigilant in seeking to reduce the costs and increase the reliability of his product. He realizes that these conflicting objectives require a search for the utmost simplicity. Great engineering is simple engineering. Many programmers, by contrast, revel in complexity, finding excitement in projects of a complexity slightly beyond their comprehension. Hoare comments: "Among manufacturers' software one can find what must be the worst engineering products of the computer age. No wonder it was given away free—and what a very expensive gift it was to the recipient" [7].

Third, an engineer uses designs based on sound mathematical theories and computational techniques. These designs are represented in manuals, textbooks, and codes of practice. The typical programmer makes up new program structures for each problem, with no mathematical basis.

An engineer respects his tools and demands from them the highest precision, convenience, quality, reliability, and the minimum cost. He has developed an intuitive ingrained mastery of his tools so that his mental effort and creativity focuses entirely on the customer's problem. A fatal attraction to the programmer, however, is the complexity of software which would "revolt the instincts of any engineer, but which to the clever programmer masquerades as power and sophistication" [7]. The programmer's use of unreliable operating systems and so on excuses the unreliability of his own code; their inefficiency excuses the inefficiency of his own programs; their complexity protects his work from close scrutiny by his client or manager.

The technique described in this book seems worthy of the name "software engineering." It is simple, elegant, and mathematically based. It allows designers to create error-free mechanisms of minimal complexity. It permits users to obtain and employ the provable mechanisms of others. *In conjunction with other non-procedural tools and design techniques* it could solve most of the problems described in this chapter.

The system designer of the future will employ a tool kit at a computer workstation. Like other craftsmen, he needs a variety of different tools and must know how to select the best tool for a given task. The design process needs to be automated as fully as possible. Some excellent tools are now available for this. The book describes one with unique properties which we think are particularly valuable—the ability to eliminate inconsistencies and errors in specifications and to decompose rigorous specifications into code.

The big problem that remains is how to convert a multibillion-dollar industry with vast vested interests in earlier techniques. Conventional programming in conventional languages has the momentum of a giant freight train. It will not be deflected from its course quickly.

One of the tragedies of the computer industry today is that while true engineering techniques *do exist* for avoiding slow, ad hoc, error-prone, programming, most DP executives are sending their staff to courses which teach variants of the messy, nonrigorous, manual methods.

REFERENCES

1. J. Fox, *Software and Its Development*, Prentice-Hall, Inc., Englewood Cliffs, NJ, 1982.

2. *Hearings on Cost Escalations in Defense Procurements*, Department of Defense Authorization for Appropriation for Fiscal Year 1975, Committee on Armed Services, U.S. House of Representatives, 93rd Congress, 1974.

3. *Hearings Before the Subcommittee on Federal Spending Practices, Efficiency, and Open Government*, Committee on Government Operations, U.S. Senate, 94th Congress, 1st Session, June–July 1975.

4. *Hearings on Military Posture and H.R. 5068*, Department of Defense Authorization for Appropriations for Fiscal Year 1978, Committee on Armed Services, U.S. House of Representatives, 95th Congress, 1st Session, February–March 1977.

5. F. A. Comper, "Project Management for System Quality and Development Productivity," *Guide and Share Application Development Symposium, Proceedings*, Share, New York, 1979.

6. M. Hamilton and S. Zeldin, "The Functional Life Cycle Model and Its Automation," submitted to *Journal of Systems and Software*, 1982.

7. C. A. R. Hoare, "The Engineering of Software: A Startling Contradiction," *Computer Bulletin* (British Computer Society), December 1975.

2 SPECIFICATION LANGUAGES

In the early days of the computer industry, computer languages were thought of only as programming languages. Initially they were close in syntax to the instruction set of the machine. Human language is very different from machine language and so attempts were made to humanize the programming languages by employing English words.

The standardization of languages like COBOL, FORTRAN, and Ada presented programmers with what in effect were theoretical computers hiding the physical details of actual computers which differed from machine to machine. The programming language, however, remained a statement of *how* to execute a set of operations in terms of computer resources.

Understanding the requirements of a complex system and writing specifications for it needs a very different type of language. In the early days (and often still today) requirements and specifications were expressed in English. Human language, however, is ambiguous and imprecise. Specifications written in English were usually incomplete and almost always open to misinterpretation. The effort to make them more thorough led to documents more voluminous than Victorian novels and far more boring. It became clear that many of the problems with systems were not the programmers' fault but the fault of the specifiers.

Because of this a variety of techniques grew up for designing and specifying systems. A new type of language began to emerge—specification languages. These languages had little or no resemblance to programming languages. They took a variety of different forms. Sometimes a formal language was used; sometimes a diagramming technique. They included SADT (Structured Analysis and Design Technique) [1], SREM (Software Requirements Engineering Methodology) [2], data flow diagramming techniques [3], HIPO (Hierarchical Input–Process Output) [4], PSL/PSA (Problem Statement Language/Problem Statement Analyzer) [5], and IDEF (ICAM Definition Method) [6].

These were all generalized techniques intended to specify any type of program. There were also specialized languages, narrow in scope, most of which were not referred to as "specification" languages. These included report definition languages, data-base query and update languages, languages that could generate certain patterns of commercial DP application [7], and languages for special functions such as financial analysis, circuit design, and coordinate geometry.

NONPROCEDURAL VERSUS PROCEDURAL LANGUAGES

At this point the term "nonprocedural language" came into use. A *procedural language* specifies *how* something is to be done. A programming language is a procedural language. It describes precisely, step by step, how something is accomplished. A *nonprocedural language* describes *what* is to be done, not *how*. A query language and a report generator language are *nonprocedural*. They describe *what* is needed, not what program instructions will be used to accomplish it.

Specification languages are nonprocedural. They describe *what* is to be done, not *how*. This chapter describes properties that good specification languages ought to have.

COMPUTABLE SPECIFICATIONS

The computer industry thus acquired two breeds of languages, one for requirements analysis, problem description, and system specification, and one for programming.

It was generally considered desirable that the specification languages be independent of machine resources or programming because the specifications were a fundamental statement about requirements and these requirements could be met with a variety of different types of hardware and software. Furthermore, the hardware and software would change while the requirements remained the same.

Programming languages had to be computable. This guaranteed rigor and sufficiency in these languages. Most of the *specification* languages and techniques that grew up were not rigorous and did not enforce logical consistency. They were not computable.

It was generally assumed that the output of the specification language was meant to be used by a programmer who then coded the programs in a different language. This led to all of the problems associated with conventional programming. *We believe that this assumption is wrong* for computing in the long term. The specification language should be processible so that program code can be *automatically generated*, as with today's report generators and application generators. This means that the specification language requires more rigor than did early specification techniques. It must be *computable*. We will use the term "computable" to mean that a language or specification contains enough detail and is precise enough to be automatically converted into program code (whether or not the conversion software exists). This does not necessarily mean that it expresses every detail, because certain types of default options are possible. A report generation statement can be computable, for example, even when it does not express the format of the report.

Most techniques for specifying systems are very sloppy and certainly not computable. There is often a pretense of rigor when it does not exist. Much bad design is perpetrated with the name "structured techniques." When programs so designed are finally debugged and systems delivered, it is often found that they were not exactly what the users wanted. Even when specification languages are used, much falls through the cracks. This is expensive because it means reprogramming. The lack of rigor in the specification techniques often causes ambiguity, incompleteness, and misunderstanding. Most such techniques should generally be regarded as useful for documentation or initial conceptualization, but not thought of as the rigorous disciplines that computing requires.

Although programming languages have the desirable property of computability, they are not suitable for stating system specifications because of their semantics. What is needed is a specification language that is computable with semantics appropriate for high-level conceptualization of systems. The property of computability will then permit resources to be allocated and programs created automatically (and hence without the errors that programmers make).

AUTOMATION OF DESIGN

Many specification techniques were designed to be used by hand. Today the hardware for running computerized tools is inexpensive, so future techniques should be designed to employ computers. It is only when computers are used that rigorous methods are practical. Human beings make too many errors and find rigorous techniques too tedious to use rapidly and thoroughly by hand. When we create design techniques to be run with computerized tools, this enormously expands the scope of what is practical.

Design will never be completely automated. Human inventiveness and creativity is its most important aspect. Human beings will always want to argue at a blackboard and draw sketches on paper, so the technique should provide ways to make simple drawings of concepts.

Figure 2.1 shows the essentials of computerized system design. There should be a specification language which is rigorous but which has an interactive user-friendly dialogue. Most people think and design with pictures, so an interactive graphics facility is desirable. The design so created should be capable of being analyzed to check its accuracy and consistency. The design *should be based on mathematics that enforces the use of provably correct constructs*. The analyzer should check that the mathematical rules have been obeyed so that the overall structure is guaranteed to be correct.

Once it has been checked the software should generate program code. Some tools generate code in conventional programming languages. This provides programs that are *portable* among different machines (insofar as the languages are portable). It is, however, more efficient to generate machine code and avoid the additional step of compilation, which can degrade code efficiency.

Strictly, the need for human programming languages disappears when we use the facilities shown in Fig. 2.1. In practice, languages such as FORTRAN, COBOL, Pascal, and Ada may be retained to aid program portability. However, we do not want programmers to tinker with, or maintain, the program code generated, because this would destroy its provably correct property, and would usually introduce errors.

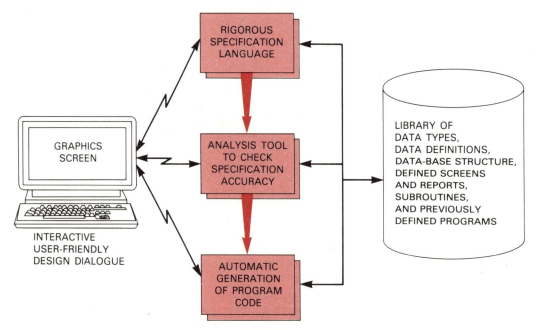

Figure 2.1   Specification languages should be user friendly and rigorous, have tools for on-line accuracy checking, employ a library for the building of complex systems, and be capable of generating code which is bug-free. The specification should be automatically checkable to eliminate inconsistencies, ambiguities, and logic errors.

STANDING ON THE SHOULDERS OF OTHERS

Isaac Newton wrote toward the end of his life that insofar as he had achieved anything worthwhile, he had done so by standing on the shoulders of giants. Richard Hamming comments that programmers do not tend to stand on each others' shoulders; they stand on each others' feet!

It is desirable that the tools we use should build ever-growing, ever-more-powerful libraries of subroutines and callable programs. If these programs obey mathematical rules such as those described in this book, we should be able to link them into new programs without interface errors. Indeed, this absence of *interface* errors is one of the major reasons for using mathematically based software. It is desirable to be able to find out what exists in the library and be able to understand it, and use it. Most large computing installations reinvent the same routines over and over again because this capability is missing.

Figure 2.1 shows the tools employing a library. As well as the code of callable routines being stored, their descriptions in the specification language are stored, and this should make them easy to understand. A directory or thesaurus of callable modules may be used to make them easy to find.

Even relatively simple programs should be built up in blocks. These blocks need to be stored and made accessible for linking to other blocks. The library mechanism should serve this short-term need as well as the long-term need of providing an encyclopedia of existing routines.

Everything in the system is built from certain semantic primitives. The proofs of correctness are applied to these primitives. If they are correct, everything that uses them and obeys the rules is also correct. The primitive mechanisms are themselves in the library. *All mechanisms added to the library, then, are defined in terms of mechanisms already in it.*

Rigorous interfacing rules throughout the library and the systems that use it should allow the library to grow in an orderly fashion and should allow modules and systems to be interchanged among libraries. The mathematically based interfacing rules distinguish this library concept from a conventional subroutine or program library.

As the library builds up the developers will have less to develop, but there will also be less to verify. All modules in the library are *already* mathematically verified.

DATA BASE

Well-managed commercial DP installations have done strategic planning of data [8], built stable models of their data [9], and stored details of them in a dictionary. A data modeling tool is an important part of the family of tools.

The data in the data model should be automatically convertible to the representations of data needed by the tools shown in Fig. 2.1. The library contains the data dictionary and representations of data needed for provably correct computing.

INTEGRATION OF DEFINITION LEVELS

We commented that with many systems the requirements definition is written in one way, usually in English; the specification is created with a different technique; and the implementation is different yet again—a programming language. When the requirements are translated into the specification there are errors, and when the specification is translated into code there are errors. It is difficult and costly to keep the requirements current once the specification is begun, or to reflect program changes back into the specifications. When the programs are maintained the documentation or higher-level systems descriptions are often not changed accordingly. They become out of date.

The specification is usually verified on a self-contained basis with only occasional *ad hoc* checks to the requirements documents. The programs are tested in a self-contained way with only occasional ad hoc checks to the specifications.

The evolution through the development phases is usually not formally traceable. The solution to this is to have *one language* which is formal input to a computerized design tool, with which requirements, specifications, and details can be expressed. The requirements statements are decomposed into greater detail and become the specifications. The specifications are decomposed into greater detail until sufficient detail is reached that code can be generated automatically. When changes are made at a lower level these are automatically reflected upward. There is then structural integrity among the requirements, specifications, and detail. In fact, these words cease to have sharp demarcations. A high-level description is decomposed into successively more detailed descriptions.

The documentation does not slip out of date when successive maintenance changes are made because these changes require regeneration of program code from the specification language. The entire structure, top to bottom, reflects the change. Subsequent maintainers will then have a clear and detailed description from which to work.

A COMMON COMMUNICATION VEHICLE

A major reason for problems with systems is inadequate communication between users and developers, or between requirements definers and programmers.

The most successful requirements definition projects are those where the implementers and users work on and understand the requirements together. The implementers understand better what the users need. The users understand better the constraints of implementation. Each group can trigger creativity in the other so that the combination produces something better than can be produced by either group alone. A few exciting projects catch fire when there is excellent understanding between the instigators and implementers.

A good specification language should build a bridge of understanding between the users, requirements planners, specifiers, and implementers. A common language should be usable by all of these. The high-level view of the users or requirements planners should be decomposable into the detail needed by the implementers. The high-level planners or specifiers should be able to choose what level of detail they want to go in specifying the system. Changes made at lower levels should reflect back into this higher-level specification to preserve integrity of the levels.

A language that provides this communication bridge accelerates the under-standing of the user requirements by the implementers, and enables the user or planner to understand his requirements better. Particularly important, it reveals misunderstanding among the users, planners, and implementers.

A developer may be better able to evaluate cost trade-off possibilities if he and the users employ a common way of looking at system specifications. This may save much money. Early feedback from the developer to the users is always beneficial.

UP-FRONT DETECTION OF ERRORS

The earlier in a project that errors are detected the less expensive they are. Figure 2.2 illustrates this.

Statistics from various organizations show that the errors detected during program testing are 10 or more times as expensive to correct as errors detected at the specification stage.

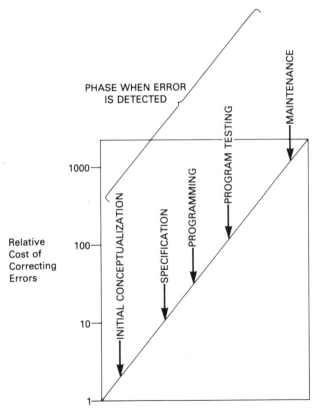

Figure 2.2　It is much less expensive to catch the error early.

Correcting errors at the maintenance stage is another order of magnitude more costly.

On one avionics system the cost per line of code, including debugging and documentation, was reported to be $70. The cost per line of code of maintenance, however, was $4000 [10]. These figures were unusually high because of the complexity of the system, but would clearly have been much, much lower if the techniques described in this book had been used.

A language with provable consistency checking which extends from the initial requirements definition down to the more detailed phases increases the chance of catching errors at the earliest and least expensive time. A language that enables users, requirements planners, and implementers to communicate greatly decreases the chance of errors slipping through to the phases where they are expensive to correct.

Traditionally, most errors are caught in the program testing or maintenance phases. As indicated earlier, many of these are specification errors which, by then, are very expensive to correct. An objective of the specification language is to find every problem as early in the development cycle as possible.

INTEGRATED TOP-DOWN AND BOTTOM-UP DESIGN

The development methodology should facilitate both top-down and bottom-up design, and should integrate them. There is a perennial argument about which is best. In practice, almost all complex systems design uses both. Pure top-down design is impractical. Pure bottom-up design would be a mess. Bottom-up design leads to interface problems, if uncontrolled. In writing a book I use a mixture of top-down and bottom-up design. Writing the details always causes me to change the table of contents. It is the same in systems design, and a tool is needed which allows the changes and inventions that occur when modules are being worked out in detail to be reflected back naturally into the higher-level specifications.

A change made in one lower-level module may affect others and it is desirable that this ripple effect be immediately traceable. The designer needs to be able to add requirements from the top or bottom. In designing systems using the technique described in this book detailed work at a lower level frequently causes data-type references to be changed at a higher level. This continual adjustment can occur easily and could be largely automatic.

Often detailed design is done on one part of a system before another. The language should permit this to occur naturally and not cause later interface problems. On some systems one component is developed to completion while specifiers are still debating the concepts of another. Detailed design in one area should not be held up waiting for complete top-down specification of the layers above. It is normal to write one or more chapters of a book before the table of contents is complete. The top level is not *really* complete until the lower levels are done and the necessary iterations have taken place.

USER FRIENDLINESS

Particularly important is the user friendliness of the specification language. We have stressed that it needs to be mathematically based to enforce correct logic and interfaces between modules. The mathematics, however, should be completely hidden because most managers and analysts are terrified of mathematics. The telephone system is exceedingly complex and designed with mathematics, but most of its users know nothing about Erlang equations. It needs to be designed so that a computer can do comprehensive consistency checking. In a complex system this becomes a major task, beyond the ability of human designers.

It is likely that different dialects of a specification language will be needed, and different forms of representation. All of these should be built from the same fundamental set of primitives.

If separate systems are defined from the same primitives, technical arguments can be resolved by breaking them down to the primitives to see whether there is real disagreement. With most requirements documents and specifications, there are no means of analyzing them into common primitives. Once the underlying structure of primitives exists, higher-level constructs should make the specification language as powerful as possible and as user friendly.

SPECTRUM OF SPECIFICATION LANGUAGES

The properties of being user friendly and being rigorous often seem in conflict. Mathematical languages are not user-friendly; user-friendly languages are generally not rigorous. We can rank them on a chart like that in Fig. 2.3. Readability, or user-friendliness, is on the vertical scale. Traditional axiomatic languages are on the right of Fig. 2.3 but at the bottom; they are difficult or impossible for ordinary analysts or users to read.

Traditional English specifications are at the extreme left of Fig. 2.3. They may be (fairly) readable but are entirely nonrigorous. Sometimes software is employed for formatting, editing, and storing specifications. This makes them easier to access, change, and manipulate, but does not make them more rigorous. Some text specification formatters have additional capabilities. They detect key words, format specification phrases, and generate tables of contents and indices. The program design language PDL [12] is an example. This improves the specification readability with clauses such as

```
IF CUSTOMER_CREDIT_CODE < 3
THEN ORDER IS REJECTED
```

It helps designers to find and cross-reference items in the specifications. It does no consistency or ambiguity checking, so there is little increase in rigor.

Another text approach advocates the use of a limited, well-defined, fairly nonambiguous subset of English [13]. This lessens the scope for misinterpretations and gives slightly more precision to the specifications. Software tools can help search for ambiguities and inconsistencies in such specifications [14].

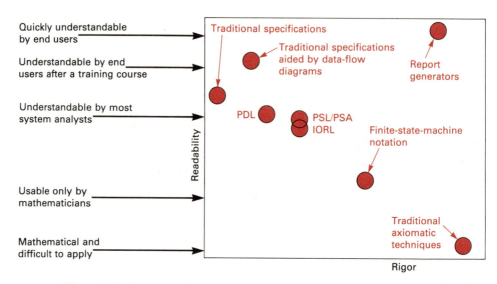

Figure 2.3 Spectrum of specification languages. (Analysts can argue about the exact positioning of the languages on the chart.) (From Ref. 11.)

Data flow diagramming techniques [3] give a step toward formality. Clear diagramming techniques in general help analysts to conceptualize systems and clarify complex flows and interrelationships. Diagrams that are too symbolic, however, are not necessarily understood by end users. Most analysts find their diagramming techniques very useful and assume that users find them useful, too. In practice, users are sometimes bewildered by the diagrams, thinking that they are more technical than they really are.

Data flow diagrams are an improvement over unstructured text in terms of formality but are still far from being rigorous. They are far from the desired property that program code could be generated from them automatically. Much more detail is needed. Much more is needed to enforce consistency and completeness.

PSL with its associated PSA (Problem Statement Language and Problem Statement Analyzer) [5] is one of the best known specification languages. It divides system functions into subfunctions, precisely specifying the inputs and outputs of each. The analyzers perform consistency checking between functions. No function, for example, is allowed to use a data item not generated by another function. PSL is farther to the right in Fig. 2.3, but it is still far from completely rigorous or capable of automatic program generation. Beside it in Fig. 2.3 is another language for functional decomposition and input/output specification: IORL (Input/Output Requirements Language) [15]. Although these do some useful specification checking, they cannot check detailed logic or specify the order and timing constraints needed in real-time systems.

A more rigorous approach is the use of *finite-state-machine notation*. This permits complex logic to be described in terms of entities which have discrete states. The analyst determines what types of stimulus cause a state to change. The state of an entity is a function of the previous state and the inputs received. The output is a function of the inputs and the state when those inputs are received. State diagrams are drawn to represent the possible states and the stimuli that change them. Associated with the diagrams is a table showing all possible states and stimuli to make sure that all combinations have been thought about.

Finite-state-machine notation has been used extensively in defining complex protocols for computer networks [16] and communications switching systems. The CCITT standards committee for international telephony and networking has a language for protocol specification based on this approach, SDL (Specification and Description Language) [17]. Other more generalized specification languages use this approach: for example, RSL (Requirements Statements Language) [2].

Finite-state-machine notation is farther to the right in Fig. 2.3. It is a major step in the direction of rigorous logic specification but not sufficiently so for automatic program generation. Some manufacturers' network software designed with finite-state-machine notation has exhibited mysterious and infuriating mis-behavior! Finite-state-machine notation is extremely difficult for most end users to understand, so it is lower on Fig. 2.3. It is not normally used in general data processing or in most scientific computing, and in general has a limited class of applications. It is possible to build software that translates finite-state-machine representation into English-like constructs to aid in user checking [18].

NARROWLY FOCUSED LANGUAGES

Computable specification languages are found in narrowly focused areas. Probably the most commonly used example is report generators. A required report can be specified by users or analysts with software which often works in conjunction with a data-base system. The program for creating the report is automatically generated. The circle at the top right of Fig. 2.3 is for report generators.

Report generators are not usually described as specification languages because their range of capabilities is so narrow. Broadening the scope somewhat, we have nonprocedural languages for querying, updating, and sometimes manipulating data bases. These are linked to graphics languages and decision support aids and form the basis of most application development without programmers [7]. Very different types of specification or problem statement languages exist for certain specific applications: for example, coordinate geometry, CAD/CAM, architects' drawings, and the building of telephone switching systems [19].

We really need, then, to add another dimension to Fig. 2.3 which indicates the *generality* of the language or the degree to which it can handle a comprehensive range of applications. This is done in Fig. 2.4. Given this way of looking at

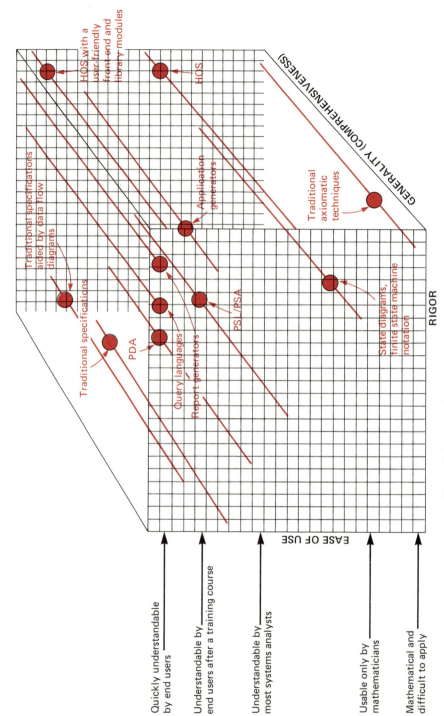

Figure 2.4 Extra dimension added to Fig. 2.3.

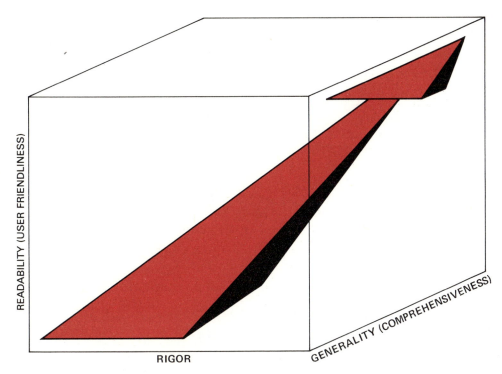

Figure 2.5   The computer industry needs to progress in the direction of the red arrow. It is now clear that there are techniques which can take us to the head of this arrow. This portends a complete revolution in software and application building.

specification languages it is clear that the computer industry needs to progress in the direction of the red arrow in Fig. 2.5.

    The HOS technique which we describe in this book appears to the author to be a major breakthrough. It is completely general and could be applied to any type of system. At its high levels it is reasonably understandable by users. English documentation can be displayed in association with any of its rigorously structured blocks. It can be linked to a variety of powerful forms of system representation for analysts or end users. Most important, it is based entirely on mathematical theorems and proofs, and introduces a new level of rigor into the design of complex specifications. It automatically generates program code that is bug-free.

    Using the HOS technique, provable modules in a library are linked into new modules which are being created. The technique eliminates interface errors so that the combined construct is provable. Increasingly large and powerful modules can be stored in the library. This seems an ideal technique for operating a software factory, and one of the world's largest software houses has adopted it.

    HOS is not high on the vertical scale of Fig. 2.4, but it is clear that mathematical rigor, like the HOS technique, can be applied to the most user-friendly means of creating specifications. The HOS software could have a report generator, screen painter, dialogue generator, encyclopedia, and a variety of user-friendly tools. Its basic method of decomposing functions into smaller modules until code can be generated could be made highly user friendly. Figure 2.5 shows a dot at the top, right, back corner indicating where a user-friendly but rigorous specification language ought to be.

A major challenge of the computer industry today is to combine HOS-like rigor with MACINTOSH-like user friendliness. It is now clear that that is possible.

SUMMARY   Box 2.1 lists the properties desirable in a specification.
Box 2.2 lists the properties desirable in a specification language. The facilities we describe in the following chapters have almost all of the properties in Box 2.2.

BOX 2.1   Desirable properties of a specification [20]

A Proper Specification Should:

- Be free from errors
- Have conceptual clarity
- Be easy to understand by managers, analysts, or programmers
- Be presentable in varying degrees of detail
- Be easy to create
- Be computable (i.e., have enough precision that program code can be generated automatically)
- Be formal input to a program code generator
- Be easy to change
- Be complete
- Be traceable when changes are introduced
- Be independent of hardware
- Employ a data dictionary
- Employ a data model based on formal data analysis
- Employ a program module library with automatic verification of interface correctness
- Employ computerized tools which make it easy to manipulate and change

BOX 2.2 Desirable properties of a specification language

- It should provide a way to think about systems which improves conceptual clarity.

- It should be easy to learn and use. At its higher levels it should be usable by non-DP personnel.

- It should be computable and program code should be generatable from it automatically.

- It should be designed for maximum automation of systems analysis, design, and programming.

- It should be rigorous and mathematically based so that its designs are built from provably correct constructs.

- Its mathematical basis should be hidden from the average user because most users are terrified of mathematics.

- It should be versatile enough to remove the need for all manual use of programming languages. (Manual programming immediately violates the requirement of provable correctness.)

- It should extend from the highest-level conceptualization of systems down to the creation of enough detail for program generation. In other words, one language should suffice for complete system creation. The more detailed versions of a specification should be a natural extension of the more general ones. The high-level specifier should be able to decide into how much detail he wants to go before handing over to the implementer.

- It should be a common communication medium among managers, designers, implementers, verifiers, maintainers, and documentors.

- It should use graphical techniques which are easy to draw and remember.

- It should employ a user-friendly computerized graphics tool for building, changing, and inspecting the design. The language should be formal input to automated design.

- It should employ testing tools which assist in verification and permit simulation of missing modules so that partially complete designs can be tested.

- It should be usable with top-down or bottom-up design and it should integrate these. Most complex systems come into existence through a combination of top-down and bottom-up design. The technique should allow certain elements of a system to be specified in detail while others, possibly parents or ancestors in the hierarchy, are not yet defined.

- It should indicate when a specification is complete.

Continued

BOX 2.2 *(Continued)*

- It should employ a hierarchy which descends into steadily increasing levels of detail. It should guarantee that each decomposition is logically valid and that each lower level completely replaces the one above it.

- When modifications are made lower in the hierarchy these should be quickly and automatically reflectable in the higher levels.

- It should employ an evolving library of subroutines and programs, and of all the constructs which the language employs. The primitive constructs will be in the library, so everything added to the library will be defined in terms of what is already there. The library becomes, in effect, an extendable requirement definition language. Everything in such a library employs the common primitives and has been verified by the software.

- It should link automatically to data-base tools, including a dictionary and directory which stores conceptual data-base models.

- It should guarantee interface consistency when subroutines or callable programs are used or when separate systems intercommunicate. Mathematical techniques should guarantee logical interface consistency as well as data consistency.

- The specification should be easy to change. It should be able to accommodate the unexpected. It should be easily changeable by persons who did not create it.

- All elements of a system should be traceable. All accesses and changes to data should be traceable throughout the system. This process should ensure that the inputs to each operation could only come from the correct source.

- The language may permit multiple dialects or multiple types of nonprocedural representation. These should all translate to a common set of control structures and a common set of rules for verifying correctness.

- A common set of primitives should be used to which the proofs of correctness apply. All nonprimitive structures and semantics should then translate to the primitives. The common primitives provide definitive communication between users employing different semantics or dialects.

- Default options may be used where they simplify specification, for example with the formatting of screens or reports.

- The language should be independent of hardware or other resources which are likely to change. It should be translatable into multiple different resource environments.

When specification languages with the properties described in Box 2.2 are used, they change the whole nature of systems development. The development life cycle is different, as discussed in Chapter 18. The improvements in correctness, maintainability, and user communication are clearly desirable, but, in addition, the development process is speeded up and the cost reduced by typically an order of magnitude.

True software "engineering" needs the properties in Box 2.2. To build software without provably correct constructs will one day seem like building a bridge without stressing calculations.

REFERENCES

1. D. Ross, "Structured Analysis (SA): A Language for Communicating Ideas," *IEEE Transactions on Software Engineering*, Vol. SE-3, No. 1 (1977): 16–34.

2. M. W. Alford, "A Requirements Engineering Methodology for Real-Time Processing Requirements," *IEEE Transactions on Software Engineering*, Vol. SE-3, No. 1 (1977).

3. T. DeMarco, *Structured Analysis and System Specification*, Yourdon Press, New York, 1978.

4. *HIPO—A Design Aid and Documentation Technique*, IBM Manual Ref. GC20-1851, IBM Corp., White Plains, NY.

5. D. Teichroew and E. A. Hershey III, "PSL/PSA: A Computer-Aided Technique for Structured Documentation and Analysis of Information Processing Systems," *IEEE Transactions on Software Engineering*, Vol. SE-3, No. 1 (1977).

6. SofTech, Inc., *Architect's Manual: ICAM Definition Method*, IDEF, Version 0, 1978; Version 1, 1978, Waltham, MA.

7. James Martin, *Application Development Without Programmers*, Prentice-Hall Inc., Englewood Cliffs, NJ, 1981.

8. James Martin, *Strategic Data-Planning Methodologies*, Prentice-Hall Inc., Englewood Cliffs, NJ, 1982.

9. James Martin, *Managing the Data-Base Environment*, Prentice-Hall, Inc., Englewood Cliffs, NJ, 1983.

10. W. L. Trainer, "Software—From Satan to Saviour," *Proceedings, NAECON Conference*, May 1973.

11. Diagram adapted from one by Alan M. Davis in "The Design of a Family of Application-Oriented Requirements Languages," *Computer*, May 1982.

12. S. H. Caine and E. K. Gordon, "PDL—A Tool for Software Design," *AFIPS Conference Proceedings*, Vol. 44, 1975 NCC, AFIPS Press, Montvale, NJ.

13. B. E. Casey and B. J. Taylor, "Writing Requirements in English: A Natural Alternative," IEEE Workshop on Software Engineering Standards, San Francisco, CA, August 1981.

14. R. Balzer et al., "Informality in Program Specifications," *IEEE Transactions on Software Engineering*, Vol. SE-4, No. 2 (March 1978).

15. C. R. Everhart, "A Unified Approach to Software System Engineering," *Proceedings, COMPSAC '80*, IEEE Computer Society, Los Alamitos, CA, October 1980.

16. James Martin, *Architectures for Distributed Processing*, Chap. 2, Savant Technical Report 6, Savant Institute, Carnforth, Lancashire, UK, 1979.

17. CCITT, *SDL User Guidelines*, Study Group X1, Working Paper 3-1, 3-4.

18. A. M. Davies, "Automating the Requirements Phase: Benefits to Later Phases of the Software Life-Cycle," *Proceedings, COMPSAC '80*, IEEE Computer Society, Los Alamitos, CA, October 1980.

19. One specific example is the COSS-RL language designed for the definition of central office switching systems at GTE Laboratories, Waltham, MA.

20. M. Hamilton and S. Zeldin, *Integrated Software Development System/Higher Order Software Conceptual Description*, Research and Development Technical Report ECOM-76-0329F, U.S. Army Electronics Command, Fort Monmouth, NJ, 1976.

PART **II** THE HOS METHODOLOGY

3 MATHEMATICALLY PROVABLE CONSTRUCTS

INTRODUCTION Program designers generally use ad hoc, undisciplined methods far removed from the precise disciplines of most branches of engineering. This results in code that is impossible to debug completely. We have learned to live with the idea that programs sometimes do strange things because it is not possible to detect all of their hidden anomalies.

MATHEMATICAL PROOFS OF CORRECTNESS Many authorities have expressed the view that mathematical approaches to program design must eventually be the solution to building better-quality software. Ever since Dijkstra's early writing about a programming calculus [1,2], a small number of researchers have attempted to apply mathematics to programming to produce provably correct code. A variety of different approaches have been used to derive correctness proofs [1,2–14].

Mathematical techniques have been applied to proving programs correct and to creating specification techniques for verifiable programs. The techniques have worked with certain fairly small programs. A variety of approaches have been used. These are summarized in Fig. 3.1, which is designed to act as a guide to the literature. A concise summary is provided in Berg et al. [15].

Almost no programmer uses such techniques in practice, for two reasons. First, they require a high level of mathematical sophistication. Even for simple programs a level of mathematical maturity is needed *far* beyond that of ordinary DP analysts and programmers. The mathematical proofs involved are often several times longer than the program derived. So the whole subject has tended to be relegated to the world of exotic research with almost no attention being paid to it by DP executives and staff. Second, they do not work with most real-life programs because these programs are too complex and unruly. The programs do not fit the mathematics.

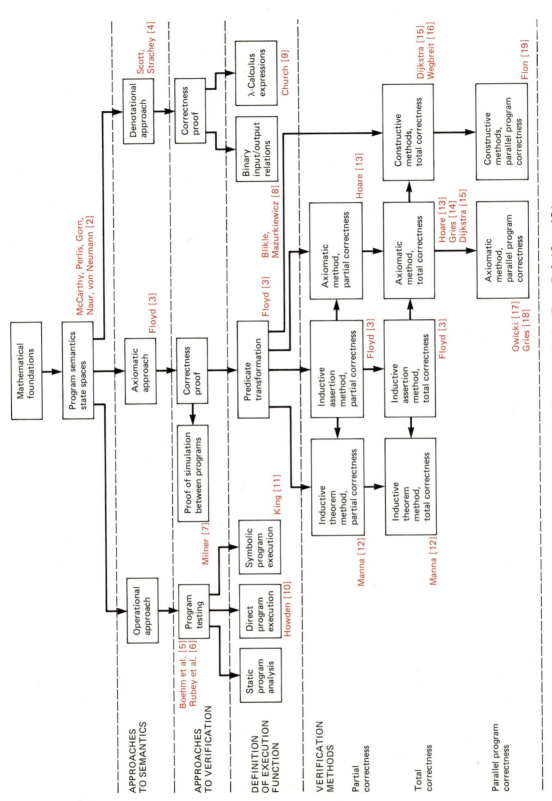

Figure 3.1 Taxonomy of verification methods. (From Ref. 15, p. 15.)

Today's programming languages permit all manner of constructs which defy mathematical verification. They were not designed with mathematical verification in mind.

The approach described in this book is different. Instead of applying ad hoc programming constructs, it employs only constructs which are built with mathematical axioms and proofs of correctness. A library of correct *operations* is built. The operations manipulate precisely defined *data types* by means of provably correct *control structures*. As the library of defined operations and data builds up, complex systems can be linked together. Most important, the mathematics is hidden from the typical user so that the method is easy to use. Non-computer professionals quickly learn to think about the systems they need using the basic approach.

The term ''provably correct code'' or ''provably correct specification'' has been used in the literature in two ways. In its purest sense it means that the problem to be computed can be stated with concise precision, as with a mathematical equation, and the logic of the program can be proven to give the required results. The program steps for evaluating a factorial, for example, may be mathematically proven to give the correct results. Unfortunately, in commercial data processing the processes that need automation do not yield to such precise mathematical description. They have large complex data bases and masses of random events, conditions, and exceptions. The dependencies among processes form complex *ad hoc* patterns. In this environment we need to impose orderliness on the way the systems analyst describes the events, conditions, data bases, and so on, and translate this orderliness into correct programs. We can use mathematics and computing to enforce the orderliness, verify the consistency of complex specifications, and translate the specifications automatically into bug-free code. But we cannot ''prove'' that the statement of the problem is correct. We *can* make the design *internally* consistent and correct.

To make this book user friendly, the mathematics appears only in the appendixes. The approach begins by ignoring existing programming languages. Only in this way can its provable constructs be built. However, the software used automatically generates code to implement the systems so designed. Code can be generated in conventional languages such as FORTRAN, Pascal, COBOL and C.

Although it was generally thought that mathematically provable software was a long way in the future, this new technique emerged from the work of Margaret Hamilton and Saydean Zeldin, which is both highly powerful and practical [14,16–21,24]. The technique has been automated so that bug-free systems can be designed by persons with no knowledge of either mathematics or programming. The software automatically generates bug-free program code. Whereas most mathematical techniques have been applied only to small programs, Hamilton and Zeldin's technique has been used successfully with highly complex systems. The technique is used not only for program design but, perhaps more important, for high-level specification of systems. The design is extended all the way from the highest-level statement of system functions down to the automatic generation of code. At the high level it is a tool for computer-aided thinking about systems, which helps designers to conceptualize the system functions.

THE IMPOSSIBILITY OF CONVENTIONAL DEBUGGING   The following illustrates the difficulty of conventional debugging:

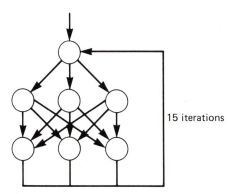

15 iterations

There are over 206 trillion unique paths through this module. If it were possible to test each of them in a millisecond, the total time taken for the complete test would be over 6000 years.

It is clearly impossible to perform a complete test. We would therefore saturation-test the module, checking as many different unique paths as we could, hoping that if the ones we have tested are correct, the others which we have not tested are also correct.

Conventional structured design seeks to lessen the number of unique paths that have to be tested. It does this by making the modules small (modular design), keeping the interfaces between modules simple, and limiting the control structures to ones which are easier to test. With nontrivial programs, however, there are still too many paths for complete testing. Furthermore, changes to the program, which often have to be made, cause unpredictable effects. Complex programs remain a minefield in which we can never be sure that all the mines have been removed.

Mathematically provable design takes a different approach. It limits the designer to the use of constructs which are provably correct. The use of hierarchies of such constructs permits the building of highly complex systems. Because mere human beings cannot be trusted to follow the rules, each step in the design is meticulously checked with software.

HIGHER-ORDER SOFTWARE

The technique created by Hamilton and Zeldin is called *Higher-Order Software* (HOS) and software which implements it is available from a corporation of that name [22]. The software automatically generates program code, thus eliminating the need for conventional programmers. A systems analyst or specially trained end user can generate the program he requires.

Chapter 8 describes the software. This chapter and the next describe the theory of HOS. Chapter 9 illustrates some systems built with the technique.

HOS BINARY TREES

The HOS methodology represents systems by means of binary trees. Each node of a binary tree has zero or two subordinate nodes. The node at the top of the tree is called the *root*. The nodes with no subordinates are called *leaves*. The following are binary trees:

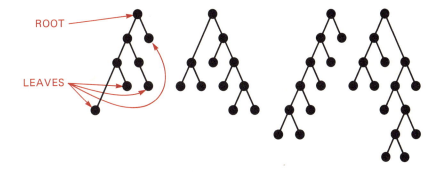

The following is a six-level tree:

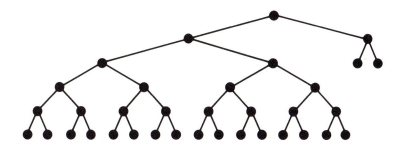

The following are *not* trees:

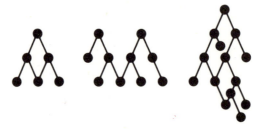

Each subordinate node is drawn below its superior in our diagrams; that is, there are no horizontal lines. A branch is described as *entering* a node if it comes from above. It is described as *leaving* a node if it goes to a subordinate node.

If a branch leaves node A and enters node B, node B is referred to as the *offspring* of A. Node A is the *parent* of B.

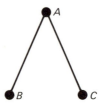

A node of a tree may be regarded as the root of another tree—a tree within a tree. The tree of which an intermediate node is a root is called a *subtree*.

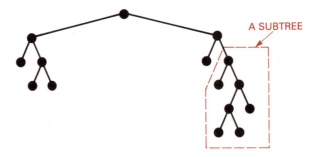

A SUBTREE

FUNCTIONS

Each node of a HOS binary tree represents a *function*.

A function has one or more *objects* as its input and one or more *objects* as its output.

An object might be a data item, a list, a table, a report, a file, a data base, or it might be a physical entity such as a circuit, a missile, an item undergoing manufacturing scheduling, a train, tracks, switching points, and so on.

In keeping with mathematical notation, the *input* object or objects are written on the right side of the function; the *output* object or objects are written on the left of the function.

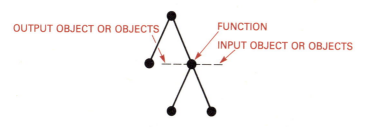

OUTPUT OBJECT OR OBJECTS   FUNCTION   INPUT OBJECT OR OBJECTS

The function may be a mathematical function. For example:

$$y \ = \ \text{SQUARE ROOT OF} \ \ x$$

OUTPUT OBJECT   FUNCTION   INPUT OBJECT

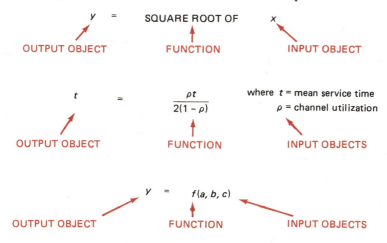

$$t \ = \ \frac{\rho t}{2(1 - \rho)}$$

where t = mean service time
ρ = channel utilization

OUTPUT OBJECT   FUNCTION   INPUT OBJECTS

$$y \ = \ f(a, b, c)$$

OUTPUT OBJECT   FUNCTION   INPUT OBJECTS

The function may be a programmed algorithm. For example:

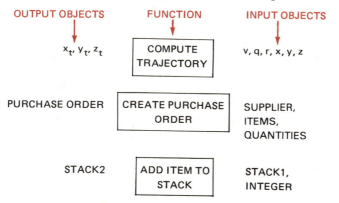

OUTPUT OBJECTS   FUNCTION   INPUT OBJECTS

x_t, y_t, z_t | COMPUTE TRAJECTORY | v, q, r, x, y, z

PURCHASE ORDER | CREATE PURCHASE ORDER | SUPPLIER, ITEMS, QUANTITIES

STACK2 | ADD ITEM TO STACK | STACK1, INTEGER

It may be a statement in a nonprocedural language:

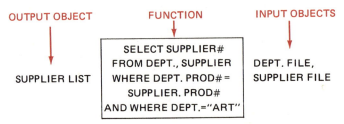

The function may be a program or subroutine specification. For example:

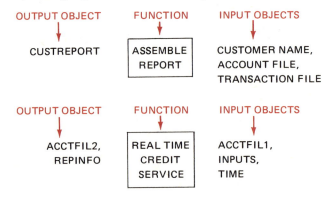

It may be a very broad statement of requirements.

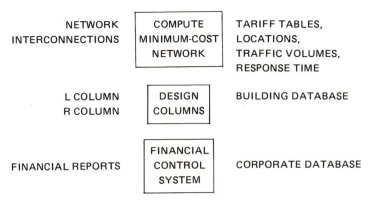

In fact, the notation can express (and decompose) operations which are not necessarily related to computing.

```
CHAIR        | MAKE    |   WOOD 1,
             | CHAIR   |   WOOD 2,
                           SCREWS

PEKING DUCK  | PREPARE |   INGREDIENTS
             | MEAL    |
```

In some cases the object that is the output from a function can be the same item type as the object that is the input. The value of the object is transformed by the function. Thus:

```
TIME2        | INCREASE     |   TIME1
             | BY ONE HOUR  |
```

TIME2 is the same data type as TIME1 but its value has changed.

```
CAR2         | WRECK |   CAR1
```

CAR2 is the same type of object as CAR1 but it is a different version.

```
STACK2       | POP |   STACK1
```

When a computer stack is "popped" this means that the top item in the stack is removed so that the next item down becomes the top item. STACK2 is similar to STACK1, but modified.

To add an item to a stack we use the function PUSH. The following inserts an integer into the stack.

```
STACK2       | PUSH |   STACK1,
                         INTEGER
```

The top function of the stack is represented with the function TOP:

```
INTEGER      | TOP |   STACK1
```

In mathematical notation we would write

$$STACK2 = PUSH\ (STACK1,\ INTEGER)$$
$$INTEGER = TOP\ (STACK1)$$

If the stack is empty when we do the latter command, the output would be a REJECT value.

In mathematical notation the output of one function is sometimes used as the input to another. Thus if we do PUSH (STACK, INTEGER1), we obtain a stack with INTEGER1 at the top. Applying the TOP function to this gives us INTEGER1.

We could write these two operations in one statement thus:

$$INTEGER_1 = TOP\ (PUSH\ (STACK,\ INTEGER_1))$$

Note that we read such mathematical statements from right to left. In $y = f(x)$ we start with x, then we apply function f to it, then we obtain output y.

With the previous example we start with the inputs STACK and INTEGER1, then apply the function PUSH to these variables, then apply function TOP to the result, then receive INTEGER1 back as output. This notation is used to state some behavior of the relation between the functions TOP, PUSH, and STACK.

FROM REQUIREMENTS STATEMENTS TO DETAILED PROGRAM DESIGN

The HOS tree charts (which are called "control maps") show how broad functions like those above are decomposed into subfunctions. The *root* of the tree is the broadest overview statement. In the tree that results from the final design, the leaves are functions which do not need to be decomposed further. The leaves may be primitive functions, functions already existing and stored in a library, or functions obtainable from an external source.

Design may proceed in a top-down or bottom-up fashion. With top-down design the broad overview is successively decomposed into functions which contain more detail. With bottom-up design detailed modules are aggregated to form higher-level modules until the overall goal of the system is reached.

In many methodologies the requirements statements, the specifications, the high-level design, and the detailed program design are done with different (and usually incompatible) languages. With HOS one language is used for all of these. An appealing feature of the methodology is that the binary tree, formally expressed, goes all the way from broad requirements statements to detailed program design. Automatic checks for errors, omissions, and inconsistencies are applied at each stage. The resulting tree is processed to create the application code automatically.

THREE PRIMITIVE CONTROL STRUCTURES

Unlike most structured methodologies, the HOS decomposition of a function into subfunctions (in other words, the relationship between a node in the tree and its two offsprings) is mathematically precise. It is this formality which enables the creation of complex specifications that are internally consistent and bug-free.

When a function is decomposed into its two offsprings this is done with a *control structure*. *Three primitive control structures* are used. They are called JOIN, INCLUDE, and OR. Other control structures can be defined as combinations of these three.

JOIN

Suppose that a high-level function is MAKE-A-STOOL. The stool is to be made from two types of wood: TOPWOOD and LEGWOOD.

We write $y = f(x)$ in mathematics, where y is the result of applying function f to data x. Similarly, to describe our requirement for making a stool, we write

STOOL = **MAKE**-A-STOOL (TOPWOOD, LEGWOOD)

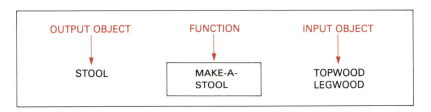

In order to make a stool, two operations are needed. We have to make the legs and the top, and then assemble these parts. The MAKE-A-STOOL function can be subdivided into a MAKE-PARTS function and an ASSEMBLE-PARTS function. Two objects are *output* from the MAKE-PARTS function: TOP and LEGS. These objects are *input* to the ASSEMBLE-PARTS function.

STOOL = MAKE-A-STOOL (TOPWOOD, LEGWOOD)

is then composed of the following two functions joined together:

TOP, LEGS = MAKE-PARTS (TOPWOOD, LEGWOOD)
STOOL = ASSEMBLE-PARTS (TOP, LEGS)

In the tree notation we represent this as follows:

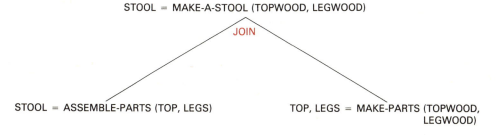

This is an illustration of the use of a JOIN control structure. Here one offspring depends on the other. The output of the right-hand function (i.e., TOPS, LEGS) must be the input to the left-hand function.

The input to the right-hand function is the same as the input to the parent. The output from the left-hand function is the same as the output from the parent. The effect of the parent function is thus reproduced.

The diagram must be read from right to left. (TOPWOOD, LEGWOOD) is the input to MAKE-PARTS, which results in TOP, LEGS, which is the input to ASSEMBLE-PARTS, which results in STOOL. Data enter each function from the right and leave it on the left. (Mathematicians sometimes do things differently from ordinary people. The tree is read right to left, not left to right, and it has its root at the top and leaves at the bottom.)

INCLUDE

The MAKE-PARTS function can be decomposed into two functions, MAKE-TOP and MAKE-LEGS. The top must be made with TOPWOOD and the legs must be made with LEGWOOD. The two functions composing make parts are thus

TOP = MAKE-TOP (TOPWOOD)
LEGS = MAKE-LEGS (LEGWOOD)

These are combined by means of an INCLUDE control structure, thus:

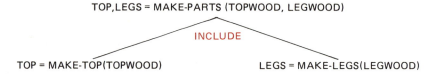

TOP,LEGS = MAKE-PARTS (TOPWOOD, LEGWOOD)

INCLUDE

TOP = MAKE-TOP(TOPWOOD)   LEGS = MAKE-LEGS(LEGWOOD)

In this control structure the two offsprings are independent of one another. They can operate separately and could even be executed on separate machines. Together both offsprings use the input data of the parent function, and together they produce the output data of that function.

OR

Let us suppose that the legs can be made in one of two ways, either with a TURN function or with a CARVE function. We have *either* LEGS = TURN (LEGWOOD) *or* LEGS = CARVE (LEGWOOD). In order to decide which to do, a Boolean expression is used which can be either true or false. An OR control structure is used as follows:

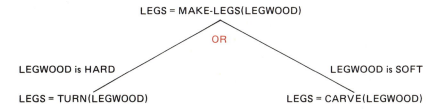

In this control structure, one or other of the offsprings achieves the effect of the parent, but not both. The resulting output of each offspring is the same as that of the parent (i.e., LEGS). Figure 3.2 summarizes the three primitive control structures.

CONTROL MAPS

We can combine the three control structures above into one tree as shown in Fig. 3.3. Diagrams like Fig. 3.3 are called *control maps*. Glancing ahead, the reader can see a collection of control maps in Chapter 9.

DYNAMICS GRAPH REPRESENTATIONS

Figure 3.4 represents the primitive functions in the form of a dynamics graph [23]. This representation makes it clear that the JOIN represents a sequence of operations; the INCLUDE breaks a function into separate *independent* activities; the OR represents a choice between *alternative* operations.

The dynamics graph is a projection of the tree representation and is a useful translation for certain purposes. It may aid an implementer in understanding the timing and storage relationship trade-off from a different viewpoint. A dynamics graph could be annotated with timing information in the physical design.

However, the dynamics graph tends to hide the hierarchical relationships (as do data flow diagrams). The HOS control maps could be automatically translated into dynamics graphs.

The INCLUDE function could be implemented with two separate processors. A system with multiple INCLUDEs could run on a multiprocessing computer configuration.

With the JOIN, in Fig. 3.4, f_2 cannot complete its processing before f_1 has been processed. The storage for z does not need to be allocated until f_1 has generated its value. The storage for y need not be allocated until its value is generated by f_2. When f_2 has completed its references to z, the storage for z may be released. The storage for f_1's instruction may be released when z is generated. If z is a single object, then f_1 must be sequentially processed before f_2. However, if z has a structure $z_1, z_2, \ldots, z_n$, the execution of f_2 may begin before f_1 has finished.

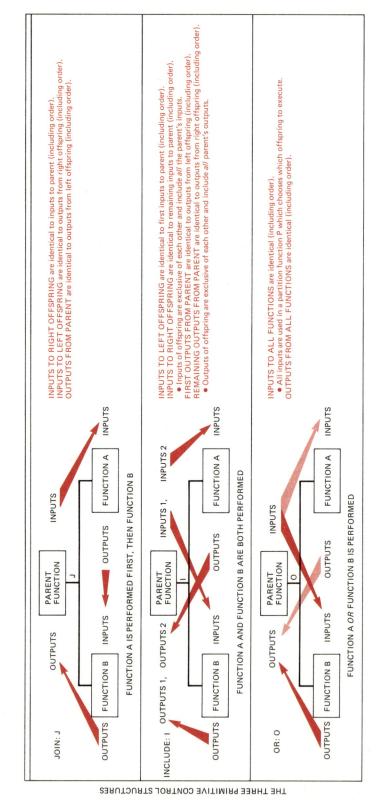

Figure 3.2 The three primitive control structures.

THE THREE PRIMITIVE CONTROL STRUCTURES

50

Figure 3.3   HOS binary tree using the three primitive control structures: JOIN, INCLUDE, and OR. They are each illustrated in this figure. Other control structures can be defined as combinations of these three. Diagrams like this are called control maps.

Similar implementation considerations apply to the other functions. This affects the techniques used for generating program code from the HOS tree.

GENERATION OF CODE
By breaking functions down with binary decomposition with the JOIN, INCLUDE, and OR constructs, control structures can be achieved which are mathematically provably correct [18]. The functional decomposition continues until leaf nodes of the binary tree are reached which are *primitives* which are known to be correct or *subroutines* which have themselves been created with this method. When all parts of the tree reach such leaf nodes the design is complete. *Program code can then be automatically generated from the resulting structures.* At each step in the design its correctness can be automatically checked.

FOUR TYPES OF LEAF NODES
The tree structures have *functions* as their nodes. The *function* is also called an *operation*. Every function is decomposed into lower-level functions showing more

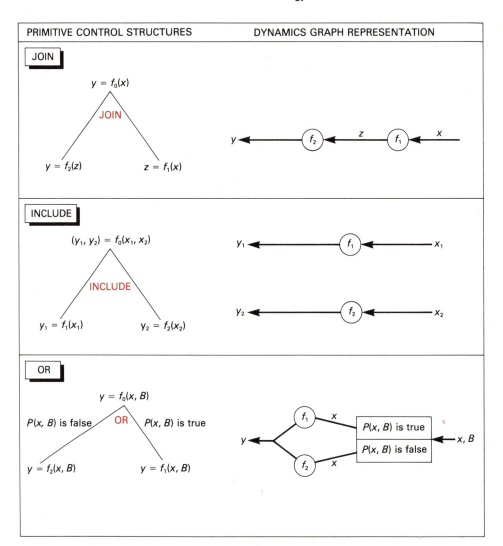

Figure 3.4 Examples of the three primitive control structures shown with a dynamics graph representation. With a JOIN the functions are executed sequentially. With an INCLUDE both are executed independently. With an OR one or other function is executed.

detail, except for those which are leaf nodes of the tree. There are four types of leaf nodes:

P: Primitive Operation

This is an operation that cannot be decomposed into other operations. It is defined rigorously with mathematical axioms.

OP: Operation Defined Elsewhere

This function will be further decomposed in another control map, which may be part of the current design or may be in a library.

R: Recursive Operation

This is a special node that allows looping. We discuss it in Chapter 5.

XO: External Operation

This function is an external program which is not written with HOS methodology. It may be manufacturer's software or previously existing user programs. Needless to say, the HOS software cannot guarantee its correctness.

If there is no non-HOS software (external operations), every operation is ultimately broken down into *primitive operations* which are described mathematically.

The repetitive use of predefined functions is essential. Without this the binary structures would have too many nodes to be practical for human design. Complex programs require the building of libraries of defined structures and defined operations (e.g., subroutines). These include completely general structures such as user-specifiable *loop* control structures, mathematical operations, elaborate application-independent functions such as data-base operations and report generators, and operations which are specific to given applications such as a backorder subroutine.

STATIC AND DYNAMIC TESTING OF PROGRAMS

We may distinguish between static and dynamic program testing.

Dynamic program testing is necessary with all programs not built with a rigorous mathematical technique (which includes the vast majority of programs in existence today). Each branch and usable combination of branches must be tested. As discussed earlier, there are usually so many combinations of branches that it is impossible to be sure that all have been tested. Consequently, saturation testing is done, but in practice, not all combinations of paths are exercised and not all possible errors in the code are revealed. Complex software is notorious for containing subtle bugs which can be extremely difficult to track down. Most large programs never become completely bug-free.

Static testing refers to verification that the functions, data types, and control structures have been used in accordance with rules that guarantee correctness. This verification can be performed by a computer with absolute precision. When this static verification is done, there is no need to dynamically test *all* of the control paths in the control map through the hierarchical structure. A few instances of control paths will be checked to ensure that correct results are being produced.

It is still necessary to check that the specifications are correct and are what the users really need, and that nothing has been omitted. Does the example above completely represent the making of a stool, for example, or is there something else needed other than legs and a top? The HOS method eliminates most of the effort in saturation testing and tracking down obscure logic errors.

Dynamic testing does not *guarantee* that code is error-free. You may search for flying saucers but just because you cannot find any that does not mean that they do not exist—especially as you do not know what you are really looking for.

EMBELLISHMENTS

We have now described the basic structures of the HOS methodology. Logic created with these structures is provably correct. In a sense, all that follows in this book is embellishment. However, much embellishment is needed to make the technique easy to use and powerful.

It has been proven that a computer could execute all arithmetic and logic with only three instructions. However, if you programmed such a computer you would need tools to make the programming easier—compilers, macroinstructions, libraries of subroutines, report generators, and so on. The same is true with the HOS language. Now that we have the sound foundation we can build higher-level control structures out of the three primitives. We can have libraries of defined operations. We can convert data-base models into HOS notation. We can use the HOS language to build report generators, create data flow diagrams, or translate other problem definition languages into computable HOS terms. We can specify a computer designed to implement the HOS constructs which can take advantage of future VLSI circuit costs and use multiple parallel processors.

We can make the methodology user friendly, and hide all the mathematics under the covers but know that it is there to protect us.

OVERVIEW

To summarize, complex systems can be decomposed hierarchically. Unlike conventional structured techniques, this can be done in a manner which is mathematically rigorous and gives provably correct decomposition to provably correct primitives.

The hierarchical chart, called a *control map*, can be built quickly at a graphics terminal with user-friendly software which we describe in Chapter 8. The software analyzes the chart, checks it for accuracy, helps the user to make adjustments until it is correct, and then generates accurate executable program code.

The chart has three types of constructs:

> FUNCTIONS
> OBJECTS (which are usually data variables)
> CONTROL STRUCTURES

FUNCTIONS are the nodes of the tree. Each function is decomposed into lower-level functions unless it is a leaf node. There can be four types of leaf nodes:

> P: Primitive operation
>
> OP: Operation defined elsewhere
>
> R: Recursive operation (Chapter 5)
>
> XO: External operation

OBJECTS, the input and output of the functions, are often data items, records, files, or data bases. They can also be physical or non-computer-related objects: for example, trains, tracks, and switching points.

CONTROL STRUCTURES show how a function is divided into lower-level functions. There are three primitive control structures which are rigorously defined mathematically:

> JOIN
> INCLUDE
> OR

Other, more powerful control structures are used, but these are all built from the three primitive control structures. The functions, thus, decompose into primitive functions which are mathematically rigorous. The means of decomposition itself is proven to be correct in terms of the three primitive control structures which are mathematically rigorous. The data types used by the functions have properties that are mathematically rigorous. From these three mathematical bases, great cathedrals of complex logic can be built.

REFERENCES

1. E. W. Dijkstra, *A Discipline of Programming*, Prentice-Hall, Inc., Englewood Cliffs, NJ, 1976.

2. E. W. Dijkstra, "The Humble Programmer," *Communications of the ACM*, Vol. 15 (October 1972).

3. A. Blikle and A. Mazurkiewicz, "An Algebraic Approach to the Theory of Programs, Algorithms, Languages and Recursiveness," *Mathematical Foundations of Computer Science*, Warsaw, Poland, 1972.

4. A. Church, *The Calculi of Lambda-Conversion*, Annals of Mathematical Studies, Vol. 6, Princeton University Press, Princeton, NJ, 1951.

5. W. E. Howden, "Methodology for Generation of Program Test Data," *IEEE Transactions on Software Engineering*, Vol. 2, No. 3 (1976).

6. J. A. Darringer, and J. C. King, "Application of Symbolic Execution to Program Testing," *Computer*, Vol. 11, No. 4 (1978).

7. Z. Manna, "The Correctness of Programs," *Journal of Computer and System Sciences*, Vol. 3, No. 2 (1969).

8. C. A. R. Hoare, "An Axiomatic Approach to Computer Programming," *Communications of the ACM*, Vol. 12, No. 10 (1969).

9. D. Gries, "An Introduction to Current Ideas on the Derivation of Correctness Proofs and Correct Programs," *IEEE Transactions on Software Engineering*, Vol. 2, No. 4 (1976).

10. B. Wegbreit, "Constructive Methods in Program Verification," *IEEE Transactions on Software Engineering*, Vol. 3, No. 2 (1977).

11. S. Owicki, "Axiomatic Proof Techniques for Parallel Programs," Ph.D. thesis, Department of Computer Science, Cornell University, 1975.

12. S. Owicki and D. Gries, "Verifying Properties of Parallel Programs: An Axiomatic Approach," *Communications of the ACM*, Vol. 19, No. 5 (1976).

13. L. Flon, "On the Design and Verification of Operating Systems," Ph.D. thesis, Department of Computer Science, Carnegie-Mellon University, 1977.

14. M. Hamilton and S. Zeldin, "The Relationship Between Design and Verification," *Journal of Systems and Software*, Vol. 1 (1979): 29–56.

15. H. K. Berg, W. E. Boebert, W. R. Franta, and T. G. Moher, *Formal Methods of Program Verification and Specification*, Prentice-Hall, Inc., Englewood Cliffs, NJ, 1982.

16. M. Hamilton and S. Zeldin, "The Manager as an Abstract Systems Engineer," *Digest of Papers, Fall COMPSAC '77*, Washington DC, IEEE Computer Society Cat. No. 77CH1258-3C, September 1977.

17. M. Hamilton and S. Zeldin, *AXES Syntax Description*, Technical Report 4, Higher Order Software, Inc., Cambridge, MA, December 1976.

18. M. Hamilton and S. Zeldin, *The Foundations of AXES: A Specification Language Based on Completeness of Control*, Doc. R-964, Charles Stark Draper Laboratory, Inc., Cambridge, MA, March 1976.

19. M. Hamilton and S. Zeldin, *Integrated Software Development System/Higher Order Software Conceptual Description*, Technical Report 3, Higher Order Software, Inc., Cambridge, MA, November 1976.

20. M. Hamilton and S. Zeldin, "Higher Order Software—A Methodology for Defining Software," *IEEE Transactions on Software Engineering*, Vol. SE-2, No. 1 (1976): 9–32.

21. M. Hamilton and S. Zeldin, "Reliability in Terms of Predictability," *Proceedings, COMPSAC '78*, Chicago, IEEE Computer Society Cat. No. 78CH1338-3C, November 1978.

22. Higher Order Software, Inc., P.O. Box 531, 2067 Massachusetts Avenue, Cambridge, MA 02140, Tel: (617)661-8900.

23. Wm. R. Hackler and A. Samarov, *An AXES Specification of a Radar Scheduler*, Technical Report 23, Higher Order Software, Inc., Cambridge, MA, November 1979.

24. M. Hamilton and S. Zeldin, "The Functional Life Cycle Model and Its Automation: USE.IT," *Journal of Systems and Software*, Vol. 3, No. 1, March, 1983, pp. 25–62.

ADDITIONAL READINGS

B. W., Boehm, R. K. McClean, and D. B. Urfreg, "Some Experience with Automated Aids to the Design of Large Scale Reliable Software," *IEEE Transactions on Software Engineering*, Vol. 1, No. 1 (1975).

R. W. Floyd, *Assigning Meanings to Programs*, Proceedings, Symposium on Applied Mathematics, Vol. 19, American Mathematical Society, Providence, RI, 1967.

R. Milner, "An Algebraic Definition of Simulation Between Programs," *Proceedings 2nd International Joint Conference on Artificial Intelligence*, London, 1971.

R. J. Rubey, J. A. Dana, and P. W. Biche, "Quantitative Aspects of Software Validation," *IEEE Transactions on Software Engineering*, Vol. 1, No. 2 (1975).

J. E. Stoy, *Denotational Semantics: The Scott–Strachey Approach to Programming Language Theory*, The MIT Press, Cambridge, MA, 1977.

4 CO-CONTROL STRUCTURES

INTRODUCTION   The HOS mathematical axioms relate to the three primitive control structures, JOIN, INCLUDE, and OR. These structures, however, are often confining. The user can be provided with other control structures which themselves are built out of the primitive structures. Employment of these other structures is automatically verified for correct use.

HOS provides four commonly used nonprimitive control structures:

> COJOIN
> COINCLUDE
> COOR
> CONCUR

These provide more flexibility in dividing the parent variables among the offspring functions. In addition to these, the user can design his own control structures rather like macroinstructions, or can use already existing designed structures from a library.

Suppose, for example, that the input to the MAKE-PARTS function discussed in Chapter 3 includes the tools needed.

> TOP, LEGS = MAKE-PARTS (TOPWOOD, LEGWOOD
> LATHE, HANDSAW, HANDTOOLS)

We cannot split these inputs into separate discrete lists, one for MAKE-TOP and one for MAKE-LEGS. To solve this problem a function similar to the INCLUDE function is used but with more flexibility in handling repeatedly used values. It is called COINCLUDE.

COINCLUDE, like INCLUDE, allows two offspring functions to be combined into one parent function. MAKE-TOP and MAKE-LEGS, for example, can be combined into MAKE-STOOL. The inputs to the offspring functions are

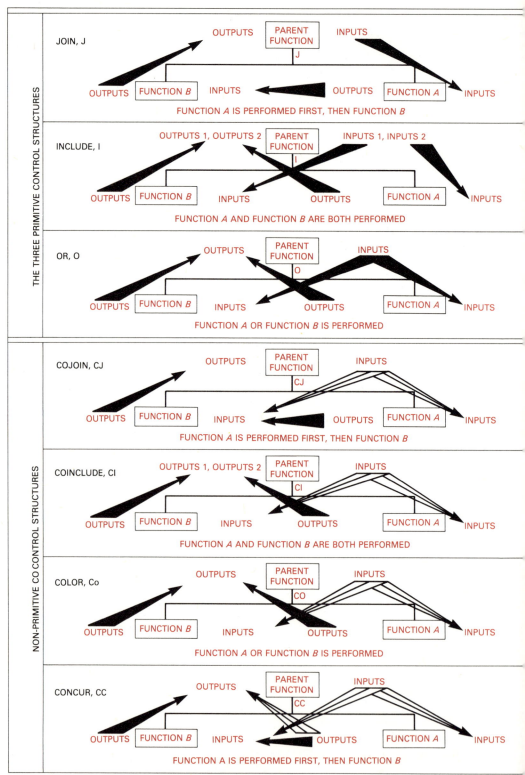

THE THREE PRIMITIVE CONTROL STRUCTURES

JOIN, J

OUTPUTS · PARENT FUNCTION · INPUTS
J
OUTPUTS · FUNCTION B · INPUTS · OUTPUTS · FUNCTION A · INPUTS

FUNCTION A IS PERFORMED FIRST, THEN FUNCTION B

INCLUDE, I

OUTPUTS 1, OUTPUTS 2 · PARENT FUNCTION · INPUTS 1, INPUTS 2
I
OUTPUTS · FUNCTION B · INPUTS · OUTPUTS · FUNCTION A · INPUTS

FUNCTION A AND FUNCTION B ARE BOTH PERFORMED

OR, O

OUTPUTS · PARENT FUNCTION · INPUTS
O
OUTPUTS · FUNCTION B · INPUTS · OUTPUTS · FUNCTION A · INPUTS

FUNCTION A OR FUNCTION B IS PERFORMED

NON-PRIMITIVE CO CONTROL STRUCTURES

COJOIN, CJ

OUTPUTS · PARENT FUNCTION · INPUTS
CJ
OUTPUTS · FUNCTION B · INPUTS · OUTPUTS · FUNCTION A · INPUTS

FUNCTION A IS PERFORMED FIRST, THEN FUNCTION B

COINCLUDE, CI

OUTPUTS 1, OUTPUTS 2 · PARENT FUNCTION · INPUTS
CI
OUTPUTS · FUNCTION B · INPUTS · OUTPUTS · FUNCTION A · INPUTS

FUNCTION A AND FUNCTION B ARE BOTH PERFORMED

COLOR, Co

OUTPUTS · PARENT FUNCTION · INPUTS
CO
OUTPUTS · FUNCTION B · INPUTS · OUTPUTS · FUNCTION A · INPUTS

FUNCTION A OR FUNCTION B IS PERFORMED

CONCUR, CC

OUTPUTS · PARENT FUNCTION · INPUTS
CC
OUTPUTS · FUNCTION B · INPUTS · OUTPUTS · FUNCTION A · INPUTS

FUNCTION A IS PERFORMED FIRST, THEN FUNCTION B

The nonstriped arrows indicate that *all* variables are transferred.
The striped arrows indicate that *some but not necessarily all* variables are transferred.

INPUTS TO RIGHT OFFSPRING are identical to inputs to parent (including order).
INPUTS TO LEFT OFFSPRING are identical to outputs from right offspring (including order).
OUTPUTS FROM PARENT are identical to outputs from left offspring (including order).

INPUTS TO LEFT OFFSPRING are identical to first inputs to parent (including order).
INPUTS TO RIGHT OFFSPRING are identical to remaining inputs to parent (including order).
  ● Inputs of offspring are exclusive of each other and include *all* the parent's inputs.
FIRST OUTPUTS FROM PARENT are identical to outputs from left offspring (including order).
REMAINING OUTPUTS FROM PARENT are identical to outputs from right offspring (including order).
  ● Outputs of offspring are exclusive of each other and include *all* parent's outputs.

INPUTS TO ALL FUNCTIONS are identical (including order).
  All inputs are used in a Partition function P which chooses which offspring to execute.
OUTPUTS FROM ALL FUNCTIONS are identical (including order).

INPUTS TO RIGHT OFFSPRING are a subset of the parent's inputs.
INPUTS TO LEFT OFFSPRING come from either the parent's inputs or the
  outputs of the right offspring.
OUTPUTS FROM PARENT are identical to the outputs from the left offspring.

INPUTS TO RIGHT AND LEFT OFFSPRINGS come from the parent's inputs.
ALL OUTPUTS FROM PARENT come from *either* the outputs of the left offspring
  or the right offspring.
  The first outputs of the parent are identical to those of the left offspring.
  The last outputs of the parent are identical to those of the right offspring.

INPUTS TO BOTH OFFSPRINGS are a subset of the inputs to the parent.
  A partition function P uses some input from the parent to determine which offspring function is used.
OUTPUTS FROM ALL FUNCTIONS are identical.

INPUTS TO RIGHT OFFSPRING are a subset of the inputs to the parent.
INPUTS TO LEFT OFFSPRING come from the outputs of the right offspring and
  from the inputs to the parent; none must necessarily come from the parent.
OUTPUTS FROM THE PARENT come from the outputs of the left and right offspring. Each offspring contributes
  at least one output of the parent.

Figure 4.1 HOS control structures and movement of variables.

61

taken freely from the inputs to the parent functions. The outputs from the offspring functions (but not necessarily all of them) are combined into the outputs of the parent function.

The decomposition of MAKE-PARTS may, for example, be as follows:

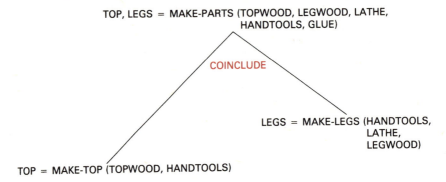

Here there is more freedom than with an INCLUDE structure in *ordering*, *selecting*, *omitting*, and *repeating* variables.

The parent's input variables are *reordered* in the input to the right offspring. With the three primitive structures the ordering of variables is important.

Only certain parent inputs and offspring outputs are *selected* for use. GLUE is *omitted* as an offspring input. HANDTOOLS is *repeated* as an input to both offsprings.

As with the primitive control structures, exact rules govern the use of variables in the co-control structures. These structures and their rules are summarized in Fig. 4.1.

To illustrate the co-control structures we will draw dynamics graph projections of them (as we did with the primitive structures in Chapter 3). These, like data flow diagrams, show functions as circles and the transfer of data types as lines. We draw the flow going from right to left because this is how an HOS chart is read.

COJOIN

The following are examples of uses of the COJOIN structure:

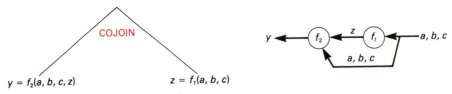

1. Here, unlike a primitive JOIN, the left offspring uses the inputs to the parents.

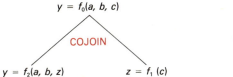

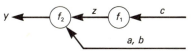

2. Here the input variables to the parent are split into separate inputs to the two offspring.

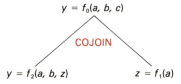

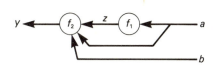

3. Here c, an input to the parent, is not used by either offspring. The offspring share a, but only the left offspring uses b.

COINCLUDE

The following are examples of uses of the COIN-CLUDE structure:

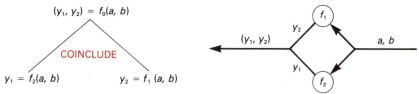

1. Unlike a primitive INCLUDE, the offspring here share the variables from the parent.

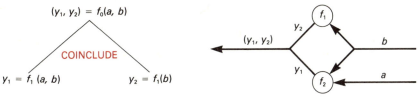

2. Here both offspring use b but only the left offspring uses a.

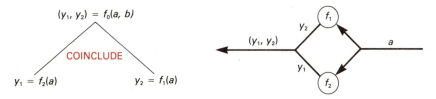

3. Here, one of the inputs to the parent, b, is ignored. Both offspring use the other input, a.

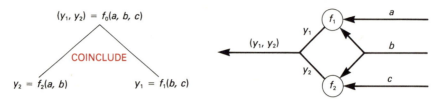

$$(y_1, y_2) = f_0(a, b, c)$$

COINCLUDE

$$y_2 = f_2(a, b) \qquad y_1 = f_1(b, c)$$

4. Here different offspring use different parent inputs, and the first output of the parent is from the right, not left, offspring.

COOR

The following are examples of uses of the COOR structure. In each of them a condition, $P(B)$, is tested. One or other of the offspring is used depending on whether the condition is TRUE or FALSE.

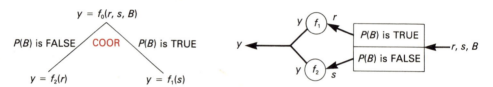

$$y = f_0(r, s, B)$$

$P(B)$ is FALSE   COOR $P(B)$ is TRUE

$$y = f_2(r) \qquad y = f_1(s)$$

1. Here, unlike a primitive OR structure, the two offspring use different variables from the parent's input.

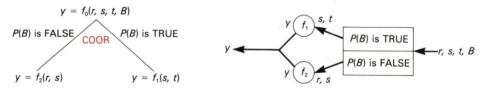

$$y = f_0(r, s, t, B)$$

$P(B)$ is FALSE   COOR $P(B)$ is TRUE

$$y = f_2(r, s) \qquad y = f_1(s, t)$$

2. The offspring may share some of the parent's variables and not others.

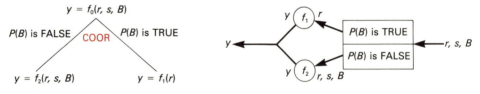

$$y = f_0(r, s, B)$$

$P(B)$ is FALSE   COOR $P(B)$ is TRUE

$$y = f_2(r, s, B) \qquad y = f_1(r)$$

3. Here one of the offspring employs the Boolean itself.

CONCUR

The following are illustrations of uses of the CONCUR structure:

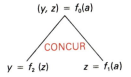

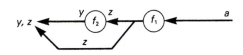

1. Here, unlike a JOIN or COJOIN, the output of the right offspring appears in the output of the parent.

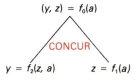

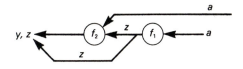

2. Here the input to the parent is used as input to the left offspring, together with z.

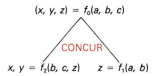

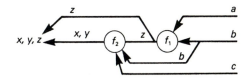

3. Here the parent inputs are split between the two offspring, with b being shared by them.

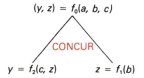

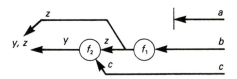

4. Here one of the inputs to the parent is not used.

Figure 4.2 shows the four co-control structures applied to the acquisition of stools.

LOCAL VARIABLES   Programs often employ local variables which are not part of their input or output. They are generated and used internally in the program.

The same is true with HOS control maps. A JOIN or COJOIN produces

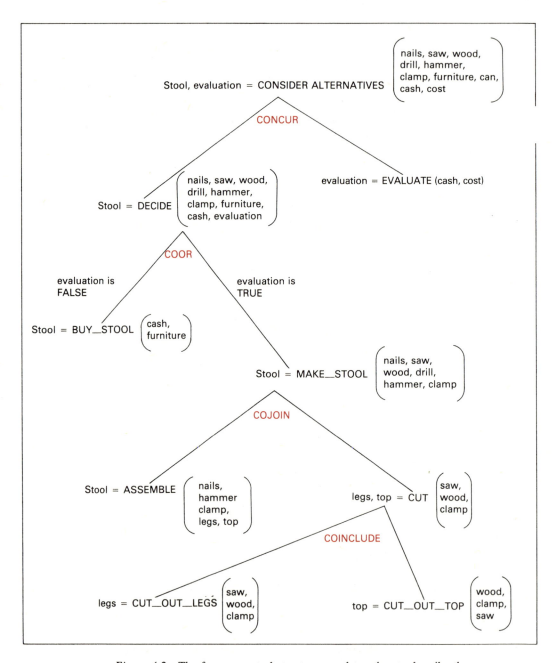

Figure 4.2 The four co-control structures used together to describe the acquisition of a stool.

and uses a local variable. Z in the following structure is a local variable:

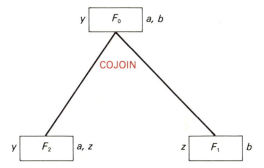

Local variables are the only ones which are not part of the input or output of the top node of the control structure.

N-ARY BRANCHES   So far we have drawn binary trees. HOS also permits one parent node to have more than two offspring. In this case the offspring are dealt with a pair at a time from right to left.

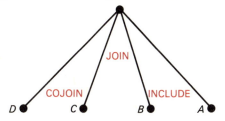

In the diagram above, an INCLUDE operation is performed between A and B. The results of that are then used in a JOIN operation with C. The results of that are then used in a COJOIN operation with D. An n-ary branch in the tree is thus a shorthand way of drawing multiple binary branches.

Figures 4.3 and 4.4 show n-ary branches with their binary equivalents. Figure 4.5 shows a typical example of a chart with n-ary branches printed by the HOS software.

If in doubt about whether a certain n-ary branch is valid, the user should break it down into its binary equivalent. Let us ask the reader, for example: Is the following valid?

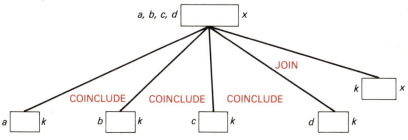

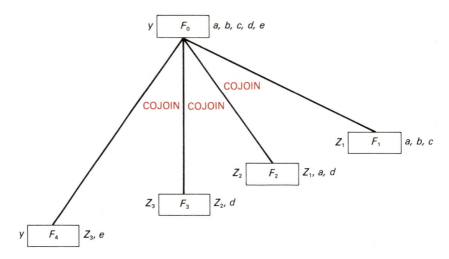

This n-ary branch is a short-hand way of showing the control map below which only has binary branches:

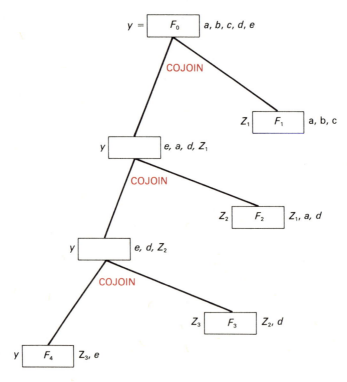

Figure 4.3 An *n*-ary branch giving a shorthand way of showing three CO-JOINs.

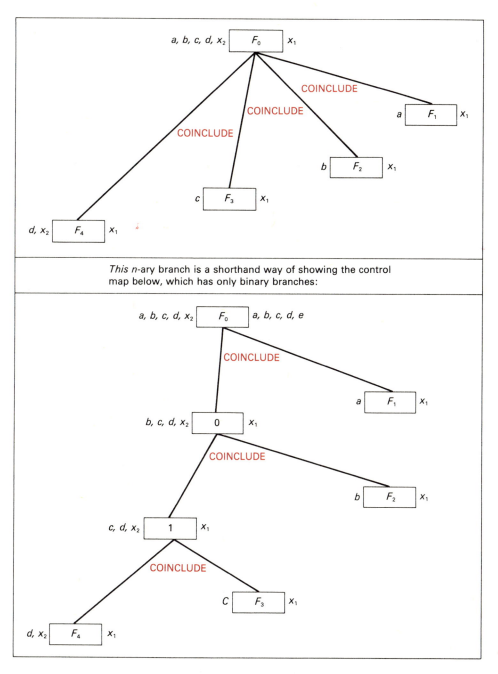

This *n*-ary branch is a shorthand way of showing the control map below, which has only binary branches:

Figure 4.4 An *n*-ary branch giving a shorthand way of showing three COIN-CLUDEs.

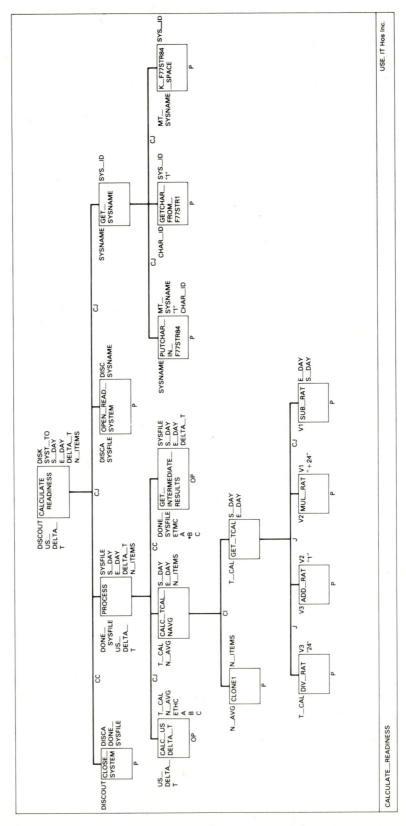

Figure 4.5 Typical example of a chart with *n*-ary branches printed by the HOS software.

This is a particularly useful construct. We often need to use an intermediate result, k in this case, in multiple operations. To see whether it is valid, break it down into its equivalent binary tree.

HELP FOR THE DESIGNER

It can be somewhat tedious to work out exactly which control structures are needed as a complex operation is decomposed. Software can help with this. The designer names the functions and sketches their decomposition into lower-level functions; he keys the data types used against the blocks, and then the software works out in detail the COJOINs, COINCLUDEs, and so on. The designer checks and may modify the result. This creative partnership of person and machine enables a rigorous design to be built quickly.

To make the design process as fast as possible, other powerful designer-friendly constructs are needed.

5 LOOPS AND RECURSION

INTRODUCTION   Many computer programs need to carry out the same function repeatedly with different variables—in other words, execute loops. Loops are represented in an HOS tree structure by means of *recursion*.

RECURSIVE NODES   Figure 5.1 illustrates recursion. It shows an early design for the jacket of this book (which was not used). The design incorporates itself and consequently it repeats many times. A similar technique is used in HOS control maps. A recursive control map is one that incorporates itself.

In Fig. 5.2 the block at the top of the control map is called REPEATING PROCESS. The control map expands REPEATING PROCESS into its components. One of those components is a block called REPEATING PROCESS. When this is reached, the whole control map is executed again. Some input to REPEATING PROCESS has to be different each time it is used.

REPEATING PROCESS in Fig. 5.2 is called a *recursive* node. A recursive node appears twice in a control map in such a way that it incorporates itself. It will then cause itself to be reexecuted over and over.

STOPPING THE LOOP   A problem with Fig. 5.1, as the artist discovered, is that it repeats infinitely. There is nothing to stop the recursion, except perhaps the artist's patience. The same is true in Fig. 5.2. There is nothing which stops the repetition.

A loop must have something to terminate it to prevent it from executing indefinitely. In an HOS tree a loop must have a decision structure (e.g., an OR) to test whether the looping is to continue. Figure 5.3 shows this. The looping stops if the Boolean *B* is *true*.

Figure 5.1   Illustration of recursion.

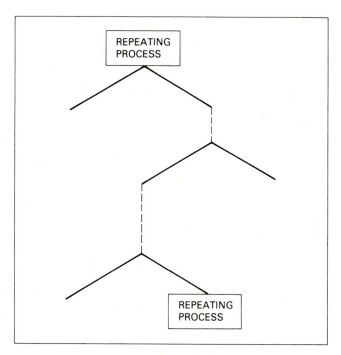

Figure 5.2 The operation REPEATING PROCESS is decomposed in this control map. It contains itself, just as the book jacket design of Fig. 5.1 contains itself. Therefore, it reexecutes and again encounters itself. This continues until something stops the loop.

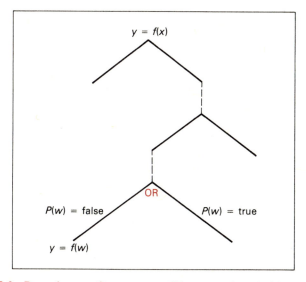

Figure 5.3 Recursion must have some condition to stop it. A decision structure is used (e.g., an OR). Here condition $P(w)$ is tested before the node $y = f(w)$. If the condition is true, the loop stops. If the condition is false, $y = f(w)$ is executed. This is the same as the original $y = f(x)$ except that now it has different input.

$y = f(x)$ is the node at the top of the tree. It is decomposed into multiple activities and one of its progeny is itself with different input: $y = f(w)$. When $y = f(w)$ is reached, the entire tree is executed again. This continues as long as the condition $P(w)$ is *false*. When some operation in the tree makes the condition $P(w)$ *true*, the looping stops.

Let us return to the MAKE-A-STOOL illustration of Chapter 3 (Fig. 3.3).

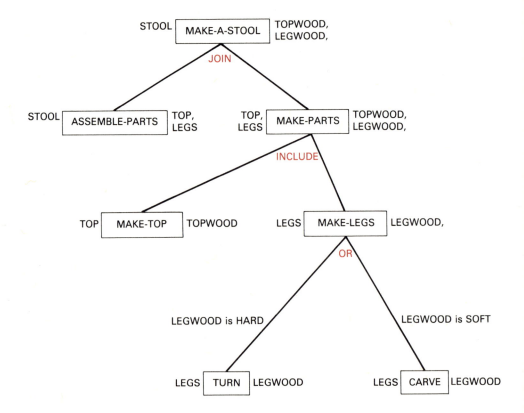

Suppose that we were really serious about the stool-making business and decided to mass-produce them. We have an inventory of stools and add stools to it as we manufacture them:

We use INVENTORY1 as input and INVENTORY2 as output to show that the inventory value is changed by the ADD-TO-INVENTORY operation.

STOOL is an output of the MAKE-A-STOOL operation and an input to the

ADD-TO-INVENTORY operation. Together these operations might constitute an overall operation called PRODUCTION:

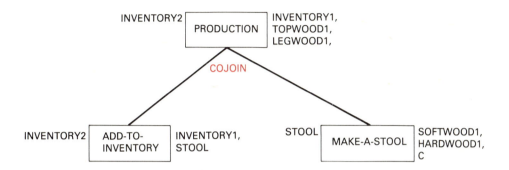

The problem with this is that it adds only one stool to the inventory. We want to make many, so we need a loop.

PRODUCTION can be our looping (i.e., recursive) function. We must have some way of stopping the loop. Suppose that we decide to make a batch of N stools. We use a count which must be set to zero before we execute PRODUCTION. Each time we execute PRODUCTION we add 1 to the count until it reaches N. This counting can be done in the ADD-TO-INVENTORY operation:

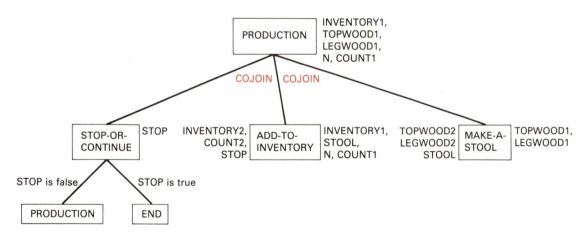

Each time this procedure reaches the lower-level block, PRODUCTION, it will execute the entire PRODUCTION control map over again. What causes it to stop? The ADD-TO-INVENTORY function creates a Boolean called STOP. STOP is set to "true" when COUNT1 reaches N.

ADD-TO-INVENTORY must *include* two operations, adding stools to the inventory and counting the stools to see whether there are N of them yet:

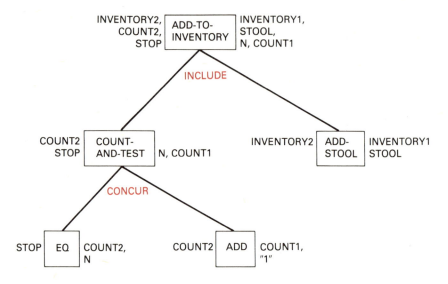

COUNT-AND-TEST encompasses two primitive operations, ADD, which adds 1 to the counter, and EQ, which sets the Boolean STOP to "true" when COUNT2 equals N. Figure 5.4 shows a count routine which counts up to N. Its COUNT-AND-TEST operation is the same as that above.

Where an output object of a recursive block is a modified version of an input object, for example, COUNT or FILE, we need three versions of this object because the inputs to the two recursive blocks must be different. Thus if COUNT1 is the input to the top LOOP block, as in Fig. 5.4, COUNT2 may be the input to the bottom LOOP block. The output of both must be the same, in this case a third version of COUNT which we might call COUNT3. Figure 5.5 illustrates this.

The recursive node, PRODUCTION, must have the same data types in both of its appearances. These have to be carried down through the STOP-OR-CONTINUE operation:

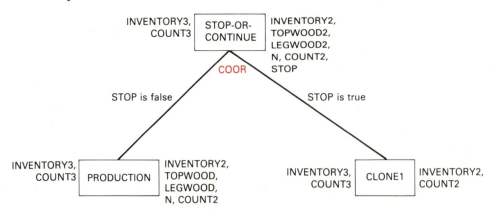

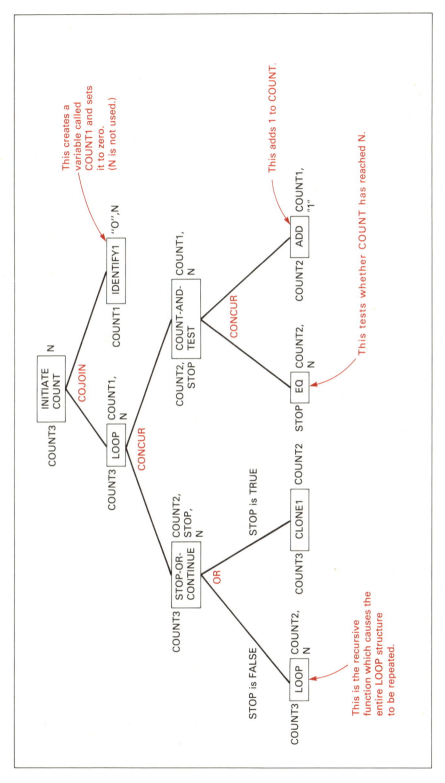

Figure 5.4 Counter that counts up to N, then stops. STOP is a Boolean that is set to TRUE by the EQ primitive operation when COUNT = N.

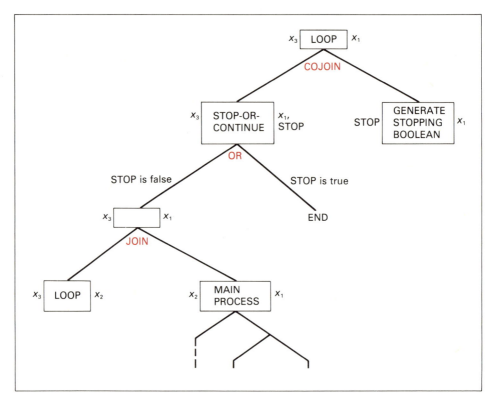

Figure 5.5 Where versions of the same variable are both the input and output of the LOOP block, three versions of this variable are needed because the lower LOOP block must have different input from the top LOOP block.

When the loop stops, CLONE1 is executed. This function provides outputs with the same values as its inputs. This is a function which makes INVENTORY3 and COUNT3 identical to INVENTORY2 and COUNT2 so that the output is the inventory containing N stools.

Figure 5.6 shows the whole operation of making a batch of stools. The IDENTIFY1 node creates the variable COUNT1 and sets it equal to the first item in the input list, which is "O".

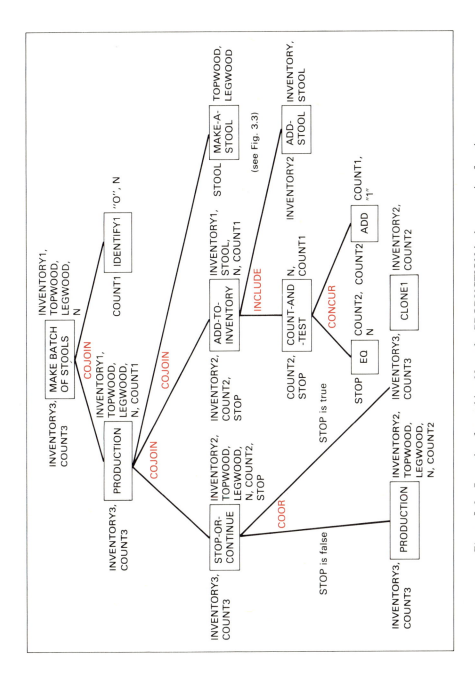

Figure 5.6 Operation for making N stools. PRODUCTION is the recursive function.

81

EVALUATION OF A FACTORIAL

Consider the evaluation of a factorial.

$$\text{Factorial}(n) = n(n - 1)(n - 2)\cdots 1$$

where n is an integer > 0. We can use the following recursion:

$$\text{Factorial}(n) = n \cdot \text{Factorial}(n - 1)$$

$y = n \cdot \text{Factorial}(n - 1)$ can be mapped as follows:

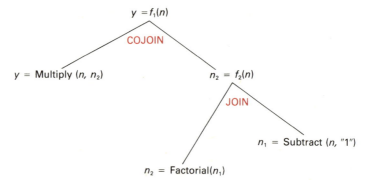

To create the recursive loop we must have a stopping condition. If $n = 0$, we want to stop. An OR structure is used to stop the recursion:

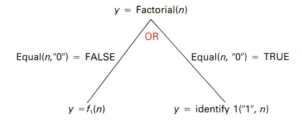

If $n = 0$, then y, the value of the factorial, is 1 (by definition of a factorial).

Figure 5.7 combines these two structures. Suppose that we execute the structure in Fig. 5.7 with $n = 4$. At the first iteration we obtain

$$\text{FACTORIAL}(4) = 4.\text{FACTORIAL}(3)$$

from the F_1 block. We evaluate FACTORIAL(3), reexecuting the entire structure. We obtain

$$\text{FACTORIAL}(3) = 3.\text{FACTORIAL}(2)$$

from the F_1 block. We evaluate FACTORIAL(2) and obtain 2.FACTORIAL(1).

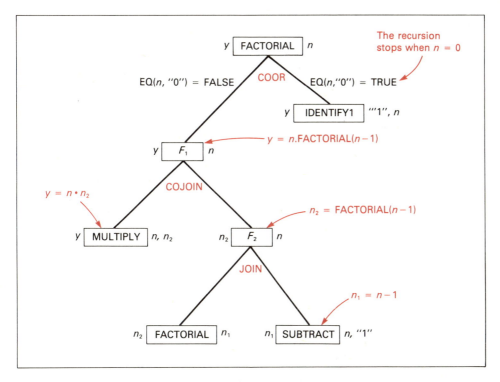

Figure 5.7   Use of recursion to evaluate the factorial of n, where n is an integer ≥ 0. The operation FACTORIAL at the bottom left causes the entire structure to be reinvoked each time control passes to it. This recursion stops when $n = 0$. On successive iterations we obtain FACTORIAL (n); n.FACTORIAL$(n-1)$, $n. (n-1)$. FACTORIAL$(n-2)$; $n. (n-1). (n-2)$. FACTORIAL$(n-3)$; until finally: $n(n-1)(n-2)(n-3)\cdots 1$.

We evaluate FACTORIAL(1) and obtain 1.FACTORIAL(0). We evaluate FACTORIAL(0) and now the condition switches us to the IDENTIFY block, which gives FACTORIAL(0) = 1.

DO-WHILE AND REPEAT-UNTIL LOOPS

Programs commonly contain two types of loops: DO-WHILE loops and REPEAT-UNTIL loops.

A DO-WHILE loop tests to see whether a certain condition is true at the start of the loop. A REPEAT-UNTIL loop tests to see whether a certain condition is true at the end of the loop.

In a DO-WHILE loop we need an OR or COOR structure at the start of the loop, immediately after the top node. In a REPEAT-UNTIL loop we need a decision structure (e.g., OR or COOR) at the end of the loop before the recursive function.

The loop in Fig. 5.7 is a DO-WHILE loop. The test to see whether $n = 1$ occurs at the start of the structure. We continue to DO the operation WHILE n is not equal to 1.

The loop in Fig. 5.6 is a REPEAT-UNTIL loop. The STOP-OR-CONTINUE operation occurs after MAKE-A-STOOL, ADD-STOOL, and COUNT-AND-TEST. We continue making stools until COUNT2 = N.

Figure 5.8 shows a DO-WHILE and REPEAT-UNTIL loop. It is often a good idea for HOS designers (or programmers) to become used to always employing one or the other. HOS designers should adopt the habit of always using

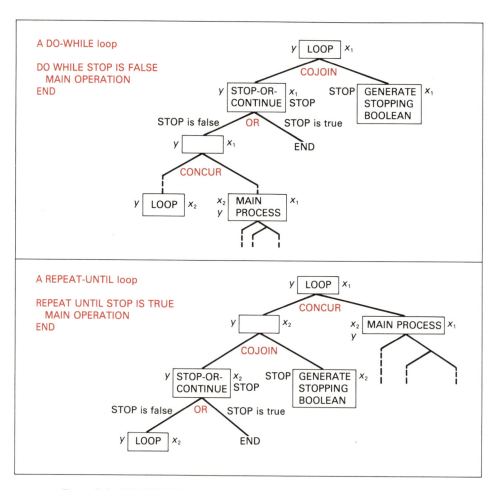

Figure 5.8   DO-WHILE loop and REPEAT-UNTIL loop. STOP is the Boolean which is tested to see whether to stop the loop.

a DO-WHILE loop formed like that at the top of Fig. 5.8 because many applications want to handle the possibility of executing the loop zero times.

FILE PROCESSING   A common form of loop is a batch run where all the records in a file are processed. The Boolean that terminates the loop is *true* when the end of the file is reached.

We will use it in a DO-WHILE loop:

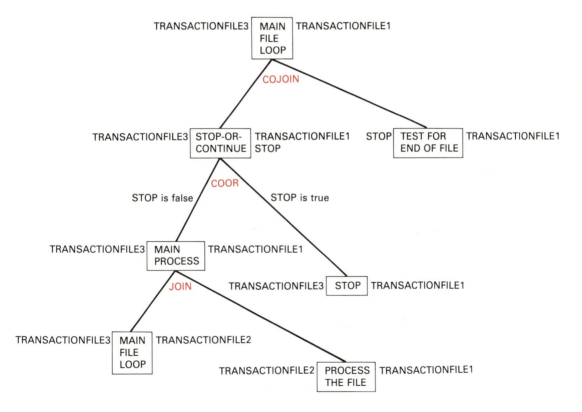

Figure 5.9 uses this in a typical masterfile update run. The transaction file contains a batch of transactions which updates a master file.

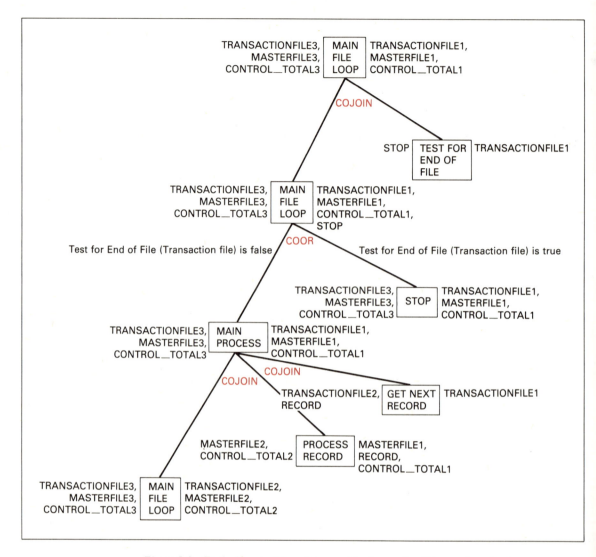

Figure 5.9 Typical masterfile update run. The transaction file contains a batch of records which are used to update a masterfile. A running control total is maintained of the transactions processed.

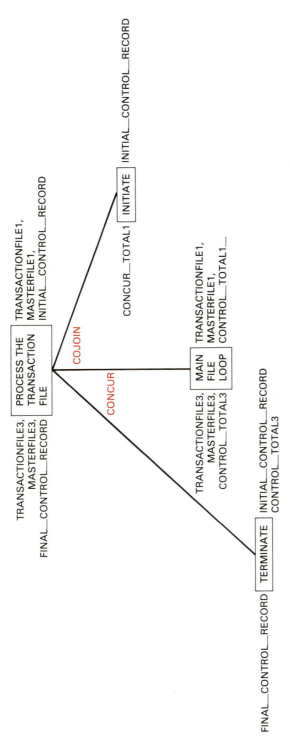

Figure 5.10 **Run initiation and termination operations used in conjuction with the main file loop of Fig. 5.9.**

INITIAL AND FINAL OPERATIONS

Usually, a loop requires some initial operation before it starts and some final operation after it completes. This typically uses two JOINs or COJOINs as follows:

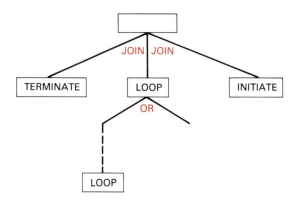

Figure 5.10 shows initiation and termination operations used with the masterfile update run of Fig. 5.9.

6 DATA

INTRODUCTION   As discussed earlier, an object in HOS is something which forms the input or output of a function. Examples of objects are CUSTOMER#, MASTERFILE, STOOL, STOP, CONTROL TOTAL, X1, X2, X3, and so on.

A data type is a set of data objects characterized by certain defined properties. Examples of data types are *integers* such as +7, *rational numbers* such as 3.9417, *floating-point numbers, Booleans* which are either true or false, a *set of values, character strings*, and so on.

The properties of each data type are rigorously defined by giving axioms that characterize their behavior. Many different objects may be used in an operation provided that they are of the specified data type. For example, if an operation employs a character string, many different character strings (i.e., different character string values) may be used.

Most programming languages permit a given number of data types to be used. FORTRAN, for example, permits a small number of data types. Newer languages such as Pascal and Ada permit users to define data types in terms of existing or previously defined data types, but not purely abstractly, in terms of axioms that characterize their properties.

The meaning of a *type* of data value is determined by the set of primitive operations that can be performed on values of that type according to axioms which state some specified behavior. What it means to be an integer, for example, is determined by the set of primitive operations that can be performed on integers. Operations out of which other operations can be built, but which are themselves defined axiomatically, are said to be *primitive operations* on their data types.

This distinguishes the HOS use of data types from the use of data types in a language like Ada. Normal programming languages used for specification merely list the primitive operations without axiomatizing them. HOS defines the data-type behaviors with axiomatic rigor.

To achieve provable correctness, the set of primitive operations that can be performed on data types must be specified with mathematical rigor. To specify a data type in the HOS methodology, a set of primitive operations and a set of axioms are defined which completely characterize the data type. Appendix III gives details of how six data types are specified mathematically in HOS.

When new data types are defined in HOS, the definition may be done in terms of existing data types, but it can also be done without reference to other data types, if the primitive operations and axioms do not require such reference. In either case, the definition must be done with mathematical rigor.

HOS provides a library of data types, and nonmathematical users are likely to employ the data types in that library rather than define their own data types. However, users who have become skilled with creating data-type axioms may define special data types of their own.

DIVERSE DATA TYPES   Whereas languages such as FORTRAN and COBOL allow the use of only certain data types, the HOS language is completely general.
In Fig. 6.1, for example, there is a rich mixture of data types. BEAR__COUNT1 is a natural. STOP is a Boolean. ZOO-NAME is an alphabetic field. ANIMAL__ FILE is a file. BEAR__RECORD is a record which is part of ANIMAL__FILE. How about BEAR and GORILLA? They are physical objects. They are not fields in a computer or simulated objects; they are real hairy animals. Hairy animals is not a data type that is permissible in FORTRAN. But HOS is a specification language which has *physical objects* as data types on some of its control maps. The MAKE-A-STOOL illustrations earlier use *physical data types*.

In Fig. 6.1 we have both the catching of bears and gorillas (a physical activity) and the recording of the results (a data processing activity) going on at the same time. A real-world example of physical activity and data processing going on together would be where a human being interacts in a complex way with a computer system: for example, the design of operating procedures for a nuclear power station.

When the software checks the control map in Figure 6.1 we may possibly not yet have told it anything about the data types. It then has to make what assumptions it can. It can conclude that STOP is a *Boolean* because of its use in a COOR structure. It can assume that BEAR__COUNT1 is a *natural* because it is set to 0. It can assume that BEAR__COUNT2 is a natural because it is obtained by adding 1 to BEAR__COUNT1. For data types about which it can make no deductions it assigns the data type ANY until the user gives it more information.

In employing the HOS language we may retain the data type ANY for abstract objects which do not have specific data types assigned to them yet. We may, for example, not have all the axioms which determine the precise behavior of BEAR or GORILLA, so they remain an ANY data type.

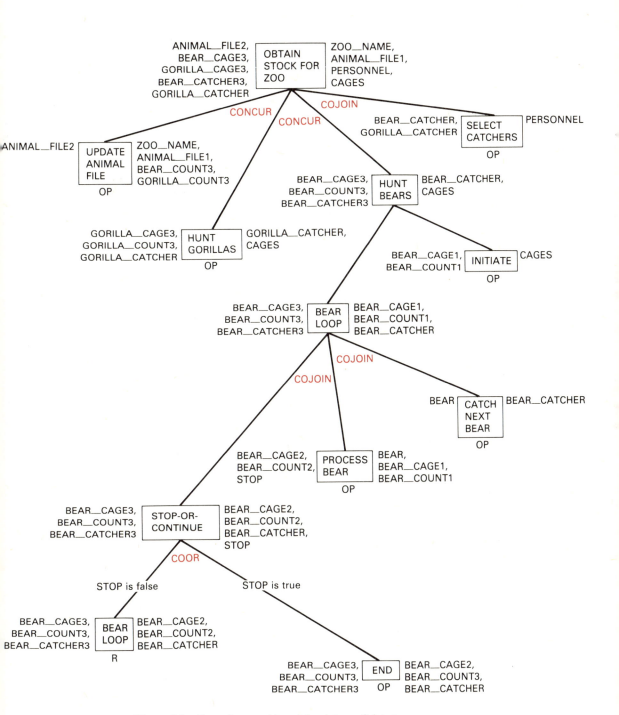

Figure 6.1 Control map with a rich mixture of data types.

DATA AGGREGATION

All the input and output data used in an operation is represented at the top node of its tree. If several hundred data items are used, nobody would want to list all of them against the higher nodes of the tree. Instead, aggregate names are used which encompass many data items.

CUSTOMER, for example, may refer to the various data-item types which are in the customer record. DATA-BASE may refer to a group of associated record types, each of which itself has a group of data-item types. PERSONNEL in Fig. 6.1 includes BEAR__CATCHER and GORILLA__CATCHER.

In this way data can be broken into greater levels of detail as one progresses from top to bottom of a control map, just as operations are exploded into greater levels of detail.

SPECIFICATION OF DATA ITEMS

In a well-managed commercial data processing environment the definitions of data types are often the responsibility of a data administrator. He maintains a data dictionary and ensures that different systems analysts use consistent data definitions.

The .WHERE: statement is used for assigning data types to variables. Thus:

> .WHERE: variable 1: datatype
> .WHERE: variable 1, variable 2, variable 3: datatype.

For example:

> .WHERE: c# 1: CUSTOMER#
>
> .WHERE: CN1: CUSTOMER__NAME
> .WHERE: CA2: CUSTOMER__ADDRESS
> .WHERE: GORILLA, BEAR: ANIMALS
> .WHERE: CUSTOMER, EMPLOYEE: PEOPLE

SPECIFICATION OF RECORDS

Data items are often grouped into records. The customer record, for example, may be as follows:

CUSTOMER

CUSTOMER#	CUSTOMER__NAME	ADDRESS	CREDIT__RATING	TELEPHONE#

The data administrator can describe this record and its data items with five primitive operation (.PRMOP) statements:

```
.DTYPE: CUSTOMER
.PRMOP: CUSTOMER# = CUSTOMER#(CUSTOMER)
.PRMOP: CUSTOMER_NAME = CUSTOMER_NAME(CUSTOMER)
.PRMOP: ADDRESS = ADDRESS(CUSTOMER)
.PRMOP: CREDIT_RATING = CREDIT_RATING(CUSTOMER)
.PRMOP: TELEPHONE# = TELEPHONE#(CUSTOMER)
```

For any specific data item in a record he might write one or more axioms which constrain how the data item is used. He might write axioms which limit its range of values, for example. He might write axioms for security purposes to limit who can read or change the data item. He might write axioms which invoke a control map of functions whenever a data item is read or modified (e.g., INVOICE_TOTAL is the sum of the LINE_ITEM_TOTALs).

SPECIFICATION OF PRIMARY KEYS

A particularly important data item is the *primary key* of a record. This is a *unique identifier* of the contents of that record. CUSTOMER#, for example, is the primary key of the record above.

To show that CUSTOMER# is a unique identifier, the following axiom is written:

```
.WHERE: C1, C2 are in a SET_OF_CUSTOMERs
.AXIOM: EQ(CUSTOMER#(C1), CUSTOMER#(C2))=>EQ(C1, C2)
```

This says that if two CUSTOMER#'s are the same, the CUSTOMER records of which they are part are the same.

ASSOCIATIONS BETWEEN RECORDS

In data-base systems groups of data items (called records, segments, tuples, or simply data-item groups) are linked with one-to-one or one-to-many associations. A one-to-one association is drawn as a line with a small bar across it (like a "1"). A one-to-many association is drawn as a line with a crow's-foot on it. The following is a typical association:

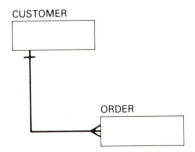

The crow's-foot link shows that a CUSTOMER record can have several ORDER records associated with it. The one-to-one indicator shows that an ORDER record is associated with a single CUSTOMER record.

The one-to-one association is described with the following primitive operation:

.PRMOP: CUSTOMER = CUSTOMER(ORDER)

This associates each ORDER with just one CUSTOMER.

The one-to-many association is described with the following primitive operation:

.PRMOP: SET OF ORDER = SET_OF_ORDERS_FOR CUSTOMER
                              (ORDERS_DATABASE, CUSTOMER)

This associates each CUSTOMER with a set of ORDERs.

Using this notation a data model created either by hand or by a data-base design tool can be entered into the library of the HOS software. Figure 6.2 shows a simple data model and the representative AXES data types of that model. When this model has been entered, the HOS software will check that the data are used correctly in the control maps that employ them. Data-base models are discussed later in the book.

SPECIFYING NEW DATA TYPES

Although most users will employ data types which are in the library, for special purposes it is possible to specify new data types. These can be specified in terms of primitive operations and axioms, as we have discussed, or in terms of core data types that are already defined. The latter process is called *data layering*— the implementation of one data type in terms of another.

To define new data types the user can specify the necessary primitive operations and axioms which specify their behavior. Using data layering, the primitive operations on noncore data types can be modeled in the same fashion as defined operations. Control maps may be developed which show the behavior of each primitive operation.

A HARDWARE MEMORY

Although this book is mainly about software design, the HOS methodology has also been used for hardware design. One such design needed a data type for computer memory [1].

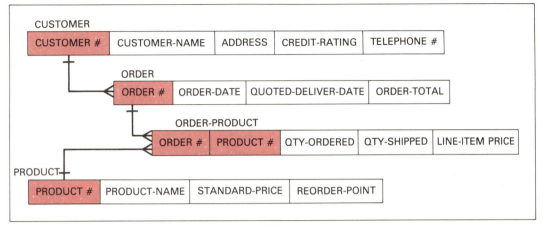

(a)

- DTYPE: CUSTOMER
- PRMOP: CUSTOMER# = CUSTOMER# (CUSTOMER)
- PRMOP: CUSTOMER__NAME = CUSTOMER__NAME(CUSTOMER)
- PRMOP: ADDRESS = ADDRESS (CUSTOMER)
- PRMOP: CREDIT__RATING = CREDIT__RATING(CUSTOMER)
- PRMOP: TELEPHONE# = TELEPHONE#(CUSTOMER)

- DTYPE: ORDER
- PRMOP: ORDER# = ORDER#(ORDER)
- PRMOP: ORDER__DATE = ORDER__DATE(ORDER)
- PRMOP: QUOTED__DELIVERY__DATE = QUOTED__DELIVERY__DATE(ORDER)
- PRMOP: ORDER__TOTAL = ORDER__TOTAL(ORDER)

- DTYPE: PRODUCT
- PRMOP: PRODUCT# = PRODUCT# (PRODUCT)
- PRMOP: PRODUCT__NAME = PRODUCT__NAME (PRODUCT)
- PRMOP: STANDARD__PRICE = STANDARD__PRICE (PRODUCT)
- PRMOP: REORDER__POINT = REORDER__POINT (PRODUCT)

- DTYPE: ORDER__PRODUCT
- PRMOP: ORDER# = ORDER#__FROM__ORDER__PRODUCT (ORDER__PRODUCT)
- PRMOP: PRODUCT# = PRODUCT#__FROM__ORDER__PRODUCT (ORDER__PRODUCT)
- PRMOP: QTY__ORDERED = QTY__ORDERED (ORDER__PRODUCT)
- PRMOP: QTY__SHIPPED = QTY__SHIPPED (ORDER__PRODUCT)
- PRMOP: LINE__ITEM__PRICE = LINE__ITEM__PRICE (ORDER__PRODUCT)

- DTYPE: ORDERS__DATABASE
- PRMOP: CUSTOMER = CUSTOMER__WITH__ORDER (ORDERS__DATABASE,ORDER)
- PRMOP: SET__OF__ORDER = SET__OF__ORDERS__FOR__CUSTOMER (ORDERS__DATABASE,CUSTOMER)
- PRMOP: ORDER = ORDER__OF__ORDER__PRODUCT (ORDERS__DATABASE,ORDER__PRODUCT)
- PRMOP: SET__OF__ORDER__PRODUCT = SET__OF__ORDER__PRODUCTS__FOR__ORDER (ORDERS__DA-TABASE,ORDER)
- PRMOP: PRODUCT = PRODUCT__OF__ORDER__PRODUCT (ORDERS__DATABASE,ORDER__PRODUCT)
- PRMOP: SET__OF__ORDER__PRODUCT = SET__OF__ORDER__PRODUCTS__FOR__PRODUCT (ORDERS__DATABASE,PRODUCT)

(b)

Figure 6.2 Simple data model and representation of this model in HOS software. The HOS description of the data should be generated automatically from the output of a data modeling tool, as described in Chapter 12.

The data type MEMORY, like any other new data type, had to be specified with primitives and axioms. Its description involved another data type already specified rigorously, called NATURAL. This represents the natural numbers with which we count: 0, 1, 2, and so on.

MEMORY is defined to have a LENGTH and a WIDTH. Both of these are natural numbers, and so we describe them with primitive operations:

$$\text{NATURAL} = \text{LENGTH (MEMORY)}$$
$$\text{NATURAL} = \text{WIDTH (MEMORY)}$$

A FETCH operation employs MEMORY and an address. The address is a natural number. The result of the FETCH operation is also a natural number. Therefore, we write

$$\text{NATURAL} = \text{FETCH (MEMORY, NATURAL)}$$

A STORE operation employs MEMORY and stores an input which is a NATURAL at an address which is a NATURAL. The result is MEMORY now modified because it contains what we stored in it. We write

$$\text{MEMORY} = \text{STORE (MEMORY, NATURAL, NATURAL)}$$

When we use STORE, the first natural is an address, the second is a datum.

$$\text{MEMORY} = \text{STORE (MEMORY, address, datum)}$$

If we then FETCH from the same address, we will receive the datum, that is,

$$\text{datum} = \text{FETCH (STORE(MEMORY, address, datum))}$$

This is one example of an axiom.

To the primitive operations and axiom above we need to add some further axioms.

1. If we use an address greater than LENGTH (MEMORY), a FETCH results in a reject, and a STORE leaves the memory unaffected. We state this in an axiom as follows:

$$\text{If } A \geq \text{LENGTH (M)}$$
$$\text{Then}$$
$$\text{FETCH (M,A)} = \text{REJECT}$$
$$\text{And}$$
$$\text{STORE (M,A,D)} = M$$

2. Storing in one cell of MEMORY does not affect the rest of MEMORY. If A and B are different addresses, FETCH (M,B) gives the same result as a FETCH after MEM-

ORY has been changed to STORE (M,A,D). The axiom is as follows:

> If A,B < LENGTH (M) and A = B
> Then
> FETCH (STORE(M,A,D),B) = FETCH (M,B)

3. If D is a natural number larger than the memory's width will allow, only that portion of the data which fits will be retained. If the width of the memory is 8 and we store 257, we will actually store 1. If we store datum D in a memory of width 8, we will actually store $MOD(D,2^8)$. We state this axiom as follows:

> If A < LENGTH (M)
> Then
> FETCH (STORE(M,A,D),A) = $MOD(D,2^{WIDTH(M)})$

Figure 6.3 gives the complete description of a data type MEMORY. This description describes only its behavior. It could be implemented in a variety of

```
DATA TYPE: MEMORY;

PRIMITIVE OPERATIONS:

    NATURAL = LENGTH(MEMORY)

    NATURAL = WIDTH(MEMORY)

    MEMORY = STORE(MEMORY, NATURAL, NATURAL)

    NATURAL = FETCH(MEMORY, NATURAL)

AXIOMS:

    (1)  FETCH (STORE(MEMORY,ADDRESS,DATUM)) = DATUM

    (2)  If A≥LENGTH(M)
         Then
         FETCH(M,A) = REJECT
         And
         STORE(M,A,D) = M

    (3)  If A,B<LENGTH(M) AND A ≠ B
         Then
         FETCH(STORE(M,A,D),B) = FETCH(M,B)

    (4)  IF A≥LENGTH(M)
         Then
         FETCH(STORE(M,A,D),A) = MOD(D,2^WIDTH(M))
```

Figure 6.3   Specification of the data type MEMORY used in creating a design for computer hardware. (From Ref. 1.)

different ways. Other descriptions are also possible for different notions of memory.

REFERENCES

1. *Introduction to the Application of HOS to Hardware Design: The CORDIC Algorithm*, IDA Study of Hardware Description Languages, National Academy of Sciences, Woods Hole, MA, 1981. Prepared by Higher Order Software, Inc., Cambridge, MA.

7 DEFINED STRUCTURES

INTRODUCTION   The three basic control structures of HOS are those described in Chapter 3; the JOIN, INCLUDE, and OR. The co-control structures, COJOIN, COINCLUDE, COOR, and CONCUR, which HOS users employ extensively, are built out of the three basic structures. The original mathematics applies to the JOIN, INCLUDE, and OR and control structures built out of these are consequently provably correct (see the appendices).

OTHER CONTROL STRUCTURES   It is possible to build other control structures out of the primitives. In fact, a long-term question for HOS product developers is: What types of control structures would benefit the users most?

Other control structures could be created in two ways. First, they could be new primitives created with new axioms and mathematics which proves them correct. This would require considerable mathematical skill and is not likely to be attempted by HOS users in general.

Second, they could be built out of existing control structures and invoked when needed. Employing this approach a user can build his own control structures. They are called *defined structures*.

There are two ways of extending the power and usability of the HOS tool. The most common is to build a library of operations, like building a library of subroutines and callable programs. Almost every HOS control map contains blocks labeled OP (Operation defined elsewhere), or XO (External Operation). The user creates OP blocks all the time for operations that he has not yet specified in detail, or which he *has* already specified elsewhere (see Figs. 9.1 to 9.6, for example). As time goes by, a large library of defined operations grows up.

CREATING ONE'S OWN LANGUAGE

The second way of extending the usefulness is to create defined structures. This is rather like *creating one's own language,* or at least *dialect,* in HOS. Some classes of users already have languages or language constructs which they want to use. They may want to use DO-WHILE or REPEAT-UNTIL loops, for example. They may want to use menu selection. They may draw data-base action diagrams [1] and want to convert them into HOS. There are a variety of such constructs with which different users are familiar, and they would like to employ them to make HOS system development easier.

Defined structures can be used to define programming language-like structures (e.g., Repeat-until, Do-while, etc.). However, users can define much more general purpose structures using the defined structure mechanism.

An important aspect of the future of HOS is the building of higher-level constructs or languages for special purposes, which employ HOS. Unlike other computer languages, they would have two important properties, first provable correctness of the resulting logic, and second the ability to drop from the higher-level constructs down to the constructs of the previous chapters for building detailed and often complex logic.

THE COMPOSITION OF A COJOIN

In a sense the co-control structures are defined structures, because they are each composed of the three primitives. Figure 7.1 for example, shows how a CO-JOIN is built from a JOIN and INCLUDE structure. Appendix I gives other examples.

SIMPLIFICATION

The basic reason for employing defined structures is to simplify control maps and to specify commonality. Certain operations appear cumbersome when created with control maps. Because they are designed interactively at a screen, the designer can build and check them quickly. However, it is desirable to replace or simplify the most commonly used logic.

An example of this is shown in Figs. 7.2 and 7.3. An operator responds to a menu on a screen with a digit, as on videotex systems, for example. The response triggers one of 10 possible actions. Figure 7.2 shows this built with the standard control structures.

The menu response may be a common occurrence. We can create an easy-to-use *defined structure* for handling it. Let us call it MENUSELECT. Its use is shown in Fig. 7.3. The use of MENUSELECT causes the control map of 7.2 to be employed.

A COJOIN structure

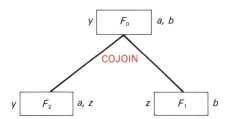

The composition of this COJOIN structure

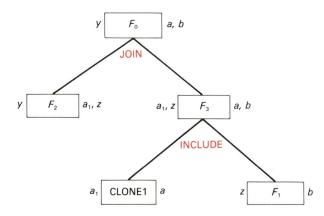

Figure 7.1   A COJOIN structure is built from primitive structures JOIN and INCLUDE. In a similar way we can build higher-level defined structures.

USER FUNCTIONS
EMPLOYED
IN A DEFINED
STRUCTURE

When a defined structure is used, the offsprings of a parent are blocks which exist in the original control map from which the defined structure was built.

Figure 7.4 shows a control map which is repetitively used. When it is used the nodes which are colored red may be different. They are OP (Operation defined elsewhere) or XO (External Operation) blocks, and may be defined by the user.

The control map is defined to be a *defined structure*. It is given a name: DS__NAME. When the user employs it he must provide the three red blocks as offsprings of the parent whose behavior is described with the defined structure DS__NAME. The bottom of Fig. 7.4 shows a user employing the defined structure.

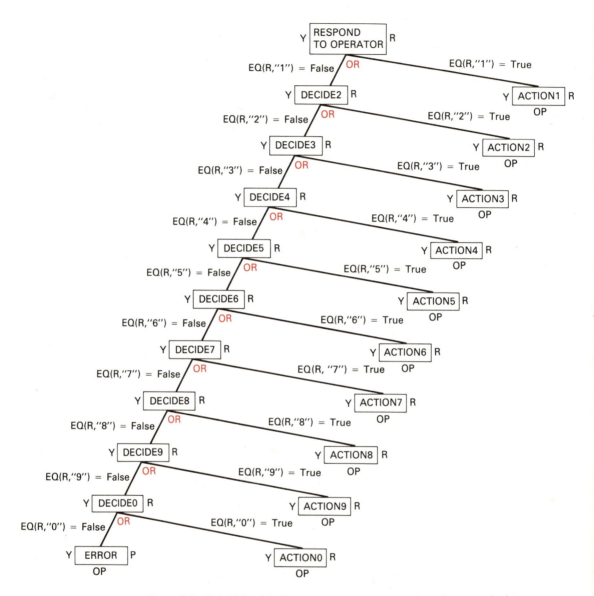

Figure 7.2 R (which might be a user response to a menu) can have any single-digit value. This decides which action is taken. This control map can be replaced with the use of a defined structure as shown in Fig. 7.3.

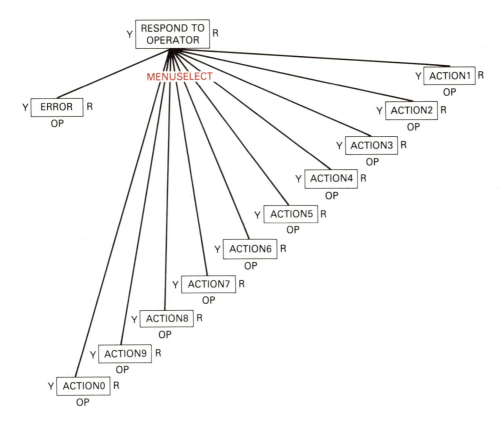

Figure 7.3 Use of the defined structure called MENUSELECT to instantiate the more complex control map of Fig. 7.2.

CRYPTOGRAPHY EXAMPLE

Figures 7.5 and 7.6 show a defined structure in use in cryptanalysis [2]. The structure in Fig. 7.5 is used repetitively with different operations in the position of those labeled F1, F2, and F3. The user creates a structure definition which he calls "FOR EACH EDGE." The structure contains a loop which searches the queues in question.

A structure definition has some functions which are undefined. Here, F1, F2, and F3 are undefined. When this defined structure is used it must follow the usage syntax given at the bottom of Fig. 7.5.

Figure 7.6 shows this defined structure in use in a cryptanalysis program. Q1 is replaced by AQ2, Q2 is replaced by AQ3, and INPUT is replaced by V1, V2, G, E1.

Operation F1 is replaced by the operation called "END POINT IS CURRENT END POINT." Operation F2 is replaced by "COMPARE WEIGHTS

A control map which we want to use as a defined structure:

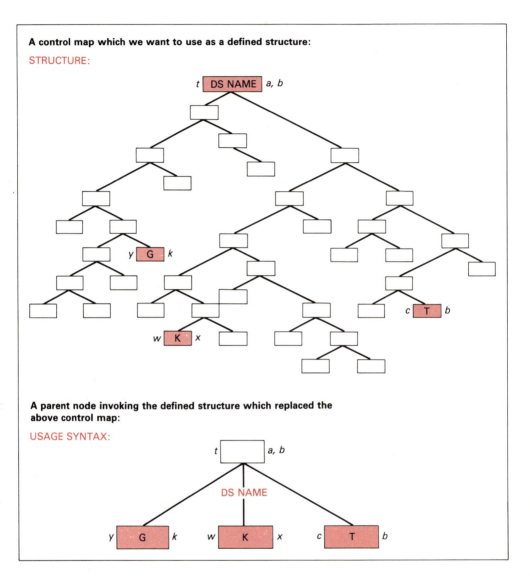

A parent node invoking the defined structure which replaced the above control map:

Figure 7.4

104

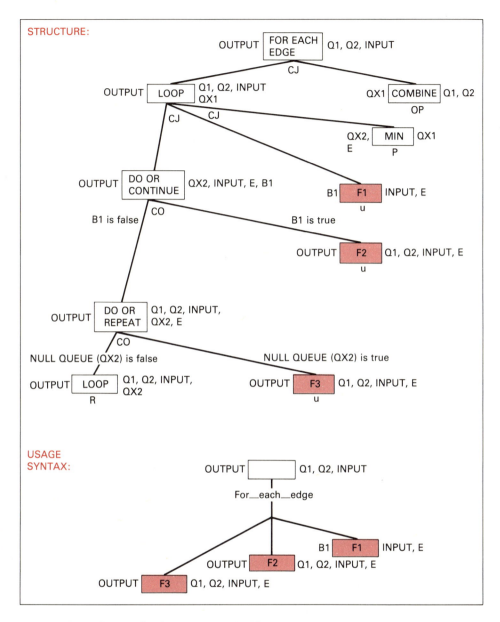

STRUCTURE:

OUTPUT [FOR EACH EDGE] Q1, Q2, INPUT
CJ

OUTPUT [LOOP] Q1, Q2, INPUT QX1
CJ   CJ

QX1 [COMBINE] Q1, Q2
OP

QX2, [MIN] QX1
E   P

OUTPUT [DO OR CONTINUE] QX2, INPUT, E, B1
B1 is false   CO

B1 [F1] INPUT, E
u

B1 is true

OUTPUT [F2] Q1, Q2, INPUT, E
u

OUTPUT [DO OR REPEAT] Q1, Q2, INPUT, QX2, E
CO

NULL QUEUE (QX2) is false   NULL QUEUE (QX2) is true

OUTPUT [LOOP] Q1, Q2, INPUT, QX2
R

OUTPUT [F3] Q1, Q2, INPUT, E
u

USAGE SYNTAX:

OUTPUT [ ] Q1, Q2, INPUT
For__each__edge

B1 [F1] INPUT, E

OUTPUT [F2] Q1, Q2, INPUT, E

OUTPUT [F3] Q1, Q2, INPUT, E

Figure 7.5 Defined structure called "FOR EACH EDGE." This defined structure is used in the cryptography operation shown in Fig. 7.6. The user employs his own operations in nodes F1, F2, and F3. The functions labeled Ⓐ, Ⓑ, and Ⓒ in Fig. 7.6 are substituted into this definition, resolving this structure into an operation where all functions are defined.

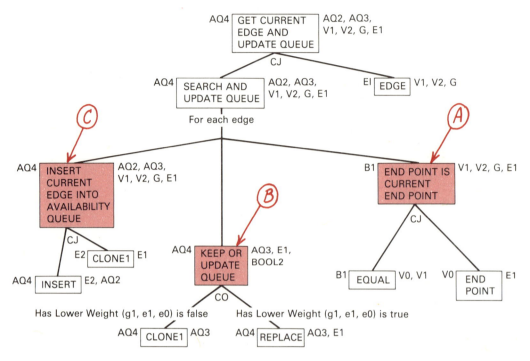

Figure 7.6 Operation used in cryptography which employs the defined structure shown in Fig. 7.5. Q1 has been replaced by AQ2. Q2 has been replaced by AQ3. INPUT has been replaced by V1, V2, G, E1. OUTPUT has been replaced by AQ4. The red nodes in Fig. 7.5 are replaced with the user's red nodes in the structure above.

AND CONTINUE." Operation F3 is replaced by "INSERT CURRENT EDGE IN AVAILABILITY QUEUE."

SINGLE-OFFSPRING PARENTS   All the nodes we have illustrated so far have two or more offspring. With a defined structure it may make sense for a node to have one offspring.

Chapter 5 showed an example of a typical masterfile update run, which is repeated in Fig. 7.7. We might perhaps want to make this a defined structure.

The parent node that uses MAIN FILE LOOP is constrained to always have three data types as input, and also as output. It may have one offspring node which replaces the node called PROCESS RECORD, which is colored red in Fig. 7.7.

Control maps using this defined structure are shown in Figs. 7.8 and 7.9. In Fig. 7.8, CUSTOMER MASTERFILE1 is substituted for MASTERFILE1 and X1 is substituted for CONTROL TOTAL1. In Fig. 7.9, ACCOUNT FILE1 is

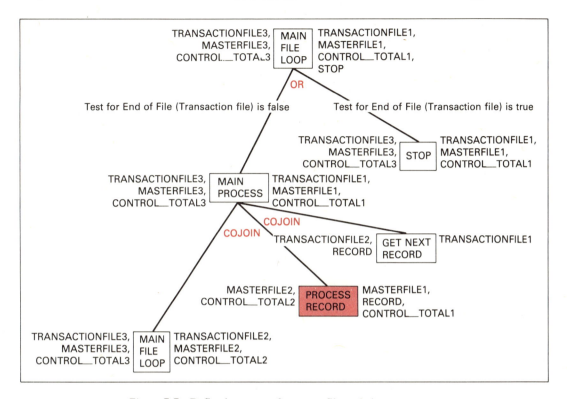

Figure 7.7   Defined structure for masterfile updating.

substituted for MASTERFILE1, DEPOSIT RECORD is substituted for record, and DEPOSIT TOTAL1, ACCOUNT TOTAL1 is substituted for CONTROL TOTAL1.

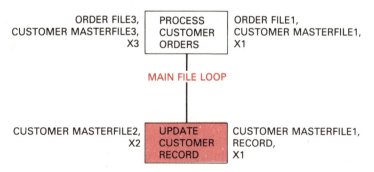

Figure 7.8   Control map using a defined structure called "MAIN FILE LOOP" which causes the control map shown in Fig. 7.7 to be executed. The red offspring above replaces the red node of Fig. 7.7.

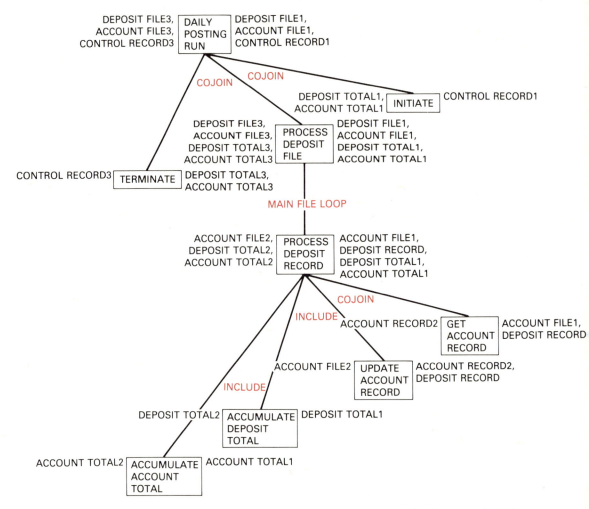

Figure 7.9 Daily banking operation which uses the defined structure, MAIN FILE LOOP, shown in Fig. 7.7.

REFERENCES

1. James Martin and Carma McClure, *Diagramming Techniques for Analysts and Programmers*, Prentice-Hall, Inc., Englewood Cliffs, NJ, 1985.

2. S. Cushing, *A Priority-Queue Based Algorithm for Computing Minimum Spanning Trees*, HOS Educational Series Memo No. 7, Higher Order Software, Inc., Cambridge, MA, 1982.

8 HOS SOFTWARE

INTRODUCTION   The technique described in the previous chapters for generating mathematically provable logic would be tedious to do by hand. Its general usability depends on automation with user-friendly software.

Software for applying such techniques requires the following components:

1. A language for expressing functions and their decomposition into other functions
2. An interactive screen facility for constructing and manipulating the control maps, and allowing the user to correct errors interactively
3. A library of data types, primitive functions, and previously defined modules
4. An analyzer routine for automatically checking that all the rules that give provably correct logic have been followed
5. A generator that automatically generates program code

HOS software provides all of these. It may be regarded as a system specification tool which, unlike other such tools, precisely checks the logic of the specification. It is much more than this because it automatically generates the required code.

It may be regarded as an application generator. Most generators can generate reports, or data-entry software or data-base operations, but cannot create *any* type of software. They can usually generate only a specified class of applications. The HOS system can generate *any* application and is particularly useful with highly complex logic.

The HOS software that generates code is separate from the software that allows the logic of the application to be specified and built. The logic of the application remains independent of machines and of programming languages. It can operate on any computer in any language for which a generator module exists.

A program generated as FORTRAN or Pascal could thus be regenerated as COBOL or Ada.

USE.IT   The software for executing the HOS methodology is called USE.IT [1]. USE.IT consists of three major components: AXES, ANALYZER, and RAT, shown in Fig. 8.1.

AXES is the language for describing the functions, data types, and control structures. Unlike a programming language, it can express a broad statement of requirements such as

$$STOOL = MAKE\text{-}STOOL(TOP,LEGS,LATHE,HANDTOOLS)$$

This statement of requirements is successively broken down as described in the previous chapters until primitives or predefined modules are reached from which program code can be generated. The target system objects provide a foundation for the user's statement of the problem, and need not necessarily be computer oriented.

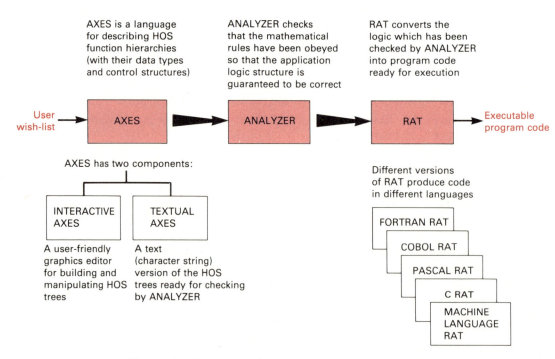

Figure 8.1 Components of USE.IT, the software for implementing the HOS methodology.

There are two major components of AXES: a powerful graphics editor which allows the HOS trees to be built and manipulated on a graphics screen in a user-friendly fashion, and a textual version of the same information which makes the control maps ready for checking by ANALYZER.

ANALYZER checks that the mathematical rules have been obeyed. It checks for syntactical errors first, then checks that the data type transfers are correct and that there are no omissions or inconsistencies in the data types or function descriptions.

RAT (Resource Allocation Tool) uses the output of ANALYZER and automatically generates executable program code. There are several versions of RAT which generate programs in different languages: a FORTRAN RAT, a Pascal RAT, a COBOL RAT, and so on. A machine-language RAT would avoid the need for a subsequent compilation step.

The word RAT is used as a verb. We talk about the AXES control charts being ''ratted'' into different languages. (The word RAT was invented and is much used by the creators of HOS, Margaret Hamilton and Saydean Zeldin, two charming women who would probably stand on a chair if they saw a mouse.)

INTERACTIVE GRAPHICS EDITOR

The key to making the HOS method easy to use is an interactive graphics editor. The HOS tree structures can be displayed on a screen and manipulated in a quick-and-easy manner.

The designer can work in a top-down fashion decomposing high-level functions, or in a bottom-up fashion combining together low-level functions. At each stage the design is checked for correctness. The designer can add comments to any node. Rather like a film editor, he can cut out subtrees and save them, hanging them on a ''hook'' for future use.

A designer working at a low-level node may discover the need for a data type which is not included in the nodes at the top of the tree. He can add this data type and quickly include it in the higher-level nodes.

The graphics editor displays three types of images. These are shown in Figs. 8.2, 8.3, and 8.4.

Figure 8.2 shows the editor in *display tree mode*. An overview of an HOS tree is shown, giving only the names of the nodes. If the entire tree is too big to show on one screen, the user can in effect move the screen ''window'' around the tree.

With a cursor positioned at some point in the tree the user may switch to the *edit mode*. He then sees details of up to six nodes, as shown in Fig. 8.3. He can move the cursor to any part of this diagram and can make changes to functions, data types, or control structures. If he moves the cursor off the screen, the node to which he moves it becomes the center node.

To see more details of a node, the user can move to the *display documentation mode*. He then obtains a screen like Fig. 8.4 with only one node but with

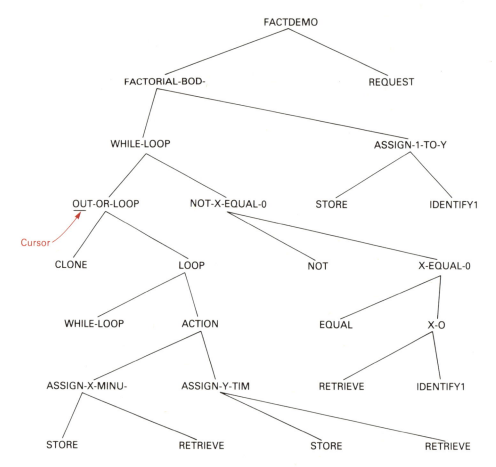

Figure 8.2 Graphics editor in the display tree mode. With the cursor in the
position shown the user may transfer to the edit mode and receive the screen
shown in Fig. 8.3.

documentation and error details. The other modes also give abbreviated error
messages.

In the *insert-documentation mode* the user can enter comments into a screen
like Fig. 8.4.

The input and output data are shown at the right and left, respectively, of
the boxes in Figs. 8.3 and 8.4. Sometimes a node has too many data types to
display. Three dots, as in Fig. 8.3, indicate this and the user can scroll up and
down a list of data.

Underneath each box on the screens are details about control structures.
The letters J, I, O, CJ, CI, CO, and CC under a box mean JOIN, INCLUDE,
OR, COJOIN, COINCLUDE, COOR, and CONCUR, respectively. DS means
DEFINED STRUCTURE. A function that was decomposed as a defined structure

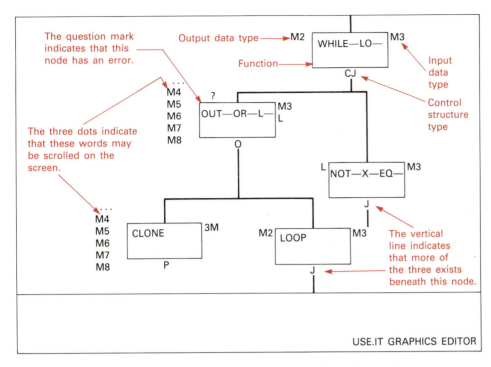

Figure 8.3 Graphics editor in the edit mode.

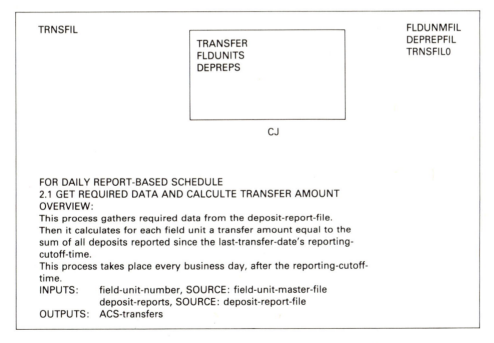

Figure 8.4 Graphics editor in the documentation display mode.

would have the name of the defined structure under the box, for example DO-WHILE LOOP.

If the box is a leaf node and requires no more functional decomposition, one of the following appears under the box:

P:	Primitive operation
OP:	Operation defined elsewhere
R:	Recursion
XO:	External operation

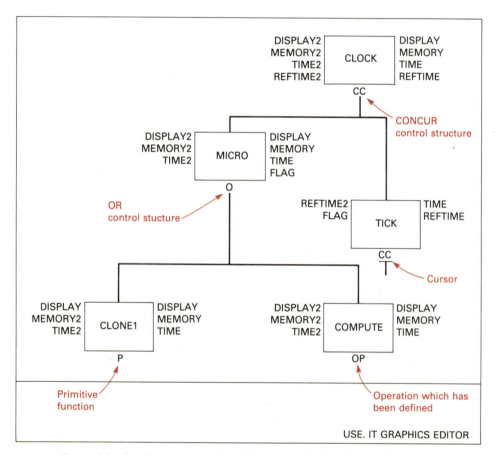

Figure 8.5 Graphics representation of the design of a digital clock. The cursor is on the control structure under TICK. By pressing the ↓ key, the user obtains the chart of TICK shown in Fig. 8.6.

Figure 8.5 shows a design for a digital clock [2]. On the screen shown is one primitive operation, CLONE 1, which simply makes an extra copy of its input variable. There is one OP node (Operation defined elsewhere). The cursor is placed at the CC indicator under the TICK function. By pressing the ↓ key the user can display details of the CC structure as shown in Fig. 8.6.

The graphics editor is easy to use. Its syntax is simple but powerful. Most commands are entered by only one keystroke. A systems analyst can build a complete function tree quickly if he understands the application well enough, and can check it for consistency and completeness. He has available to him a library of data types, primitives, previously defined operations, and previously defined control structures.

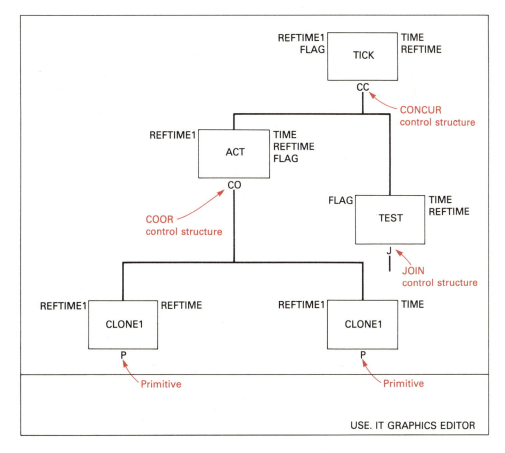

Figure 8.6 Expansion of the control structure for TICK in the design of the digital clock shown in Fig. 8.5.

Pressing the ↑ , →, ↓ or ← keys moves the cursor from box to box, or to boxes which are off the screen. Pressing the space bar moves the cursor around the lettering of a box in a clockwise fashion: first the output, then the function, then the input, then the structure description under the box. The designer may change or insert lettering.

Like most graphics software, the user syntax is rapidly being improved with such facilities as a mouse, windows on personal computers, pop-on menus, and so on. There is much scope for making the software smarter and improving the speed with which users obtain results.

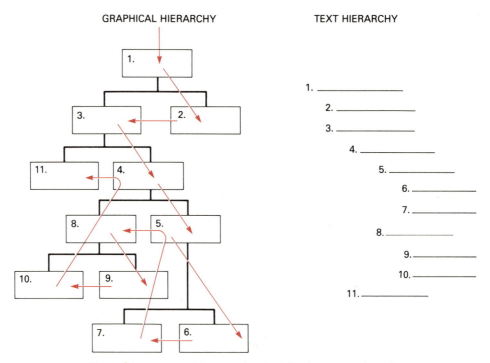

The tree is represented in text using the following sequencing rules:

- Start at the top.
- If a node has offsprings, list the right offspring first.
- When the descendants beneath the right offspring
  are listed, list the left offspring.
- Use indentations equivalent to the depth in the tree.

Figure 8.7 Top-to-bottom, right-to-left sequencing of an AXES tree structure in AXES text.

```
.MODEL/CLOCK
DISPLAY2,MEMORY2,TIME2,REFTIME2 = CLOCK(DISPLAY,MEMORY,TIME,REFTIME) [CC]
    REFTIME2,FLAG = TICK(TIME,REFTIME) [CC]
      DISPLAY2,MEMORY2,TIME2 = MICRO(DISPLAY,MEMORY,TIME,FLAG [O]
        DISPLAY2,MEMORY2,TIME2 = COMPUTE(DISPLAY,MEMORY,TIME [OP]
        DISPLAY2,MEMORY2,TIME2 = CLONE1(DISPLAY,MEMORY,TIME [P]
  .END
```

Figure 8.8   AXES text version of the control structure for CLOCK in Fig. 8.5.

CONVERTING CONTROL MAPS TO TEXT FORM

In converting the tree structure to text, the nodes are listed by the editor, in a given sequence. Top-to-bottom, right-to-left sequencing is used as shown in Fig. 8.7.

After each node in the text the node-type indicator beneath the node in the graphics version is enclosed in square brackets. For a leaf node this indicates the type of leaf, for example [**P**]. For a nonleaf node the square bracket shows the control structure with which it is decomposed, for example [**CI**].

Various AXES language keywords punctuate the text, each beginning with a period. For example, the text may start with a .MODEL: statement and finish with an .END statement, as in Fig. 8.8. .MODEL: in Fig. 8.8 is followed by the name of the model.

Comments can be displayed or inserted with the graphics editor. Inserted comments statements can be placed between or at the end of the text lines. They begin with a semicolon, as shown in Fig. 8.9. Comments inserted by the ANALYZER begin with an asterisk.

MODULARITY

HOS programs are normally built up in modules. Each module is checked with ANALYZER.

To ensure that the modules link together correctly, an interface statement is needed. A template of the form

DATATYPE1,. . . . OPERATION NAME(DATATYPEm,. . . .)

is generated by the system and placed in an interface template file.

ANALYZER infers what it can about the data types in a module, and compares these with the template in the template file to ensure that the interface is correct. If there is a mismatch, an error message is produced.

```
;NEXTCHAR.HOS
.MODEL:NEXTCHAR
.LIBOP:NATURAL,INTEGER,BOOLEAN = NEXTCHAR (IAR32,NATURAL)


;      DATE:   4/28/82

;      AUTHOR:   HOS

;      REVISED:   5/13/82 — Replaced AR32 with IAR32

;      VERSION:   1.2

;

;

; This model gets the next character from an array, checking first to
; see if the end of the array has been reached. Blanks, tabs, and
; newline characters are skipped. The Boolean output indicates whether
; or not the end-or-array condition was encountered.
CTRX,CX,BX = NEXTCHAR (L,CTR) CJ
          B1 = EQ (CRT, "132") P              ;test for end-of-line
CTRX,CX,BX = TEXT (L,CTR,B1) CO               ;IF end-of-line:
       CTRX,CX,BX = CLONEOUT (CTR) CJ
          BX = INDENTIFY1 ("TRUE",CTR)   P        ;1) set Bool to "TRUE"
                          .
                          .
                          .
```

Figure 8.9   Comment statements in an AXES file are preceded by a semicolon. They can be read and inserted with the graphics editor, as in Fig. 8.4.

When program code is generated with the RAT, *unique module names* are generated which ensure correct linkage of program modules.

This control of the linkage between modules permits portions of a total system to be analyzed and ratted independently of one another. The separate modules of programs that are generated may be tested via *simulation*.

SIMULATION

It is sometimes desirable to run a module and examine its operation before a system is completely defined. This is done by simulating manually the portion which is as-yet undefined.

The designer inserts into the module file a statement naming each operation which he wishes to simulate. When ANALYZER is used in such a case, it prompts the user for the names of the data types to be employed.

Following this, the RAT may generate program code and insert *prompts* into each node that reference an undefined operation. When the system is executed, it will operate normally until it reaches one of these nodes.

Consider a system that will calculate a runner's pace per mile. The AXES chart is as follows:

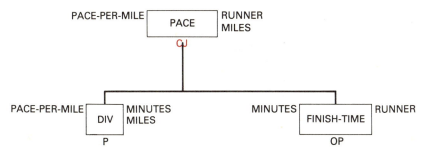

Suppose that in this specification FINISH-TIME is an as-yet undefined operation that does a data access to find the value of MINUTES for each value of RUNNER.

We can test the incomplete code for the PACE module above because USE.IT allows us to manually simulate the as-yet unimplemented node FINISH-TIME.

To test the module we enter the RUN command for the module in the MASTER SYSTEM MENU. The system analyzes the module, generates code for it, and executes it.

```
⟨EXECUTING SYSTEM "PACE"⟩
Enter Input: RUNNER:INT
        ⟨INT⟩:=
```

We respond by entering the runner's number: 123. The system then asks for the other top-node input:

```
Enter Input: MILES:RAT
⟨RATIONAL⟩:=
```

We respond by typing in a number: 24.1. The system then attempts to execute the code and reaches the unimplemented operation FINISH-TIME.

It gives the name of the pseudonode, tells us its input, and asks us to supply the output:

```
PSEUDO-NODE: MINUTES=FINISH__TIME(RUNNER)
                Input: RUNNER
⟨INT⟩:=            123
              Output: MINUTES
⟨RATIONAL⟩:=
```

We enter the expected output: 128.4, and then the program module completes its operation and prints the value of PACE__PER__MILE:

```
Output: PACE__PER__MILE:   RAT
⟨RATIONAL⟩ =               5.327800
Do you wish to run PACE again (YES OR NO)? ■
```

EXTERNAL MODULES OF CODE

Sometimes previously existing programs need to be incorporated into code generated by USE.IT. USE.IT RATs can generate interfaces to such programs provided that:

1. They are callable in the language in question.

2. The non-RAT-generated programs have valid interfaces and work correctly.

Of course, the RAT cannot ensure the correctness of program code from outside sources.

The module that calls the outside program must have a node in it which represents the interface to that outside program. This is a leaf node in the HOS tree labeled [XO] for External Operation.

The input list and output list of the node must contain the arguments and return parameters of the called routine. These data types must be declared with a .WHERE statement. Apart from the module's name a call to an external operation then appears the same as a call to an [OP] RAT-generated module.

REFERENCES

1. *USE.IT Reference Manual,* Higher Order Software, Inc., Cambridge, MA, 1982.

2. *Annotated Model of a Digital Clock,* Educational Series 1, Higher Order Software, Inc., Cambridge, MA, May 1982.

9 APPLICATIONS OF THE HOS METHOD

A WAY TO THINK ABOUT SYSTEMS

The systems design methodology of HOS has been applied to a startling diversity of situations. The technique provides a powerful way to think about axioms and logic generally, not only in computer systems.

The technique has been used to design hardware as well as software (see Appendix II). It has proven valuable in the design of integrated circuits and electronic hardware [1,2]. It has been used to design a digital clock [3]. A complex radar system was specified in the AXES language [4,5], as we will discuss later.

It was used to specify a portion of the NAVPAK satellite communications system. Its Boolean logic can describe basic electronic functions such as NAND and NOR circuits. These primitive structures can then be combined into complex circuits. The behavior of such circuits can be simulated before the hardware is built.

Front-end system specification methodologies have been adjusted so that they can be converted into HOS control maps, for example, SADT, IDEF (used for ICAM definition), and data-base action diagrams. This provides a rigorous semantic foundation for an already established user community, and helps automate the generation of programs from these methodologies by formalizing an already existing syntax into a syntax with computable semantics.

The control maps can be used to specify a logically consistent design for noncomputer systems, or systems which involve people as well as machines. They have been used for project management, assigning tasks, resources, and relationships. They clearly identify sequential and parallel activities.

Its use was proposed in Harvard Law School for the study of laws and their relation to the U.S. Constitution. Complex branches of law, for example tax law, could be clarified and made consistent using the AXES language. Computerized aid to both lawmakers and lawyers could lessen the ever-growing burden of legal costs.

AXES was used to analyze the programming language Ada [6,7]. Such analysis assists in compiler, interpreter, or implementation design, but it goes beyond that. It gives a context-free grammar (syntax) showing the structure of strings of a computer language which guides the assigning of semantic values to the strings. This could produce a language specification which is completely formal. The language specification in AXES is completely machine independent and is logically verifiable. A compiler or optimization of a compiler could be simulated with HOS tools. AXES provides a powerful way to study and specify new languages.

The HOS technique has been used to design a microprocessor. Particularly intriguing is the possibility of designing a computer intended to run programs created with this method. It is desirable that future computers should use multiprocessing with many cheap microprocessors combined to form a larger machine. Such multiprocessor architectures have been built, but it has proven difficult to break down programs so that they can employ multiple processors operating in parallel. Programs designed with AXES may be broken down for parallel operation. The INCLUDE construct, for example, requires that two activities are performed which are independent. A large system has many INCLUDEs and CO-INCLUDEs, which permit parallel processing.

New machines need new operating systems. The operating systems of the past have been plagued with subtle bugs which are sometimes extremely difficult to find. Seemingly trivial modifications to operating systems have triggered chain reactions of unanticipated problems. Flaw fixing introduces new flaws, and more and more time is spent on fixing these secondary problems rather than correcting the structure that caused the original problem. After his experience in building OS 360, Fred Brooks lamented: ''Program maintenance is an entropy-increasing process, and even its most skilful execution only delays the subsidence of the system into unfixable obsolescence'' [8]. If operating systems were designed with a language such as AXES, this would not be true. Changes could be made without triggering chain reactions of bugs. Logically guaranteed code would remove most timing, deadlock, and other problems. A library of provably correct operating system modules would steadily grow. Operating systems would at last be based on a sound engineering discipline.

To build an operating system without such a technique is like building a bridge without stressing calculations. The early bridge builders used massive structures just to be sure. Even then, their bridges sometimes collapsed. The massive quantities of code in today's operating systems could be replaced with much smaller, tighter, provably correct constructs.

COMPLEX SPECIFICATIONS

The predominant use of HOS software at the time of writing is for designing complex specifications. There are a variety of different application generators on the market. Most can generate reports or applications with relatively simple logic. HOS seems to be unique in its capability to represent complex specifications in a way that gives error-free design.

The author examined one set of highly complex specifications created with conventional techniques, which were later redone with HOS. The rigorous tool revealed thousands of errors, omissions, and inconsistencies in the original specifications (which contained many person-years of work). Most complex specifications are similarly inadequate. The human mind simply cannot spot the ambiguities, inconsistencies, and incompleteness in highly complex specifications. And a team of human minds is worse because they create pieces that do not mesh exactly. A tool for creating *computable* specifications enforces completeness, consistency, and lack of ambiguity in the specifications; otherwise, it cannot generate code from them.

Specifications created with HOS are relatively easy to modify, compared with the difficulties of modifying traditional complex systems. The control maps *are* the documentation and modifications are made at the control map level. The documentation cannot slip out of sync with the code, which is what usually happens with traditional systems. Partly because of this, one of the world's largest software houses made a commitment to redevelop all of it systems using HOS.

In this chapter we show illustrations of HOS applications. We have selected relatively simple examples for tutorial purposes. In practice most uses of HOS are much more complex and generate much larger control maps. The reader should extrapolate from the simple examples shown to the complexity of the real world. It is, indeed, on complex applications, rather than simple ones, that HOS software is of the most value.

SPECIFICATION OF BUILDINGS

We will now describe a system created for the Buildings Division of Butler Manufacturing Company [9]. This Division's Construction group undertakes the design and erection of large building projects, often in conjunction with several hundred local Butler builders.

A Butler customer gives an order for a building, and this building must be designed. At the highest level we therefore have

BUILDING__DESIGN | DESIGN | CUSTOMER__ORDER

One subsystem of this overall operation was created—a subsystem with a customer request as input and part of the design as output. A data base of building types and information about components was also required as input:

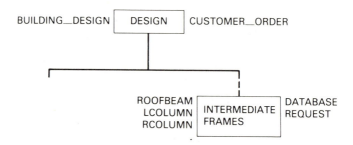

The process of designing roof beams, left columns, and right columns from the customer request is referred to with the function name INTERMEDIATE FRAMES. We will describe this operation.

The entire design process took one person 11 days. During this time he had to learn the application, interacting strongly with the end users and studying a manual giving details of how Butler designs buildings. The resulting programs contained about 10,000 lines of efficient FORTRAN. Department of Defense statistics indicate that their FORTRAN programmers average 10 lines of debugged code per day. This system would have taken about 1000 person-days, but this is only for programming. In 11 days the HOS analyst did the system specifications and design as well as creating the code. *Prior to this the analyst was unfamiliar with the application and the Butler environment. He had never written a program and had no computing experience before using the HOS technique.*

A library was built up of operations such as the procedure for obtaining bay-length values and load keys (Figs. 9.11 to 9.14). The functional decomposition technique identifies functions which are used repetitively. These become either primitive operations [P] or operations designed with their own HOS chart [OP]. As such commonality is abstracted, the overall specification is simplified.

It is certain that substantial modifications will be needed to the programs as the corporation evolves its product line. A customer may specify different forms of building, and changes in construction technique and parts and materials will occur. With the USE.IT graphics editor and library, such changes can be made quickly and with the certainty that they are not causing chain reactions of hidden errors.

DESIGN OF INTERMEDIATE FRAMES

The customer's request may be for a building with a standard or nonstandard frame. To have a standard frame the *building type* must be standard, it must have a standard *width and height,* the *load code* must be standard, and the *bay length* must be standard. If any one of these four items is nonstandard, then a nonstandard frame is required.

Figures 9.1 and 9.2 show the function ALL REQUESTS—STANDARD. ANSWER1, ANSWER2, ANSWER3, and ANSWER4 show whether each of

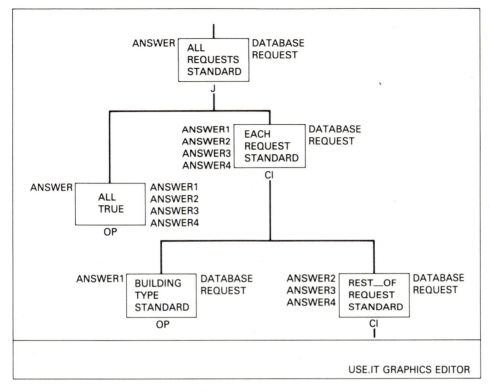

Figure 9.1

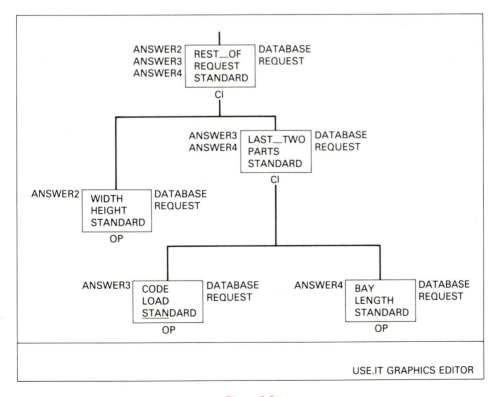

Figure 9.2

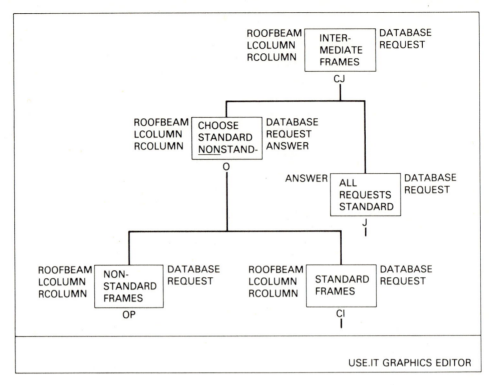

Figure 9.3

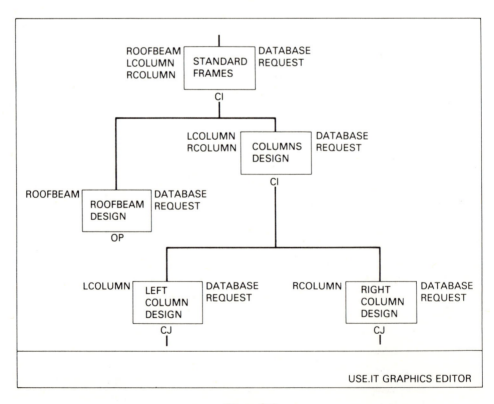

Figure 9.4

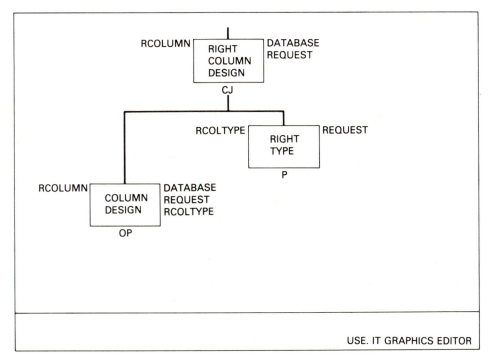

Figure 9.5

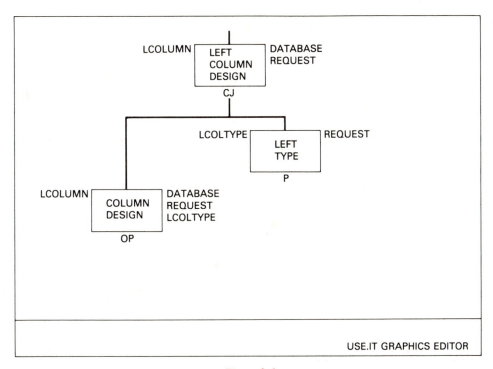

Figure 9.6

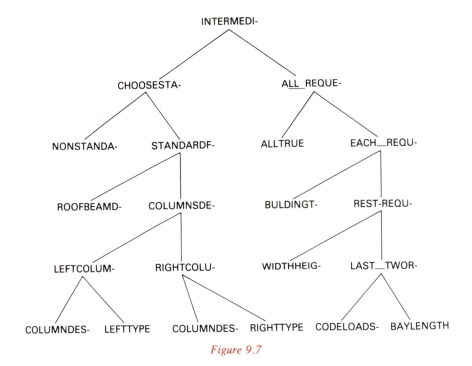

Figure 9.7

the four requests are standard. These four data types form input to the ALL.TRUE function. Its output, ANSWER, is a Boolean which is *true* if all four inputs are *true*.

CHOOSE—STANDARD—NONSTANDARD employs this Boolean in an OR structure in Fig. 9.3. If the building type is all standard, the STANDARD—FRAMES function is employed. This is expanded on the AXES screens in Figs. 9.4, 9.5, and 9.6.

There are two main types of operations needed in designing the standard frames: the design of the columns and the design of the roof beam. The design of the left column is different from the design of the right column. Figure 9.4 shows this breakdown. Figure 9.5 shows the right-column design and Fig. 9.6 shows the left-column design.

The function INTERMEDIATE—FRAMES has now been decomposed into primitives and defined operations. Putting the graphics editor into the *display-tree mode* gives an overview of what has been done (Fig. 9.7). The program code for this can now be generated with the RAT.

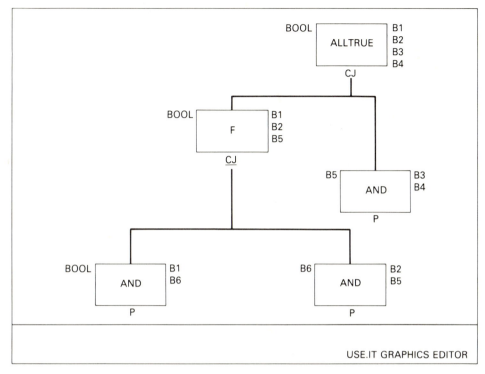

Figure 9.8 If the Booleans B1, B2, B3, and B4 are all true, then the output Boolean, BOOL, is true.

INTERFACES TO THE DEFINED OPERATIONS

The defined operations (labeled OP under the function boxes of the graphics editor) now need to be specified. Figure 9.8 shows the first of these. The next four check the various data types in the user's request against the data base. Figure 9.9 shows the operation that checks whether the bay length is standard, for example.

COLUMN DESIGN

COLUMNDESIGN and ROOFBEAMDESIGN are more complex operations. There are several different types of columns. An operation determines what type of column meets the customer's requirements. There is a design function for each type of column. Figures 9.10 to 9.18 show the design of a girt column.

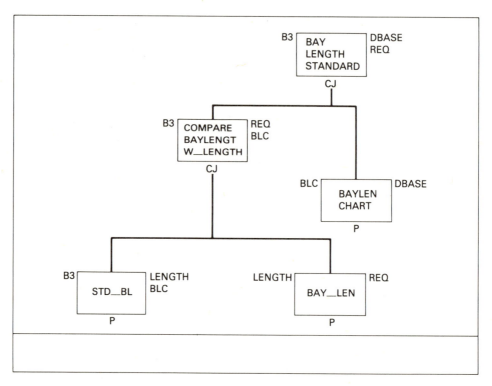

Figure 9.9 This operation checks that the bay length (LENGTH) in the customer's request (REG) is one of a set of standard bay-length values (BLC) which are derived from the data base (DBASE). If it is, the Boolean B3 is set to be true, and is used in Fig. 9.8.

Figure 9.10 divides GIRT COLUMN DESIGN into two operations: first BAYLENGTH LOADKEY PAIR, then DO GIRT. GIRT COLUMN DESIGN must establish two values, BAYLENGTH and LOADKEY.

BLV, bay-length value, has only certain permitted values. In Fig. 9.14 the bay length in the customer's request is adjusted to one of the permitted values.

Next it is necessary to find the LOAD KEY, LK. This is done in Figs. 9.12 and 9.13. Different states have different codes regulating building design. The code, CD, wind load, WL, and live load, LL, are determined from the customer's request in Fig. 9.13.

The *load key code* is obtained from the data base, in Fig. 9.12. With this chart, the wind load, live load, and code are used to determine the load key, LK.

Figure 9.11 is a defined operation which produces the bay-length value, BLV, and the load key, LK. This operation becomes a subroutine when the program code is generated. It is used in other parts of the design of the building

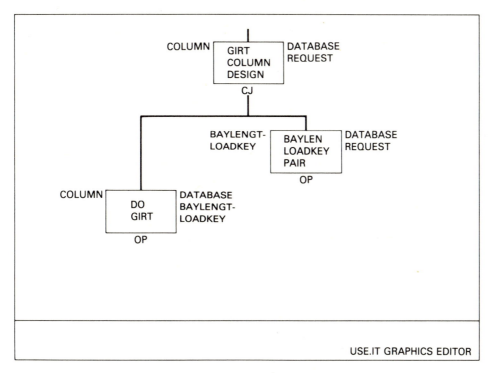

Figure 9.10

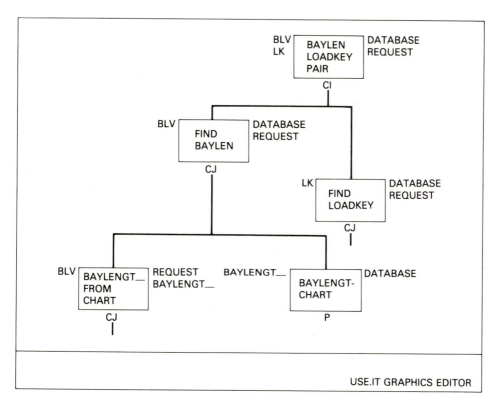

Figure 9.11

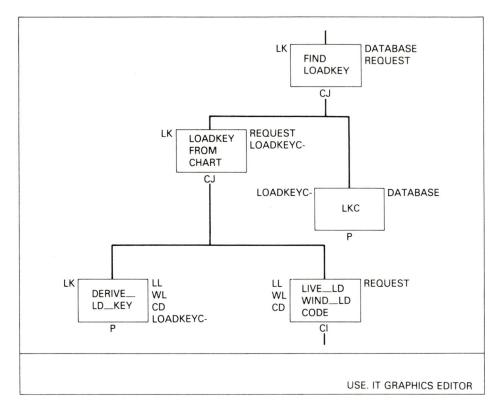

Figure 9.12

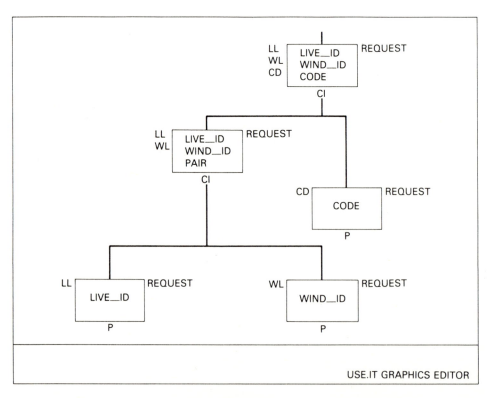

Figure 9.13

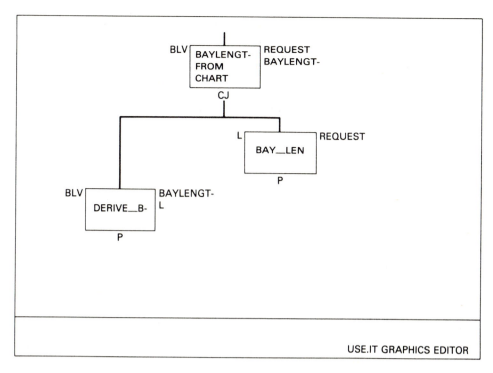

Figure 9.14

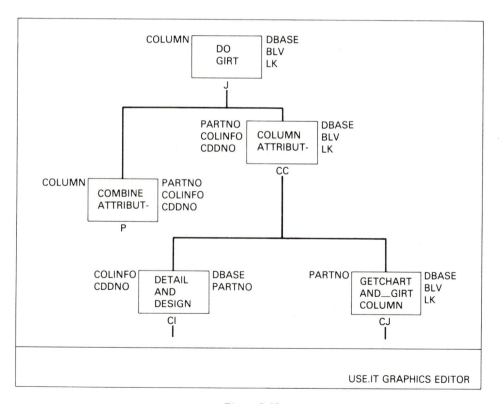

Figure 9.15

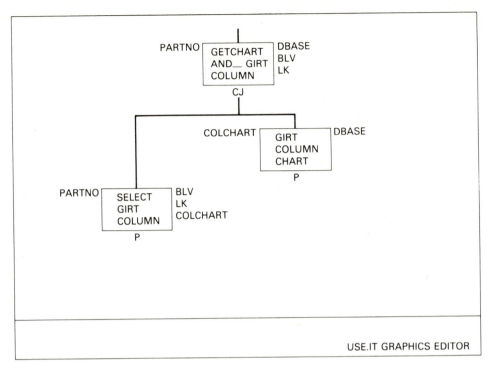

Figure 9.16

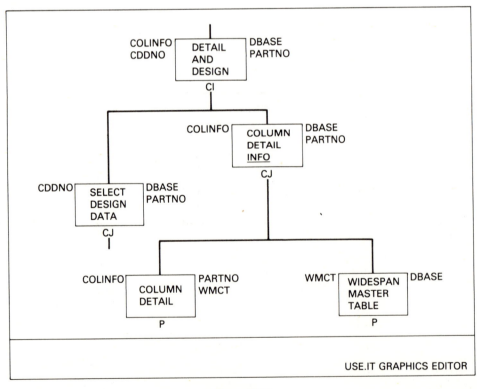

Figure 9.17

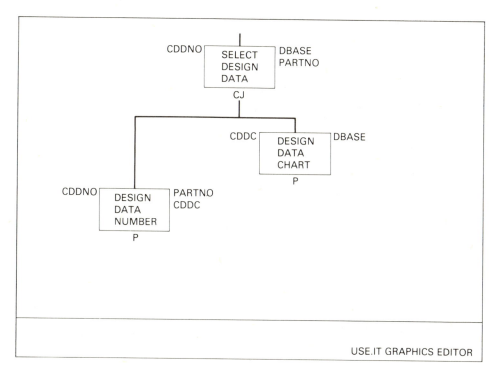

USE.IT GRAPHICS EDITOR

Figure 9.18

frame as well as in designing girt columns, as in Fig. 9.10. These values are fed with a CO-JOIN into the DO GIRT operation of Fig. 9.10 to design the girt column. DO GIRT is expanded in Figs. 9.15 to 9.18.

A BALLISTIC MISSILE DEFENSE SYSTEM

The preceding example, like most commercial data processing, involved multiple data-base references and relatively simple calculations. Now let us examine an application requiring extremely complex computation. This example could not have been approached with any of the common "application generators" or higher-level data-base languages.

The objective was to specify the software for a ballistic missile defense system and generate the code. The module that was developed first is discussed here. This is a radar subsystem [4]. It is characteristic of the overall ballistic missile defense system software.

When the work began, a specification existed which included:

1. A flowchart, showing a mixture of flow of data and flow of control

2. English text mixed with mathematical formulas

3. An input/output list

4. Appendices of file contents and symbol definitions

There were difficulties in trying to extract the intended meaning from this description. It is almost always the case that loosely described specifications of this type contain ambiguities and missing components. Often some of these problems are not discovered until code has been written and tested. It is then extremely expensive and time consuming to solve the problems.

The HOS methodology enforces the creation of nonambiguous and complete specifications. This has a major effect on the resulting code and maintenance problems.

Creating the HOS tree gave the team working on this system the ability to gain knowledge in parallel, different people working on the decomposition of different higher-level nodes. This accelerated the information-gathering process, and aided in design verification.

The algorithm expressed in the original flowchart and text became modified as the HOS tree was built. Various errors became apparent. Many common functions were identified that could be used multiple times. The overall algorithm was modified, so that all calculations necessary to prepare radar search pulses were done at the start and not in the midst of the scheduling operation.

RADAR SYSTEM   The ballistic missile defense system *includes* the radar system (Fig. 9.19). The radar scheduling system is

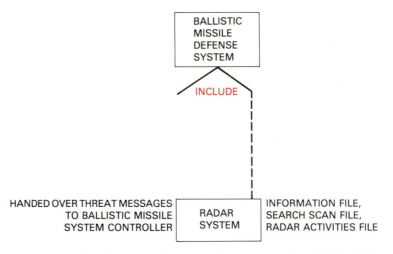

Figure 9.19   The radar scheduling system is one component of the ballistic missile defense system. Figure 9.22 gives a functional breakdown of this.

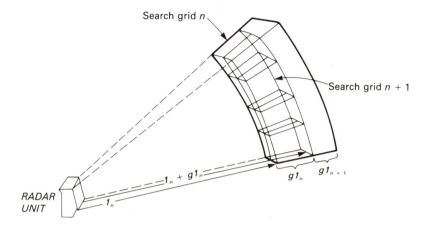

1_n is the distance of the near edge of grid n.

$g1_n$ is the depth of grid n.

Figure 9.20   The radar unit divides its search into grids of cubes.

fairly complex. Let us piece together our understanding of it in a *bottom-up* fashion.

The radar unit itself is a device that sends pulses into the sky and receives signals back if an object is present. The sky is divided into grids of cubes as shown in Fig. 9.20.

The goal is to find objects in the sky and then determine whether they are possible threats. Knowledge of all objects is sent to a control facility for tracking. The radar system needs to be able to react in a flexible manner and return reliable information to its controller in the midst of many possible attack scenarios.

A scheduler gives orders to the radar unit requesting it to send a search pulse to look at a sky location. The RADAR UNIT itself has a buffer in which it stores these orders. As it scans the sky it sends out pulses according to these orders and receives a set of *returns*. These are also stored in a buffer. We have

RADAR RETURNS BUFFER | RADAR UNIT | RADAR ORDERS BUFFER

The radar returns have to be processed, so the contents of the *radar returns buffer* are passed to a RADAR RETURNS PROCESSING function. This function examines the characteristics of all returned pulses and performs a correlation. It eliminates invalid returns and noise. To do so it needs a *radar information file* giving details about the schedule of pulses, and a *general information file*. The output of this function is referred to as the *verification return queue:*

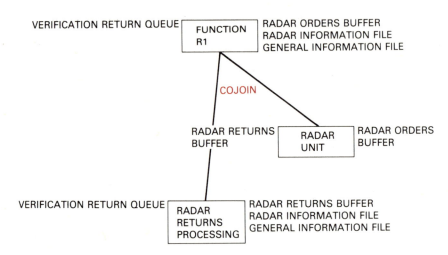

The foregoing step produces a set of radar returns which have been verified by more than one radar scan. A function is now required which will determine whether or not pulses returned to the radar, and verified, constitute a threat. This is done by a bulk filtering process and a series of repeated tests performed on new pulses which are transmitted to recheck the characteristics of the possible threat object. This function is called OBJECT DETECTION AND DESIGNA-TION. It requires the *verification return queue,* the *general information file,* a *radar activities file,* and an ordered set of *radar search requests.* The output is an updated *radar activities file,* an updated set of *radar search requests,* and a *Boolean* indicating whether the object detection and designation is complete.

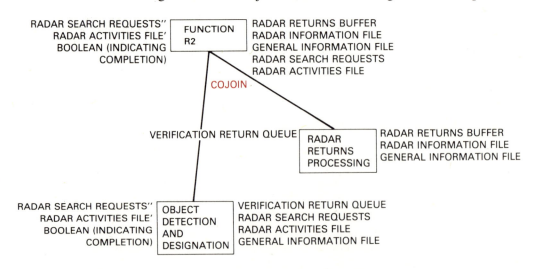

The foregoing functions can be combined into one trinary node:

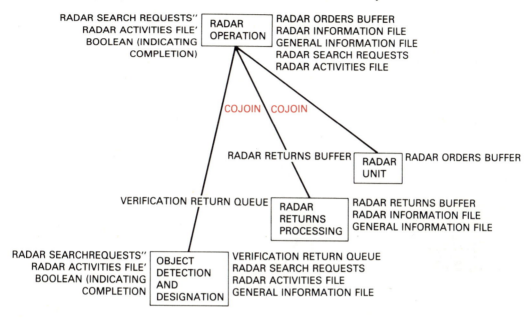

In order to examine a potential threat thoroughly, the OBJECT DETECTION AND DESIGNATION function creates a new set of *radar search requests*, each giving the location of the possible threat and the requested time to retest it.

The timing of the pulses is coordinated by a RADAR SCHEDULER function. This creates the orders that go into the *radar order buffer* which is input to the RADAR UNIT. It also creates the *radar information file* which is used in the RADAR RETURNS PROCESSING function, and updates a set of *radar search requests* which are input to the OBJECT DETECTION AND DESIGNATION function. It employs the *general information file* and *radar activities file:*

```
RADAR ORDERS BUFFER ┌──────────┐ RADAR ACTIVITIES FILE
RADAR INFORMATION FILE │  RADAR   │ GENERAL INFORMATION FILE
RADAR SEARCH REQUESTS' │ SCHEDULER│ RADAR SEARCH REQUESTS
                       └──────────┘
```

Linking this to the functions described above gives the control map in Fig. 9.21.

The overall output of the RADAR SYSTEM is a set of *threat messages* which are handed over to the ballistic missile controller. The overall input to the processing is a *search scan file, radar activities file,* and *general information file:*

```
THREAT MESSAGES ┌────────┐ SEARCH SCAN FILE
                │ RADAR  │ RADAR ACTIVITIES FILE
                │ SYSTEM │ GENERAL INFORMATION FILE
                └────────┘
```

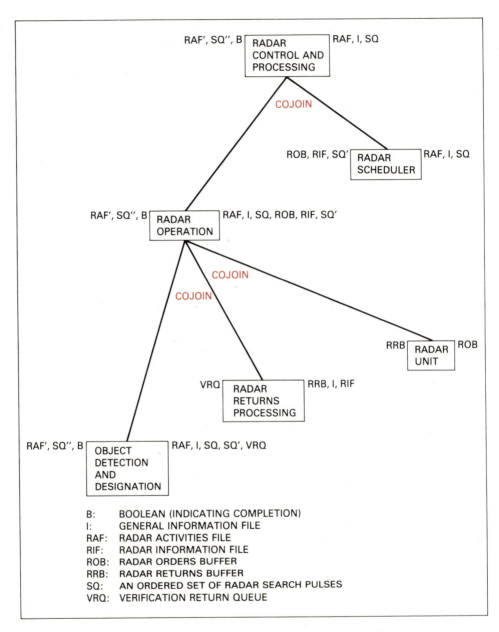

Figure 9.21 Part of the radar system (shown in Fig. 9.22).

The *threat messages* are obtained by processing the updated *radar activities file* and new *search requests* from Fig. 9.21, which encompasses the activities so far described. The Boolean indicates whether the object detection and designation is complete:

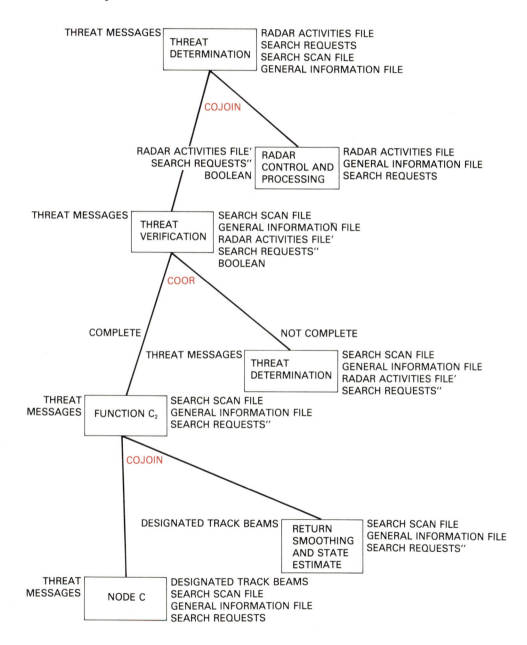

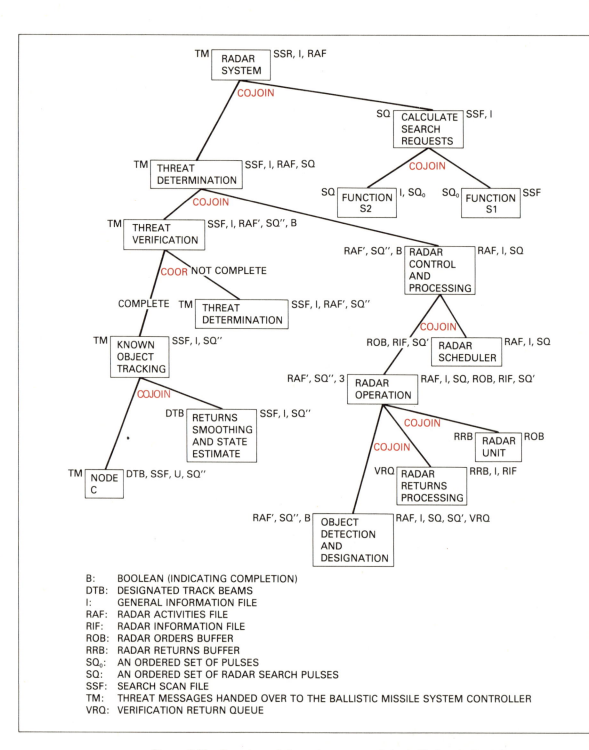

B: BOOLEAN (INDICATING COMPLETION)
DTB: DESIGNATED TRACK BEAMS
I: GENERAL INFORMATION FILE
RAF: RADAR ACTIVITIES FILE
RIF: RADAR INFORMATION FILE
ROB: RADAR ORDERS BUFFER
RRB: RADAR RETURNS BUFFER
SQ_0: AN ORDERED SET OF PULSES
SQ: AN ORDERED SET OF RADAR SEARCH PULSES
SSF: SEARCH SCAN FILE
TM: THREAT MESSAGES HANDED OVER TO THE BALLISTIC MISSILE SYSTEM CONTROLLER
VRQ: VERIFICATION RETURN QUEUE

Figure 9.22 Overview of the radar system of the ballistic missile defense system.

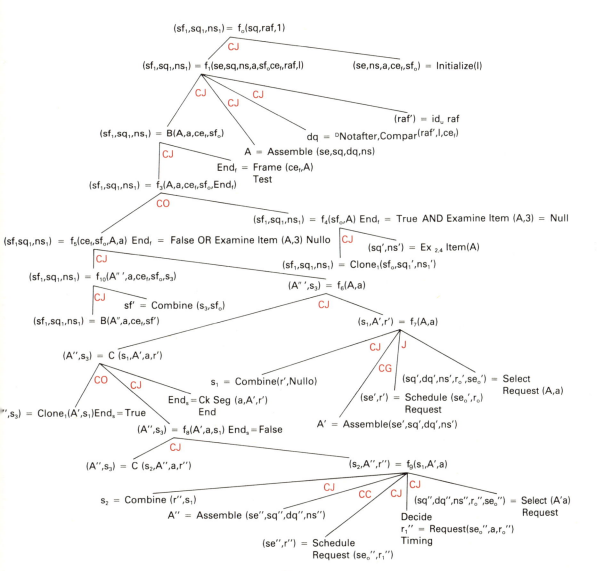

Figure 9.23 Radar scheduling mechanism for a frame. This is part of the RADAR SCHEDULER function shown in Fig. 9.22. (From Ref. 4.)

The original set of search requests is calculated from the *search scan file* and the *general information file*.

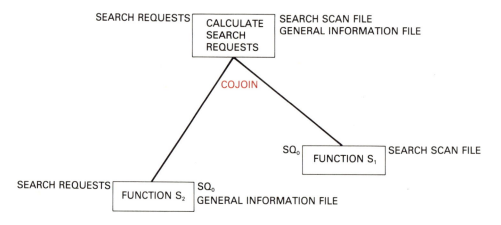

Putting all of this together we have the overall operation of the RADAR SYSTEM, shown in Fig. 9.22. The functions in this figure have to be expanded into much more detail. Figure 9.23 gives an example of this detail. This is a part of the RADAR SCHEDULER function. The level of detail in Fig. 9.23 can be used for automatic generation of code.

At each stage in this bottom-up and top-down design the specifications can be automatically checked for completeness, consistency, and correctness of logic. It is often the case that the data requirements are incompletely stated at a higher-level node. As the node is decomposed the data requirements become better understood. Detailed data requirements discovered low in the tree can be propagated up the tree as necessary. This can be done very quickly with the graphics editor and ANALYZER.

PAYROLL

I thought this ballistic missile defense system was a pretty interesting example, but when I showed it to a typical DP executive, he said, "That's fine, but can HOS do the payroll?" Figures 9.24 to 9.26 illustrate the design of a payroll system [10].

The payroll program has three main branches:

· INITIATE
· LOOP
· TERMINATE

The INITIATE branch opens all files and passes them to the LOOP branch, which is the main operation. The TERMINATE branch closes all of the input and output files.

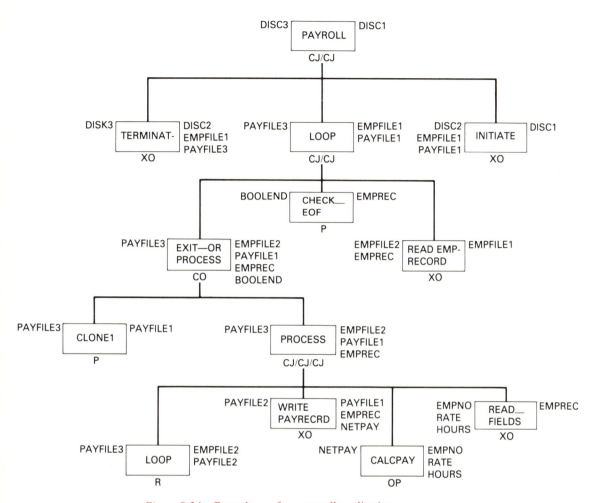

Figure 9.24 Control map for a payroll application.

The main routine, LOOP, reads records from the input file, checks for End of File, processes the data, and writes computed results to an output file.

Figures 9.25 and 9.26 explode the CALCPAY operation into more detail. All file manipulation functions are specified as External Operations [XO]. These functions are externally supplied software. Their interface to the HOS control map is specified as a Function Name, list of input arguments, and list of output arguments. The HOS analyzer checks the consistency of this interface while it verifies the logic of the control map and its defined operations, but it cannot, of course, validate the logic of externally supplied software.

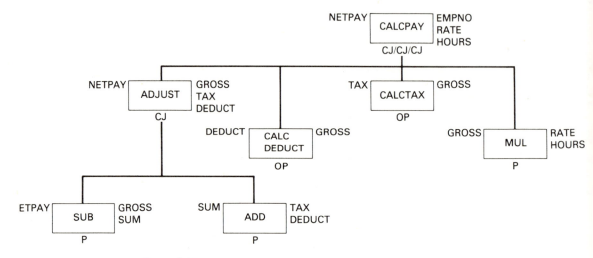

Figure 9.25   The defined operation CALCPAY in Fig. 9.24 is expanded here. CALCTAX, here, is further expanded in Fig. 9.26.

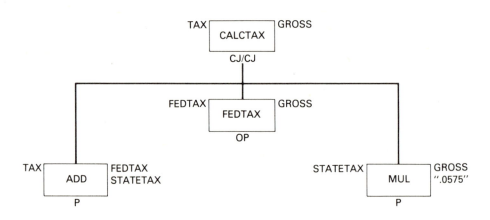

Figure 9.26   CALCTAX in Fig. 9.25 is further expanded here.

HARDWARE LOGIC   HOS has been used for hardware logic design as well as software design [1]. Figure 9.27 shows the functions of NAND and NOR gates.

Figures 9.28 to 9.32 show the electrical behavior of a NAND gate [2]. A NAND gate, if we watch its behavior on an oscilloscope, *outputs* a time-varying voltage under stimulus by a pair of *input* time-varying voltages. If we look at times when all three signals are stable, we can attach a Boolean interpretation to the relative voltages among them. If we look when the input signals are rapidly

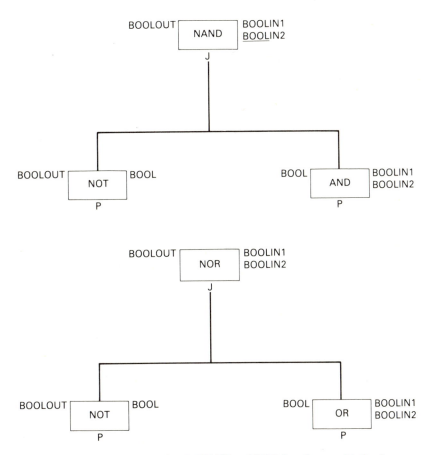

Figure 9.27   Control maps for the NAND and NOR functions used in hardware logic design.

changing, or at abnormal levels, the behavior is erratic. If the logic device is to operate rapidly, rapidly changing voltages will occur. If they change too fast, erratic behavior will result. The hardware designer requires the electrical behavior of combinations of devices to allow a logic interpretation. He must simulate the behavior of combinations of gates with time-varying voltages.

Figure 9.31 shows an HOS description of the electrical behavior of a NAND gate. Figure 9.32 illustrates the behavior of this model. Two input voltages are plotted, SIGIN1 and SIGIN2, together with the resulting output voltage SIGOUT1. The output voltage here exhibits some unwanted spiking.

A hardware designer is concerned with complex combinations of logic gates. He can simulate their behavior with HOS control maps showing multiple functions, like the one shown in Fig. 9.31.

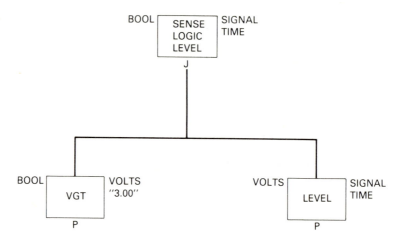

Figure 9.28 Logical interpretation for voltage signals: signals are *true* when greater than 3 volts, and false otherwise. (From Ref. 2.)

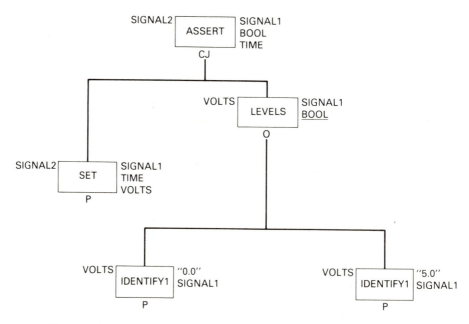

Figure 9.29 Electrical interpretation of logical levels: 5 volts for true, and 0 volts for false. (From Ref. 2.)

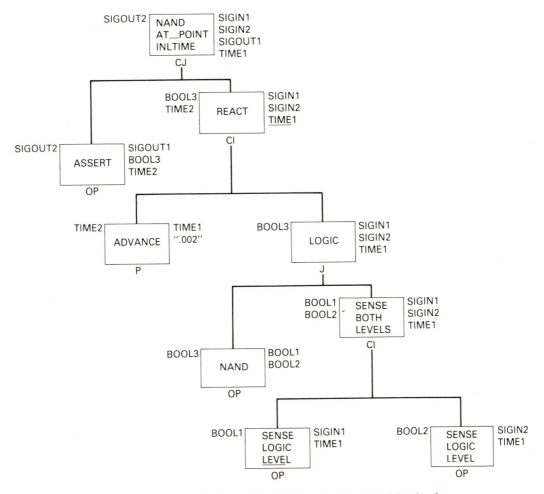

Figure 9.30 Instantaneous behavior of a NAND gate. The logical levels of
the input signals are NANDed, and the reject asserted to the output delayed by
2 nanoseconds. (From Ref. 2.)

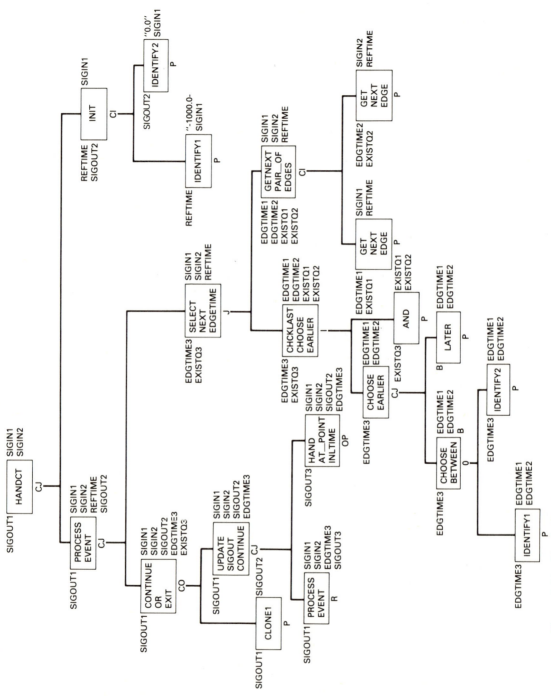

Figure 9.31 The full NAND gate is modeled by "integrating" its instantaneous behavior over time. Only times when inputs are in transition are considered in the model. The integral is being treated discretely. (From Ref. 2.)

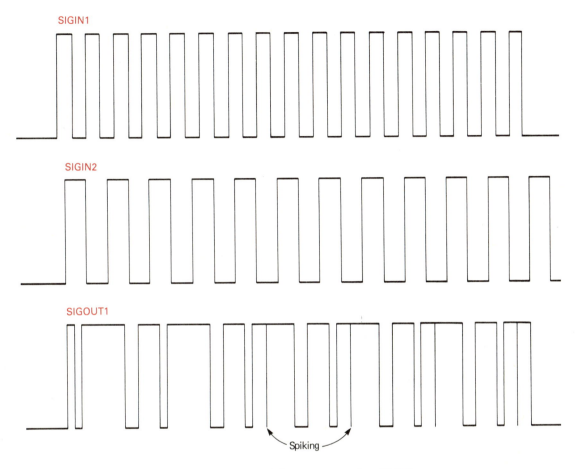

Figure 9.32   Example of output when modeling a test setup for a NAND gate. The top two curves show the inputs; the bottom one shows the output. In this illustration some unwanted spiking occurs in the output. The hardware designer simulates the behavior of many logic gates in combination, using functions like that in Fig. 9.31. (From Ref. 2.)

REFERENCES

1. *Introduction to the Application of HOS to Hardware Design: The CORDIC Algorithm,* IDA Study of Hardware Description Languages, National Academy of Sciences, Woods Hole, MA, 1981. Prepared by Higher Order Software, Inc., Cambridge, MA.

2. Allen Razdow and Gary Goates, *Using AXES as a Hardware Description Language,* Educational Series 8, Higher Order Software, Inc., Cambridge, MA, 1982.

3. *Annotated Model of a Digital Clock,* Educational Series 1, Higher Order Software, Inc., Cambridge, MA, May 1982.

4. W. R. Hackler and A. Samarov, *An AXES Specification of a Radar Scheduler,* Technical Report 23, Higher Order Software, Inc., Cambridge, MA, November 1979.

5. R. Hackler, "An AXES Specification of a Radar," *Proceedings, Fourteenth Hawaii International Conference on System Sciences,* Vol. 1, Western Periodicals Company, Honolulu, Hawaii, January 1981.

6. *Specifying ADA Semantics in HOS,* Technical Report 34, Higher Order Software, Inc., Cambridge, MA, May 1982.

7. M. Hamilton, "The ADA Environment as a System," *Proceedings of the ADA Environment Workshop,* sponsored by Dod High Order Language Working Group, Harbor Island, San Diego, CA, November 1979.

8. F. Brooks, *The Mythical Man-Month,* Addison-Wesley Publishing Co., Inc., Reading, MA, 1975.

9. *USE.IT for Building Buildings,* Educational Series 2, Higher Order Software, Inc., Cambridge, MA, June 1982.

10. Pieter R. Mimno, *Mathematically Provable Software: A Major New Technology,* Higher Order Software, Inc., Cambridge, MA, 1982.

III **BROADER CONTEXT**

Part II of this book has described the HOS methodology. It has been used with impressive results on stand-alone systems for both software creation and hardware design. In the broader context of information systems in a large enterprise it needs to be linked to data-base planning and information resource planning in general. Other methodologies for overall planning are valuable and benefit greatly from being interpreted in HOS notation or coupled directly to HOS software. AXES-defined structures and defined operations can be written to build this connection.

In Part III we look at this broader context, particularly the techniques of data administration without which fully adequate corporate information systems cannot be built.

10 DATA-BASE PLANNING

INTRODUCTION In the first decades of computing, software has become an unruly mess, far removed from the orderliness one would normally associate with an engineering discipline. A methodology like that of HOS could (in time) gain control of software and eliminate the chaos and redundancy.

In data processing there is another mess—the data. The tape and disc libraries have vast numbers of volumes containing redundant, inconsistent collections of data, chaotically organized. What are, in effect, the same data are represented in numerous different incompatible ways on different tapes and discs. The grouping of data items into records is such that it leads to all manner of anomolies and maintenance problems.

The use of HOS for computation alone would not eliminate these problems without overall management and control of the *data* in an enterprise. One of the important objectives of the HOS methodology is to avoid having unpleasant surprises in the later stages of system development. We stressed in Chapter 2 that discovering problems or changes needed in specifications late in the development life cycle is much more expensive than discovering them early.

In commercial data processing there can be very expensive surprises late in the development phases, and more often in the maintenance phase, when good *data-base planning* has not been done. The data needed for technical applications, like the radar scheduler of Figs. 9.22 and 9.23 or the building of a spacecraft operating system, are tractable as the specifications are being developed. The data for commercial data processing can be much more numerous and are entangled with many other applications. A large commercial volume library has tens of thousands of tapes and discs, most of them containing different types of data items. One commercial application receives data from, or passes data to, many other applications. If these applications are developed without integrated planning of the data, chaos results. Higher management cannot extract data which need to be drawn from multiple systems. Expensive conversion is needed and often important business options are lost because the data are not available in the right form.

The evidence with the use of nonprocedural languages in commercial DP indicates that thorough data-base administration is a vital key to their success. They make systems development easier than with traditional programming and it is only too easy for developers serving a particular user group to develop their own data, ignoring the needs of other users. A Tower of Babel grows up in the data if a data administration does not have firm control.

The HOS library is designed to store data objects as well as operations and structures, and to ensure correct interfacing of separately developed HOS systems. If all systems in an organization were developed with a common HOS library and HOS and its library became management standards, interfacing problems could be dealt with. Unfortunately, most applications are not developed with HOS at this time, so the interfacing problems have to be dealt with, for the time being, by human administration.

SEPARATE DEVELOPMENTS WITH INCOMPATIBLE DATA

Traditionally, each functional area in an organization has developed its own files and procedures. There has been much redundancy in data. A medium-sized firm might have many departments each doing their own purchasing, for example. Before computers, this did not matter; it was probably the best way to operate. After computers, it did matter. There might be a dozen sets of purchasing programs to be maintained instead of one. There might be a dozen sets of incompatible purchasing files. The incompatibility prevented overall management information from being pulled together.

Earlier data processing installations implemented one application at a time. (Many still do.) Integrating the different applications seemed too difficult. Integration grew slowly *within* departments or functional area. To achieve integration *among* functional area would have needed new types of management.

Each functional area had its own procedures which it understood very well. It did not understand the procedures of other areas. Each area kept its own files. The structure of these files was unique to the responsibilities of that area. Unfortunately, data had to pass among the areas, and management data needed to be extracted from multiple areas. These data were usually incompatible. Worse, individual areas frequently found the need to change their data structures, and often did so without appreciating the chain reaction of problems this would cause. Figure 10.1 shows the environment of this style of data processing.

In this nonintegrated environment, most communication of changes is done by paperwork—which is error-prone, time consuming, and highly labor intensive. Suppose, for example, that the Engineering department prepares an engineering change report. It makes multiple copies, one for Production Control, one for

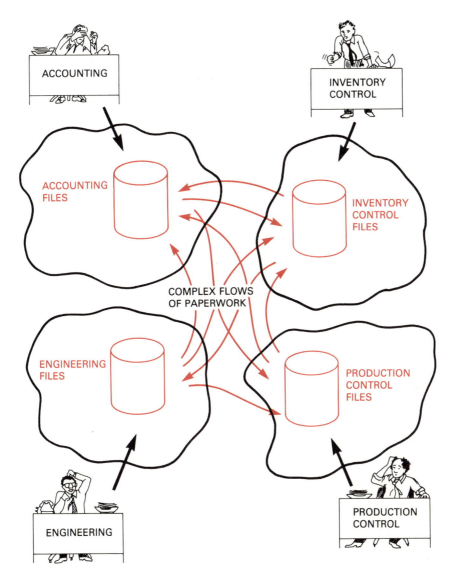

Figure 10.1 Traditionally, each functional area has it own files and procedures. Because of this there is a complex flow of paperwork between the areas to reflect changes in all versions of the data. When this is computerized with separate files, the system is complex and inflexible. Data for different areas are separately designed and not equivalent. Accuracy is lost. Items "slip through the cracks" in the paperwork processes. Maintenance and change are difficult to accomplish, so the procedures become rigid. Management information spanning the areas cannot be extracted.

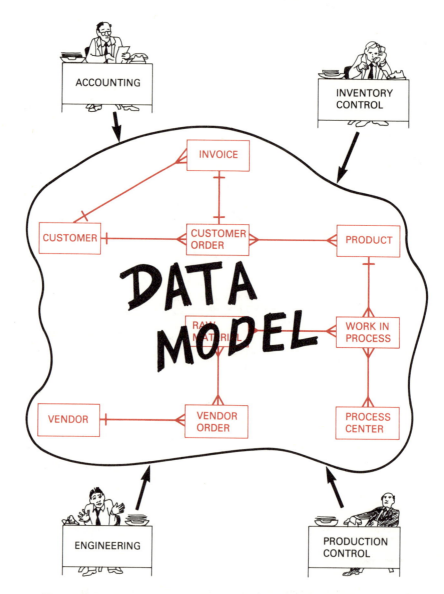

Figure 10.2 When data are consolidated into an integrated data base, data modeling is the key to success. The data structures become more complex but the data flows are greatly simplified. The data are consistent and accurate. New forms of management information can be extracted quickly with fourth-generation languages. Changes in procedures can be made rapidly with these languages. Paperwork is greatly lessened. The administrative procedures of the organization need to be completely rethought. Fundamentally different analysis and design techniques are needed.

Inventory Control, one for Accounting, and so on. Production Control concludes that the engineering change requires changes to be made to its product file. It requires a new request for materials to be sent to Inventory Control. Inventory Control must determine the effects of the change on its purchasing operations. These affect the costs of raw materials and parts. Inventory Control communicates these to Accounting. Accounting concludes that a change in sales price is necessary to retain profitability. It communicates this to Marketing. And so on.

When data for different areas are separately defined and incompatible, this passing of information among the separate systems is complex and inflexible. Manual handling of paperwork is needed. Accuracy is lost. Items slip through the cracks. Changes made to one system can play havoc with others. To prevent harmful effects of change, the management procedures become rigid and change is made difficult.

In one factory more than $1 million worth of work-in-progress was unaccounted for on the shop floor due to items "slipping through the cracks" in the paperwork process. This unaccountability was a major motivation for the end-user management to create an on-line system, and that totally changed the administrative procedures of the factory.

The solution to the problems illustrated by Fig. 10.1 is centralized planning of the data. It is the job of a data administrator to create a model of the data needed to run an organization. This model spans the functional areas. When it is modularized it is broken up by data subjects rather than by departmental or organization-chart boundaries. Figure 10.2 illustrates the use of a common data model.

STABLE FOUNDATION STONE

In well-organized commercial DP the data models become a foundation stone on top of which the procedures are built. A basic reason why this has proven to be practical is that the types of data used in an enterprise do not change very much. Although the information requirements of executives change from month to month, the basic entities in an enterprise remain the same unless the enterprise is itself drastically changed.

An entity is anything about which data can be stored: a product, a customer, a salesman, a part, and so on. A data model shows the relationships between entities: a *salesman* is an *employee*; a *branch office* has many *salesmen*, and so on.

We store *attributes* giving data about the entities. For example, a salesman has a given address, territory, quota, salary, has sold a certain percentage of his quota, and so on. The data model shows what attributes relate to each entity.

The types of entities and attributes that are used in running a corporation usually remain the same with minor changes. They are the foundation of data processing. Their *values* change constantly. The *information* or types of reports which we extract from that collection of data may change substantially. The technology that we use for storing or updating the data will change.

When a corporation changes its administrative procedures, the entities and attributes usually remain the same. It may require a small number of new entities or some new attributes for existing entities, so the foundation data model grows somewhat over the years.

A typical medium-sized corporation has several hundred entities (when redundancies are removed). A large diversified corporation has more, and a separate data model might be created for each of its subsidiaries. There are often 10 or so attributes to each entity on average.

The author worked in a large bank when computers were first introduced. There was batch processing, many manual procedures, no terminals, and much form filling. Today the customers use automated teller machines on-line to distant computers; there are large numbers of terminals and the administrative procedures have entirely changed. However, the raw types of data that are stored are the same as 20 years earlier. There has been a huge change in automation, but if a data model had been created 20 years ago it would still be valid today with minor changes. Of course, if the bank decided to diversify into the whisky distillation business (appropriate for some bankers), a fundamentally different data model would have to be created and added to the existing model.

With some data-base management software new attributes can be added without causing disruption. New entities can be added. Some types of data system software have more flexibility than others. An appropriate choice is needed.

It might be argued that some enterprises change more than banks in their types of data. That is true, so their data models need to be updated, preferably in an automated fashion.

STABLE DATA BASES

There is a huge difference between data bases that are specifically designed to be *stable*, and the files that have been used in traditional data processing. Typical *file* structures tend to change continually because the requirements of users change. No enterprise is static and management perceptions of what information is needed change rapidly.

Because of the intertwined nature of commercial data illustrated in Fig. 10.1, and much more complex than Fig. 10.1 in reality, we seek to isolate the programs from the changes in data structures. We use the term *data independence*. *Data independence* means that when the data structure changes, the programs keep running because they are isolated from that change. The programs have a ''view'' of the data which can be preserved even though the actual, physical structure of the data changes.

Data independence is achieved by means of data-base management systems. The most important difference between a data-base management system and a file management system is that data-base management translates between the application program's view of data and the actual structure of the data. It preserves the program's view of data when the actual view changes in either a logical or a physical manner. With data-base systems many application programs can have different views of the same data.

The use of a good data-base management system does not, by itself, give us the protection we need. We also need good logical design of the data structures used.

LOGICAL DESIGN OF DATA BASES

Unless controlled, systems analysts tend to group together in records any collection of data items which they perceive as being useful. All manner of anomolies can arise because of inappropriate grouping of data items. Some of these anomolies are subtle and often not perceived.

A data base contains hundreds (and sometimes thousands) of types of data items. These data-item types have to be associated into a data-base structure. How do you organize them into a logical structure? What is the best logical structure?

This question is vitally important because that logical structure is the foundation stone on which most future data processing will be built. Not only will conventional programs be written to use the data base but, increasingly, higher-level data-base languages will be used which enable users to extract the information they need from the data base directly, and sometimes to update the data bases. The future corporation will be managed with data-base resources, networks to access the data bases, and end-user software for employing and updating the data.

If the logical structures are designed badly, a large financial penalty will result. A corporation will not be able to employ the data bases as it should, so productivity will suffer. The data bases will constantly have to be modified, but they cannot be modified without much application program rewriting. The end users will not be served as they need, and because of this many try to create their own alternatives to employing the data base.

In the late 1970s it became clear that many data-base installations were not living up to the publicized advantages of data base. A few rare ones had spectacularly improved the whole data processing function and greatly increased application development speed and productivity. Time and time again the difference lay in the design of the overall logical structure of the data.

One of the arguments for using data-base management systems is that they greatly reduce maintenance. In practice, data-base techniques have often not succeeded in lowering the maintenance costs because a need is felt to create new data bases as new applications come along. The reason for this again lies in the logical structuring of the data.

The following two chapters describe logical structuring of data. Chapter 11 describes *normalization* of data. Chapter 12 describes *canonical data structures* and the automation of stable data modeling. Together with these approaches good understanding of the nature and definitions of data is needed and this requires close interaction with those end users who are experts on the data.

OVERALL CONTROL OF DATA   Real corporations are much more complex than Figs. 10.1 and 10.2. Many early attempts to build integrated data bases failed. This occurred for several reasons:

- The magnitude of the task was underestimated.
- Organizational politics prevailed, partly because of a lack of strong management with a clear perception of what was to be accomplished.
- Methodologies for the design of stable data structures were not understood.
- An appropriate design methodology was not understood.
- There was not an overall architect who could use the design methodology.
- Data model *design* was confused with *implementation*.

BOX 10.1   Essentials for overall control of data in an enterprise

- Strategic planning should be done of the entities in an enterprise [1]. All entities should be represented in a rough entity model.
- The rough entity model should be expanded into detailed data models in stages, as appropriate.
- The detailed data model should represent all functional dependencies among the data items.
- All records should be in third normal form (Chapter 11).
- Stability analysis should be applied to the detailed data model [2].
- The data model should be designed with an automated tool [3].
- The data modeling tool should provide *automatic* input to the library of the specification language tool [4].
- Submodels should be extractable from the overall model when needed for specific projects.
- If the data model is adjusted or added to in the application design process, the data administrator should feed these changes into the overall model.
- Defined operations may be associated with the data to ensure integrity, accuracy, and security checks are applied to the data, independent of applications.

In order to achieve overall control of data, the factors listed in Box 10.1 are needed. The objective is to do data planning across an enterprise so that incompatible data are largely eliminated and stable data models form the foundations of information systems.

Without the planning and controls listed in Box 10.1, the use of AXES or other nonprocedural facilities for application building will not be enough to avoid severe problems with incompatible data.

REFERENCES

1. James Martin, *Strategic Data-Planning Methodologies*, Prentice-Hall, Inc., Englewood Cliffs, NJ, 1982.

2. James Martin, *Managing the Data-Base Environment*, Prentice-Hall, Inc., Englewood Cliffs, NJ, 1983.

3. For example, Data Designer, available from Database Design, Inc., Ann Arbor, MI.

4. The output of Data Designer can be converted automatically to the HOS representation of data.

11 THIRD NORMAL FORM

NORMALIZATION OF DATA

The term *normalization* of data refers to the way data items are grouped together into record structures. *Third normal form* is a grouping of data designed to avoid the anomalies and problems that can occur with data. The concept originated with the mathematics of E. F. Codd, which is given in Appendix IV. This chapter takes what Codd described mathematically and explains it in a manner that is easy to understand.

With third-normal-form data each data item in a record refers to a particular key which uniquely identifies that data. The key itself may be composed of more than one data item. Each data item in the record is identified by the whole key and not just part of the key. No data item in the record is identifiable by any other data item in the record which is not part of the key.

The basic simplicity of third normal form makes the data records easy to understand, and easier to change than when data are organized in less rigorous ways. It formally groups the data items which are associated with each entity type (and also those which are associated with more than one entity type), and separates the data items which belong to different entity types. Third normal form prevents anomolies which can occur otherwise. It permits rules to be established for controlling semantic disintegrity in query languages.

Data exist in real life as groups of data items. They exist on invoices, weighbills, tax forms, driving licences, and so on. These groupings are usually not in a normalized form. Not surprisingly, systems analysts have often implemented computer records that are also not normalized. However, data which are not normalized can lead to various subtle problems in the future.

Experience has shown that when computer data are organized in third normal form the resulting data structures are more stable and able to accommodate change. Each attribute relates to its own entity and is not mixed up with attributes relating

BOX 11.1   Conversion to third normal form

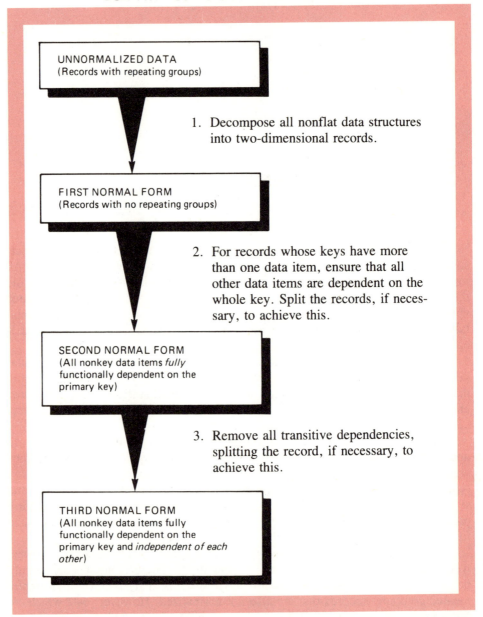

UNNORMALIZED DATA
(Records with repeating groups)

1. Decompose all nonflat data structures into two-dimensional records.

FIRST NORMAL FORM
(Records with no repeating groups)

2. For records whose keys have more than one data item, ensure that all other data items are dependent on the whole key. Split the records, if necessary, to achieve this.

SECOND NORMAL FORM
(All nonkey data items *fully* functionally dependent on the primary key)

3. Remove all transitive dependencies, splitting the record, if necessary, to achieve this.

THIRD NORMAL FORM
(All nonkey data items fully functionally dependent on the primary key and *independent of each other*)

to different entities. The actions that create and update data can then be applied with simple structured design to one normalized record at a time.

At the time of writing, only a small proportion of existing data bases are in third normal form. Some corporations have several years of experience of operation of third-normal-form data structures. There is no question that they have greatly benefited from this type of design, especially when it is combined with other steps which are part of good data administration [1].

Reacting to the perceived benefits, some corporations have incorporated into their data base standards manuals the requirement that all data base structures be in third normal form. Usually, this form of design is better in terms of *machine requirements* as well as in logical structuring, but this is not always the case. Sometimes the physical designer finds it desirable to deviate from third normal form. A compromise is then needed. Which is preferable: somewhat better machine performance or better protection from maintenance costs? Usually, the potential maintenance costs are much the more expensive.

The data base standards manual should say that all data will be *designed* in third normal form, but that the physical implementation may occasionally deviate from third normal form if the trade-off is fully explored and documented.

To put data into third normal form, three steps may be used. It is put into *first normal form*, then *second normal form*, then *third normal form*. Box 11.1 summarizes these. The rules for achieving fully normalized data can be expressed in the AXES language, and correct accesses to such data enforced.

The basic ideas of this normalization of data are simple, but the ramifications are many and subtle, and vary from one type of data base usage to another. It is important to note that normalization decribes the *logical* representation of data, not the physical. There are multiple ways of implementing it physically.

Box 11.2 gives the terminology used in discussing data.

BOX 11.2   Vocabulary Used in Discussing Data

The reader should distinguish clearly between the terms *data type* and *data-item type*.

Data type refers to an attribute of data itself, that is, data about data. Examples of data types are *integer, rational number, Boolean*, and *alphabetic string*.

Entity type refers to a given class of entities, such as *customer, part, account, employee*, and so on.

Attribute refers to a characteristic of an entity type, for example, *color, shape, shipment-date, type-of-account, dollar-value*, and so on.

When we say *data-item type* we are referring to either an *entity type* or an *attribute*.

Data item refers to a field which expresses an attribute or entity identifier (a special type of attribute) in computable form.

(Continued)

BOX 11.2   *(Continued)*

> *Data-item type* refers to a given class of data items. Examples of data-item types are *customer#*, *account#*, *address*, *dollar-value*, *color*, and so on.
>
> Entities and data items are *instances* of entity types and data-item types. For example, DUPONT is an instance of the entity type *customer*. RED is an instance of the attribute *color*. Data item 4789123 is an instance of the data-item type *employee number*.
>
> In discussion of data we sometimes use a shorthand. We say "entity" when we mean "entity type," "data item" when we mean "data-item type," and so on. "Data type" is never abbreviated. That term is especially important in the HOS methodology.

FIRST NORMAL FORM   *First normal form* refers to a collection of data organized into records which have no repeating groups of data items within a record. In other words, they are flat files, two-dimensional matrices of data items. Such a flat file may be thought of as a simple two-dimensional table. It may, however, contain many thousands of records.

Most programming languages give programmers the ability to create and refer to records which are not *flat*, that is, they contain repeating groups of data items within a record. In COBOL these are called *data aggregates*. There can be data aggregates within data aggregates—repeating groups within repeating groups.

The following COBOL record contains two data aggregates, called BIRTH and SKILLS.

```
RECORD NAME IS PERSON

01            EMPLOYEE# PICTURE "9(5)"
01            EMPNAME TYPE CHARACTER 20
01            SEX PICTURE "A"
01            EMPJCODE PICTURE "9999"
01            SALARY PICTURE "9(5)V99"
01            BIRTH
       02        MONTH PICTURE "99"
       02        DAY
       02        YEAR PICTURE "99"
01            NOSKILLS TYPE BINARY
01            SKILLS OCCURS NOSKILLS TIMES
       02        SKILLCODE PICTURE "9999"
       02        SKILLYEARS PICTURE "99"
```

PERSON

EMPLOYEE#	EMPNAME	SEX	EMPJCODE	SALARY	BIRTH			SKILLS	
					MONTH	DAY	YEAR	SKILLCODE	SKILLYEARS

Birth causes no problems because it occurs only once in each record. SKILLS can occur several times in one record, so that record is not in first normal form. It is not a *flat*, two-dimensional record. To *normalize* it the repeating group SKILLS must be removed and put into a separate record, thus:

PERSON

EMPLOYEE#	EMPNAME	SEX	EMPJCODE	SALARY	BIRTH		
					MONTH	DAY	YEAR

SKILLS

EMPLOYEE# + SKILLCODE	SKILLYEARS

The lower record has a concatenated key EMPLOYEE# + SKILLCODE. We cannot know SKILLYEARS (the number of years of experience an employee has had with a given skill) unless we know EMPLOYEE# (the employee number whom this refers to) and SKILLCODE (the skill in question). In general, a nonflat record is normalized by converting it into two or more flat records.

If the normalized records above were implemented in a CODASYL, DL/1, or other nonrelational data-base management system, we would not repeat the field EMPLOYEE# in the lower record. A linkage to the upper record would imply this key:

A relational data base *would* employ a separate SKILLS record (relation) with a key EMPLOYEE + SKILLCODE; it thus avoids pointer mechanisms in the logical representation of data.

Here we are concerned, not with how the physical implementation is done, but with the overall *logical* representation of data. We need to analyze and chart an enterprise's information resources and how they are used. We draw the lower record with its complete concatenated key so that it can stand alone and the key uniquely identifies the data in the record.

FUNCTIONAL DEPENDENCE

In attempting to lay out the relationships between data items, the designer must concern himself with which data items are *dependent* on which other. The phrase *functionally dependent* is defined as follows: *Data item B of a record R is functionally dependent on data item A of R if, at every instant of time, each value in A has no more than one value in B associated with it in record R* [2].

Saying that **B** is functionally dependent on **A** is equivalent to saying that *A identifies B*. In other words, if we know the value of **A**, we can find the value of **B** that is associated with it. For example, in an employee record, the SALARY data item is functionally dependent on EMPLOYEE#. For one EMPLOYEE# there is one SALARY. To find the value of SALARY in a data base you would normally go via EMPLOYEE#. The latter is a key that identifies the attribute SALARY.

We will draw a functional dependency with a line which has a small bar (like a ''1'') on it, thus:

EMPLOYEE#————————+ SALARY

This indicates that one instance of SALARY is associated with each EMPLOYEE#.

Consider the record for the entity EMPLOYEE:

EMPLOYEE#	EMPLOYEE-NAME	SALARY	PROJECT#	COMPLETION-DATE

The functional dependencies in this record are as follows:

EMPLOYEE#	is dependent on EMPLOYEE-NAME
EMPLOYEE-NAME	is dependent on EMPLOYEE#
SALARY	is dependent on either EMPLOYEE-NAME or EMPLOYEE#
PROJECT#	is dependent on either EMPLOYEE-NAME or EMPLOYEE#
COMPLETION-DATE	is dependent on EMPLOYEE-NAME, EMPLOYEE#, or PROJECT#

EMPLOYEE# is not functionally dependent on SALARY because more than one employee could have the same salary. Similarly, EMPLOYEE# is not functionally dependent on PROJECT# but COMPLETION-DATE is. No other data item in the record is fully dependent on PROJECT#. We can draw these functional dependencies as follows:

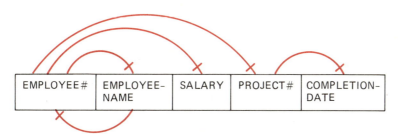

A data item can be functionally dependent on a *group* of data items rather than on a single data item. Consider, for example, the following record, which shows how programmers spent their time:

PROGRAMMER–ACTIVITY

PROGRAMMER#	PACKAGE#	PROGRAMMER-NAME	PACKAGE-NAME	TOTAL-HOURS-WORKED

TOTAL-HOURS-WORKED is functionally dependent on the concatenated key (PROGRAMMER#, PACKAGE#).

The functional dependencies in this record can be drawn as follows:

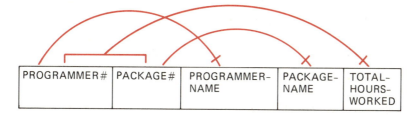

FULL FUNCTIONAL DEPENDENCY

A data item or a collection of data items, B, of a record R can be said to be *fully functionally dependent* on another collection of data items, A, of record R if B is functionally dependent on the whole of A but not on any subset of A.

For example, in the record above, TOTAL-HOURS-WORKED is fully functionally dependent on the concatenated key (PROGRAMMER#, PACKAGE#) because it refers to how many hours a given programmer has worked on a given package. Neither PROGRAMMER# alone nor PACKAGE# alone identifies TOTAL-HOURS-WORKED.

TOTAL-HOURS-WORKED, however, is the *only* data item which is fully functionally dependent on the concatenated key. PROGRAMMER-NAME is fully functionally dependent on PROGRAMMER# alone, and PACKAGE-NAME is fully functionally dependent on PACKAGE# alone. The lines with bars above make these dependencies clear.

SECOND NORMAL FORM

We are now in a position to define second normal form. First a simple definition: *Each attribute in a record is functionally dependent on the whole key of that record.*

Where the key consists of more than one data item, the record may not be in second normal form. The record above with the key PROGRAMMER# + PACKAGE# is not in second normal form because TOTAL-HOURS-WORKED depends on the whole key, whereas PROGRAMMER-NAME and PACKAGE-NAME each depends on only one data item in the key. Similarly, the following record is not in second normal form:

PART#	SUPPLIER#	SUPPLIER-NAME	SUPPLIER-DETAILS	PRICE

There are a few problems that can result from this record *not* being in second normal form:

1. We cannot enter details about a supplier until that supplier supplies a part. If the supplier does not supply a part, there is no key.

2. If a supplier should temporarily cease to supply any part, the deletion of the last record containing that SUPPLIER# will also delete the details of the supplier. It would normally be desirable that SUPPLIER-DETAILS be preserved.

3. We have problems when we attempt to update the supplier details. We must search for every record which contains that supplier as part of the key. If a supplier supplies many parts, much redundant updating of supplier details will be needed.

These types of irregularities can be removed by splitting the record into two records in second normal form, as shown in Fig. 11.1. Only PRICE is fully functionally dependent on the concatenated key, so all other attributes are removed to the separate record on the left which has SUPPLIER-NUMBER only as its key.

Splitting to second normal form is the type of splitting that natural database growth tends to force, so it might as well be anticipated when the data base is first set up. In general, every data item in a record should be dependent on the *entire* key; otherwise, it should be removed to a separate record.

Figure 11.1 illustrates the splitting of the record above into second-normal-form records.

CANDIDATE KEYS

The *key* of a normalized record must have the following properties:

1. *Unique identification.* For every record occurrence the key must uniquely identify the record.

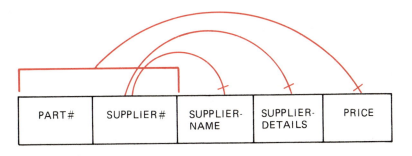

An instance of this record:

PART#	SUPPLIER#	SUPPLIER-NAME	SUPPLIER-DETAILS	PRICE
1	1000	JONES	x	20
1	1500	ABC	x	28
1	2050	XYZ	y	22
1	1900	P–H	z	30
2	3100	ALLEN	z	520
2	1000	JONES	x	500
2	2050	XYZ	y	590
3	2050	XYZ	y	1000
4	1000	JONES	x	80
4	3100	ALLEN	z	90
4	1900	P–H	z	95
5	1500	ABC	x	160
5	1000	JONES	x	140

To convert the records above into second normal form, we split it into two records, thus:

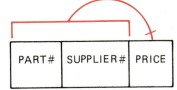

An instance of the above pair of records:

SUPPLIER#	SUPPLIER-NAME	SUPPLIER-DETAILS
1000	JONES	x
1500	ABC	x
2050	XYZ	y
1900	P–H	z
3100	ALLEN	z

PART#	SUPPLIER#	PRICE
1	1000	20
1	1500	28
1	2050	22
1	1900	30
2	3100	520
2	1000	500
2	2050	590
3	2050	1000
4	1000	80
4	3100	90
4	1900	95
5	1500	160
5	1000	140

Figure 11.1   Conversion to second normal form.

2. *Nonredundancy*. No data item in the key can be discarded without destroying the property of unique identification.

It sometimes happens that more than one data item or set of data items *could* be the key of a record. Such alternative choices are referred to as *candidate keys*.

One candidate key must be designated the *primary key*. We will draw the functional dependencies for candidate keys which are not the primary key *underneath* the record, thus:

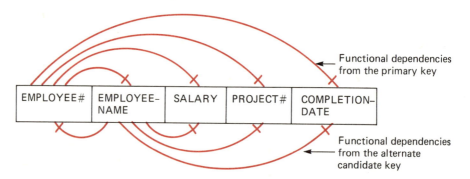

In this illustration EMPLOYEE-NAME is regarded as a candidate key—an alternative to EMPLOYEE#. This is not generally done in practice because two employees *might* have the same name. Only EMPLOYEE# is truly unique. The possible existence of candidate keys complicates the definitions of second and third normal form.

A more comprehensive definition of second normal form is: *A record R is in second normal form if it is in first normal form and every nonprime data item of R is fully functionally dependent on each candidate key of R* [2].

In the EMPLOYEE record above the candidate keys have only one data item, and hence the record is always in second normal form because the nonprime data items *must* be fully dependent on the candidate keys. When the candidate keys consist of more than one data item, a first-normal-form record may not be in second normal form.

THIRD NORMAL FORM

A record that *is* in second normal form can have another type of anomaly. It may have a data item which is not a key but which itself identifies other data items. This is referred to as a *transitive dependence*. Transitive dependencies can cause problems. The step of putting data into *third normal form* removes transitive dependencies.

Suppose that **A**, **B**, and **C** are three data items or distinct collections of data items of a record **R**. If **C** is functionally dependent on **B** and **B** is functionally dependent on **A**, then **C** is functionally dependent on **A**. If the inverse mapping is nonsimple (i.e., if **A** is not functionally dependent on **B** or **B** is not functionally dependent on **C**), **C** is said to be *transitively dependent* on **A**.

In a diagram **C** is transitively dependent on **A** if

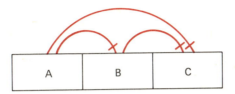

Conversion to third normal form removes this transitive dependence by splitting the record into two, thus:

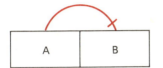 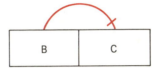

The following record is not in third normal form because COMPLETION-DATE is dependent on PROJECT#.

EMPLOYEE

EMPLOYEE#	EMPLOYEE-NAME	SALARY	PROJECT#	COMPLETION-DATE

A few problems might result from this record not being in third normal form.

1. Before any employees are recruited for a project the completion date of the project cannot be recorded because there is no EMPLOYEE record.

2. If all the employees should leave the project so that the project has no employees until others are recruited, all records containing the completion date would be deleted. This may be thought an unlikely occurrence, but on other types of files a similar danger of loss of information can be less improbable.

3. If the completion date is changed, it will be necessary to search for all records containing that completion date, and update them all.

A simple definition of third normal form is: A record is in second normal form and each attribute is functionally dependent on the key and *nothing but the key*.

A more formal definition which incorporates candidate keys is as follows: *A record R is in third normal form if it is in second normal form and every nonprime data item of R is nontransitively dependent on each candidate key of R* [2].

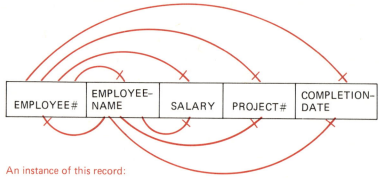

EMPLOYEE#	EMPLOYEE-NAME	SALARY	PROJECT#	COMPLETION-DATE

An instance of this record:

EMPLOYEE#	EMPLOYEE-NAME	SALARY	PROJECT#	COMPLETION-DATE
120	JONES	2000	x	17.7.84
121	HARPO	1700	x	17.7.84
270	GARFUNKAL	1800	y	12.1.87
273	SELSI	3600	x	17.7.84
274	ABRAHMS	3000	z	21.3.86
279	HIGGINS	2400	y	12.1.87
301	FLANNEL	1800	z	21.3.86
306	MCGRAW	2100	x	17.7.84
310	ENSON	3000	z	21.3.86
315	GOLDSTEIN	3100	x	17.7.84
317	PUORRO	2700	y	12.1.87
320	MANSINI	1700	y	12.1.87
321	SPOTO	2900	x	17.7.84
340	SCHAFT	3100	x	17.7.84
349	GOLD	1900	z	21.3.86

To convert the above record into third normal form we split it into two records, thus:

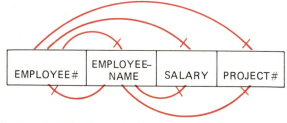

EMPLOYEE#	EMPLOYEE-NAME	SALARY	PROJECT#

PROJECT#	COMPLETION-DATE

An instance of the above pair of records:

EMPLOYEE#	EMPLOYEE-NAME	SALARY	PROJECT#
120	JONES	2000	x
121	HARPO	1700	x
270	GARFUNKAL	1800	y
273	SELSI	3600	x
274	ABRAHMS	3000	z
279	HIGGINS	2400	y
301	FLANNEL	1800	z
306	MCGRAW	2100	x
310	ENSON	3000	z
315	GOLDSTEIN	3100	x
317	PUORRO	2700	y
320	MANSINI	1700	y
321	SPOTO	2900	x
340	SCHAFT	3100	x

PROJECT#	COMPLETION-DATE
x	17.7.84
y	12.1.87
z	21.3.86

Figure 11.2 Conversion to third normal form.

Figure 11.2 show the conversion of the EMPLOYEE record above to third normal form. The conversion to third normal form produces a separate record for each entity—normalized record. For example, Fig. 11.2 produced a separate record for the entity PROJECT. Usually, this normalized record would be needed anyway. We need data separately storing for each entity.

STORAGE AND PERFORMANCE   The concept of third normal form applies to all data bases. Experience has shown that the records of a CODASYL system, the segments of a DL/1 system, or the group of data items in other systems can benefit from being in third normal form.

Objections to third normal form are occasionally heard on the grounds that it requires more storage or more machine time. A third-normal-form structure usually has more records after all the splitting described above. Isn't that worse from the hardware point of view?

Not necessarily. In fact, although there are more records they almost always take less storage. The reason is that non-third-normal-form records usually have much *value* redundancy.

Compare the records in Fig. 11.1. Here records not in second normal form are converted to second normal form by splitting. It will be seen that the lower red part of Fig. 11.1 has fewer *values* of data written down than the red part at the top. There are fewer values of SUPPLIER-NAME and SUPPLIER-DETAILS. This shrinkage does not look very dramatic on such a small illustration. If there had been thousands of suppliers and thousands of parts, and many attributes of both, the shrinkage would have been spectacular.

Again, compare the red parts of Fig. 11.2. Here a record is converted to third normal form by splitting. The number of *values* of data shrinks. There are fewer values of COMPLETION-DATE recorded after the split. Once more, if there had been many employees, many projects, and many attributes of those projects, the shrinkage would have been dramatic. Conversion to third normal form almost always reduces the amount of storage used, often dramatically.

What about machine time and accesses? Often this is less after normalization. Before normalization many aspects of the data are tangled together and must all be read at once. After normalization they are separated, so a small record is read.

Also because there is less value redundancy in third normal form, there is less duplicated updating of the redundant values. Suppose that project x slips its completion date (which it does every week!). In the record at the top of Fig. 11.2, the completion date has to be changed seven times; in the third normal form version it has to be changed only once. A similar argument applies to SUPPLIER-NAME and SUPPLIER-DETAILS in Fig. 11.1. The argument would have more force if the examples had hundreds of employees, thousands of suppliers, and many attributes that have to be updated.

There are, however, exceptions to this. On rare occasions a designer may consciously design non-third-normal-form records for performance reasons. For our purposes throughout most of this book third normal form relates to the logical structure of data, not the physical.

SEMANTIC DISINTEGRITY

A further reason for using third normal form is that certain data-base queries can run into problems when data are not cleanly structured. A query, perhaps entered with a data-base query language, can appear to be valid, but in fact have subtle illogical aspects sometimes referred to as *semantic disintegrity*. When the data is in third normal form, rules can be devised for preventing semantic disintegrity or warning the user about his query. This is discussed in Chapter 13.

CLEAR THINKING ABOUT DATA

Third normal form is an aid to clear thinking about data. It is a formal method of separating the data items which relate to different entities. A record in third normal form has the following clean, simple structure:

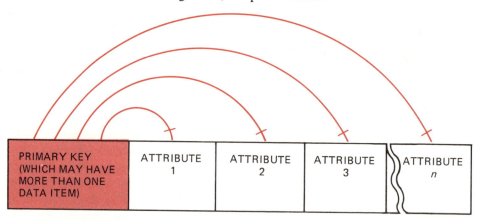

The functional dependency lines all come from the primary key. There are no hidden dependencies not relating to the key. If the key is concatenated, all data items are dependent on the entire key.

We can give a loose definition of third normal form, which has the advantage of being easy to remember: *Every data item in a record is dependent on the key, the whole key, and nothing but the key.*

If a systems analyst remembers this definition (understanding that it is not rigorous like those earlier in the chapter), he can quickly spot and modify records which are not in third normal form. He should be familiar enough with this that alarm bells go off in his mind whenever he sees records which are not in third normal form. This clean, simple, data grouping is easy to implement and to use. There will be complications in store in the future if more complex record structures are used.

For the data-base administrator, third normal form is an aid to precision. A data base in third normal form can grow and evolve naturally. The updating rules are straightforward. A third-normal-form record type can have records added to it or can have records deleted without the problems that could occur with non-third-normal-form record types. Third-normal-form structuring gives a simple view of data to the programmers and users, and makes them less likely to perform invalid operations.

Figure 11.3 gives a simplified illustration of the three steps in achieving third-normal-form structures.

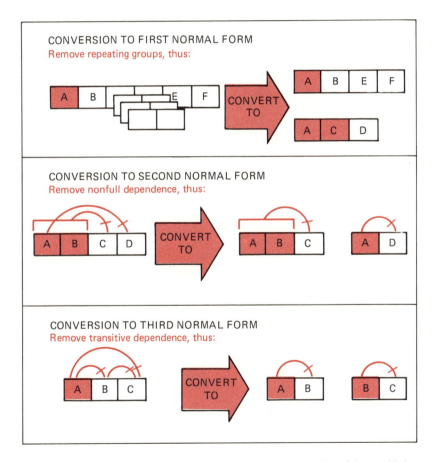

Figure 11.3   Simple illustration of the three steps in conversion of data to third normal form. Figure 11.4 gives an illustration with real data.

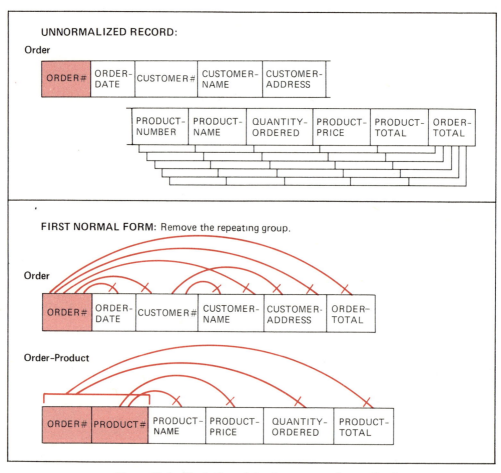

Figure 11.4 Illustration of the three stages of normalization.

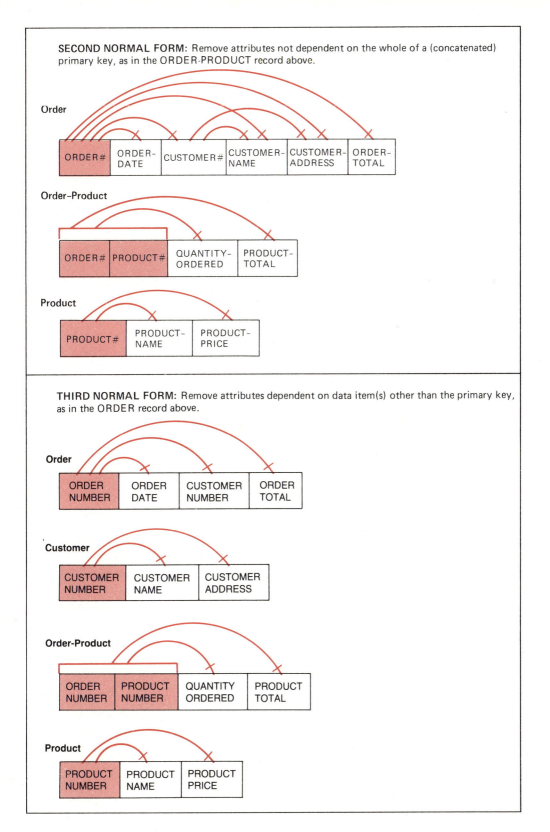

SECOND NORMAL FORM: Remove attributes not dependent on the whole of a (concatenated) primary key, as in the ORDER-PRODUCT record above.

Order

ORDER#	ORDER-DATE	CUSTOMER#	CUSTOMER-NAME	CUSTOMER-ADDRESS	ORDER-TOTAL

Order–Product

ORDER#	PRODUCT#	QUANTITY-ORDERED	PRODUCT-TOTAL

Product

PRODUCT#	PRODUCT-NAME	PRODUCT-PRICE

THIRD NORMAL FORM: Remove attributes dependent on data item(s) other than the primary key, as in the ORDER record above.

Order

ORDER NUMBER	ORDER DATE	CUSTOMER NUMBER	ORDER TOTAL

Customer

CUSTOMER NUMBER	CUSTOMER NAME	CUSTOMER ADDRESS

Order-Product

ORDER NUMBER	PRODUCT NUMBER	QUANTITY ORDERED	PRODUCT TOTAL

Product

PRODUCT NUMBER	PRODUCT NAME	PRODUCT PRICE

Probably the best way for a data processing user to become convinced of the value (or otherwise) of normalization is to take a section of his files and write down what third-normal-form records would be used to represent them. A group of systems analysts should then list all the plausible changes that might occur to the files as data processing evolves in the years ahead, and see how many of these changes would necessitate restructuring the records in such a way that previously written application programs would have to be changed. Compare this with what reprogramming would be needed if the same changes were applied to the existing records.

In examining existing data bases it has been my experience that time and time again they are not in third normal form. This spells trouble for the future. Unless it was the conscious policy of management to create third-normal-form structures, the design has been far from these principles.

**AN EXAMPLE OF
NORMALIZATION**
Earlier in the chapter we referred to an ORDER record with the following unnormalized structure:

ORDER   *(order number,* order date, customer number, customer name, customer address ((product number, product name, quantity ordered, product price, product total)), order total.)

Applying the three normalization steps to this example is illustrated in Fig. 11.4.

Application of the *first normal form* rule (remove repeating groups) creates two records: ORDER and ORDER-PRODUCT. The primary key is made up of *Order#* and *Product#.* (ORDER-PRODUCT is, in fact, the ORDER LINE ITEM record which we discussed above.)

Second normal form removes the product name from the ORDER-PRODUCT record into a new record: PRODUCT. Product name is wholly dependent on product number; it is only partially dependent on the primary (combined or compound) key of ORDER-PRODUCT: *Order#* + *Product#.*

Third normal form removes the customer details from the ORDER record to a separate CUSTOMER record. Customer name and address are wholly dependent on customer number; they are not dependent at all on the primary key of ORDER (i.e., *Order#*). (A customer will not change his name and address with each new order . . . unless he doesn't intend to pay for it!)

The four resulting records in Fig. 11.4—ORDER, CUSTOMER, ORDER-PRODUCT, and PRODUCT—are in third normal form. Normalization has, in fact, produced the four records we discussed earlier, which we intuitively felt were necessary to accommodate business change more readily.

The CUSTOMER and PRODUCT normalized records would be needed for other purposes and created by other analysts. We need to synthesize the data that result from multiple normalization processes, as discussed later in the book.

EXPRESSING NORMALIZED DATA IN HOS   A central tenet of HOS is that data are described by primitive operations on those data, with axioms describing the behavior of those operations. This technique allows the complete integration of facts about data into the specification of the system. System functions which are rigorously specified are the interface between data and processes.

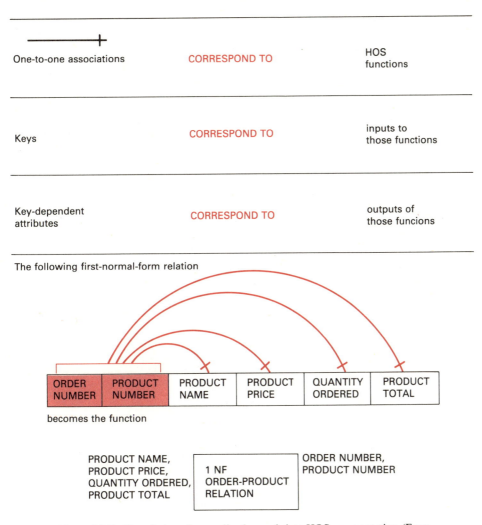

Figure 11.5   Translation of normalized records into HOS representation.(From Ref. 3.)

A data model is described as a set of primitive operations on data types. The integration of this model into the rest of the system is immediate. One can immediately begin specifying applications which use those primitive operations, and their behavior is guaranteed by the axioms on them. The resulting system specifications are immediately automatically verifiable for correctness according to the HOS methodology: syntactic correctness, data-flow correctness, and interface correctness.

The control map may employ hierarchical, network, or relational data-base operations by means of defined operations or defined control structures, such as SELECT, PROJECT, JOIN, GET-NEXT, and so on, which must themselves be axiomatically specified.

The graphical means which we use for representing third-normal-form data, or data-base structures in general, can be translated directly into HOS notation. One-to-one associations correspond to HOS *functions*. Keys can correspond to *inputs* to those functions. Key-dependent attributes can correspond to outputs of those functions. The ORDER-PRODUCT relation then becomes the function shown in Fig. 11.5.

The function's complex relationship can be decomposed into simpler relationships as shown in Fig. 11.6. The CLONE2 function in the figure gives us two product numbers which are the same. We use these as we split the INF relation into two 2NF relations, as follows:

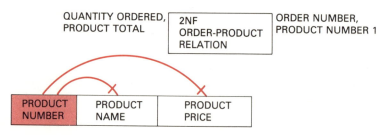

becomes the function

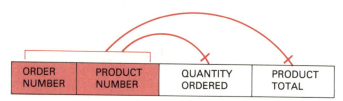

becomes the function

Decomposition to third normal form can be handled similarly.

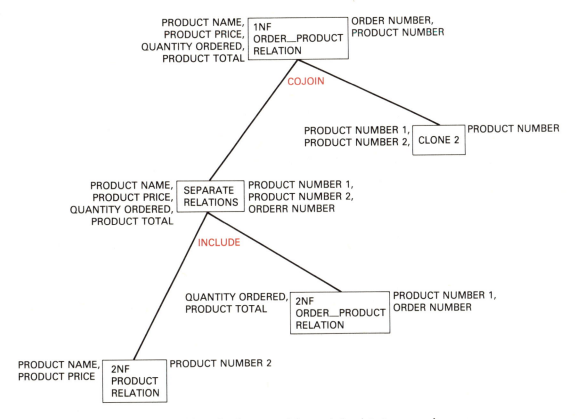

Figure 11.6 Decomposition of a first-normal-form relation into two second-normal-form relations.

DATA LAYERING

Data layering is used in HOS to show that one data type is composed of other data types. CUSTOMER DATABASE is composed of certain records. These records are composed of certain data items. It is convenient to refer to the higher aggregates of data in drawing the control maps.

Consider an organization of data types related to the first-normal-form OR-DER-PRODUCT record in Fig. 11.4. This can be decomposed into two records (ORDER-PRODUCT and PRODUCT) in a lower layer. These can be decomposed into data items. These can be described as numbers or strings. Figure 11.7 shows this hierarchical breakdown. Figure 11.8 shows the formal definitions.

At the bottom of the data-layering hierarchy in Fig. 11.7 are only *string* and *number* data types. These lowest-level data types are called *representation types*. More complex data types are built out of representation types in data layering. Axioms of the representation types are valid for all higher-level data types in the layering.

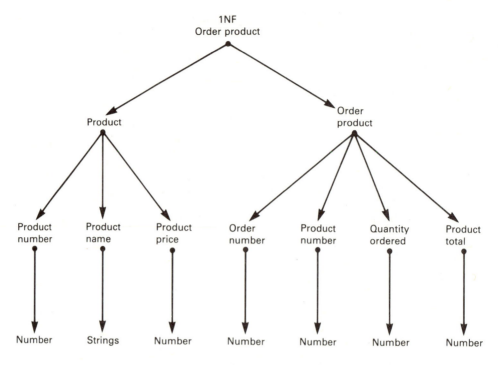

Figure 11.7   Data layering, showing a hierarchy of data types.(From Ref. 3.)

```
Data Type: 1NF Order Product (Product, Order Product)
  Primitive Operations:
    Product, Order Product = Relations of (1NF Order Product)
    1NF Order Product = Associate (Product, Order, Product, 1NF Order Product.
  Axioms:

Data Type: Order Product   (Order Number, Product Number, Quantity Ordered,
                            Product Total)

  Primitive Operations:
    Order Number, Product Number,
    Quantity Ordered Product Total = Components of (Order Product)

  Axioms:

Data Type: Product (Product Number, Product Name, Product Price)

  Primitive Operations:
    Product Price, Product Name = Price and Name of (Product)
    Product = Assign Price and Name to (Product Price, Product Name, Product)

  Axioms:

Etc.
```

Figure 11.8   Primitive operations and axioms which control data type layering such as that in Fig. 11.7.(From Ref. 3.)

INTEGRITY CHECKS

The axioms on the higher-level data types can constrain the allowable strings to those which are specific names, and can constrain the allowable numbers to certain values or ranges. In this way consistency and integrity checks can be applied to values of data in the data base. Users' data entry would be automatically checked against the permissible names and values. If the data were invalid, a prompt for correct data or an error message would result, depending on how the primitive operations were implemented.

PRODUCT TOTAL is a derived data item. Associated with this data item would be a function which shows how PRODUCT TOTAL is calculated from PRODUCT PRICE and QUANTITY ORDERED:

PRODUCT TOTAL | COMPUTE PRODUCT TOTAL | PRODUCT PRICE, QUANTITY ORDERED

The term *intelligent data base* is sometimes used to imply that certain functions are associated with data and are invoked every time it is used, whatever the application. HOS provides a mechanism for automatically invoking such functions.

The layering to a set of axiomatically specified data-manipulation primitives ensures the correct use of data, and allows value correctness checks, functions for derived data, and intelligent data-base functions to be invoked automatically with provable correctness.

REFERENCES

1. James Martin, *Managing the Data-Base Environment*, Prentice-Hall, Inc., Englewood Cliffs, NJ, 1983.

2. E. F. Codd, "Further Normalization of the Data Base Relational Model," in *Data Base Systems* (Courant Computer Science Symposia 6), R. Rustin, ed., Prentice-Hall, Inc., Englewood Cliffs, NJ, 1972. (Reproduced in Appendix IV.)

3. Richard Smaby and Ron Hackler, *Information Modeling in HOS*, Educational Series 11, Higher Order Software, Inc., Cambridge, MA, 1982. (This report was written in conjunction with this chapter.)

12 AUTOMATED DATA MODELING

Application creators can get into various subtle types of trouble if the data they use is not correctly modeled. Long and expensive experience has shown the need for thorough data analysis.

The author has picked apart many examples of specifications, data flow diagrams, and other forms of application design which are wrong because the designer has not had a correct data model. As we will show in the next chapter, data-base query languages, report generators, and other relational languages can give misleadingly wrong results if used with incorrectly modeled data.

A data model shows the functional dependencies and associations among data items. Functional dependencies in data do not depend on any specific application. They are inherent properties of the data themselves, independent of how the data are used. The data model therefore has a long-term life, whereas applications often have a short-term life. The logical model of data is a vital foundation stone for the building of data processing in an enterprise.

The data in a data model are in third normal form, as described in Chapter 11. However, we need more than simply third-normal-form design of records. We need the normalized records to be correctly associated into larger structures, and we need to avoid redundancy among data used in different areas. Different areas could have different normalized data which are highly redundant, if there is no overall data modeling.

It is the task of a *data administrator* to create and be the custodian of the data model (or models) in an enterprise. We believe that the data model should be designed and maintained with a computerized tool. The task is too tedious and error-prone to be done by hand. Organizations without computerized data models usually have all manner of inconsistencies and errors in their representation of data. These become very expensive in maintenance costs, lost application opportunities, and incorrect information for management.

The HOS technique gives consistent and error-free logic. However, we have stressed that incorrect input gives incorrect output. Inconsistent, invalid, or incomplete representations of complex commercial data are a likely form of incorrect input. In the commercial environment the HOS technique needs to be used with thorough data administration (which needs much human agreement and semantics definition as well as algorithms for data modeling).

This chapter describes an automated approach to data modeling. It helps the data administrator build thorough data models. This is a complex process which the author has described in more detail elsewhere [1]. The input to the process is simple in that it can be entered a small step at a time. It needs much human thought about the true nature and definitions of the data. The computerized output of the process can *automatically* become the descriptions of data used in the HOS language [2].

When appropriate automation is used the difficulties of data administration cease to be technical difficulties; they are the human and political difficulties of agreeing about the definitions and uses of data.

THE SYNTHESIS PROCESS

The synthesis process described in this chapter creates a minimal nonredundant data model, designed to be as stable as possible. We refer to it as a *canonical model*. There is one and only one canonical model of a given collection of data items and functional dependencies.

The canonical form of data which we derive in this chapter is independent of whether the data will eventually be represented by means of hierarchical, CODASYL, relational, or other structures. An additional step in deriving a workable schema is to convert the canonical form of the data into a structure that can be supported by whatever software is being used. This is a relatively straightforward step.

The canonical model is sometimes also called a *conceptual model* or *conceptual schema*. This model must be converted into a logical representation which the selected software can handle, and this is then represented physically.

In first deriving the canonical form of the data we will ignore the question of machine performance. Infrequently used linkages between data will be treated in the same way as linkages of high usage. The resulting minimal data structure will then be reexamined to distinguish between the high-usage and low-usage paths, or paths which are used in real-time operation and batch operation. It will often be necessary to deviate from the minimal structure because of constraints in the software that is used.

The synthesis process can be done largely automatically with a tool that produces third-normal-form structures and good documentation. Such a tool should be used on a corporate-wide basis to design, clarify, unify, and document the corporation's data structures. The tool can be used in conjunction with a data dictionary as discussed in this chapter.

This chapter introduces the canonical modeling process. It is discussed in more detail along with practical experience of using it and the role of the data administrator in the author's *Managing the Data-Base Environment* [1].

BUBBLE CHARTS

In order to communicate with the data administrator, the end users should be able to draw representations of data structures, and understand the diagrams of the data administrator. Database professionals use very complicated words. To involve end users we must communicate in simple words. Using the bubble charts described in this chapter we could explain the basic ideas of data structures to a child of 10.

Bubble charts provide a way of representing and thinking about data and the associations between data items. They explain the nature of data very simply so that end users can be taught to use them, draw them, and think about their data with them. Bubble charts drawn by end users can form a vital input to the data base design process.

DATA ITEMS

We have referred to the most elemental piece of data as a *data item*. It is sometimes also called a *field* or a *data element*.

It is the atom of data, in that it cannot be subdivided into smaller data types and retain any meaning to the users of the data. You cannot split the data item called SALARY, for example, into smaller data items which by themselves are meaningful to end users.

We will draw each type of data item as a bubble:

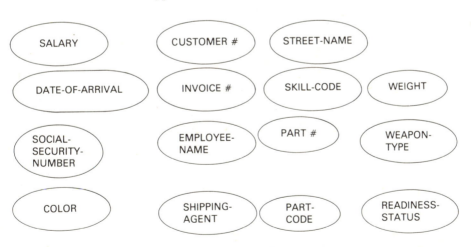

A data base contains hundreds (and sometimes thousands) of types of data items. Ten thousand or more types of data items may be used in the running of a big corporation.

To computerize the activities of a corporation, the data items it uses must be defined, cataloged, and organized. This is often difficult and time consuming because data have been treated rather sloppily in the past. What is essentially the same data item has been defined differently in different places, represented differently in computers, and given different names. Data items which were casually thought to be the same are found to be not quite the same. In one insurance company the term POLICY NUMBER was widely used but as the data bases were being defined it was found that it was used with a dozen different meanings in different places. If a simple term like POLICY NUMBER causes this problem, think of the problem with some of the more subtle terms.

The data administrator has the job of cleaning up this confusion. Definitions of data items must be agreed on and documented. Much help from end users is often needed in this process.

ASSOCIATIONS BETWEEN DATA ITEMS

A data item by itself is not of much use. For example, a value of SALARY by itself is uninteresting. It becomes interesting only when it is associated with another data item, such as EMPLOYEE-NAME, thus:

A data base, therefore, consists not only of data items but also of associations between them. There are a large number of different data-item types and we need a map showing how they are associated. This map is called a *data model*.

ONE-TO-ONE LINKS

In Chapter 11 we drew a single-headed arrow between data items to show that one data item was *functionally dependent* on another. This concept of functional dependency is vital for building clean data structures.

A single-headed arrow from data item **A** to data item **B** means that *at each instant in time, each value of A has one and only one value of B associated with it*. There is a one-to-one mapping from **A** to **B**. If you know the value of **A**, you can know the value of **B**. We say that "**B** is functionally dependent on **A**."

There is only one value of SALARY associated with a value of EMPLOYEE# at one instant in time; therefore, we can draw a line with a "one" bar from EMPLOYEE# to SALARY, thus:

It is said that EMPLOYEE# *identifies* SALARY. If you know the value of EMPLOYEE#, then you can know the value of SALARY.

ONE-TO-MANY There is another type of association between data items
LINKS which we need. This is called a *multivalued depend-ency*. We will draw this as a line with a crow's-foot.
A crow's-foot line from A to B means that *one value of A has one or many values of B associated with it*. This is a one-to-many mapping from A to B.

While an employee can only have one salary at a given time, he might have one or many PROJECTS. Therefore, we would draw

For one value of the data item EMPLOYEE# there can be one or many values of the data item PROJECT.

SYNTHESIS We can draw both of the situations above on one bubble chart, thus:

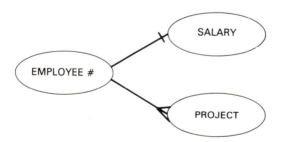

This bubble chart *synthesizes* the two previous charts into one chart. From this one chart we could derive either of the two previous charts.

The two previous charts might be two different user views, one user being interested in salary and the other in projects. We have created one simple data structure which incorporates these two user views. This is what the data admin-istrator does when building a data base, but the real-life user views are much more complicated than the illustration above and there are many of them. The resulting data model sometimes has hundreds or even thousands of data items.

A "o" is written on a link if there can be zero instances of the data item it points to, thus:

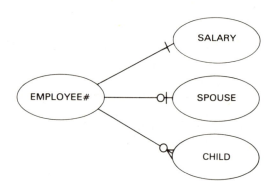

REVERSE ASSOCIATIONS

Between any two data items there can be a mapping in both directions. This gives four possibilities for forward and reverse association. If the data-item types are MAN and WOMAN, and the relationship between them represents *marriage*, the four theoretical possibilities are:

1. Conventional marriage:

2. Polygyny:

3. Polyandry:

4. Group marriage:

The reverse associations are not always of interest. For example, with the data model

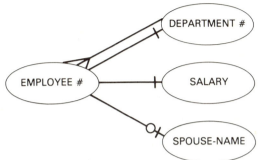

we want the reverse association from DEPARTMENT# to EMPLOYEE# because users want to know what employees work in a given department. However, there is no one-to-one mark from SPOUSE-NAME to EMPLOYEE# because no user wants to ask "What employee has a spouse named Gertrude?" If a user wanted to ask "What employees have a salary over $25,000?", we might include a crow's foot line from SALARY to EMPLOYEE#.

KEYS AND NONPRIME ATTRIBUTES

Given the bubble chart method of representing data, we can state three important definitions:

> Primary key
> Secondary key
> Nonprime attribute

A primary key is a bubble with one or more one-to-one links leaving it. Thus, in Fig. 12.1, **A**, **C**, and **F** are primary keys:

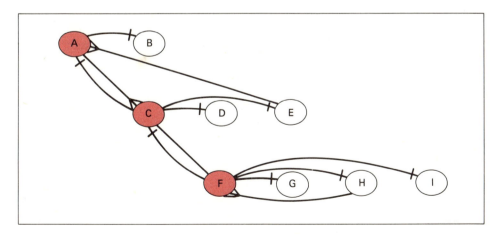

Figure 12.1

Data items that are not primary keys are referred to as *nonprime attributes*. All data items, then, are either *primary keys* or *nonprime attributes*. In the diagram above, **B, D, E, G, H,** and **I** are non prime attributes. To highlight the distinction, primary keys are colored red in our diagrams.

We can define a nonprime attribute as follows: *A nonprime attribute is a bubble with no one-to-one links leaving it.*

Each primary key uniquely identifies one or more data items. Those which are not other primary keys are nonprime attributes.

A *secondary key* does not uniquely identify another data item. One value of a secondary key is associated with zero, one, or many values of another data item. In other words, there is a crow's-foot *link* going from it to that other item. A secondary key is sometimes referred to as a *search key*.

A secondary key is a nonprime attribute with one or more crow's-foot links leaving it. In the diagram above, E and H are secondary keys.

For emphasis the box below repeats these three fundamental definitions.

A *primary key* is a bubble with one or more one-to-one links leaving it.
A *nonprime attribute* is a bubble with no one-to-one links leaving it.
A *secondary key* is an attribute with one or more one-to-many links leaving it.

DATA-ITEM GROUPS   In the bubble chart that results from combining many user views, the bubbles are grouped by primary key.

Each primary key is the unique identifier of a data-item group. It points with one-to-one links to each attribute in that data-item group.

The data-item group needs to be structured carefully so that it is as stable as possible. We should not group together an ad hoc collection of data items. There are formal rules for structuring the data-item group, which were referred to in Chapter 11 when we discussed third normal form.

A primary key and its nonprime attributes are drawn on a bubble diagram as follows:

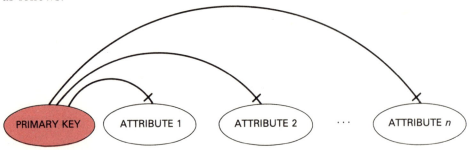

EMPLOYEE NUMBER	NAME	SEX	GRADE	DATE OF BIRTH	DEPART-MENT	SKILL CODE	TITLE	SALARY
53730	JONES BILL W	1	03	100335	044	73	ACCOUNTANT	2000
28719	BLANAGAN JOE E	1	05	101019	172	43	PLUMBER	1800
53550	LAWRENCE MARIGOLD	0	07	090932	044	02	CLERK	1100
79632	ROCKEFELLER FRED	1	11	011132	090	11	CONSULTANT	5000
15971	ROPLEY ED S	1	13	021242	172	43	PLUMBER	1700
51883	SMITH TOM P W	1	03	091130	044	73	ACCOUNTANT	2000
36453	RALNER WILLIAM C	1	08	110941	044	02	CLERK	1200
41618	HORSERADISH FREDA	0	07	071235	172	07	ENGINEER	2500
61903	HALL ALBERT JR	1	11	011030	172	21	ARCHITECT	3700
72921	FAIR CAROLYN	0	03	020442	090	93	PROGRAMMER	2100

Record structure

An occurrence of a record

An occurrence of a logical file or relation

Entity identifier

A set of values of one data-item type

Some attributes are themselves entity identifiers of another file

Values of the attributes

Figure 12.2

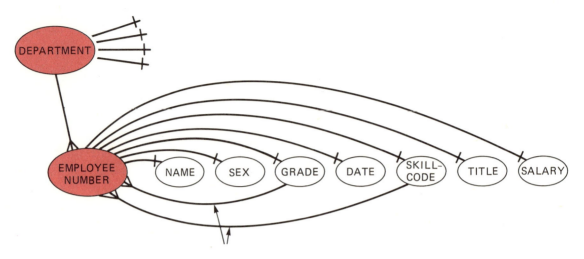

Figure 12.3 Bubble chart of the data in Fig. 12.2, assuming that DEPART-
MENT is a separate primary key.

Some data-base authorities describe data only in terms of entities, attributes,
and relations between these. There is a complication in this view of data. A data
item that appears as an attribute in one place can be primary key in another place.
The EMPLOYEE entity in Fig. 12.2, for example, has DEPARTMENT as one
of its attributes, but DEPARTMENT itself is an entity. It would be drawn on a
bubble chart as in Fig. 12.3.

**CONCATENATED
KEYS**

Furthermore, many attributes are not identified by any
single entity data item. They need more than one entity
to identify them. For example, the *price of a part* is
an attribute which may not be identified by the entity PART alone. Different
prices are charged for the same part by different suppliers and may also depend
on the *time of quotation*. Because of such complications, it is easier to refer to
primary keys and nonprime attributes. Sometimes the primary key will be a
concatenated key.

When data items cannot be identified by any one single data item in a user's
view, they need a primary key (unique identifier) which is composed of more
than one data item in combination. This is called a *concatenated key*.

Several suppliers may supply a part and each charge a different price for
it. The primary key SUPPLIER# is used for identifying information about a
supplier. The key PART# is used for identifying information about a *part*. Neither
of those keys is sufficient for identifying the *price*. The price is dependent on
both the supplier and the part. We create a new key to identify the price, which

consists of SUPPLIER# and PART# joined together (concatenated). We draw this as one bubble:

The two fields from which the concatenated key is created are joined with a " + " symbol.

The concatenated key has one-to-one links to the keys SUPPLIER# and PART#. The resulting diagram is as follows:

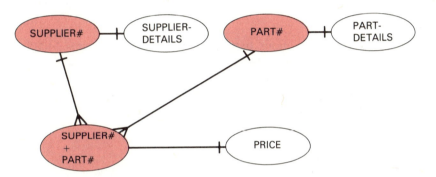

By introducing this form of concatenated key into the logical view of data, we make each data item dependent on *one* node of the chart.

Whenever a concatenated key is introduced, the designer should ensure that the items it identifies are dependent on the whole key, not on a portion of it only. In practice it is sometimes necessary to join together *more than two* data items in a concatenated key. For example, a company supplies a product to domestic and industrial customers. It charges a different price to different *types of customers*, and also the price varies from one *state* to another. There is a *discount* giving different price reductions for different quantities purchased. The *price* is identified by a combination of CUSTOMER-TYPE, STATE, DISCOUNT, and PRODUCT, thus:

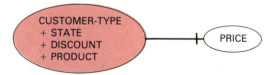

The use of concatenated keys gives each data-item group in the resulting data model a simple structure in which each attribute is fully dependent on the key bubble and nothing else:

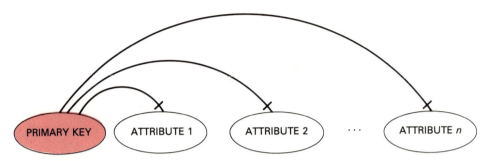

MULTIPLE ASSOCIATIONS BETWEEN DATA ITEMS

On rare occasions it is necessary to have two associations between the same two bubbles. Suppose that we have a data item called PERSON and a data item called DOG, and we want to represent which dogs a person owns and also which dogs a person has been bitten by. We would draw

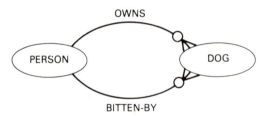

Because there are two links between the same two data items, the links are labeled.

Situations like this requiring labeled associations can usually be avoided by introducing an extra data item type, thus:

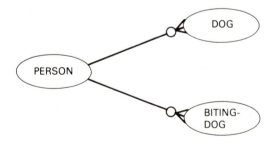

A one-to-one link may go from both of the DOG data items above to PERSON, to show who owns what dog. The owner of the biting dog may then be traced.

In general, it is recommended that labeled associations be avoided, where possible, but it cannot always be avoided.

LEVELS OF PRIMARY KEYS

Some of the primary keys themselves identify other primary keys; that is, they have one-to-one links going to other primary keys. For clarity the diagram of the data structure is often drawn with the one-to-one links between primary keys pointing upward whenever possible. This is normally done in a tree-structure representation of data. The record at the top of the tree is called the root record, and its primary key is a *root key*.

We can define a root key: *A root key is a primary key with no one-to-one links leaving it to another primary key.*

In a tree structure there is one root key. Structures more complicated than a tree structure (called *plex* or *network structures*) may have more than one root key. In Fig. 12.1, data item A is the root key.

The definition of root key is not fundamental to understanding data, as are the definitions of a primary key and secondary key. It is, however, *useful* to know which are the root keys and root records for planning the physical organization of the data.

The primary keys, or records they identify, can be arranged into levels. The highest level is the root key, and we will call this *depth 1*.

A *depth 2* primary key has a one-to-one link to a depth 1 primary key.

A *depth 3* primary key has a one-to-one link to a depth 2 primary key but no one-to-one links to a depth 1 primary key.

A *depth N* primary key has a one-to-one link to a depth $N - 1$ primary key but no one-to-one links to a depth M primary key where $M < N - 1$.

The primary keys with the greatest depth in a data structure have no one-to-one links entering them.

Levels can be indicated on a drawing by positioning the data-item groups with different amounts of offset: the depth 1 groups are the leftmost and the deepest groups the rightmost, as shown in Fig. 12.4.

SYNTHESIZING USER VIEWS

The data modeling process takes many separate user views of data and *synthesizes* them into a structure which incorporates all of them. The synthesis is done in such a way that redundant data items are eliminated where possible. The same data item does not generally appear twice in the final result. Also, redundant *associations* are eliminated where possible. In other words, a minimal number of lines connects the bubbles in the resulting bubble chart.

The synthesis process is a formal procedure following a formal set of rules. Because it is a formal procedure, it can be done by a computer. This eliminates errors in the process, provides formal documentation which is a basis for end-

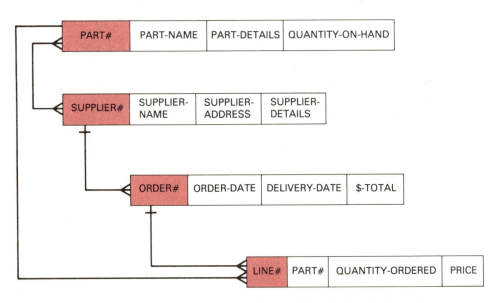

Figure 12.4   Data model with two root keys and three levels of primary key.

user discussion, and permits any input view to be changed or new views to be added and immediately reflects the effect of the change in the resulting data model. The computer output can then be *automatically* convertd to HOS data representation for inclusion in the AXES library ready for application building.

SYNTHESIS ILLUSTRATION

As a simple illustration of the synthesis process, consider the four user views of data shown in Fig. 12.5. We want to combine those into a single data model.

To start, here is view 1:

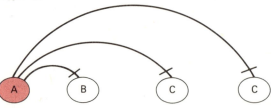

We will combine view 2 with it:

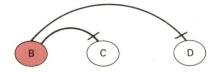

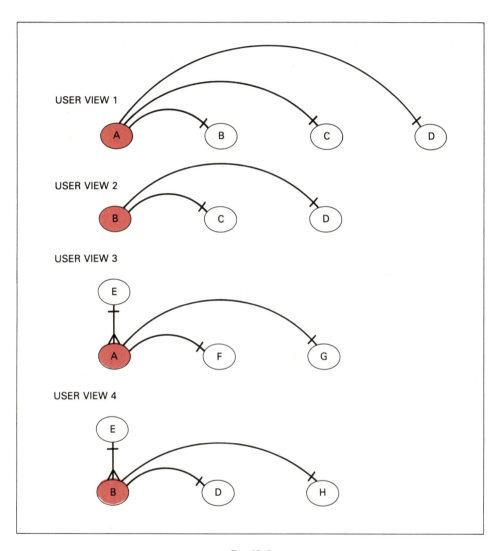

Fig.12.5

None of the data items above appear twice in the result:

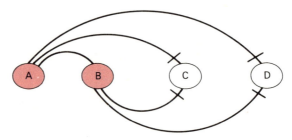

There are, however, some redundant links.

> A identifies B;
>
> And B identifies C;
>
> Therefore, A *must* identify C.
>
> Therefore, the link A———┤C is redundant.

Similarly, A identifies B and B identifies D; therefore A *must* identify D. Therefore, the link A———┤ D is redundant.

The redundant links are removed and we have

Now the third view:

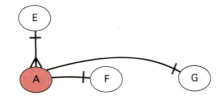

This contains three data items E, F, and G. When it is merged into the model, we get

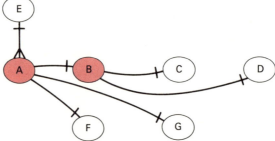

There are no new redundancies, so we will merge in the fourth view:

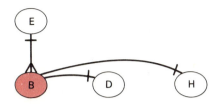

This adds one new data item to the model, H:

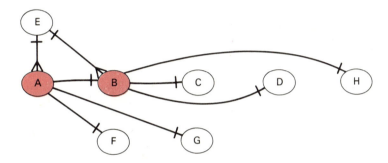

There is now one redundant link.

A identifies B; B identifies E; therefore, A *must* identify E. We can remove the one-to-one link from A to E (we cannot change the crow's-foot link from E to A):

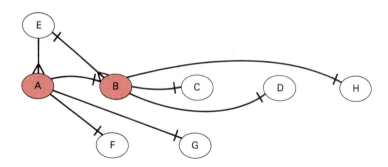

In this resulting structure there are two primary keys: A and B. (A primary key is a bubble with one or more one-to-one links leaving it.)

We can associate each primary key with the attributes it identifies:

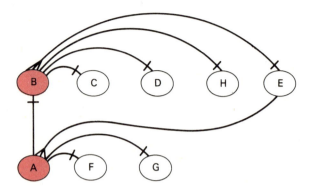

On each linkage between primary keys it is desirable to put the reverse linkage. We should therefore ask: Is the link from B to A a one-to-many link or a one-to-one link?

Suppose that it is a crow's-foot link. The following diagram draws the logical records that result from this design.

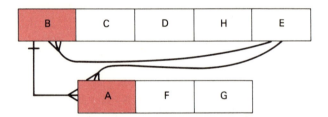

E, here, is a secondary key pointing to both A and B. In old punched card or batch processing systems secondary keys, like E, were the *sort* keys. In on-line systems secondary key paths such as those from E to A or B are followed by such means as pointers or indices.

CANONICAL DATA STRUCTURES   If we have a given collection of data items and we identify their functional dependencies, we can combine them into a nonredundant model. We combine redundant data items and redundant associations so that no redundancy remains.

There is one and only one nonredundant model of a given collection of data. We call this a *canonical model*—a model obtained by following a formal set of rules.

Secondary keys may be added to the model later as the need to search the data is identified. If we consider only primary keys and the grouping of the data items in entity records, the resulting model is *independent of how the data are used*. The structure is inherent in the properties of the data themselves.

It is because there is only one nonredundant model, and that model is independent of the usage of the data, that we say that *data designed this way in an enterprise are stable*. This constitutes a valuable structured technique. *We can structure the data independently of their usage*.

We will define a canonical schema as *a model of data which represents the inherent structure of that data in a nonredundant fashion and hence is independent of individual applications of the data and also of the software or hardware mechanisms which are employed in representing and using the data*.

We have stressed that procedures—the way people use data—change rapidly in a typical enterprise. The data themselves have a structure that will not change unless new types of data are added. As new types of data are added, the model can grow in a fashion which does not necessitate the rewriting of existing programs (if the data-base management system has good data independence).

Most structured techniques have analyzed procedures first and then decided what file or data base structures are necessary for these procedures. This has resulted in high maintenance costs because the procedures change. In good information engineering we analyze the data first and apply various steps to make it stable. Then we look for techniques which enable users to employ that data with as little programming effort as possible—query languages, report generators, and so on.

As we will see in the next chapter, these languages can produce incorrect results if the data are not correctly modeled. Canonical data models should be input to HOS application design as well as to query and report facilities.

CANONICAL SYNTHESIS

Software for data modeling should take any number of user views of data and combine them into a minimal set of canonical records with the requisite links between records.

We will represent the user views, or application views of data, by means of bubble charts and will combine them, a step at a time, eliminating redundancies. The method is tedious to do by hand but is easy to do by computer. The input to the process must correctly identify the functional dependencies. The output is then automatically in third normal form.

The technique can be applied to the narrow perspective of data bases designed for a specific set of applications, or to the broader perspective of building enterprise data models. The entities in a corporate-wide entity chart may be clustered into submodels which are, in turn, developed in detail using canonical synthesis.

ELIMINATION OF REDUNDANCIES

In the following grouping of data items, the arrow from X to Z is *probably* redundant:

If we know that X——+Y and Y——+Z, this implies that X——+Z (i.e., there is one value of Z for each value of X). In other words, X identifies Y; Y identifies Z; therefore, X identifies Z.

Why did we say that the link from X to Z is 'probably' redundant? Is it not *always* redundant?

Unfortunately, we cannot be absolutely sure unless we know the meaning of the association. As we have illustrated earlier, it is possible to have more than one association between the same two data items:

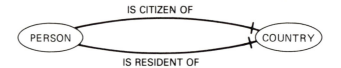

Therefore, before we delete X——+Z, we must examine the meaning of the associations to be sure that X——+Z is *really* implied by X ——+Y and Y——+Z.

In the following case we could not delete it. An employee has a telephone number:

The employee reports to a manager:

The manager also has a telephone number:

Combining these, we have

It would not be valid to assume that EMPLOYEE ——+ TELEPHONE# is redundant and delete it. The employee's telephone number is different from the
manager's and we want both:

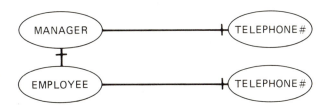

Because TELEPHONE# is an attribute, we can have a separate data item with
this name associated with both EMPLOYEE and MANAGER.

    We have trouble in the case above because of muddled thinking: MANAGER
and EMPLOYEE are really the same type of data item—a manager is an employee.
We will use the rule that one-to-one link redundancies can be removed, but each
time we use this rule we must look carefully to ensure that we have a genuine
redundancy.

    Sometimes redundancies can be removed in longer strings of links. Thus,
in the case

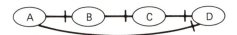

A ——+ D is a candidate for removal.

    It should be noted that one-to-many links cannot be removed. There is
nothing necessarily redundant in the following:

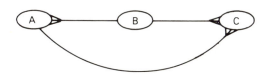

TRANSITIVE DEPENDENCIES

The input views to the synthesis process should contain
no *hidden* primary keys. In other words, there should
be no *transitive dependencies*. The following pur-
chase-order master record contains a transitive dependency:

ORDER#	SUPPLIER#	SUPPLIER-NAME	SUPPLIER-ADDRESS	DELIVERY-DATE	ORDER-DATE	$-TOTAL

ORDER# is the key. It might be tempting to diagram this record as

However, SUPPLIER-NAME and SUPPLIER-ADDRESS are identified by SUP-PLIER#. The record is therefore better diagrammed as in Box 12.1.

This process of removing transitive dependencies is essentially equivalent to the conversion to *third normal form* discussed in Chapter 11.

BOX 12.1 Avoidance of Hidden Transitive Dependencies in the Representation of User Views of Data

The record below, taken from a user's view of data, contains a hidden transitive dependency:

ORDER#	SUPPLIER#	SUPPLIER-NAME	SUPPLIER-ADDRESS	DELIVERY-DAY	ORDER-DATE	$-TOTAL

It might be tempting to diagram it thus:

However, SUPPLIER NAME and SUPPLIER ADDRESS are identified by SUPPLIER#. The record should then be diagrammed as follows:

Transitive dependencies should be removed from user's views when they are originally diagrammed. This is done before they are fed into the synthesis process.

CONCATENATED KEYS

As discussed earlier, concatenated keys may be necessary. In the example earlier, the *price* was identified by a combination of CUSTOMER-TYPE, STATE, DISCOUNT, and PRODUCT.

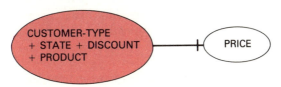

When the modeling process encounters a concatenated key such as this, it automatically makes the component fields of the key into data item bubbles in their own right in the model. In other words, it explodes the concatenated key, thus:

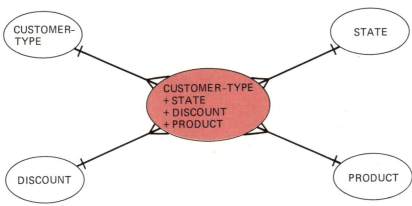

Some of these data items might become keys themselves: for example PRODUCT; others may remain attributes.

In the final synthesis those which still remain merely attributes may be deleted because they already exist in the concatenated key. They are deleted if they are not used as a separate data item.

INTERSECTION DATA

In some types of data-base software, data can be related to the *association* between data items. A part, for example, may be supplied by several vendors who each charge a different price for it. The data item PRICE cannot be associated with the PART record alone or with the SUPPLIER record alone. It can only be associated with the combination of the two. Such information is sometimes called *intersection data*—data associated with the association between records.

MANY-TO-MANY ASSOCIATIONS

It is necessary to be cautious with links which have crow's-feet pointing in both directions: many-to-many associations. In practice, when a many-to-many association is used, there will usually be *intersection data* associated with it sooner or later. If there are no intersection data to start with, they are likely to be added later *as the data-base evolves*. If intersection data are associated with records having keys **A** and **B**, those data are identified by a concatenated key **A + B**. Figure 12.6 shows two examples of intersection data and how they might be handled.

Because of the likelihood of adding intersection data, it is usually best to avoid an **A ⊁–≺B** link in a schema and instead create an extra record having the concatenated key **A + B** when the data base is first implemented. This avoids later restructuring and consequent rewriting of programs.

MAPPING BETWEEN PRIMARY KEYS

To avoid this problem, when the design procedure gives a mapping *between keys* in one direction, we will add the equivalent mapping in the opposite direction. In other words, the line between keys has arrows drawn in both directions. If we then have a many-to-many mapping between two keys **A** and **B**.

As the path in either direction might conceivably be traversed, we introduce a third key **A + B** as follows:

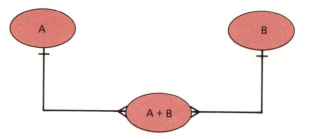

Because we use this procedure the canonical schema we create will have no many-to-many links between keys unless the association could *never* be used in one direction.

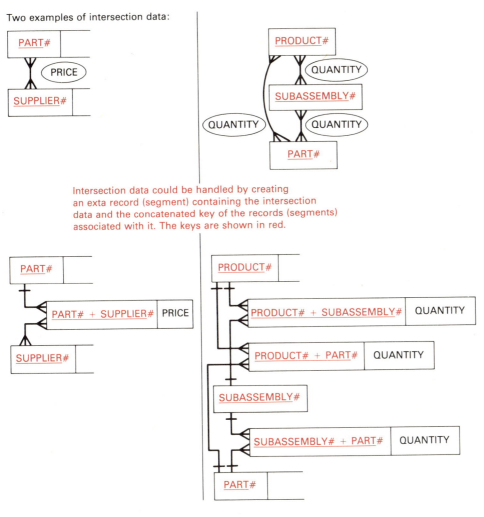

Figure 12.6   Two examples of intersection data.

INTERSECTING ATTRIBUTES

A problem which sometimes exists in the synthesized structure is that an *attribute* may be attached to more than one primary key. In other words, it has more than one one-to-one indicator pointing to it. This is sometimes called an *intersecting attribute*. It cannot remain in such a state in the final synthesis. An attribute in a canonical model can be owned by only one key.

Box 12.2 illustrates an intersecting attribute and shows three ways of dealing with it. There should be no intersecting attributes on the final canonical graph.

The following graph contains an intersecting attribute:

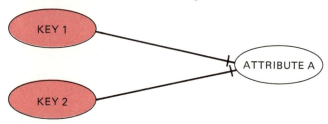

An intersecting attribute can be avoided in one of the following three ways:

1. All but one link to it may be replaced with equivalent links via an existing key:

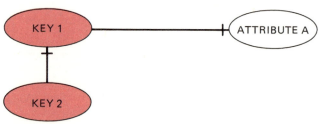

2. Redundant versions of it may be connected to each associated key:

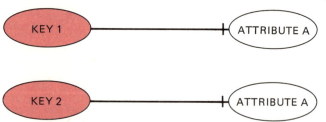

3. It may be made into a key with no attributes:

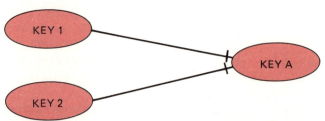

ISOLATED ATTRIBUTES

An *isolated attribute* is an attribute which is not identified by a primary key. It is a bubble with no one-to-one links entering or leaving it, although there will be one-to-many links.

An isolated attribute should be treated in one of the following ways:

1. It may be implemented as a repeating attribute in a variable-length record.

2. It may be treated as a solitary key—a one-data-item record.

Often it results from an error in interpretation of the user's data, so the meaning related to it should be carefully checked.

RECORD SEQUENCE

In certain user views the *sequence* in which the data are presented to the application program, or displayed on a terminal, is critical. However, the canonical schema does not indicate the sequence in which records are stored. *In general, it is undesirable to state a record sequence in the canonical schema because different applications of the data might require the records in a different sequence.*

In a data base of book titles, for example, one application might want a logical file of book titles in alphabetical order, another might want them ordered by author, another by Library of Congress number. The different sequencing can be indicated by secondary keys—bubbles with a crow's-foot link to BOOK-TITLE.

When the canonical schema is converted to a physical representation, it is necessary to state the record sequencing. This is a statement that should be part of the physical, rather than the logical, description of data. Some *logical* data description languages require statements about the order of records. This information must then be added when the canonical schema is converted to the software logical schema. The enthusiasts of *relational* data bases stress that the sequencing of the tuples should not be part of the *logical* data description.

AUTOMATING THE PROCEDURE

Canonical modeling done by hand is tedious, but as we have stressed, tools exist for automating it. If these tools are not available, the designer may compromise by identifying the primary keys in all the input views and building a linkage between these by hand. He then adds the attributes which these keys identify. The tool saves time, enforces discipline, helps avoid errors, and provides documents which form the basis of vital communication with end users.

Either way, the designer tackles one input view at a time, checks that it appears correct in its own right, has it merged into the model, and inspects the results. When the program deletes an apparently redundant association, it should ask the designer if he considers it to be *genuinely* redundant. Each time a programmer or user wants to add new data types or use the data base in a new way, the data-base administrator can enter the new user view and see what effect it has on the existing data base.

The bubble charts showing data, which the systems analyst or end user draws, can be fed into a computerized modeling tool one at a time. The tool synthesizes them into the model structure. It draws the resulting structure and produces various reports. The output of the modeling process should be studied by concerned users, together with dictionary output, to ensure that the data bases being designed do indeed meet their needs.

Even if the synthesis process is automated, there are several steps which require intelligent human understanding of the meaning of the data. The input must be carefully examined to ensure that the correct keys are used for all data items and that transitive dependencies are removed. When links are removed because they appear to be redundant, the data administrator must check that this reflects the true meaning of the links.

DATA DESIGNER

One tool for data modeling is DDI's Data Designer [3]. User views, portions of user views, or single functional dependencies can be fed to Data Designer one at a time. Data Designer synthesises them into a nonredundant data model, plots the result, and produces various reports for the data administrator. If the input functional dependencies are correct, the output is in third normal form.

Entries to Data Designer consist of a code character followed by a comma and an input which is usually a data item, thus:

K, EMPLOYEE#
1, EMPLOYEE-NAME
1, AGE

The code character (K and 1 above) is called a *modeling command*. Code K is used for indicating the data item at *the start of a one-to-one link* (K stands for *key*). The data item at the other end of the link is indicated with a code 1 if it is *one-to-one* association and with a code M if it is a *one-to-many* association. Thus:

is coded

K, EMPLOYEE#
1, EMPLOYEE-NAME
1, AGE

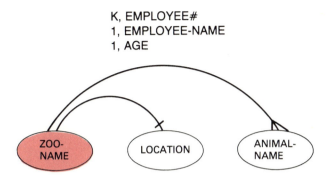

is coded

K, ZOO-NAME
1, LOCATION
M, ANIMAL-NAME

The reverse association can be coded with a 1 or M *after* the data-item name. Thus

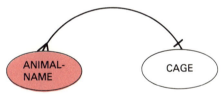

is coded

K, ANIMAL-NAME
I, CAGE, M

The data item labeled K can have a list of data items associated with it without its name being repeated. The list may not contain another K data item.

To code two links in a string, two K data items are used, thus:

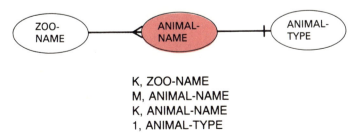

K, ZOO-NAME
M, ANIMAL-NAME
K, ANIMAL-NAME
1, ANIMAL-TYPE

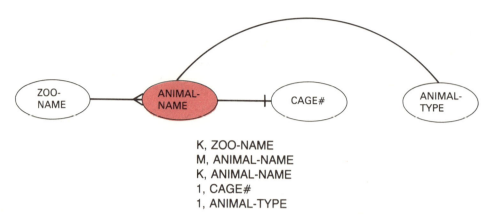

K, ZOO-NAME
M, ANIMAL-NAME
K, ANIMAL-NAME
1, CAGE#
1, ANIMAL-TYPE

To lessen the amount of typing, a name which is the same as in the previous entry need not be repeated, thus:

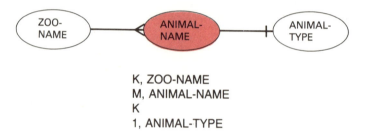

K, ZOO-NAME
M, ANIMAL-NAME
K
1, ANIMAL-TYPE

A concatenated field is represented with one of the data-item entries above, followed by one or more data items with a C code (C for *concatenated*). Thus:

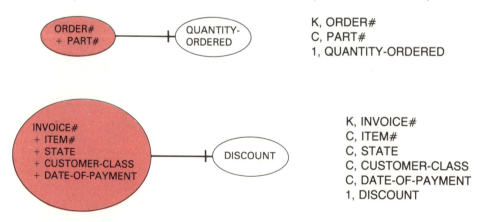

K, ORDER#
C, PART#
1, QUANTITY-ORDERED

K, INVOICE#
C, ITEM#
C, STATE
C, CUSTOMER-CLASS
C, DATE-OF-PAYMENT
1, DISCOUNT

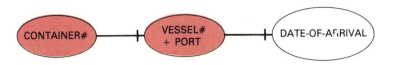

	or
K, CONTAINER#	K, CONTAINER#
1, VESSEL#	1, VESSEL#
C, PORT	C, PORT
K, VESSEL#	K
C, PORT	1, DATE-OF-ARRIVAL
1, DATE-OF-ARRIVAL	

In the example above, on the right the blank K field picks up the value of the entire concatenated field (the entire bubble), not just part of it.

Using this simple form of coding, one user view after another can be fed to the data modeling tool. It synthesizes them into a structure designed to be stable (a canonical, third-normal-form structure). It prints reports and draws diagrams such as that in Fig. 12.7 describing the resulting model.

Data models produced in this way ought to be thoroughly checked by users who are experts on the data. The objective of the design and checking is to make the data as stable as possible. A set of steps called *stability analysis* are described in the author's *Managing the Data-Base Environment* [1].

CONVERSION TO HOS NOTATION

Figure 12.7 shows HOS code for a data model. This code can be created automatically. There should be an automated link between a tool that gives third-normal-form design of data and the library of data types in HOS. The mathematical constructs of Codd should be linked automatically to the mathematical constructs of Hamilton and Zeldin.

REFERENCES

1. James Martin, *Managing the Data-Base Environment*, Prentice-Hall, Inc., Englewood Cliffs, NJ, 1983.

2. This refers to the linkage of the data modeling tool Data Designer (below) to the HOS tool USE.IT.

3. Data Designer and associated tools for data administration are available from DDI, 2020 Hogback Road, Ann Arbor, MI 48104.

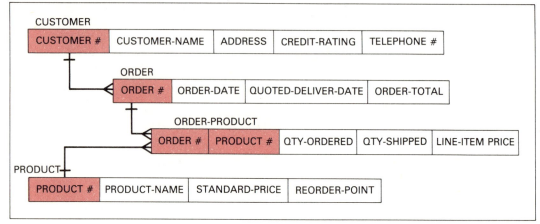

(a)

```
• DTYPE:   CUSTOMER
• PRMOP:   CUSTOMER# = CUSTOMER# (CUSTOMER)
• PRMOP:   CUSTOMER__NAME = CUSTOMER__NAME(CUSTOMER)
• PRMOP:   ADDRESS = ADDRESS (CUSTOMER)
• PRMOP:   CREDIT__RATING = CREDIT__RATING(CUSTOMER)
• PRMOP:   TELEPHONE# = TELEPHONE#(CUSTOMER)

• DTYPE:   ORDER
• PRMOP:   ORDER# = ORDER#(ORDER)
• PRMOP:   ORDER__DATE = ORDER__DATE(ORDER)
• PRMOP:   QUOTED__DELIVERY__DATE = QUOTED__DELIVERY__DATE(ORDER)
• PRMOP:   ORDER__TOTAL = ORDER__TOTAL(ORDER)

• DTYPE:   PRODUCT
• PRMOP:   PRODUCT# = PRODUCT# (PRODUCT)
• PRMOP:   PRODUCT__NAME = PRODUCT__NAME (PRODUCT)
• PRMOP:   STANDARD__PRICE = STANDARD__PRICE (PRODUCT)
• PRMOP:   REORDER__POINT = REORDER__POINT (PRODUCT)

• DTYPE:   ORDER__PRODUCT
• PRMOP:   ORDER# = ORDER#__FROM__ORDER__PRODUCT (ORDER__PRODUCT)
• PRMOP:   PRODUCT# = PRODUCT#__FROM__ORDER__PRODUCT (ORDER__PRODUCT)
• PRMOP:   QTY__ORDERED = QTY__ORDERED (ORDER__PRODUCT)
• PRMOP:   QTY__SHIPPED = QTY__SHIPPED (ORDER__PRODUCT)
• PRMOP:   LINE__ITEM__PRICE = LINE__ITEM__PRICE (ORDER__PRODUCT)

• DTYPE:   ORDERS__DATABASE
• PRMOP:   CUSTOMER = CUSTOMER__WITH__ORDER (ORDERS__DATABASE,ORDER)
• PRMOP:   SET__OF__ORDER = SET__OF__ORDERS__FOR__CUSTOMER (ORDERS__DATABASE,CUSTOMER)
• PRMOP:   ORDER = ORDER__OF__ORDER__PRODUCT (ORDERS__DATABASE,ORDER__PRODUCT)
• PRMOP:   SET__OF__ORDER__PRODUCT = SET__OF__ORDER__PRODUCTS__FOR__ORDER (ORDERS__DA-
           TABASE,ORDER)
• PRMOP:   PRODUCT = PRODUCT__OF__ORDER__PRODUCT (ORDERS__DATABASE,ORDER__PRODUCT)
• PRMOP:   SET__OF__ORDER__PRODUCT = SET__OF__ORDER__PRODUCTS__FOR__PRODUCT (ORDERS__
           DATABASE,PRODUCT)
```

(b)

Figure 12.7 A canonical representation of data and the HOS description of those data. The HOS code, above, should be generated automatically from the output of a data modeling tool.

220

13 SEMANTIC DISINTEGRITY IN RELATIONAL OPERATIONS

INTRODUCTION Query languages and report generators provide a powerful way for computer users to obtain information from computers. Many such languages now exist, some of which are well human-factored and very easy to use. They represent a major advance in making information systems valuable to users.

Unfortunately it is possible to obtain invalid results with such languages unless certain controls are applied. Users can express a query that appears to be correct but in fact lacks semantic integrity. The users can obtain seemingly correct answers which in fact are wrong.

Consider IBM's language SQL (Structured Query Language) for example. Suppose that a user wanted to see a *list of all suppliers who supply Department 291*. Two data-base records are available as follows:

DEPARTMENT

DEPARTMENT#	PART

SUPPLIER

SUPPLIER#	SUPPLIER-NAME	PART

The user can enter a query

```
SELECT SUPPLIER-NAME
  FROM SUPPLIER, DEPARTMENT
    WHERE SUPPLIER.PART = DEPARTMENT.PART
    AND DEPARTMENT# = 291
```

This says "Select SUPPLIER-NAME from the combination of the SUPPLIER and DEPARTMENT tables where PART in the SUPPLIER table is identical to PART in the DEPARTMENT table, and DEPARTMENT# is 291."

The same query could be handled with the screen language QBE (QUERY-BY-EXAMPLE):

DEPARTMENT	DEPARTMENT#	PART	
	291	X	

SUPPLIER	SUPPLIER#	SUPPLIER NAME	PART	
		P.	X	

Here the user has equated PART in the SUPPLIER table with PART in the DEPARTMENT table by putting an x, underlined, in both of them. He then indicates the DEPARTMENT# by putting 291 in the DEPARTMENT# column and puts P. in the SUPPLIER NAME column to request that this be printed.

A more automatic facility might make its own assumption about how to *join* the DEPARTMENT and SUPPLIER tables because they have only one data-item type in common. The user might then say something like

LIST SUPPLIER NAME DEPARTMENT# = 291

All of these are incorrect. Why?

They are examples of semantic disintegrity in query languages. Just because Parker Bros. supplies grappling irons and grappling irons are used by Department 291, that does not mean that Parker Bros. supplies Department 291. They might use somebody else's grappling irons.

We can prevent semantic disintegrity, or at least warn the user about it, if we apply certain rules.

RELATIONAL OPERATIONS

The query above is one that *joins* two tables. JOIN is an example of a relational operation. Many query languages employ relational operations and sometimes employ a relational data base.

Semantic disintegrity can sometimes occur with the relational operations JOIN and PROJECT. The equivalent of these operations is sometimes employed by languages for nonrelational data bases also.

> *Note*: JOIN, as used in this chapter, has no relationship to the HOS control structure, JOIN, used in the rest of the book. It is unfortunate that these terms are the same word with entirely different meanings. JOIN is a relational algebra term of old standing in common use in data-base circles. The reader is cautioned not to be confused by this homonym.

A relational operation manipulates two-dimensional tables of data. These tables are sometimes called *relations* and sometimes *files*. Let us use the word "relation." Every record (also called tuple) in the relation contains the same set of data-item types.

PROJECTION

With the PROJECT operator the user selects certain columns of a relation, and specifies in what order he wants them.

Figure 13.1 shows two projections of the relation called ENGINEER. On the right of Fig. 13.1 the user has created a result called DEPT. He wants two data-item types in the result, DEPT# and LOCATION. He writes

$$\text{DEPT} = \pi \text{ ENGINEER (DEPT\#, LOCATION)}$$

The symbol π is used as the PROJECT operator. There are a smaller number of rows in the result than in the original because redundant rows are not required in the result.

On the left of Fig. 13.1 the user has created a projection called EMP with the statement

$$\text{EMP} = \pi \text{ ENGINEER (EMPLOYEE NAME, EMPLOYEE\#, LOCATION,}$$
$$\text{SALARY)}$$

JOIN

When two relations share a common data-item type, they might be *joined*. The *projection* operation splits relations, selecting certain columns. The *join* operation puts together columns from different relations.

The symbol * is used as the join operator. The statement EMPLOYEE = EMP * DEPT does the opposite of the operation shown in Fig. 13.1 and forms the relation EMPLOYEE from the relations EMP and DEPT.

A user may wish to form a relation out of two or more separate relations, which does not use all the attributes of these relations. For example, in joining EMP and DEPT he may wish to create a relation which gives only the employees' names and locations. This can be done with the statement

$$\text{EMPLOC} = \text{EMP} * \text{DEPT (EMPLOYEE NAME, LOCATION)}$$

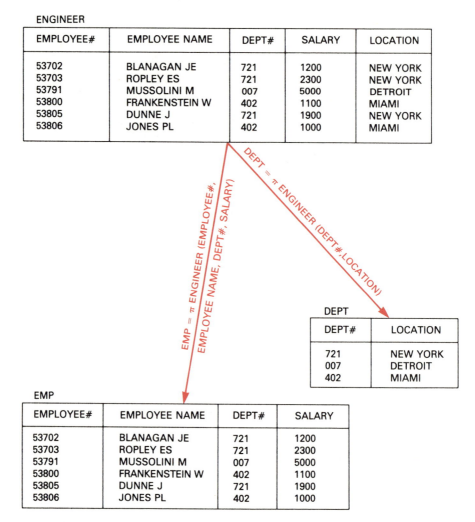

ENGINEER

EMPLOYEE#	EMPLOYEE NAME	DEPT#	SALARY	LOCATION
53702	BLANAGAN JE	721	1200	NEW YORK
53703	ROPLEY ES	721	2300	NEW YORK
53791	MUSSOLINI M	007	5000	DETROIT
53800	FRANKENSTEIN W	402	1100	MIAMI
53805	DUNNE J	721	1900	NEW YORK
53806	JONES PL	402	1000	MIAMI

EMP = π ENGINEER (EMPLOYEE#, EMPLOYEE NAME, DEPT#, SALARY)

DEPT = π ENGINEER (DEPT#, LOCATION)

DEPT

DEPT#	LOCATION
721	NEW YORK
007	DETROIT
402	MIAMI

EMP

EMPLOYEE#	EMPLOYEE NAME	DEPT#	SALARY
53702	BLANAGAN JE	721	1200
53703	ROPLEY ES	721	2300
53791	MUSSOLINI M	007	5000
53800	FRANKENSTEIN W	402	1100
53805	DUNNE J	721	1900
53806	JONES PL	402	1000

Figure 13.1   Illustration of two projections. The relation ENGINEER is split into two relations.

Figure 13.2 shows several join operations on two relations. The relations in this illustration have the domain B in common. Figure 13.3 shows a join on three relations.

When relations are joined on a given data-item type, only those tuples that share the same value of that data item appear in the result. Consequently, the resulting relation may contain fewer tuples than either of the original relations. This is seen in Fig. 13.2. The reduction effect may be used to isolate certain tuples in response to queries. A relation with only one domain, and possibly only

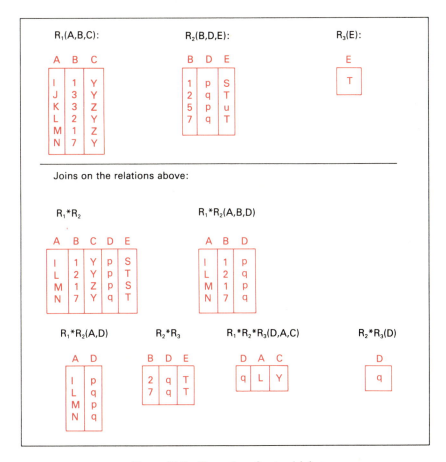

Figure 13.2 Examples of natural joins.

one data item, may be joined to other relations to extract a restricted set of the tuples. In Fig. 13.2, for example, the relation R_3 contains only one data item, E, and only one value of that data item, T. When it is joined with R_2 it produces an answer to the query "What tuples in R_2 have a value of data item E equal to T?"

The join we have described, joining on the basis of equal data-item values in shared domains and not duplicating the shared domain in the result, is called a *natural join*. Other types of joins are possible, including ones that search a domain for values *not equal*, *greater than*, or *less than* those in a given domain.

R_1 and R_2 in Fig. 13.2 could be joined because they had one data-item type in common, B. If they had no data-item type in common, they could not be joined. If they had two data-item types in common they could be joined on one, on the other, or on both.

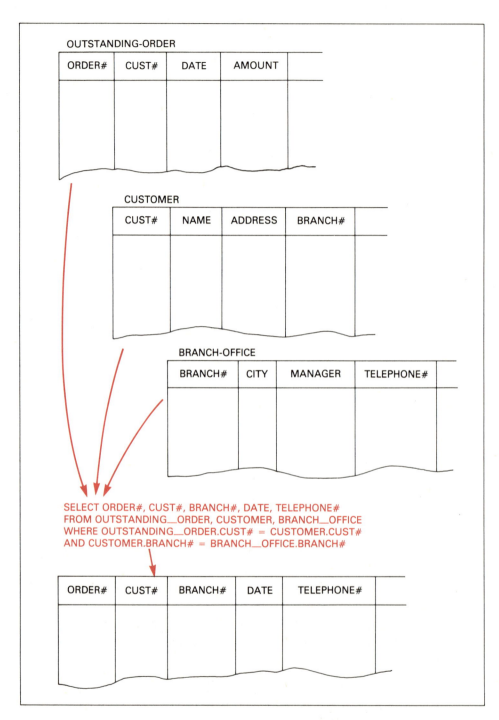

Figure 13.3 Join between three relations expressed with SQL.

The example with which we started this chapter was a JOIN. The DE-PARTMENT and SUPPLIER tables are joined using the data-item type called PART. This is expressed in SQL with the clause

WHERE SUPPLIER.PART = DEPARTMENT.PART

It was expressed in QBE by putting the same value (x) in the PART column of both the SUPPLIER and DEPARTMENT relations.

REASONS FOR INVALID OPERATIONS   A major reason why this SUPPLIER and DEPART-MENT join is invalid is that it uses incorrectly modeled data. A *PROJECT* operation can also give invalid results.

Consider the projection in Fig. 13.1 which creates the relation DEPT (DEPT#,LOCATION) from the ENGINEER relation. If the association between DEPT# and LOCATION is a one-to-one association, the projection is valid. We have the following associations:

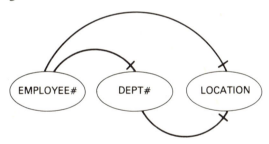

However, it may not be valid if the association between DEPT# and LOCATION is a one-to-many association (i.e., a department can have more than one location), thus:

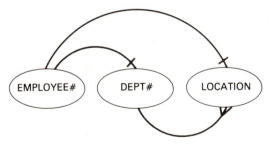

Department 721 in Fig. 13.1 might have an office in Detroit as well as New York for all we know, but the Detroit office has no engineers.

A similar argument applies to *join* operations. Suppose that two relations were joined as follows:

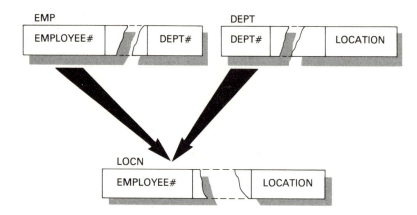

This join is valid if there is a one-to-one association between DEPT# and LO-CATION. It is not valid if there is a one-to-many association between DEPT# and LOCATION, because although a department can have more than one location, an employee works in only one location, thus:

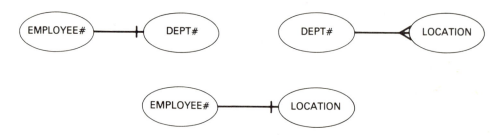

NAVIGATION PATHS

We can understand what a query or relational operation is doing by drawing a navigation path. To perform the join above, we start with EMPLOYEE# and find the associated DEPT#. For that DEPT# we find the associated LOCATION. We can draw this navigation path as follows:

Here we have only one-to-one paths, so there is no problem.

If however, there were a one-to-many path from DEPT# to LOCATION,

we would draw

This is invalid because there is *one* LOCATION, not many, for an employee.

Similarly, for the query "List all suppliers who supply Department 291," we have the navigation path

This lacks integrity because we cannot be sure which SUPPLIER# to associate with a given PART (or that any SUPPLIER# is associated with that PART for that DEPARTMENT#).

We have the possibility of semantic disintegrity if the navigation path has a one-to-many link which is not the first link. For example:

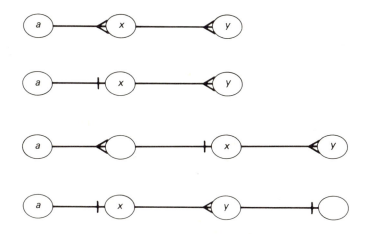

Many values of y are associated with x, but they might not *all* be associated with a.

We do not necessarily know whether such a navigation path will be valid or not. Figure 13.4 shows two queries employing a JOIN. Their data and navigation paths are similar in structure. Both use fully normalized data. The one-to-many path makes the bottom one invalid, but not the top one. Because the software cannot tell for sure, it should warn the user that the results might be invalid.

QUERY: "List all incidents that were reported on passenger JONES' voyage."

NORMALIZED DATA:

PASSENGER

PASSENGER#	PASSENGER-NAME	ADDRESS	VOYAGE#

INCIDENT

INCIDENT#	INCIDENT-NAME	DETAILS	VOYAGE#

JOIN

NAVIGATION PATH:

PASSENGER# → VOYAGE# → INCIDENT

QUERY: "List all projects that employee JONES works on."

NORMALIZED DATA:

EMPLOYEE

EMPLOYEE#	EMPLOYEE-NAME	ADDRESS	DEPARTMENT#

PROJECT

PROJECT#	PROJECT-NAME	DETAILS	DEPARTMENT#

JOIN

NAVIGATION PATH:

EMPLOYEE# → DEPARTMENT# → PROJECT#

The top join is valid because every incident on passenger JONES' voyage is needed.

The bottom join is *not* valid because employee JONES does not work on *every* project in his department.

The software does not know for certain whether the one-to-many link in the navigation path will cause trouble, so it should warn the user.

Figure 13.4 Two queries using a join, which have similar data structures.

We cannot control semantic disintegrity in data that
are incorrectly modeled. The records used in the de-
partment-supplier example are imprecise and incorrect:

DEPARTMENT

DEPARTMENT#	PART

SUPPLIER

SUPPLIER#	SUPPLER NAME	PART

Each part needs to have a unique identifier PART#. A grappling iron supplied
by Parker Bros. must have a different PART# from a grappling iron supplied
by Jones Inc. If we want to say merely "grappling iron," we use a data-item
PART TYPE.

A department has many part#s and a part# has many departments. We
therefore use intersection data in the model with the key DEPARTMENT# +
PART#. This key identifies such items as QUANTITY SOLD. The model, then,
includes the following:

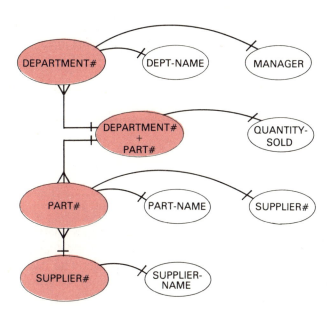

Drawing these as relations, we have the following:

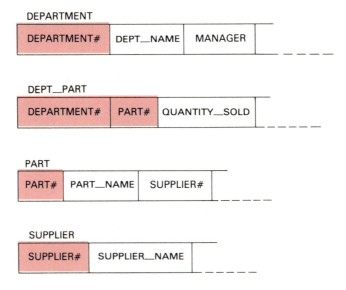

Now we can reformulate the query:

```
SELECT SUPPLIER_NAME
FROM SUPPLIER, PART, DEPT_PART
WHERE DEPT_PART.PART# = PART.PART#
AND PART.SUPPLIER# = SUPPLIER.SUPPLIER#
AND DEPARTMENT# = 291
```

The navigation path is

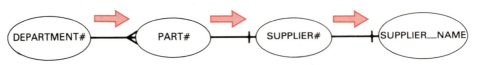

In this navigation path there is no ambiguous linking to a one-to-many path.

     Suppose an accountant is concerned that accounts receivable are becoming too high. He wants to phone any branch office manager who has a 6-month-old debt outstanding from a customer. The following record structures exist:

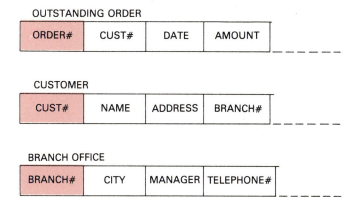

He enters the following query:

```
SELECT CITY, MANAGER, TELEPHONE#
FROM ORDER#, CUST#, BRANCH#
WHERE OUTSTANDING ORDER.CUST# = CUSTOMER.CUST#
AND CUSTOMER.BRANCH# = BRANCH_OFFICE.BRANCH#
AND DATE <5.12
```

This, in effect, joins the three records as in Fig. 13.3. We have the following navigation path:

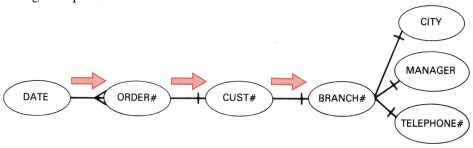

This is valid because we do not have any crow's foot links after the first. The correct normalization of the data protects us.

Suppose, however, that there was a mistake in the data modeling. A few customers are served by more than one branch office. We have

The query then has disintegrity. The accountant might be phoning the wrong branch manager.

PREVENTION OF SEMANTIC DISINTEGRITY

To ensure integrity in relational operations it is essential that the data be completely and correctly modeled as described in Chapter 12.

The following rules will prevent semantic disintegrity:

1. A relation may be projected if:

   (a) The relation is in third normal form, *and*
   (b) The resulting relation contains the same key or an equivalent candidate key.

2. Relations A and B may be joined on data-item types A.x and B.y if

   (a) the relations A and B are in third normal form, *and*
   (b) A.x is an attribute of A (including a key attribute) and B.y is a key or candidate key of B.

These rules can easily be represented with the HOS methods.

MORAL

The message of this chapter is simple and clear. Data-base query languages and report generators are very valuable for end users. Automatic navigation is a powerful data-base facility. Relational languages are here to stay and can be made very easy to use. However, if they are used on data bases on which precise data modeling has not been done, they can lead to false results.

If you use SQL, NOMAD, DATATRIEVE, and the other nonprocedural languages, you had better make sure that your data are correctly modeled as described in Chapter 12. In addition, the interpreters or compilers for such languages *ought* to warn users when their operations violate the rules above. The users can then check carefully that the data they are receiving are valid.

Unfortunately, at the time of writing many of today's data-base products do not attempt to detect semantic disintegrity in *join* and *project* operations. This does not mean that the products are not valuable; they are. It does mean that care should be taken with data modeling, and users should be encouraged to check heuristically the results they obtain.

14 DATA NAVIGATION DIAGRAMS

INTRODUCTION   Once a data model of good quality exists, the creation of procedures which use those data becomes much easier. Data-base experience has shown that thorough data analysis should precede application building. The application designers then need a simple technique for *navigating* through the data model. Using HOS, we can provide *defined structures* for data-base navigation.

Given a thorough data model, the building of complex applications can be reduced to relatively small projects. *Divide and conquer* should always be a principle of good system design. Almost all such projects can be performed *by one person*. Given one-person projects, and a library that enforces correct interfaces, most of the communication problems between developers on large projects disappear. The main communication among separate developers is via the data model and library.

A problem with many structured techniques is that they tangle up the structuring of the data with the structuring of the procedures. This complicates the techniques used. Worse, it results in data that are viewed narrowly and usually not put into a form suitable for other applications which employ the same data. We have stressed that the data administrator's work of designing the data should be separate from the structured technique for designing the procedures. Data have properties of their own, independent of procedures, which lead to stable structuring. As discussed in Chapter 12, these properties can be used to automate the creation of data models and their conversion to HOS notation.

SEQUENCE OF ACCESS   A first step in creating data-base procedures is to identify the sequence in which the records are accessed. This sequence can be overdrawn on the data model. This is referred to as a *data navigation diagram*.

From the *data navigation diagram* information can be created for both the physical data-base designer and the designer of application procedures. The data navigation diagram, if correctly drawn, can be automatically converted into an action diagram, which represents the resulting program control structure [1].

Some corporations have drawn many data navigation diagrams from an overall conceptual data model. One large aerospace corporation, for example, has created more than a thousand data navigation diagrams. These are a formal foundation for procedure creation.

SUBMODEL

The complete data model is usually too complex for the drawing of access sequences. Only certain entity types in the data model are needed. The procedure designer specifies which entity types are of concern, and includes these in a submodel.

From the data model a *neighborhood* may be printed. The neighborhood of one entity type is the set of entity types which can be reached from it by traversing one link in the data model. Usually, this means examining the next-door neighbors in a canonical model. Sometimes the data model may contain extra information saying that additional neighbors should be examined. The designer displays a list of such neighbors of the entity types he is interested in. Occasionally, the neighbor one link away may be a concatenated entity (containing intersection data) and the design inspects the other entity type(s) in the concatenated record.

The designer examines the neighborhood. He sees the records his procedure will use, plus a few more. He eliminates those he does not want. There may be some which he would not have thought about if he had not displayed the neighborhood. There may be some which have *mandatory* links to records he has specified. For example, when a *booking* record is created, the *seat inventory* record *must* be updated.

The designer settles on the group of records his procedure will use. He then has a subset of the overall data model. Usually, this is small enough to draw on one page. A computerized tool may be available to draw it. If not, it should be drawn by hand.

The designer then makes decisions about the sequence in which his procedure uses the records. He draws this sequence, perhaps with a red pen on the subset data model. He uses a single line to indicate that one occurrence of a record is accessed and a crow's-foot line to indicate that multiple occurrences of a record are accessed.

NAVIGATION DIAGRAM FOR AN ORDER ACCEPTANCE SYSTEM

Consider the design of an order acceptance application for a wholesale distributor. A third-normal-form data model exists, as shown in Fig. 14.1. The designer knows that the application requires CUSTOMER-OR-DER records and PRODUCT records. The *neighborhood* of these includes the following records:

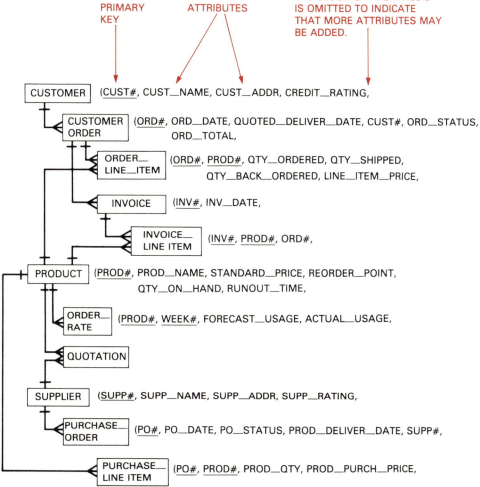

CUSTOMER ORDER
CUSTOMER
ORDER LINE ITEM
INVOICE
PRODUCT
ORDER RATE
QUOTATION
INVOICE LINE ITEM
PURCHASE LINE ITEM

PRIMARY KEY

ATTRIBUTES

THE CLOSING PARENTHESIS
IS OMITTED TO INDICATE
THAT MORE ATTRIBUTES MAY
BE ADDED.

CUSTOMER (CUST#, CUST_NAME, CUST_ADDR, CREDIT_RATING,

CUSTOMER ORDER (ORD#, ORD_DATE, QUOTED_DELIVER_DATE, CUST#, ORD_STATUS, ORD_TOTAL,

ORDER_LINE_ITEM (ORD#, PROD#, QTY_ORDERED, QTY_SHIPPED, QTY_BACK_ORDERED, LINE_ITEM_PRICE,

INVOICE (INV#, INV_DATE,

INVOICE_LINE ITEM (INV#, PROD#, ORD#,

PRODUCT (PROD#, PROD_NAME, STANDARD_PRICE, REORDER_POINT, QTY_ON_HAND, RUNOUT_TIME,

ORDER_RATE (PROD#, WEEK#, FORECAST_USAGE, ACTUAL_USAGE,

QUOTATION

SUPPLIER (SUPP#, SUPP_NAME, SUPP_ADDR, SUPP_RATING,

PURCHASE_ORDER (PO#, PO_DATE, PO_STATUS, PROD_DELIVER_DATE, SUPP#,

PURCHASE_LINE ITEM (PO#, PROD#, PROD_QTY, PROD_PURCH_PRICE,

Figure 14.1   Data model for a wholesale distributor. This model is not complete, but because it is correctly normalized it can be grown without pernicious impact to include such things as SALESMAN, WAREHOUSE, ALTERNATE ADDRESSES, and so on.

The designer examines the data items in these records. The application does not need any data in the INVOICE, INVOICE LINE ITEM, PURCHASE LINE ITEM, or QUOTATION records. The ORDER RATE record *should* be updated. The designer would have neglected the ORDER RATE record if he had not printed the neighborhood.

The designer decides, then, that he needs five records and creates a submodel containing these records as shown in Fig. 14.2. Figure 14.3 shows his first drawing of the sequence in which the records will be accessed:

1. The CUSTOMER records will be inspected to see whether the customer exists and whether the credit is okay.

2. A CUSTOMER ORDER record is created.

3. An ORDER LINE ITEM record is created, linked to the CUSTOMER ORDER record, for each line item on the order.

4. For each product on the order the PRODUCT record is retrieved.

5. The ORDER RATE record for that PRODUCT is retrieved, a new order is calculated, and the ORDER RATE record is updated.

Arrow 3 in Fig. 14.3 has a crow's-foot to indicate that there are many ORDER LINE ITEM accesses for one access to CUSTOMER ORDER. The designer (or computerized tool) may now straighten out the navigation diagram to make it easier to annotate. Figure 14.4 shows the navigation diagram of Fig. 14.3 drawn vertically. Marked against each record are the attributes that the procedure updates or retrieves.

PROCEDURE DESIGN

The designer now starts to be more precise about what needs to be done with the data. Initially, the *physical* aspects of accessing the data are ignored. Because the data are properly analyzed and structured, the Data-Base Management System can assemble the required data. From the logical point of view the data are thought of as though they existed in memory just for this designer. Later the navigation diagram may be annotated with details of numbers of accesses so that it forms valuable input to the physical data-base designer [1].

ACTION DIAGRAMS

Figure 14.5 shows an *action diagram* based on the data navigation diagram of Fig. 14.4. The diagram shows the procedure for accepting customer orders.

Action diagrams are designed to provide a simple way of drawing the control structure of programs that employ data bases. They may be based on the data navigation diagram which is drawn on data models. They are translatable directly

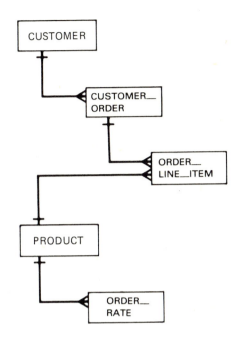

Figure 14.2 Subset of the data model in Fig. 14.1, extracted for the design of the order acceptance procedure.

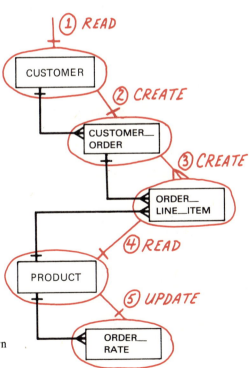

Figure 14.3 Data navigation diagram drawn on the subset data model of Fig. 14.2.

239

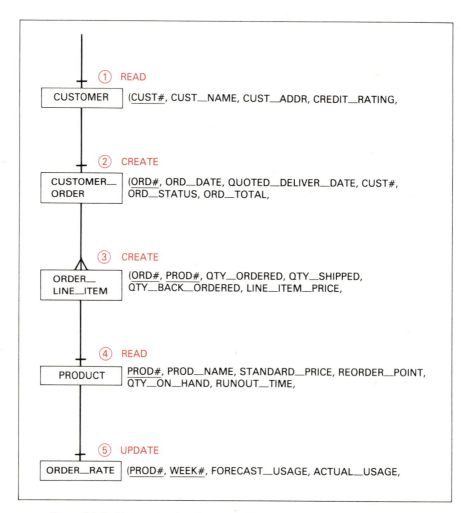

Figure 14.4   Data navigation diagram in Fig. 14.3 drawn vertically, with data-item details. The numbers and vertical positioning show the sequence in which actions are performed.

into the code of fourth-generation languages such as FOCUS, RAMIS, NOMAD, IDEAL, and so on. Once the user is familiar with them they are perhaps the clearest and easiest way to draw data-base applications and discuss them with end users. They are discussed in detail in the author's book with Carma McClure, *Diagramming Techniques for Analysts and Programmers* [1].

The vertical brackets on the action diagram represent subprocedures. The text against the top of the bracket shows the conditions governing the execution of what is in the bracket.

The middle bracket of the action diagram in Fig. 14.5 is a bracket showing

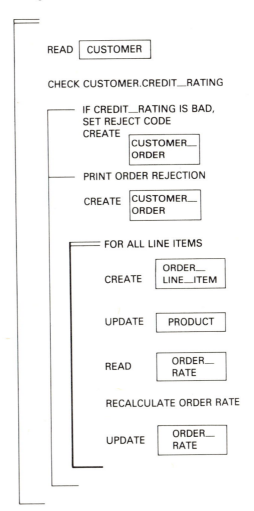

Figure 14.5   Action diagram for ORDER ACCEPTANCE created from the data navigation diagram of Fig. 14.4.

two options. First, if the customer's credit rating is bad, the first part of the bracket is executed. Second, if "ELSE" (i.e., the customer's credit rating is *not* bad), the bottom part of the bracket is executed.

The rightmost bracket of Fig. 14.5 is labeled FOR ALL LINE ITEMS. For every line item on the order the contents of this bracket are executed. This bracket, which may be executed *many* times, corresponds to the one-to-many link from CUSTOMER ORDER to ORDER LINE ITEM on the data navigation diagram.

Two types of brackets are drawn on action diagrams, single-execution brackets and repetition brackets. Both are shown on Fig. 14.5. A single-execution bracket states that if the entry conditions are satisfied, the contents of the bracket will be executed *once*. A repetition bracket states that its contents may be executed many times, as controlled by the entry clause. In other words, it represents a loop. It has a thicker vertical line and a double bar at the top:

Single-
execution
bracket

Repitition
bracket

In Fig. 14.5, we first retrieve the CUSTOMER record, and check the customer CREDIT RATING. If the CREDIT RATING is bad, we create a CUSTOMER ORDER record with a reject code set in the ORDER STATUS data item to indicate the bad rating. We print an order rejection.

If the CREDIT RATING is good, we again create a CUSTOMER ORDER record. Then for all line items on the order we do the following: create an ORDER LINE ITEM record, retrieve the requisite PRODUCT record, retrieve the ORDER RATE record for that PRODUCT, recalculate the order rate, and update the ORDER RATE record.

A DEFINED STRUCTURE FOR "FOR ALL . . ."

To make data-base navigation easy to represent in HOS, we can create *defined structures* for it. It would be convenient to have a defined structure for the FOR ALL . . . brackets in action diagrams.

Consider the single bracket in Fig. 14.5. We test the customer's credit rating to see whether it is bad:

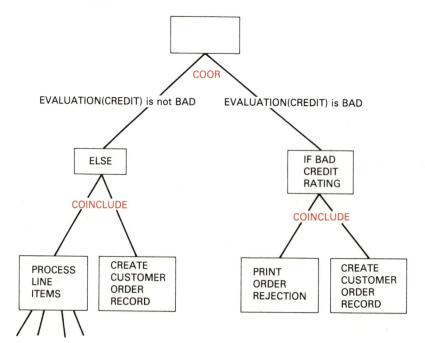

Note here, incidentally, that the operation CREATE CUSTOMER ORDER RE-CORD is used twice. These operations are identical. They have the same object types as input, although BAD would have different values. In the code generated the same subroutine would be used for both of these operations. The operation PROCESS LINE ITEMS above is the repetition bracket of Fig. 14.5, headed "FOR ALL LINE ITEMS."

It would be convenient to have a defined structure called FOR ALL which decomposes the PROCESS LINE ITEMS operation into a recursive structure which performs the same function "PROCESS LINE__ITEM" on each line item in the data structure set "LINE__ITEMS." Thus:

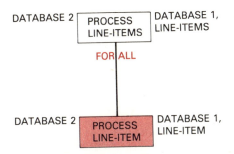

Figure 14.6 shows a control map created with the USE.IT graphics editor which is the basis of a FOR ALL *defined structure*. It has two inputs: X1, which can be any collection of objects, and SET1, which is a set of elements. The block colored red is replaced with the lower block in our FOR ALL defined structure. In the example above, DATABASE 1 and DATABASE 2 replace X1 and X3; LINE ITEMS replace SET1; LINE ITEM replaces ELEMENT.

The user does not need to know about the control map of Fig. 14.6. He can use the defined structure to do data-base navigation. Figure 14.7 shows an HOS version of the action diagram in Fig. 14.5. It uses the FOR ALL control structure to handle the repetition bracket.

AN ACTION DIAGRAM WITH THREE FOR-ALLS

Figure 14.8 shows an action diagram with three FOR ALL operations. It is derived from the data navigation chart in Fig. 14.9.

First all CUSTOMER records are obtained. Then all SERVICE records for each given CUSTOMER are obtained. Then all TRANS-ACTION records are obtained for each SERVICE record.

The control map for this operation requires three uses of the FOR ALL control structure, as follows:

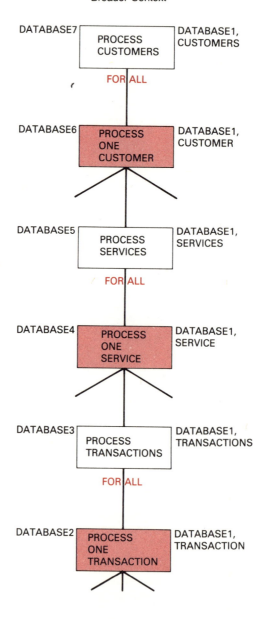

In this control map all six blocks result in some change to the data base. Figure 14.10 fills in more details, showing the primitive operations which GET the records required, and the procedures A, B, C, and D, which are marked on the action diagram in Fig. 14.8. When ANALYZEd by the HOS software, the control map in Fig. 14.10 would be verified for logical correctness in the use of the data model in question.

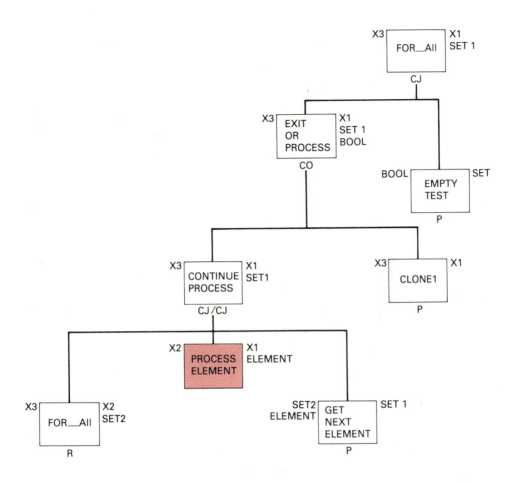

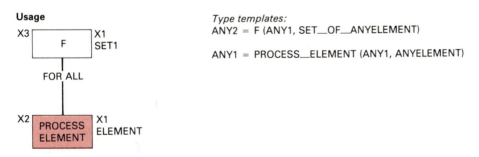

Usage

Type templates:
ANY2 = F (ANY1, SET_OF_ANYELEMENT)

ANY1 = PROCESS_ELEMENT (ANY1, ANYELEMENT)

Figure 14.6 Control map for the FOR ALL defined structure, which simplifies data-base navigation.

245

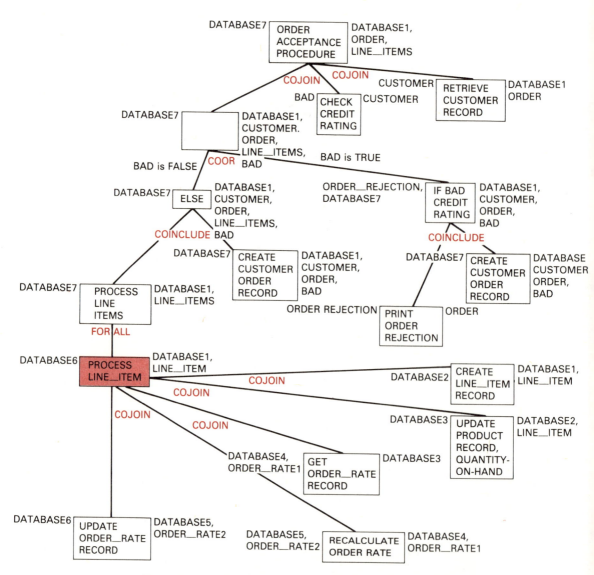

Figure 14.7 HOS representation of the action diagram in Fig. 14.5. Each labeled operation corresponds to an item on the action digram. Note that the **CREATE CUSTOMER ORDER RECORD** blocks are the same operation. The same program code would be used for both.

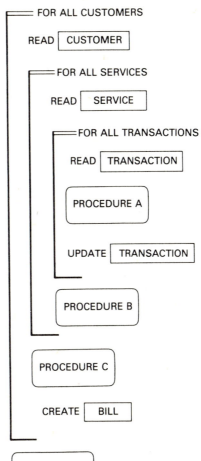

FOR ALL CUSTOMERS

READ | CUSTOMER

FOR ALL SERVICES

READ | SERVICE

FOR ALL TRANSACTIONS

READ | TRANSACTION

PROCEDURE A

UPDATE | TRANSACTION

PROCEDURE B

PROCEDURE C

CREATE | BILL

PROCEDURE D

Figure 14.8 Action diagram with three FOR ALL constructs. Figure 14.10 shows an HOS version of this.

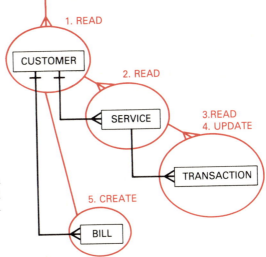

Figure 14.9 Data navigation diagram showing accesses needed on a data model during a billing run. A data-base action diagram of this is shown in Fig. 14.8.

1. READ

CUSTOMER

2. READ

SERVICE

3. READ
4. UPDATE

TRANSACTION

5. CREATE

BILL

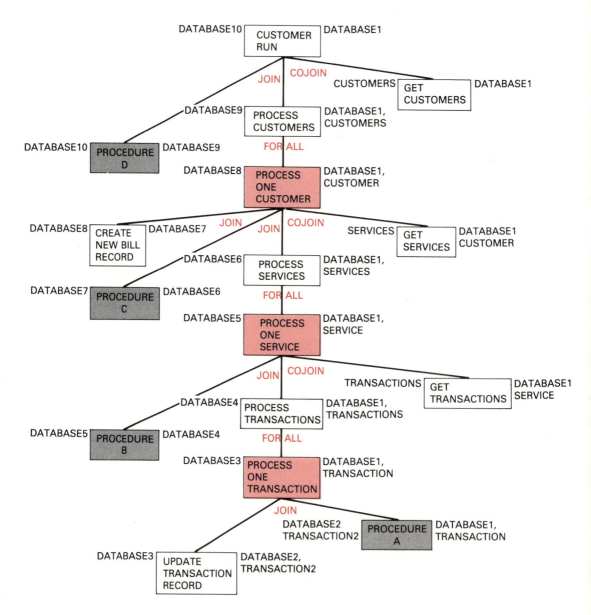

Figure 14.10 HOS version of the action diagram in Fig. 14.8 using three FOR ALL control structures.

NON-HOS FORMS OF DESIGN

In this chapter we have taken a non-HOS method of designing applications, and made it easy to represent in HOS by creating an HOS control structure for it. We can similarly take other forms of design which are familiar to particular communities and devise HOS-defined operations or defined structures which make those methods easy to represent in HOS. Code can then be generated from the ANALYZEd HOS control maps.

REFERENCE

1. James Martin and Carma McClure, *Diagramming Techniques for Analysts and Programmers*, Prentice-Hall, Inc., Englewood Cliffs, NJ, 1985.

15 DATA FLOW DIAGRAMS

INTRODUCTION   There are multiple ways to conceptualize systems. A variety of techniques for thinking about systems can be translated into HOS representation.

The HOS approach is itself a very good way to think about systems. It is necessary to ask whether it is better than other forms of conceptualization. Sometimes, analysts or specifiers will want to draw different representations of systems, and then we need to convert these into HOS control maps.

COMPUTABLE SPECIFICATIONS   The problem with most ways of conceptualizing systems is that they are imprecise. They are not computable. They are intended for human beings drawing on a sheet of paper. If we can make the human beings draw on a computer screen instead of a sheet of paper, the machine may be able to request refinements to their input so that consistency and computability is achieved.

A methodology grew up, for example, in the late 1970s, for specifying systems in connection with ICAM projects (Integrated Computer-Aided Manufacturing) [1]. The method, called IDEF (ICAM Definition Method) [2], used a type of chart with lines and boxes to show in an easily readable fashion the flow of control in complex systems. The result, however, was not computable. Like most such techniques, it provides guidelines for software development, rather than computable specifications for it. The HOS approach was applied to IDEF to refine it and make it computable. Computable IDEF interacts with the user to elicit specification definitions of sufficient precision to be computable, and then uses HOS software to generate the program code [3].

The computable specification employs previous defined operations or subsystems. A library of these builds up. It should also use previously defined descriptions of data. A conceptual model of the data grows steadily. The tool for making the specifications computable enforces consistency with preexisting operations and data.

DATA FLOW DIAGRAMS

A common way to design systems is by employing data flow diagrams. Figure 15.1 shows a typical data flow diagram. The circles in the figure are processes. The arrows are data that pass among the processes. The parallel horizontal lines represent stores of data such as files or data bases.

A circle on a data flow diagram can be exploded into another more detailed data flow diagram. In this way they can be nested like the defined operations in AXES.

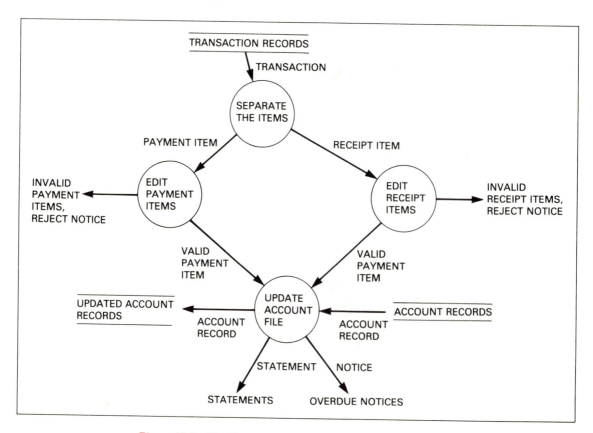

Figure 15.1 Simple example of a data flow diagram. The circles are operations. The arrows show data flows. The parallel lines show files.

Any HOS tree can be converted directly into a data flow diagram.

The dynamics graph representations that we used in Chapters 3 and 4 were in effect data flow diagrams.

We will draw flow diagrams from right to left so that the positioning of their nodes bears some relation to the right-to-left positioning in the HOS tree.

A control structure with multiple *joins* becomes a string of data flow circles as shown in Fig. 15.2. A control structure with multiple *includes* becomes a diagram with data branching into each circle as shown in Fig. 15.3.

Figure 15.4 shows multiple *ORs*. Here we have deviated from the data flow diagramming convention, for clarity. The decision point of an *OR* or *COOR* is shown as a split box rather than a circle.

In Figs. 15.2, 15.3, and 15.4, only the leaf nodes F_1, F_2, F_3, and F_4 appear as circles on the flow diagrams. In general, one-level flow diagrams show only

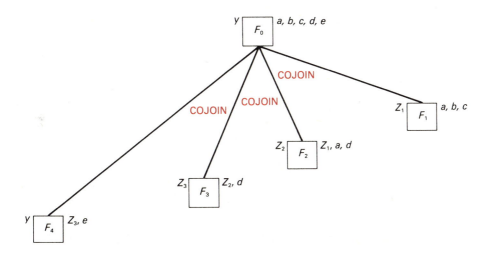

A flow diagram of the control map above:

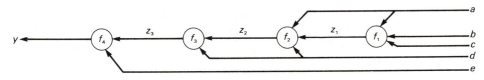

Figure 15.2 Flow diagram of multiple COJOINS.

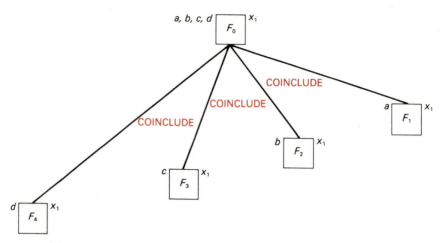

A flow diagram of the control map above:

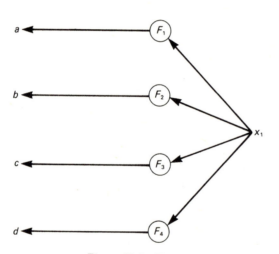

Figure 15.3   Flow diagram of multiple COINCLUDES.

leaf nodes of the tree, and nodes controlling an *OR* or *COOR*. A nonleaf node could be drawn as a ring encompassing those nodes below it.

Figure 15.5 repeats our earlier illustration of the three primitive control structures used in connection with making stools. There are four leaf nodes. Figure 15.6 shows this as a flow diagram. Figure 15.7 puts rings around parts of the flow diagram so that all of the nodes on the tree are shown.

The outer ring, labeled MAKE-A-STOOL, could be represented as one circle on a higher-level flow diagram. For example, if Fig. 5.5 were converted into a flow diagram, it would contain this MAKE-A-STOOL circle.

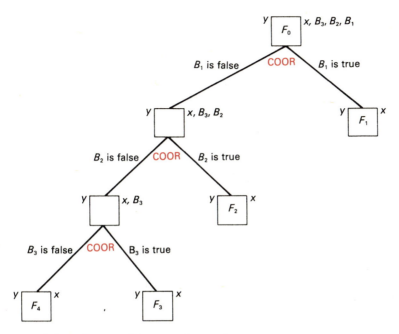

A flow diagram of the control map above:

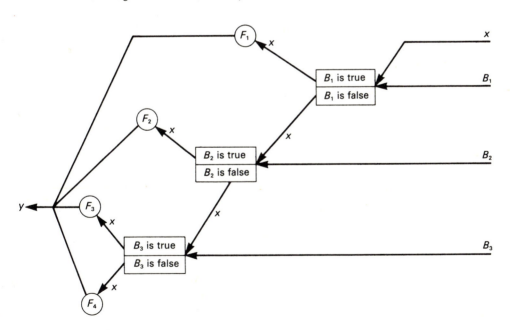

Figure 15.4 Flow diagram of multiple COORs.

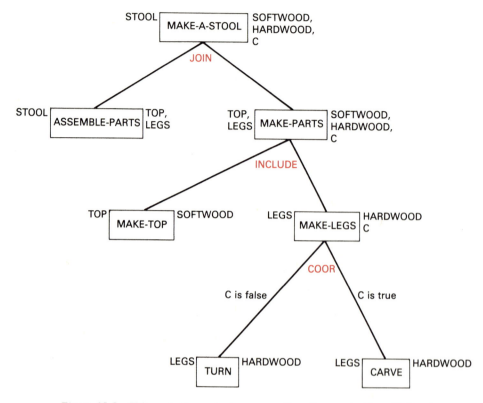

Figure 15.5 This control map is shown as a flow diagram in Figs. 15.6 and 15.7.

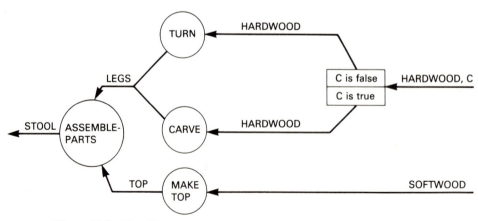

Figure 15.6 Flow diagram of the HOS tree in Fig. 15.5. Only the leaf nodes and OR or COOR decisions appear in a one-level flow diagram.

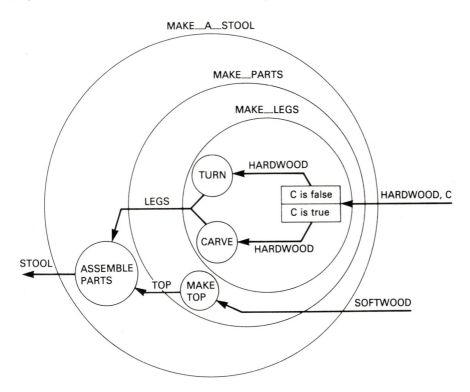

Figure 15.7　Rings drawn on the flow diagram of Fig. 15.6 to illustrate the nonleaf nodes in Fig. 15.5.

Figure 15.8 shows the control map for a radar system discussed in Chapter 9. Figure 15.9 shows a flow diagram of this control map. For some purposes the flow diagram makes it easier to visualize what is happening.

INSUFFICIENT DATA FLOW DIAGRAMS

Although any HOS tree can be converted in a data flow diagram, it is not true that the data flow diagrams drawn by most systems analysts can be converted directly into HOS trees. The reason is that they lack the precision that is necessary.

The example of a data flow diagram in Fig. 15.1 is typical of what analysts draw and structured analysis courses recommend. It has, like most such diagrams, some serious deficiencies.

To develop a more rigorous version of it, we first need to analyze the data it uses. It employs two types of records: an ACCOUNT record and a TRANS-ACTION record. These records are related and Fig. 15.10 shows a simple data model of them.

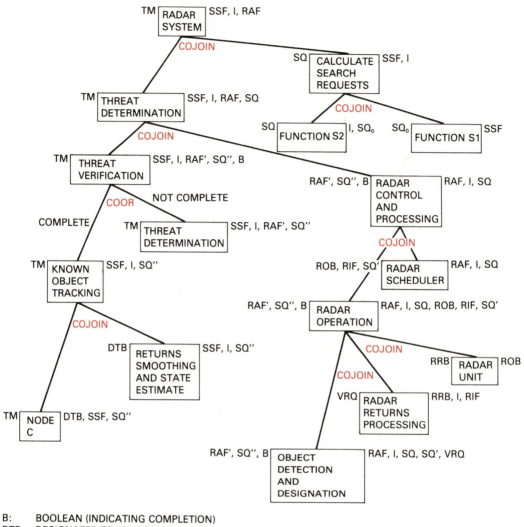

TM RADAR SYSTEM — SSF, I, RAF

COJOIN

SQ CALCULATE SEARCH REQUESTS — SSF, I

TM THREAT DETERMINATION — SSF, I, RAF, SQ

COJOIN

SQ FUNCTION S2 — I, SQ_0 SQ_0 FUNCTION S1 — SSF

TM THREAT VERIFICATION — SSF, I, RAF', SQ'', B

RAF', SQ'', B RADAR CONTROL AND PROCESSING — RAF, I, SQ

COOR   NOT COMPLETE

COMPLETE

TM THREAT DETERMINATION — SSF, I, RAF', SQ''

COJOIN

TM KNOWN OBJECT TRACKING — SSF, I, SQ''

ROB, RIF, SQ' RADAR SCHEDULER — RAF, I, SQ

RAF', SQ'', B RADAR OPERATION — RAF, I, SQ, ROB, RIF, SQ'

COJOIN

DTB RETURNS SMOOTHING AND STATE ESTIMATE — SSF, I, SQ''

COJOIN

RRB RADAR UNIT — ROB

COJOIN

VRQ RADAR RETURNS PROCESSING — RRB, I, RIF

TM NODE C — DTB, SSF, SQ''

RAF', SQ'', B OBJECT DETECTION AND DESIGNATION — RAF, I, SQ, SQ', VRQ

B: BOOLEAN (INDICATING COMPLETION)
DTB: DESIGNATED TRACK BEAMS
I: GENERAL INFORMATION FILE
RAF: RADAR ACTIVITIES FILE
RIF: RADAR INFORMATION FILE
ROB: RADAR ORDERS BUFFER
RRB: RADAR RETURNS BUFFER
SQ_0:   AN ORDERED SET OF PULSES
SQ: AN ORDERED SET OF RADAR SEARCH PULSES
SSF: SEARCH SCAN FILE
TM: THREAT MESSAGES HANDED OVER TO THE BALLISTIC MISSILE SYSTEM CONTROLLER
VRQ: VERIFICATION RETURN QUEUE

Figure 15.8   This structure is shown as a flow diagram in Fig. 15.9.

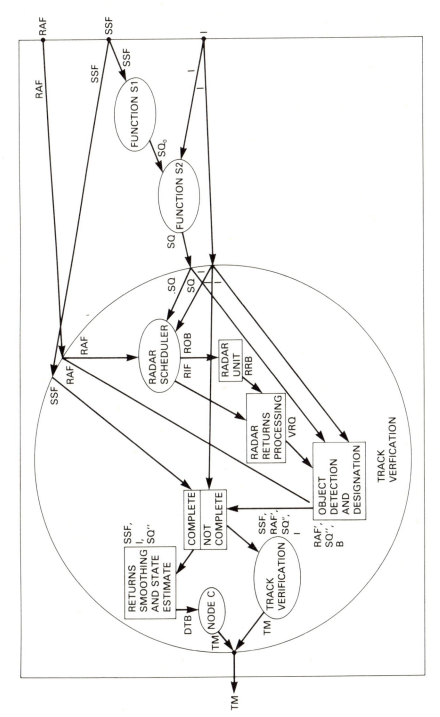

Figure 15.9 Flow diagram of the radar system in Fig. 15.8. Again only the leaf nodes of the HOS tree appear as circles on the flow diagram.

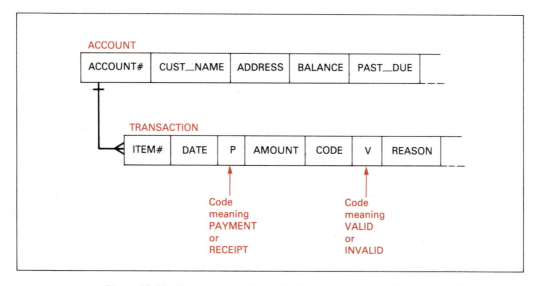

Figure 15.10 Data structure design for the processing related to the data flow diagram in Fig. 15.1.

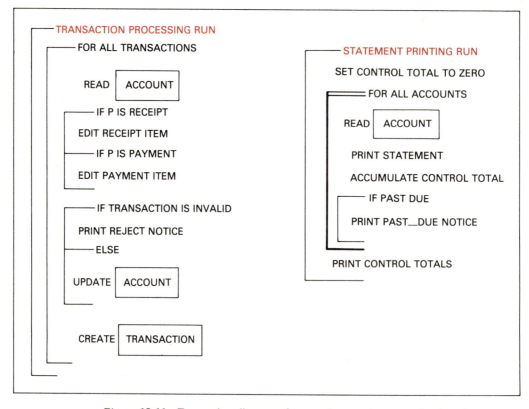

Figure 15.11 Two action diagrams for carrying out the runs related to the data flow diagram in Fig. 15.1.

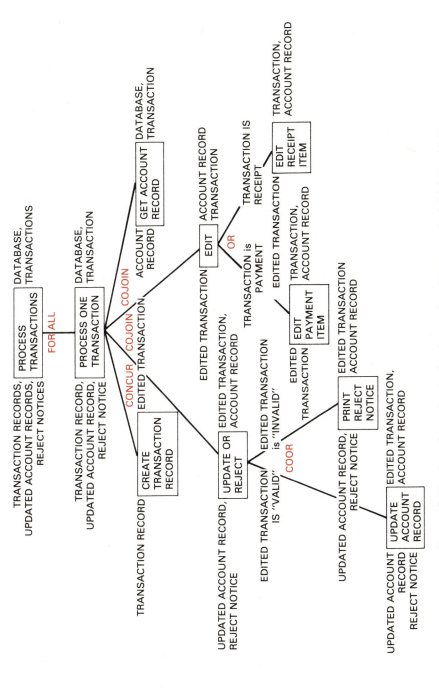

Figure 15.12 Control map for the data-base action diagram on the left of Fig. 15.11.

261

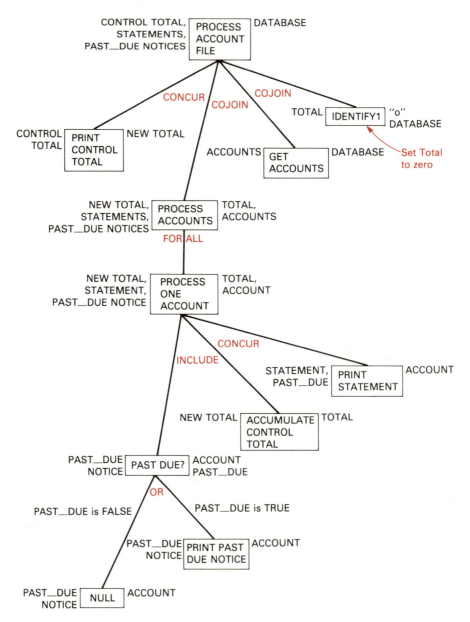

Figure 15.13 Control map for the data-base action diagram on the right of Fig. 15.11.

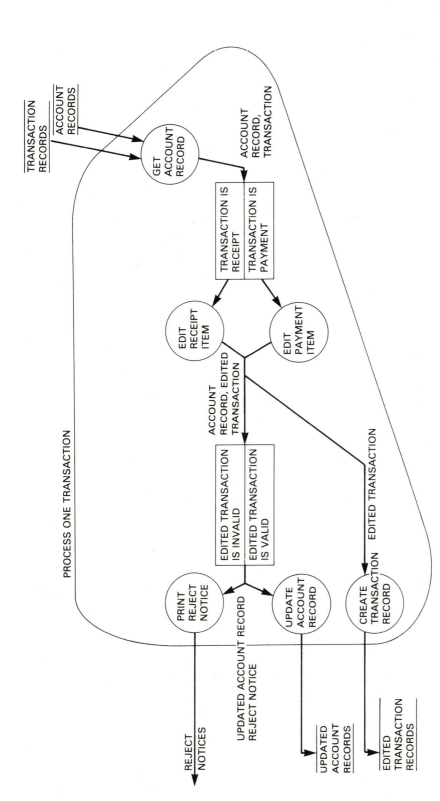

Figure 15.14 Flow diagram of the transaction processing run, drawn from Fig. 15.12.

263

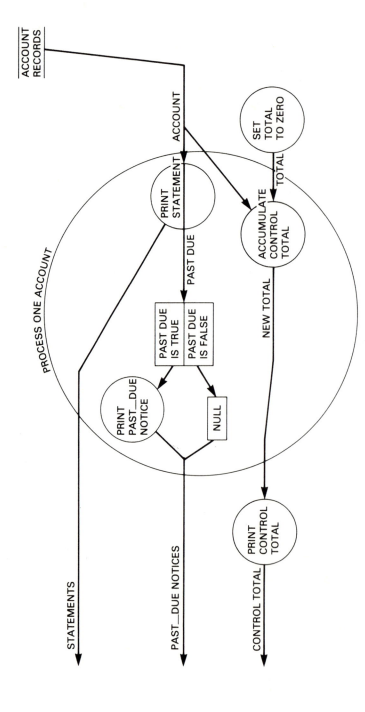

Figure 15.15 Flow diagram of the statement-printing run, drawn from Fig. 15.13. This and Fig. 15.14 replace Fig. 15.1.

Two operations are being carried out in Fig. 15.1. Input transactions are being processed, and account statements are being produced. These two activities do not occur at the same time. Statements are sent periodically—monthly, let's say. Transactions can arrive at any time. Two separate computer operations are needed, one for processing the incoming transactions and one, at a different time, for printing the monthly statements. The fact that these operations must be separate programs is not revealed in the data flow diagram.

A simple way to draw what happens in the two programs is with action diagrams. Figure 15.11 shows these for the two programs. We can convert these diagrams into HOS charts, as we did in Chapter 14. Figures 15.12 and 15.13 show the control maps derived from the action diagrams. We can now convert these back into data flow diagrams as shown in Figs. 15.14 and 15.15, which represent in a complete and consistent manner what the programs do. Figure 15.1 did not.

The shortcomings of data flow diagrams as typically drawn are often much worse than the simple example in Fig. 15.1. As a method of analysis they leave much to be desired. They help to conceptualize entangled flows of data between operations, but unless coupled to more rigorous forms of analysis, they are often misleading or wrong. They are no substitute for formal data analysis and rigorous functional decomposition. "Structured analysis" as commonly practiced gives inadequate front-end design (although it is better than unstructured text specifications), and consequently the programs created with it have many errors of specification which are expensive to correct.

REFERENCES

1. SofTech, Inc., *Integrated Computer Aided Manufacturing, Task 1—Architecture*, Waltham, MA, June 1978.

2. SofTech, Inc., *Architect's Manual: ICAM Definition Method*, IDEF, Version 0, 1978; Version 1, 1979, Waltham, MA.

3. Higher Order Software, Inc., *Computable IDEF, Preliminary Design*, Cambridge, MA, February 1982.

PART IV EFFECTS

16 ERRORS AND VERIFICATION

INTRODUCTION HOS claims that their software creates programs which are provably correct. Just what does that mean? We stressed in the first chapter that it does not eliminate errors in the *concept* of what a program should do. We can tell it to do something stupid and the methodology can create provably correct code for that stupid question. In old fairy stories a magic device such as the *Monkey's Paw* executes its users' wishes but does not check that the effects will really be good for the users.

The fairy stories warned us, philosophically, about wishing for the wrong thing. We can give wrong instructions to the HOS, not because of any philosophical problems but because we are careless. This is a new version of garbage-in-garbage-out. Ill-conceived requirements or misstated requirements lead to correctly-meshing mechanisms for executing those wrong requirements.

It is perfectly possible to create a correct control map for solving the wrong problem. The software checks that the control map is correct according to its mathematical rules, but the result is wrong because the wrong problem was solved.

The misstatement of requirements could happen by accident. It might be a careless misstatement of requirements hidden in the middle of a control map.

Suppose that a developer wants to evaluate

$$y = \frac{x(1 - x)^2}{z - 1}$$

He creates the control map shown in Fig. 16.1. This is correct from HOS's point of view, but from the user's point of view it contains a mistake. It solves a perfectly valid problem but it is not the problem the user wanted to solve.

After looking for the error the reader might say "That's a silly mistake." So it is. We sometimes make silly mistakes. We have here a perfectly valid control map to solve the wrong problem. Garbage-in-garbage-out.

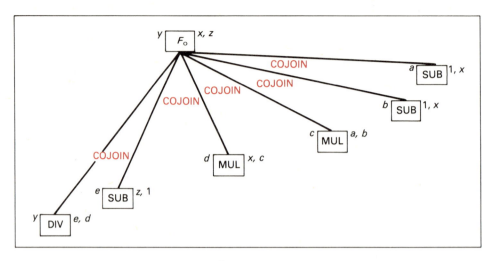

Figure 16.1

The user may be less likely to make a mistake if he could key in a conventional algebraic expression: $x*(1 - x)**2/(z - 1)$ instead of the control map above. Giving HOS user-friendly interfaces makes it both easier and quicker to use *and* less subject to garbage-in-garbage-out errors. However, it is still possible to make errors with algebraic expressions [e.g., $x*(1 - x)**2/z - 1$].

The argument for user-friendly formula translation becomes stronger when the formulas are more complex. Figure 16.2 shows a control map for evaluating

$$y = \sum_{x = 1}^{n} x^2$$

Most of the errors the user is likely to make in creating this control map are caught by the software. However, the user *could* make the silly mistake of putting the test in the wrong place so that a perfectly valid control map is created for

$$y = \sum_{x = 1}^{n + 1} x^2$$

One single test of the resulting program would catch these errors. Any program must always be tested. What we can avoid is saturation testing of every possible combination of branches in a combinatorial structure.

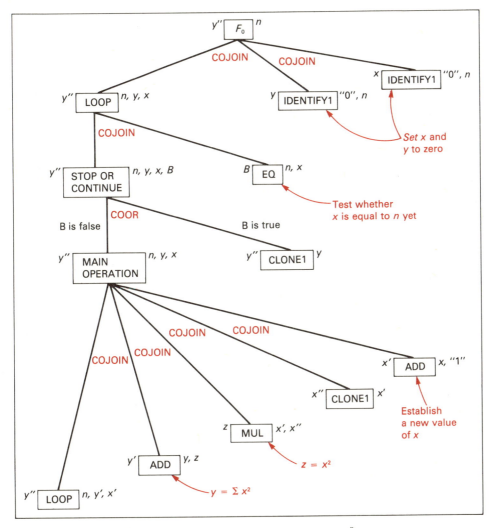

Figure 16.2   Control map for evaluating $y = \sum_{x=1}^{n} x^2$.

VERIFICATION AND TESTING

In an HOS environment we can distinguish between *verification* and *testing*. By verification we mean checking a system's specification for logical completeness and consistency and that it obeys the mathematical rules. By testing we mean checking the correctness by demonstrating that the system really works as it was intended to. *Verification* is performed automatically and statically by the HOS software. *Testing* requires specimens of the target system's behavior to be checked. Test cases are fed to the system to ensure that its algorithms give the results the designers intended.

In conventional systems development almost all testing has to be done after programming. This is expensive to do and it is even more expensive to correct the errors found at that late stage. Figure 2.2 illustrated that if errors are caught early they are less costly by one or two orders of magnitude. Using HOS, most of the errors can be caught early. The software ANALYZEs the high-level specifications and they can be successively reANALYZEd as they are broken down into detail. The designer will also do case tests on modules as he proceeds.

Verification ought to take place at every stage in a design process. Hamilton and Zeldin express this as follows:

> *Design* means to think. *Verify* means to think back. For each step of design there should be a counter-step of verification. At times, the process of design is one and the same as the process of verification. This occurs when certain design characteristics are included for the purpose of preventing unnecessary verification. In such a case, some types of verification requirements are designed out of the system [1].

In order to verify automatically one has to translate a design into a computable form. The HOS representation allows rigorous verification at each step of the design process.

BUILDING HIGHER LEVELS OF TRUST

Modules that are verified and tested are stored in the system library. These are then regarded as proven modules which do not need to be verified again. They are verified *one time only*. Their application may be tested when they are used in newly defined systems.

The library of verified modules grows and these modules may become linked to form larger modules. All new design should use as many of the library modules as possible. This lessens the amount of verification and testing required.

Systems can thus be defined using techniques that eliminate the need for certain types of verification. If techniques are enforced which eliminate data and sequence errors, there is no need to look for these errors. When you use a computer as part of a system you do not check its internal wiring. You assume that it is correct. We should similarly be able to trust as many software modules as possible, and link them together into larger trustworthy modules. The growth and maximal use of the library of verified modules is thus a very important part of the overall reduction of testing time and costs.

SYNTAX AND SEMANTICS

We can distinguish between syntax and semantics in languages. Syntax refers to *how* something is being said. Semantics refers to *what* is being said.

The *Oxford English Dictionary* defines *syntax* as "sentence construction; the grammatical arrangement of words (in language); set of rules governing this." It defines *semantic* as "relating to meaning in language."

Most compilers and interpreters check for *syntax* errors: misspelled words, commands without the required variables, missing END statements, and so on. They cannot check the *meaning* of the language. Languages of higher level than programming languages can make some checks on *what* is being said, not just *how*. We are not likely soon to have specification languages that can make complete semantic checks. This would take us into the realms of artificial intelligence, which is increasingly concerned with computer representation of meaning. Relational languages, such as powerful query languages, ought to do some checks on *what* is being asked for to warn about semantic disintegrity, as discussed in Chapter 13. The HOS software carries out as much verification as it can of *what* is being said. Do the operations and data references obey the basic axioms? There may be garbage-in-garbage-out, but the internal logic can be checked for what it is doing. This type of internal semantic check is a major step forward in automated design verification.

It is desirable to represent specifications in a technology-independent fashion because machines and software change. A fixed semantics is necessary for this. This semantics may be expressed with different forms of syntax, just as AXES is RATted into COBOL, FORTRAN, Ada, and so on. In historical methods the opposite is true. The languages have a fixed syntax but uncontrolled semantics. AXES has controlled semantics that can be translated into multiple syntaxes.

INTERNAL AND EXTERNAL SEMANTICS

We should distinguish between *internal semantics* and *external semantics*. *Internal semantics* relates to whether what is being said obeys the rules which are established in the basic axioms. *External semantics* relates to whether the system is solving the right problem. Techniques for proving program correctness can deal with internal semantics, not external semantics.

We might say to a science-fiction robot "Get me a dry blartini with a twist." It will tell us there is a *syntax* error, and ask whether the word "blartini" should be "martini."

If we tell it to get a dry martini made with Seven-Up it will tell us we have an *internal semantics* error. Our instruction violates a basic axiom of martini making.

If we want a vodka martini and only say "Get me a dry martini with a twist," it might bring a gin martini. Now we have an *external semantics* error which the software has not caught.

You might say that the robot should have detected that our specifications were incomplete. It should have known that there are two types of martini and asked: "Vodka or gin?" There are other options. It should say "With ice or straight up?" But where does it stop?

It might say "Gordon's, Juniper, Beefeater, Boodles, Tanqueray, Bombay, Schenley, Skol, London, Boston, Burnett's, Crystal Palace, Seagram's, Calvert, Booth's, Fleischmann's, S.S. Pierce, Five O'clock, Gilbey's . . .," and we lose patience and say "Fetch the damned thing."

Specifications, to be computable, have to have much detail, or else default options. Default options are common in the simpler forms of nonprocedural languages, such as report generators.

HORIZONTAL AND   We can distinguish between errors which exist within
VERTICAL ERRORS   one level of a specification and errors which exist in
                       the decomposition of a level into more detail. We will
call the first *horizontal errors,* and the second *vertical errors.*

In conventional systems design, vertical errors often occur because of misinterpretation of the semantic intent of one layer by the developers of the lower layers. Horizontal errors occur because of inconsistencies and omissions in the specification itself.

The original manual specifications for the radar scheduling system discussed in Chapter 9 had both horizontal and vertical errors in them [2]. Rebuilding the specifications in HOS representation revealed these. Typical examples of horizontal errors were:

- An initiation problem: Before the end of a radar transmit window is specified for the first time it is not clear how a certain function should perform.
- Certain parameters were placed into a queue and not used.
- An arrow was incorrect on a flowchart.
- The end time of a segment was incorrectly specified.
- There were missing parameters for certain functions.
- One variable was undefined.

Examples of vertical errors which occurred in decomposing the highest layer, were:

- It was not clear whether search pulses and designation pulses were to be kept distinct and separate.
- It was not clear how a certain parameter should be computed. There were several choices and it was not known how they affected the efficiency of the radar unit.
- It was not known what should be done when a tolerance constraint was violated.

All of these specification errors were caught and resolved at the front of the HOS development because of the rigor it enforces. With conventional techniques the errors may not have been detected until during, or after, programming. The rigorous representation enforces the asking of questions about the specification before correct code can be generated.

FOUR STAGES OF VERIFICATION

When a user of the HOS software builds a control map on the graphics screen he has four levels of verification available to him.

First the ANALYZER checks the format of functions and statements. This is a syntax check similar to those done by compilers. It indicates the elements of the control map in error and displays messages for each error, such as:

> UNKNOWN SYNTAX
> ILLEGAL FUNCTION FORM
> NAME(S) MISSING
> DUPLICATE INPUT   (a function has duplicate input variables)
> INCOMPLETE TREE   (a parent exists without two offsprings)

A second pass checks the input and output relationships between each parent and its offsprings. It ensures that the control map can be decomposed into primitive operations and primitive control structures which obey the rules. It produces such messages as:

> INPUT NOT PASSED R
> OUTPUT NOT PASSED L
> DATA NOT PASSED ACROSS   (in a JOIN or COJOIN)
> OUTPUT NOT SHARED   (in an OR or COOR)
> INPUT NOT PARTITIONED   (in an INCLUDE)
> BAD VARIABLE ORDERING
> UNUSED OUTPUT R
> NONUNIQUE FUNCTION

A third pass checks the leaf nodes and finds any interface errors. These may result from incorrect linkage to other operations or defined structures. Common causes are inconsistent use of data types and references to nodes not yet defined. This pass produces such messages as:

> SUBTREE LABEL NOT FOUND
> NO SUCH FUNCTION
> WRONG NUMBER OF VARIABLES
> TOP OF SUBTREE DIFFERS FROM REFERENCE
> NO PLUG-IN   (for a defined structure)
> EMPTY REFERENCE   (reference to a model with no control map)

The third pass also looks for recursion (looping) errors. It displays such messages as:

> INFINITE RECURSION
> NO NEW DATA IN RECURSION
> MULTIPLE RECURSION   (more than one node with the same name as the recursive node)

NO RECURSION FOUND   (no node with the same name as the recursive
                      node)

This interactive verification enables a developer to check and correct his
control map very quickly. The mistakes, once pointed out, are easy to see, and
many of them are easy to correct. Most people are surprised, as the author was,
by the speed of finding and correcting one's errors.

Once the third-pass errors are corrected (or patched over because a defined
operation does not yet exist), the developer can generate and run the program
code. This fourth level of verification is often done with simulation as described
in Chapter 8. Certain operations are not yet defined, so they are simulated. The
user enters expected output values for the missing node so that the overall program
can be run. He can then find any hidden errors of external semantics like that in
Fig. 16.1.

If there are no unimplemented data types or operations, the program is
validated in the usual manner; that is, the user selects particular data as input to
the program and determines whether or not the output conforms to his expectations.

Like a compiler or interpreter, the first of these stages catches *syntax errors*.
The second and third catch *internal semantics errors*. The fourth helps the developer to catch his *external semantics errors*.

The testing required is *black-box* testing. We can assume that the internals
of the black box are consistent. We validate the behavior of the black box. As
well as checking that it produces correct answers with normal data, we should
test unusual cases such as values equaling zero, out-of-bounds situations, special
cases such as an empty set, only one pass through a loop, and so on.

INTERFACE ERRORS

One of the particularly important aspects of the HOS
software is its catching of interface errors among different modules or separately developed subsystems.
The interfaces are rigorously defined, and most interface errors will be caught
in the third pass. With large complex systems, the majority of the errors are
interface errors, so this capability is very valuable.

Occasionally, interface errors are caused by external misconceptions rather
than by internal syntax or semantics. These are caught by black-box testing after
the modules are linked together.

COMBINATORIAL TESTING

Some programs have enormous numbers of possible
execution paths, especially those in which real-time
or interactive input can come in any sequence. We
indicated in Chapter 3 that the following module has over 206 trillion possible
unique execution paths:

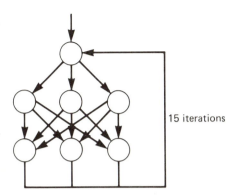

15 iterations

To *fully* debug a program created with ad hoc methods, all of its paths must be tested. In practice there is no way they could possibly all be tested thoroughly. An attempt is made at saturation testing, in which the system is flooded with large numbers of test cases. In saturation testing it may be difficult to notice or track down an error if it occurs, and many errors may lurk in paths which the saturation testing does not happen to reach.

Because of this, most large systems are never fully debugged. They occasionally do mysterious things. A high-level check is placed on them so that they do not lose accounts or have dramatic errors. Most of their minor disasters can be caught when they happen, and recovered from. On some software there is a lengthy list of bugs observed but not yet caught. There are probably many others not yet observed.

When this report was being written, *MIS Week* reported in a headline that only 30 bugs remained in a certain system [3]. We could ask: ''How do you know?'' If there are 30 bugs that you cannot find, there are probably many more hiding in the woodwork. In a later issue the publication said that 600 out of 900 bugs had been fixed on the same system.

One of the more extraordinary phenomena of the present computer age is the Big Eight accounting firms charging large sums for ''certifying'' certain programs when there can be no possible assurance that these programs work correctly. If they were created with the HOS tools, they could, honestly, be certified.

When a complex system is developed with HOS, including one with many loops, all possible paths are built from primitives which are mathematically verified. *There are no unknown paths.*

Dynamic program testing is necessary with all programs not built with a rigorous mathematical technique (which includes the vast majority of programs in existence today). Each branch and usable combination of branches ought to be tested if this were possible. With HOS most errors are caught with *static* verification, and some with tests of specific instances to ensure that correct results are being created.

ERROR STATISTICS   On some large projects detailed analysis has been done of the errors made. It is interesting to look back and estimate how many errors could have been avoided with the technique described in this report.

Figure 16.3 shows statistics of the preflight software errors in NASA's moonshot Project Apollo [4]. These were errors discovered *after* implementation and delivery of code. Far more errors were presumably caught by programmers during implementation. Seventy-three percent of the problems were software–software interface errors. This is common on large projects. If all software for a project were developed with a methodology like that in this book, there should be no interface problems discovered *after* implementation. The interfaces are defined with mathematical precision, and details of all modules and their interface definitions are in the library. The interface linkages are checked by the ANALYZER when the implementer creates new modules. Forty-four percent of the errors were found manually and many by *dynamic* testing runs. With HOS most would be found in *static* verification.

It was estimated that 30% of the errors would have been avoided with better programming style—a good structured programming method. Eighty-seven percent of the errors in the bottom chart of Fig. 16.3 would have been caught by HOS verification methods, before code delivery. Thirteen percent of the errors were conceptual problems or problems of changing requirements which would not have been caught by mathematical verification. Typically, the specification was incomplete or inconsistent with the original intent of the designer.

Hamilton and Zeldin refer to this residual 13% of errors as the ''13% problem.'' If code generation and verification are automated, and precision is enforced in specification, developers can spend more time at the front of projects checking the high-level HOS charts with the end users and management, trying to flush out any specification faults and omissions.

Seeing results as quickly as possible and being able to perform simulations at the terminal help developers to catch external semantics errors. Better front-end methodologies for helping to achieve accurate system conceptualization may reduce the 13%. These include thorough data modeling and event diagramming.

HUMAN SYSTEM COMPONENTS   A particularly interesting error occurred on Project Apollo Mission 11. Just prior to landing on the moon a warning signal informed the astronauts that the capsule should not land. This hair-raising signal was incorrect.

The error was caused by an incorrect entry in the astronaut's checklist of procedures. This caused the astronaut to take an incorrect action with the hardware, which in turn caused the software to think something was true which was not true. Here we have a system error where the system includes interacting hardware, software, and human being.

The HOS technique can be applied to broad systems, in which the interaction

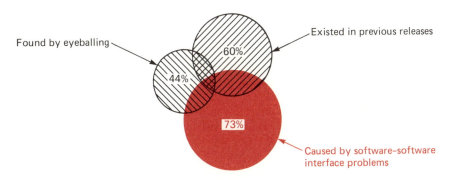

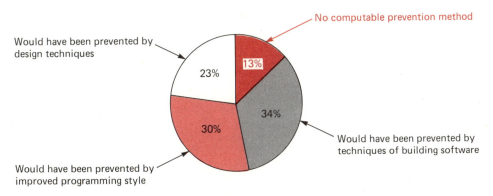

Figure 16.3   Breakdown of the official preflight software anomalies of Project Apollo.(From Ref. 4.)

of the hardware, software, and human beings is diagrammed, so that human checklists can be proved as well as other system components. This would have prevented some of the problems with nuclear power station operating procedures, for example.

REFERENCES

1. M. Hamilton and S. Zeldin, "The Relationship Between Design and Verification," *Journal of Systems and Software,* Vol. 1 (1979).

2. W. R. Hackler and A. Samarov, *An Axes Specification of a Radar Scheduler,* Technical Report 23, Higher Order Software, Inc., Cambridge, MA, 1979.

3. *MIS Week,* February 10, 1982, p. 1 (Fairchild Business Newspaper).

4. M. Hamilton and S. Zeldin, "Higher Order Software—A Methodology for Defining Software," *IEEE Transactions on Software Engineering,* Vol. SE-2, No. 1 (March 1976).

17 SOLUTIONS TO DP'S PROBLEMS

PROBLEMS WITH DP

There are many problems with today's data processing. Box 17.1 lists the major causes for concern. These problems are not new. Much effort has gone into attacking them, but many of them are steadily becoming worse. Articles are appearing referring to the "failure of the structured revolution" [1]. It is clear that most of these problems will not be solved with *manual* techniques and improved management. What is needed is a higher level of automation of data processing.

In much of this book we have been concerned with errors in code. We should also be concerned with changeability of programs. Maintenance is a nightmare in many installations, becoming steadily worse as the installation ages. The need to change programs arises constantly.

Users are becoming much more sophisticated about computing. Their understanding and expectations are growing. Their imaginations are going to work about how computers could help them. They want results, accurate results, fast, and they often want to change the procedures.

Users of computers, and particularly high-level management, need to make many changes to their methods of working. Often they are told that a certain change cannot be achieved because the computer programs cannot be changed.

APPLICATION BACKLOG

In most well-managed corporations the demand for new applications is rising faster than DP can supply them. The imbalance between demand and supply is steadily becoming worse. Because of this, the backlog of needed applications is growing. One New York bank executive informed us that the bank's *effective* backlog was seven years. An airline DP executive said his backlog was 1500 person years. Faster and better methods of creating applications must be found.

BOX 17.1   Problems with computing

Problems of Computing As Seen by Users and Management

- They cannot obtain applications when they want them. There is often a delay of years.

- It is difficult or impossible to obtain changes they need in a reasonable amount of time.

- The programs have errors in them or sometimes do not work.

- Systems delivered often do not match the true user requirements.

- It is difficult to understand DP and communicate precise requirements.

- Specifications, on which they have to sign off, are difficult to check.

- Systems cost much more to develop and to maintain than anticipated.

Technical Problems that Cause the Concerns Listed Above

- Programming in conventional languages takes too long.

- Program testing takes too long.

- After testing too many subtle errors remain.

- Vendors' software is of poor quality.

- Systems software causes many problems and consumes too much of the machine's resources.

- Programs do not match specifications. There are misinterpretations.

- Specifications do not match requirements. There are misinterpretations.

- Requirements are always changing—even after the specifications become frozen.

- Users do not check and understand the details of specifications before coding begins.

- Specifications are verbose, ambiguous, incomplete, unspecific, inconsistent, incorrect.

- When programs are maintained the specifications are not updated correspondingly.

- Structured techniques have not improved productivity sufficiently.

- Different programmers have different ideas of structured programming.

- The design of programs is not rigorous.

BOX 17.1 (*continued*)

- Usage and modification of variables are not traceable.
- Seeming small changes to programs set off chain reactions of problems.
- Maintenance successively degrades the code quality.
- The design tools and languages are not integrated.
- Methodologies are not integrated.
- There are many interface problems among separately developed systems, and even between modules within programs.
- There is excessive redundancy in program functions.
- There is no organization-wide data planning.
- The same data are represented incompatibly in different systems.
- Programs are not transferrable.
- There is a lack of understanding of newer, better methodologies.
- There is resistance to new methodologies and adherence to obsolete ones.
- The DP standards manual enforces old, inappropriate techniques.
- An excessive bureaucracy has grown up around old-fashioned methods.
- Managers operate constantly in fire-brigade mode because of problems listed above.
- Managers tied down by detail are unable to plan better ways of operating.

The long backlog and inability of computer departments to respond to end users' needs quickly is very frustrating for them. In many cases the end users have felt that they cannot wait and have obtained their own departmental minicomputer or microcomputers.

INVISIBLE BACKLOG　　　　Even though today's application backlogs are so long, they reveal only part of the story. When the documented backlog is several years (as it is in most installations), the end users do not even consider making requests for many of the applications they need. There is thus an *invisible backlog*.

The invisible backlog cannot easily be measured. Its size is indicated in those installations where end users have acquired a capability to develop their own application quickly. Such examples indicate that the *invisible backlog* is often larger than the *documented backlog*.

The Sloan Business School set out to measure the invisible application backlog in typical Fortune 500 corporations [2]. It concluded that in the organizations it studied the invisible backlog was about 168% of the formal measured backlog. In other words, many users need applications that would be valuable to them, but do not ask for them because of the DP overload.

THE NEED FOR VASTLY IMPROVED PRODUCTIVITY

User demands will become worse. Computing power is dropping in cost rapidly, and end users are becoming much more knowledgeable about how they could use computers. The more computers drop in cost, the more end users are challenged to put them to work to improve their decision-making capabilities and power, eliminate time-wasting paperwork, improve productivity, and build more advanced facilities.

End users from scientists to clerks are improving their ideas about how computers could help them. The problem is that until recently most of these ideas could not be implemented because the processes of systems analysis and programming were too slow. Most application programs are individually designed and hand coded with very slow methods. Imagine the automobile industry if cars were still built by craftsmen with hand tools. Most organizations have not yet reached the era of the Model T Ford in application creation.

Application programming is one of the most labor-intensive jobs known. We are now beginning to perceive how to automate much of it. To do so we need better software, which is becoming available. We also need new approaches to the analysis and design of information systems. To change the building of cars from individual hand-tooling to mass production needed a substantial infrastructure to be put into place. The same is true with the move to information system automation. The necessary infrastructure takes some time to build and costs money (though not much compared with the maintenance and hand-crafting of earlier systems).

In the next 10 years computers, on average, will increase in speed by a factor of 10 or more. If the most advanced goals of the Japanese and others are realized, the increase will be 1000 or more, this large number being made possible by highly parallel architectures incorporating many processors which are cheaply mass-produced. As computers plunge in cost, many more will be sold. The number of applications in today's data processing centers is growing by 45% per year, according to an IBM survey. Ten years' growth at 45% multiples the number of applications by 41.1. At the same time the number of installations is growing greatly because of small cheap mainframes, minicomputers, and desktop machines.

Most estimates of future computing power indicate that the *productivity of application development needs to increase by two orders of magnitude* in the next 10 years.

INSUFFICIENT IMPROVEMENTS FROM STRUCTURED TECHNIQUES

The main hope for improving programming productivity in the 1970s was *structured techniques*. We can now survey extensive experience with the techniques advocated by Yourdon, Constantine, Gane and Sarson, Michael Jackson, and others. Research into the impact of these techniques shows that there are few installations where the move to structured programming by itself gives an overall programming productivity increase of greater than 25% [3]. Usually, it is less. In installations where it is used well, Jackson methodology [4] appears to give a better improvement than other forms of structured programming which are in common use. Structured analysis as commonly practiced usually takes longer than conventional systems analysis (albeit for good reason). It is clear that much better techniques are both possible and essential as computers continue to plunge in cost.

The effectiveness of the move to conventional structured techniques is addressed in extensive research done by T. C. Jones [3]. He divides programming productivity improvements into four ranges and discusses what techniques have achieved improvements within these ranges:

1. Improving Productivity up to 25%

Most of the success stories and firm evidence of productivity improvement with conventional languages lie in the 25% range. Often the baseline for comparison is programs which are unstructured, designed in a bottom-up fashion, with no formal reviews or inspections prior to testing, and no use of interactive methods. If this is the starting point, almost *any* step toward structured techniques or interactive development will give results. These results are rarely more than a 25% improvement (if there is no change in language and no move to programmers of greater talent).

Small programs written by individual programmers benefit from interactive methods [5]. Large programs needing multiple programmers benefit from the better discipline of structured methods [6, 7] and from inspections [8].

2. Improving Productivity by 25 to 50%

Achieving more than a 25% improvement is more difficult because programming is so labor-intensive. Real people in real life, Jones concludes, cannot move a great deal faster than they already do. To achieve more than 25% improvement requires techniques that replace human effort in some way.

Jones concludes: "It can almost definitely be stated that no *single technique* by itself can improve productivity at the 50% level for programs larger than trivial ones," except for a change in programming language. Jones stated that there are a few success stories at the 35 to 40% improvement level. Sometimes these related to an unusually backward installation so that the improvement looked better than it perhaps should have.

3. Improving Productivity by 50 to 75%

Jones concluded that there are only two general ways to achieve programming productivity gains that approach 75%:

(a) Search out those programmers and analysts who have exceptionally high personal achievement. There are a few isolated stories of abnormally high productivity, such as the programming of the New York Times information system (87,000 instructions in one year by three people: Harlan Mills, Terry Baker, and an assistant who checked the code). This is a productivity four or five times higher than the norm. It is sometimes quoted as a triumph of structured programming, which it is, but it is more a triumph of selecting brilliant individuals and giving them the fullest support.

(b) Use program generators, very high level languages, shared systems, or other forms of program *acquisition* in place of program *development*.

4. High Productivity Gains

In stark contrast to the surveys of programmer productivity improvement are the results that have been achieved with data-base user languages, report generators, graphics packages, and application generators. With these, productivity improvements of over 1000% are not uncommon [10]. Unfortunately, they can generate only certain well-defined classes of applications. Code generators are needed which generate much broader ranges of software.

HOW TO IMPROVE PRODUCTIVITY

There is a major imbalance of supply and demand in computer applications. Box 17.2 lists approaches which are important in improving the productivity of creating applications.

This box does not mention structured programming. This is not because we have anything against structuring programs; *structured programs are clearly much better than nonstructured ones*. However, structured programming as commonly practiced has been demonstrated to increase productivity much less than is needed. The way to change productivity is to *avoid* hand coding in languages such as COBOL, FORTRAN, and Ada. DP organizations should be seeking every opportunity to avoid writing such programs.

Not only do the so-called structured techniques have too small an effect on productivity; they also have too small an effect on the numbers of errors made. The techniques described in this book are an advanced form of structured design. They have a major effect on errors and the subsequent costs of testing, reprogramming, retrofitting, and maintenance. By comparison the methods of the so-called "structured revolution" are ill-structured. Perhaps we should refer to "structured techniques" that lack rigor as "ill-structured structured techniques."

MAINTENANCE

The problems of DP and software development are made worse by the maintenance problem. The term "maintenance" is used to refer to the rewriting of old programs to make them accommodate new requirements or make them work with changed system resources. Reprogramming is often needed because separately developed programs do not fit together, or interface problems exist when data are passed from one system to another. A needed change in one program sets off a whole chain reaction of changes that have to be made to other programs.

Maintenance, if not consciously controlled, tends to rise as the numbers of programs grow. The interactions among programs grow roughly as the square of the number of programs, unless deliberately controlled.

The growing maintenance burden greatly worsens the application backlog. In many organizations, and often those moving fastest into on-line and interactive systems, the ratio of maintenance activity to new application development has reached 80%. Large corporations often have some systems or application areas where 100% of the programmer effort is spent on maintenance.

It is often thought by systems analysts that existing programs that work well can be left alone. In reality, the data such programs create or use are needed by other applications and are almost always needed in a slightly different form, unless thorough logical data-base analysis has been performed.

The maintenance mess has become a nightmare in some large corporations. It is alarming to reflect what it would be like 20 years from now if more and more applications and systems were added with conventional methodologies.

Under appropriate conditions, microbes can multiply exponentially like today's computers. But if they multiply when shut in an enclosed laboratory dish, they eventually drown in their own excrement. One top DP executive compared this to his maintenance problems. New growth, he said, was being stifled by the use of old COBOL and PL/1 systems. If new techniques were not widely accepted and used, the programming team would eventually drown in its own maintenance.

IMPROVEMENTS IN PRODUCTIVITY

Early experiences with the HOS tools show major increases in application development productivity. There are several reasons for this:

1. Highly complex specifications can be made consistent, unambiguous and error-free.

2. Most programming is avoided; the code is automatically generated.

3. Most dynamic testing and error correction, which consumes so much time, is avoided.

4. When an error is corrected or a change is made, the effects of this on other parts of

BOX 17.2 How to improve program development productivity

- Automation of code generation; avoidance of manual coding in languages such as COBOL, FORTRAN, and Ada whenever possible
- Discovery of errors as early as possible in the development cycle
- Elimination of as many errors as possible by techniques that give provably correct logic
- Replacement of dynamic program testing with static verification whenever possible
- Verification of design at the design phase
- Employment of end-user languages where possible (e.g., query languages, report generator, application generators) where these can give results that do not lack integrity
- Use by systems analysts of the highest-level nonprocedural languages and techniques
- Prevention of mismatches between requirements and specifications
- Prevention of mismatches between specifications and program creation
- Use of a single, common, user-friendly language for stating requirements, specifications, and implementation
- Avoidance of redundant development of operations and functions
- Use of a library system that solves interface problems and enables developers to employ easily operations, functions, and data which have been designed and verified previously
- Use of self-documenting techniques
- Use of techniques that make all use of variables and operations traceable
- Use of techniques and tools that make modifications and maintenance easier
- Conversion of systems with expensive maintenance using techniques that drastically reduce maintenance costs
- Competent organization-wide data administration which produces sound stable data models
- Automation of data modeling and generation of implementers' data
- Organization-wide strategic data planning to prevent the spread of incompatible data
- Use of the most powerful data-base techniques
- Prevention of interface problems among separately developed systems
- Avoidance of systems analysis techniques which are slow, nonrigorous, and lead to ambiguity
- Change of the development life cycle to incorporate the highest-productivity methods, automation of techniques where possible, formal verification of design up front, and thorough data administration

the system are *rigorously* detected and quickly modified, with the graphics editor and ANALYZER.

5. The control maps, although they become large and complex, are highly modular and are created and manipulated quickly and easily with the graphics editor.

6. *Defined operations* and *defined structures* are created to form a powerful macrolanguage for specific application areas or system viewpoints.

7. The library facility largely eliminates interface problems among separately created system modules.

8. The library facility encourages the maximum repetitive use of code modules and the minimum redundant code creation.

9. Complex systems have been specified by one person, thus avoiding the problems that are associated with large teams.

One simple application of USE.IT was the design of a digital clock [11]. This was used as a test case to compare conventional programming with USE.IT development. An exceptionally high-speed programmer tackled the problem with FORTRAN. He claimed to be a 5000-line-per-month programmer. The Department of Defense statistics for FORTRAN coding shows an average of 200 lines per month, so he had a capability perhaps an order of magnitude better than the average. He took 3 full man-days. With USE.IT the HOS staff took 4 hours.

The Butler design of buildings illustrated in Chapter 9 resulted in 10,000 lines of FORTRAN. This was generated by one person in 11 days. This averages 909 lines of code per day, as opposed to the Department of Defense's average of 10 lines of code per day. The DOD average, however, covers only programming and testing, whereas this example covers specification, design, and generation of provably correct code. The person in question was brilliant and highly motivated but *had never programmed*, and *had no computer experience* except with the HOS tools. He was a musician who ran a rock band and also operated his own moving company. The staff who developed the radar scheduler example in Chapter 9 generated an average of 300 lines of code per day—30 times the speed of the average Department of Defense programmer.

There are now many nonprocedural languages and code generators in use. It is typical to observe an order-of-magnitude improvement in productivity with the good ones [10]. USE.IT seems to give similar improvements. However, most generators generate relatively simple applications, whereas USE.IT can generate exceedingly complex logic.

COST SAVINGS　　　　Figure 17.1 shows a typical breakdown of classical life-cycle costs for a large software project [12]. Employing the HOS software, programming (which is only 18.5% of the costs in Fig. 17.1) disappears. Verification and testing costs would be drastically reduced by employing the HOS software. Let us assume that it is cut by 75% (assuming that 25% are conceptual errors of the designers which cannot be caught by

PERCENTAGE OF COSTS

	DEVELOPMENT EFFORT	FINDING AND FIXING ERRORS	TOTAL
INITIAL DEVELOPMENT			
Specification and Design	5	5	10
Programming	5		5
Verification and Testing		10	10
TOTAL	10	15	25
MAINTENANCE			
Residual Errors		7.5	7.5
Specification and Design	13.5	13.5	27
Programming	13.5		13.5
Verification and Testing		27	27
TOTAL	27	48	75
OVERALL TOTAL	37	63	100

Figure 17.1   Classical life-cycle costs. (Derived from Ref. 12.)

PERCENTAGE OF COSTS

	DEVELOPMENT EFFORT		FINDING AND FIXING ERRORS		TOTAL	
INITIAL DEVELOPMENT						
Specification and Design	5	2.5	5	1.25	10	3.75
Programming	5	0			5	0
Verification and Testing			10	2.5	10	2.5
TOTAL	10	2.5	15	3.75	25	6.25
MAINTENANCE						
Residual Errors			7.5	1.875	7.5	1.875
Specification and Design	13.5	6.75	13.5	3.375	27	10.125
Programming	13.5	0			13.5	0
Verification and Testing			27	6.75	27	6.75
TOTAL	27	6.75	48	12	75	18.75
OVERALL TOTAL	37	9.25	63	15.75	100	25

Figure 17.2   Estimated reduction in life-cycle costs when using the software described in Chapter 8 are shown in red. Three-fourths of the total project cost is saved.

mathematical rigor). Much of the time the customer does not get what is really needed because these needs are not adequately communicated to the developer. The top-to-bottom communication of HOS, speeded up by the graphics editor, has cut the specification and design costs by half on some early examples which appear representative.

Using these figures, the resulting cost savings are shown in Fig. 17.2. Three quarters of the life-cycle costs are saved. Such figures are likely to vary substantially from one project to another. On some projects development programming and maintenance programming account for much more than 18.5% of the total costs, and here the savings might be a higher proportion.

THE EFFECT OF PROGRAM SIZE

Lower programmer productivity is achieved with large programs than with small programs. Figure 17.3 shows a typical distribution. The productivity achieved with superlarge programs is almost one-tenth of that achieved with small programs [5].

There are several reasons why productivity with large programs is worse than with small ones. First, the programming team is larger. This requires more formal interaction between people and gives more scope for miscommunication. There is substantial overhead required to fit together all the pieces of a large program.

Small programs are often created by one person who has all the pieces in his head. With large systems, planning and paperwork is needed to control the development cycle. The various forms of paperwork with large systems sometimes contain an aggregate of over 50 English words for each line of source code in the system [12, 13].

In large systems where the programmer works on one project for more than a year, his interest and productivity often decline substantially. On a small program the programmer can keep working fast to complete the work quickly.

The testing is disproportionately time consuming with very large programs. The number of combinations that need to be tested tend to increase roughly as the square of the program size. The problems with interfaces between modules become numerous and severe on large programs. Saturation testing becomes lengthy and unsatisfactory in that many bugs are not found. When a bug is corrected it can have unforeseen consequences in other parts of the program, which in turn are difficult to find.

The HOS technique has a direct effect on all of these problems. It rigorously controls the interfaces among modules. The modules fit together in a provably correct fashion. The generation of code is so much faster than hand coding that a large team of people is not needed. One person can replace 10 programmers. Three people can replace a team of 30. This shrinkage greatly reduces the problems of communication among people. The different members of the team all interact with the same graphics representation and library. When any change is made,

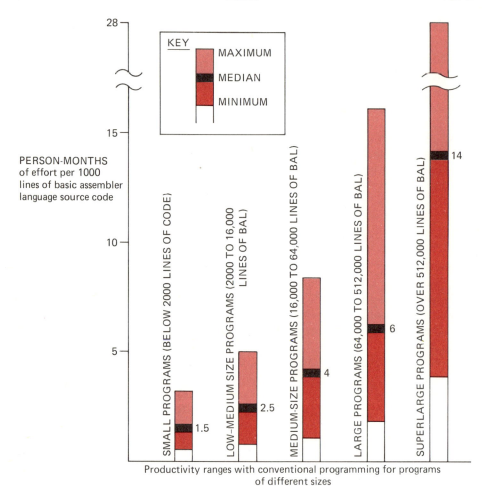

28 —

KEY

MAXIMUM

MEDIAN

MINIMUM

15 —

PERSON-MONTHS
of effort per 1000
lines of basic assembler
language source code

10 —

5 —

SMALL PROGRAMS (BELOW 2000 LINES OF CODE)

LOW-MEDIUM SIZE PROGRAMS (2000 TO 16,000 LINES OF BAL)

MEDIUM-SIZE PROGRAMS (16,000 TO 64,000 LINES OF BAL)

LARGE PROGRAMS (64,000 TO 512,000 LINES OF BAL)

SUPERLARGE PROGRAMS (OVER 512,000 LINES OF BAL)

1.5

2.5

4

6

14

Productivity ranges with conventional programming for programs
of different sizes

Figure 17.3   Lower programmer productivity is achieved with large programs
than with small programs. (From Ref. 5.)

the consequences of that are automatically shown on the screen and can be quickly
adjusted. The finding of most errors is brought to the front of the development
cycle. Saturation testing is largely replaced by static verification. Individual modules, or portions of the system with missing modules, can be tested on-line in a
simulated fashion.

In a typical large development project a programmer sits at his desk and is
greeted each morning with a set of memos or documents about changes. He often
regards them cynically feeling that he has neither the time to read them nor the
ability to remember to react to them. Somebody, he hopes, is filing them. With

HOS, change control is largely automatic. The areas affected by each change are revealed automatically and the system ensures that all consequential adjustments are made. These adjustments then reside in the on-line graphic representation of the system which every developer uses.

ONE-PERSON PROJECTS

There is much to be said in all complex human endeavor for having one-person projects. If one-person projects are practical, that one person can be carefully selected, motivated, and measured. He is responsible for his own work and can become excited about it. He has no excuses about other team members lessening his effectiveness. He cannot pass the buck. He is more likely to be proud of his work. The large overhead of human communication, and error correction caused by it, is avoided.

With nonprocedural languages and code generators, many team programming efforts shrink to one-person projects. This can be enhanced by firm high-quality data administration techniques [14].

Tools that give a person the power to build systems by himself greatly encourage his creativity. He can have ideas and make them work. He is cut free from bureaucratic inhibitions.

AVOIDING MISMATCHES BETWEEN DESIGN LEVELS

A major reason for problems in traditional program development is that the specifications are incomplete and inconsistent. There is often a misinterpretation as requirements are translated into detailed specifications, specifications are translated into designs, and designs are translated into program code.

The HOS methodology overcomes most of the misinterpretation problems by having one language and diagramming technique for requirements, specifications, and design. Indeed, it becomes impossible to distinguish sharply between these activities. The process starts with a high-level overview and successively breaks it down into finer detail until code can be generated.

At each step the ANALYZER enforces consistency in the control maps. These must be consistent and internally complete before they are accepted into the library. As more detail is worked out it often reveals incompleteness higher in the control map. New variables are needed which must be inputs from the top.

A rigorous specification is seldom created in one shot. There will be much successive refinement as the system is steadily broken down into more detail. Different persons are likely to be involved at different levels of detail. All use the same type of chart. At the highest level the chart has relatively few blocks which represent the broad requirements of the system.

Suppose that we want to build a circulation system for a magazine. We might ask the management: "What do you need in a circulation system?" The management says that the system must be concerned with circulation information and advertizing information. Subscriptions will be processed and stored in a circulation data base. An advertizing data base will be used together with this to generate analysis reports. This requirement is drawn as follows:

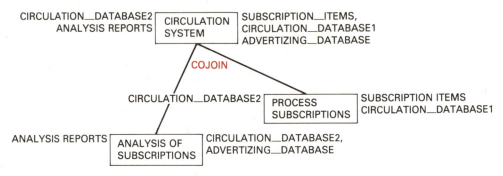

The requirements analyst might ask: "What does ANALYSIS OF SUB-SCRIPTIONS consist of?" Management replies that there must be advertizing analysis as well as subscriber analysis. "Do they relate?" Yes. Subscriber statistics are needed in order to do the advertizing analysis. The analyst adds this to the chart:

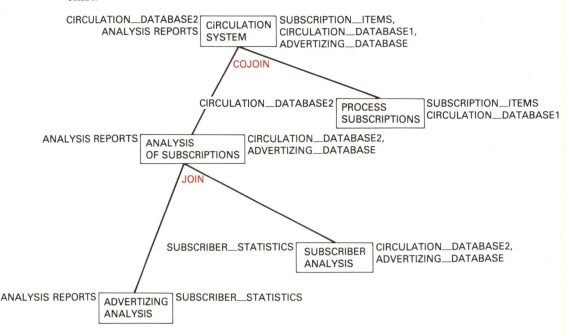

The analyst breaks down the PROCESS SUBSCRIPTIONS block as follows:

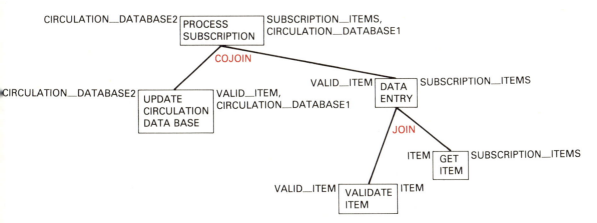

"What type of subscriber statistics are needed?" The new subscriptions are of four types: *renewals, gift subscriptions, special offers*, and *regular subscriptions*. A breakdown of these is needed in order to analyze the effectiveness of the advertizing. "What about cancellations?" Yes, we must also have statistics on those.

UPDATE CIRCULATION DATA BASE must be decomposed to reflect the different item types. These are all processed differently. The analyst draws the following:

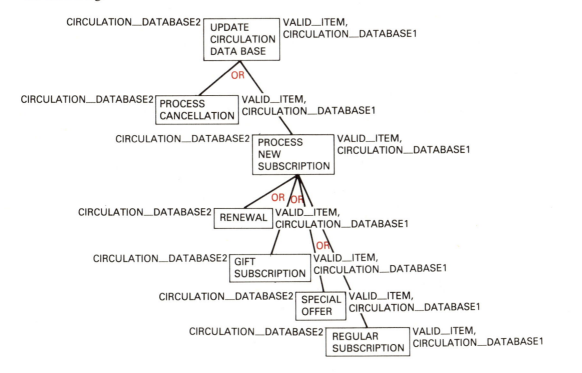

REQUIREMENTS ANALYST AND DETAIL ANALYST

The ANALYZER software would reject the preceding diagram because the OR control structures do not yet have the requisite Booleans. More detail is needed to correct this. The HOS software assists the designer by selecting the co-control structures that would be valid. A *requirements analyst* might at this point want to work with a *detail analyst*, who quickly adds to the control map the detail required to make it acceptable to the ANALYZER.

A good way to organize the HOS development team is to have requirements analysts and detail analysts. The requirements analyst works with users and management to understand their needs. He creates broad specifications like the above, and documents them with the HOS software, as in Fig. 8.5. This is an alternative to our earlier suggestion of one-person projects. It has the advantage that it separates the talents of the high-level requirements analyst and the detail implementor while using a rigorous technique to prevent communication problems. He may employ other front-end analysis methods which are represented with HOS defined structures and defined operations. He uses the HOS charts as a precise way to think about systems and hands them over to a detail analyst to develop them to the stage where they can be RATted. The detail analyst comes back to the requirements analyst with questions and adjusted charts from the graphics software until their interaction results in a complete and correct set of control maps.

SUMMARY OF THE EFFECTS OF THE METHODOLOGY

Box 17.3 summarizes the effects of the HOS methodology. To achieve good results, a variety of changes in DP management are needed. These are discussed in the following chapter. The software development life cycle needs to be substantially changed.

Many of the best results from HOS techniques are often achieved with people who are not programmers. New graduates often learn the technique more quickly. Experienced programmers and analysts have much to *unlearn* in using the technique. They tend, often subconsciously, to map it against old familiar methods to which it does not relate.

When organizations experiment with the technique, they should be aware of this culture-shock phenomenon and select staff who have the ingenuity to adapt to new techniques quickly, and employ new graduates, perhaps from business schools, to develop the first systems. The results can then be measured.

HOS VERSUS OTHER PRODUCTIVITY TOOLS

In the last few years a variety of application generators and high-productivity languages have come into use [15]. How does USE-IT relate to these other tools for solving DP problems?

In selecting productivity tools one wants to be

BOX 17.3 Advantages of HOS methodology

Problems With Traditional Development	*Effects of the Methodology in This Book*
Development takes too long.	Development is much faster.
Development costs are too high.	Major reduction in development costs.
Programming is manual.	Programming is automatic.
Most errors are found *after* coding.	Most errors are found *before* implementation.
Most errors are found manually or by *dynamic* runs.	Most errors are found by *automatic* and *static* analysis.
Some errors are *never* found.	Almost all errors are found.
Mismatch between requirements and specifications. Mismatch between specifications and design. Mismatch between design and coding.	Each level is a precise expansion of the previous level.
Incomplete specifications Inconsistent specifications	Internally complete, consistent specifications are enforced.
Many interface errors and mismatches between subsystems (73% of the errors on Project Apollo).	Rigorous, provably correct, interfaces between subsystems.
No guarantee of function integrity after implementation.	Guarantee of function integrity after implementation.
Large developer teams: severe communication problems.	Small or one-person teams: few communication problems.
Massive paperwork for management control.	Elimination of most paperwork.
Much redundant code development.	Identification of common modules. Use of common modules made easy.
Separate developers reinventing the wheel.	Library mechanism with rigorous interfaces encourages the building of reusable constructs.
Difficult to maintain.	Easy to maintain.
Modifications trigger chain reactions of new bugs.	The effects of all modifications are made explicit and clear.
Successive maintenance degrades the code quality.	High-quality code is regenerated after each change.
Portability problems.	A design can be re-RATted to different environments.

able to build computer systems and software that is reasonably efficient *with the minimum amount of work*. Debugging and maintenance problems cause a severe amount of work and need to be included in the overall assessment of effort.

For simple applications such as producing a report or chart, the nonprocedural report generators give results very quickly. For somewhat more involved applications such as processing orders or creating invoices, the application generators give fast results. However, for complex applications such as electronic fund transfer networks, radar systems, process control, vehicle scheduling, or applications involving intricate logic, the application generators are not usable. Here we need a tool that enables us to generate consistent, logically correct, and complete specifications, and convert these specifications into code. For these more complex applications USE-IT, at the time of writing, has no competition.

In the world of fourth-generation languages and generators it is important to select the right tool for a given task. An attempt to build a system with an inappropriate tool can be disastrous. The range of systems for which USE-IT would be the best choice would be greatly extended if USE-IT encompassed the powerful techniques for report generation, screen painting, data-base manipulation, etc., which are found in the nonprocedural languages. We will discuss this in the next chapter.

REFERENCES

1. P. R. Mimno, *Mathematically Provable Software: A Major New Technology*, Higher Order Software, Inc., Cambridge, MA, 1982.

2. R. B. Rosenberger, "The Information Center," *Proceedings, SHARE No. 56*, Session M372, March 1981.

3. T. Capers Jones, "The Limits to Programming Productivity," *Guide and Share Application Development Symposium, Proceedings*, Share, New York, 1979.

4. M. Jackson, *Principles of Program Design*, Academic Press, Inc. (London) Ltd., London, 1977.

5. G. W. Willett et al., *TSO Productivity Study*, American Telephone and Telegraph Long Lines, Kansas City, April 1973.

6. P. Freeman and A. I. Wasserman, *Tutorial on Software Design Techniques*, IEEE Computer Society Cat. No. 76CH1145-2, 1977.

7. C. V. Ramamoorthy and H. H. So, "Survey of Principles and Techniques of Software Requirements and Specifications, *Software Engineering Techniques 2*," Invited papers, Infotech International Ltd., Nicholson House, Maidenhead, Berkshire, UK, 1977, pp. 265–318.

8. M. E. Fagan, "Design and Code Inspections to Reduce Errors in Program Development," *IBM Systems Journal*, Vol. 15, No. 3 (1976). (Reprint Order No. G321-5033.)

9. J. Fox, *Software and Its Development*, Prentice-Hall, Inc., Englewood Cliffs, NJ, 1982.

10. James Martin, *Application Development Without Programmers*, Prentice-Hall, Inc., Englewood Cliffs, NJ, 1982.

11. *Annotated Model of a Digital Clock*, Educational Series 1, Higher Order Software, Inc., Cambridge, MA, May 1982.

12. D. K. Lloyd and M. Lipow, *Reliability: Management Methods and Mathematics*, Prentice-Hall, Inc., Englewood Cliffs, NJ, 1972.

13. T. C. Jones, "Optimizing Program Quality and Programmer Productivity," *Guide 45, Proceedings*, Atlanta, GA, November 1977.

14. T. C. Jones, "A Survey of Programming Design and specification Techniques," *IEEE Symposium on Specifications of Reliable Software*, April 1979, IEEE Order No. 79CH1401-9C.

15. *The Martin Report on High-Productivity Languages,* Washington Street, Marblehead, MA.

18 THE CHANGING DEVELOPMENT LIFE CYCLE

INTRODUCTION   It is clear that use of the HOS methodology completely changes the traditional development life cycle.

The life cycle was illustrated in Fig. 1.2. Various organizations have their own version of it. Figures 18.1 and 18.2 show two of them.

Formal management of system development requires that certain documents are created and reviews are conducted at each stage. The phases of the life cycle are decomposed into subcycles and checklists as illustrated in Fig. 18.3. These components of the cycle are important for telling development staff what to do, giving them guidelines, and ensuring that nothing important is forgotten.

Management standards associated with the life cycle have acquired the force of law in many organizations. Some corporations refer to their development life cycle manual as the *Bible* of DP. It has become heresy to suggest that this Bible is wrong and that things should be done differently. And yet there are obviously great problems associated with the traditional life cycle, as illustrated in Box 18.1. The historical life cycle grew up before the following tools and techniques existed:

- Nonprocedural languages
- Techniques that generate program code automatically
- Computable specification languages
- Rigorous verification techniques
- On-line graphics tools for design
- Formal data modeling tools
- Strategic data planning techniques
- Languages for rapid prototyping
- Languages for end users

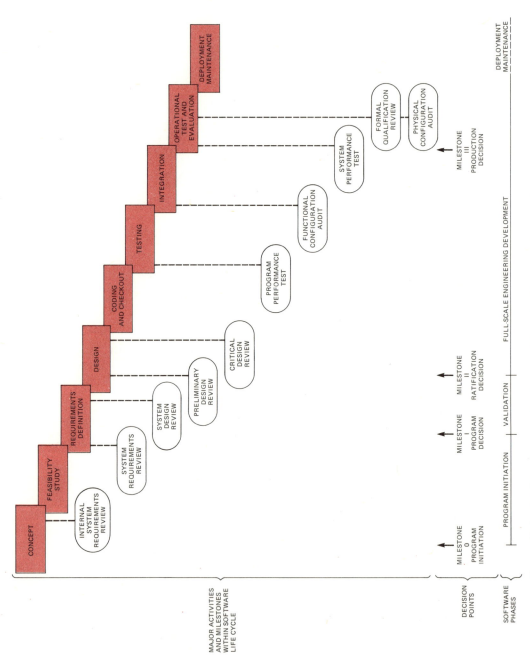

Figure 18.1 Traditional system development life cycle. The reviews and milestones shown here are those required in the U.S. Department of Defense.

SYSTEM DEVELOPMENT LIFE CYCLE

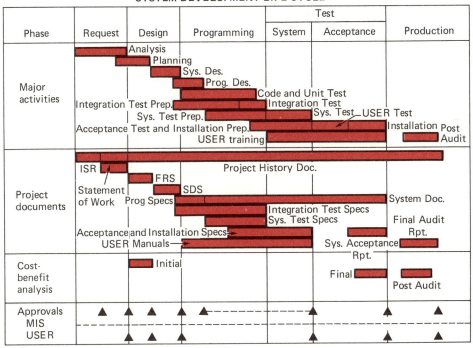

Figure 18.2   System development life cycle in a DP standards document of a large aerospace corporation.

- Distributed processing
- The information center concept
- The personal computer

All of these tools and techniques have a major impact on the effectiveness of computer usage. Any one of them would change the historical life cycle. In combination they render it obsolete. It needs complete redesign, retaining those checklist items that ensure thorough planning. At each stage the life cycle needs to be reexamined to *maximize the degree of automation* of systems engineering, *build in thorough data modeling* which is often independent of specific projects, ensure flexibility so that systems can be *easily changed when necessary*, and provide end users with facilities for *extracting and themselves manipulating* the information they need.

With HOS software, the program coding phase disappears, testing and integration testing are radically changed and shortened, and the requirements, specification, and design of the logic are completely changed and integrated.

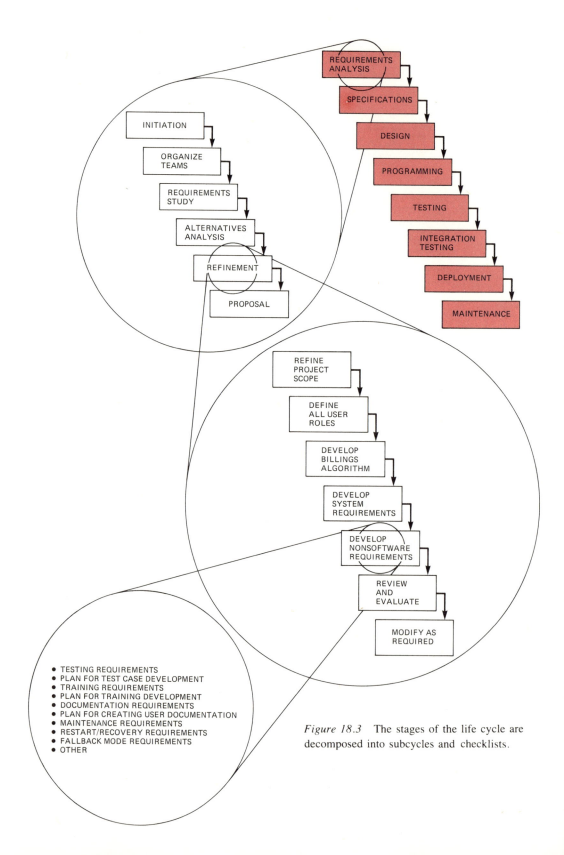

Figure 18.3 The stages of the life cycle are decomposed into subcycles and checklists.

REQUIREMENTS ANALYSIS

SPECIFICATIONS

DESIGN

PROGRAMMING

TESTING

INTEGRATION TESTING

DEPLOYMENT

MAINTENANCE

INITIATION

ORGANIZE TEAMS

REQUIREMENTS STUDY

ALTERNATIVES ANALYSIS

REFINEMENT

PROPOSAL

REFINE PROJECT SCOPE

DEFINE ALL USER ROLES

DEVELOP BILLINGS ALGORITHM

DEVELOP SYSTEM REQUIREMENTS

DEVELOP NONSOFTWARE REQUIREMENTS

REVIEW AND EVALUATE

MODIFY AS REQUIRED

- TESTING REQUIREMENTS
- PLAN FOR TEST CASE DEVELOPMENT
- TRAINING REQUIREMENTS
- PLAN FOR TRAINING DEVELOPMENT
- DOCUMENTATION REQUIREMENTS
- PLAN FOR CREATING USER DOCUMENTATION
- MAINTENANCE REQUIREMENTS
- RESTART/RECOVERY REQUIREMENTS
- FALLBACK MODE REQUIREMENTS
- OTHER

Box 18.1   What do we need in DP methodologies?

- *Automation*. As much as possible of the analysts' and programmers' jobs should be automated.

- *Avoidance of hand programming*. Hand programming is too slow, clumsy, and error-prone. The maximum use should be made of code generators.

- *Speed*. Techniques are needed that obtain results very quickly.

- *Changeability*. Techniques are needed that enable programs to be changed quickly without the cost and slowness of traditional maintenance.

- *Verification of correctness*. All syntax and internal semantics errors should be caught automatically. Maximum assistance should be provided in catching external semantics errors easily.

- *Avoidance of most dynamic testing*. Dynamic testing is slow, expensive, and does not catch all errors.

- *Techniques that facilitate communication with end users*. The knowledge of the users must be harnessed and their needs responded to flexibly. Users should be able to check every stage of system evolution.

- *User-driven computing*. Users should be able to employ their own query and update languages, report generators, decision-support languages, and specification languages.

- *Stable data-base design*. Automation of data modeling is necessary, linked to techniques to make the data bases a stable foundation stone.

- *Fast data-base languages*. Languages should be adopted that enable new information to be extracted from the data bases for management immediately when they need it.

- *Enterprise-wide data planning*. Data should be planned to avoid the Tower of Babel effect of different analysts creating the same data incompatibly.

- *Overview planning*. Complex organizations need overview planning for converting to and streamlining on-line procedures.

- *Aids to eliminate redundancy*. A methodology is needed that avoids redundant development and reinventing the wheel.

- *Modularity*. Systems should be divided into easily comprehensible modules. Changes should be able to be made locally *within* a module. Any effect of changes outside a module should be *rigorously* traceable.

- *Control of interoperability*. A formal, rigorous technique is needed to ensure that separately developed systems and modules operate together correctly.

- *Truly usable library control*. There should be an ever-growing library of program modules with a methodology for making these known to and usable by all developers.

BOX 18.1 (*continued*)

- *Automated change control.* When changes are made the consequences of these should be revealed automatically and the complete set of consequential corrections should be represented in the library.

- *Evolving power.* The methodology should encourage an evolving set of more powerful mechanisms, built with lower-level mechanisms.

- *Alternate dialects.* Alternate means for conceptualizing, drawing, and designing systems may be permitted where helpful and converted automatically to the standard representation.

- *An integrated set of tools.* Tools that achieve the objectives listed above should work together and avoid manual bridges which introduce errors. They should use common syntax and graphics where possible.

ARGUMENT AGAINST CHANGE

Many computer executives hear the reasons for change but do not know what to do about it. They have too much invested in present systems to be able to change, or so they think. This argument becomes worse with time as more becomes invested, and the old systems become more difficult to change.

This argument is a lethal trap. The old systems become steadily worse and DP becomes even more unable to respond to needs for changes and new systems. Newcomers have a major competitive edge by moving directly into high-productivity techniques.

The solution in most established organizations is to set up separate systems development groups charged with investigating the latest highest-productivity methods and using them on certain selected new systems. The intention is that this new-technology group shall grow, finding the best methods and using them on increasing numbers of systems. The old-methodology group should be steadily migrated across to new techniques. As old systems become too expensive to maintain, or need major changes, they are rebuilt with high-productivity methods.

THE METHODOLOGY ZOO

Realizing the seriousness of the problems in Box 17.1, many organizations have undertaken to create and sell "methodologies" for system planning and development. Methodologies are sold by manufacturers, software houses, consultants, accounting firms, university professors, and new companies formed for this purpose. Managers reading *Computerworld* are confronted with such a zoo of methodologies that they often ignore them all and continue to work with techniques with which they are familiar.

Many of the methodologies are utterly obsolete, including some of those with high prices, voluminous documentation, and impressive salespeople. To use them guarantees low productivity, high maintenance costs, and inability to change. They formalize the ways of the past, fail to automate system development, and encourage excessive, unnecessary bureaucracy.

The DP executive should be aware that computing is going through the greatest changes in its history and should meticulously avoid methodologies that fossilize the manually oriented techniques of the past.

What should a manager look for in new methodologies? Above all, *automation*. We must automate the job of the analyst and programmer as fully as possible. It is sometimes commented that systems analysts are prone to automate every job except their own. This automation needs to harness the knowledge of end users, communicate well with the end users, and be adaptable to their changing needs in a flexible fashion.

LIFE-CYCLE STAFFING

In the traditional life cycle the number of persons employed grows toward the end of the cycle as shown in Fig. 18.4. There are more programmers than specifiers, and much effort is needed in testing. Sometimes concern builds up about a project slipping its schedule and additional programmers are added late in the cycle (often with disastrous results).

Structured analysis grew up in the 1970s because of concern that the front end of the cycle was inadequate. It was clear that poor quality and incomplete specifications were giving rise to inappropriate coding. Poorly defined specifications cause the wrong thing to be coded, make testing difficult, destroy management control, and often cause project failures.

The analysis phase was often glossed over because it did not lend itself to the use of precise tools such as programming languages. As more precise tools and techniques have evolved, more attention has been paid to front-end analysis. The shape of Fig. 18.4 changed somewhat. More effort at the front resulted in less effort at the end. Structured analysis, however, was still far from being a precise discipline. It is only with computable specification languages that we begin to see high precision at the front end. This has a high payoff at the back end and substantially shortens the entire cycle.

Figure 18.5 shows the timing and people consumption with an HOS life cycle. Program coding has disappeared. Program testing has been reduced to a low level. Verification is moved to the front of the cycle, where it is much lower in cost. The overall development time is much shorter, and the costs drastically reduced, as indicated in Fig. 17.2.

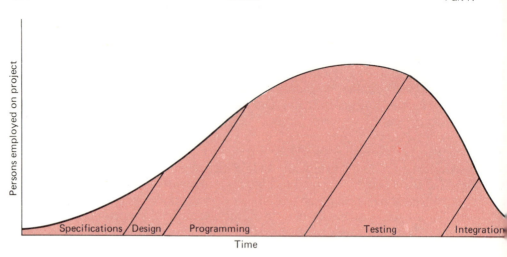

Figure 18.4   People requirements with the traditional life cycle.

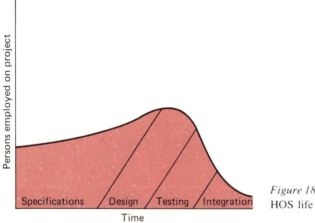

Figure 18.5   People requirements with the HOS life cycle.

ELIMINATION OF UNNECESSARY TOOLS AND PROCEDURES

As traditional life-cycle management has evolved, many procedures and tools have been created to solve its problems. The procedures have become rigidified in order to achieve management control of the life cycle.

Many of the original problems disappear with the HOS technique and hence the procedures and tools associated with them are no longer needed. The life cycle procedures need to be critically examined and eliminated where appropriate. This eliminates much time-consuming work.

Among the problems that gave rise to time-consuming procedures and tools were:

- Problems of managing large teams.
- Nonautomated change control.
- Management of manual documentation.
- Problems of dynamic testing.
- Tools for saturation testing.
- Difficulty of tracking the effects of changes or bug correction (the ripple effect). Correcting one bug often gave rise to other bugs.
- Difficulty of controlling source-code changes.
- Communication problems among programmers.
- Interface errors.
- Mismatch of requirement language (normally English), specification diagrams, and program design.
- Errors in converting the design to coding.

These problems are taken care of to a large extent by the HOS technique and its software. Eliminating time-consuming, tedious, or expensive procedures is an important part of the life-cycle change.

Not only can procedures be deleted but also much software. Much software is performing tasks which are unnecessary. High-level programming languages, compilers, testing aids, maintenance aids, and many operating system functions become unnecessary. Compilers for languages such as FORTRAN have complex functions to deal with the problems that FORTRAN causes. These problems can be made to disappear. Operating systems have functions to deal with uncontrolled interrupts, deadly embraces, and other problems that can be removed in the original design. Networking software has highly complex functions to help recovery from subtle deadlocks and interference problems. Many such problems should not occur with HOS-like design. Testing tools spend much time testing over and over again for errors that should be provably absent.

A challenge, then, of new software techniques, application generators, and nonprocedural languages is to throw overboard as much unnecessary baggage as possible. We should eliminate as much of the procedures, documentation, maintenance, training, computer time, compilers, testing aids, unnecessary software mechanisms, recovery aids, and people time as is practical. Some of these can be eliminated by development methods; some go to the heart of complex software and require new generations of such software to evolve.

INTRODUCING TECHNIQUES

How should an organization set about introducing a technique like HOS? System development in a large organization cannot be switched overnight from traditional techniques to HOS. Fundamentally new methods need to be introduced a stage at a time. Furthermore, HOS must take its place among other powerful

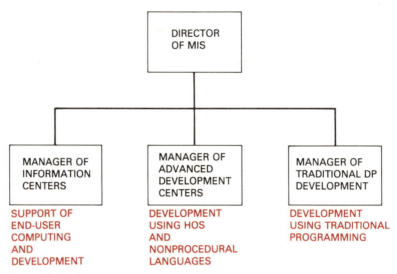

Figure 18.6   Computing today can be split into three development areas: development and maintenance using traditional programming, development using higher-level techniques, and support of end-user-driven computing. The objective should be progressively to minimize traditional programming.

new languages such as query languages, report generators, application generators, and languages designed for end users.

It is generally desirable to establish a separate development group to use HOS and other new techniques. We will refer to this as an *advanced development center*. It is staffed by computer professionals some of whom may be new graduates, because new graduates often learn and apply HOS faster than do traditional analysts and programmers.

In progressive organizations today we are seeing a rapid growth of user-driven computing in which end users either create their own applications or else work hand in hand with specialists doing interactive development with non-procedural, or fourth-generation, languages (such as ADRS, FOCUS, RAMIS, NOMAD, IDEAL, SQL, MAPPER, SAS, MARK V, NATURAL, CORTEX FACTORY, DATATRIEVE, etc.). The organization that supports this user-driven computing is often called an *information center*.

In addition to its traditional DP development, every medium-sized or large enterprise ought to have an *information center* and an *advanced development center*. Many need multiple such centers.

An MIS executive may divide his organization into three areas as shown in Fig. 18.6. He may have a manager who oversees all information centers, and another who oversees all advanced development centers.

The objective should be to progressively minimize and ultimately eliminate traditional programming, because of the problems we have discussed. This will not be done quickly in old-established DP organizations because of the mass of existing programs that have to be maintained or converted, and because of the difficulty of making traditional DP staff adopt new methods.

The three areas in Fig. 18.6 should, in effect, be in competition with one another. The ones that produce the most satisfactory results should be made to grow the fastest. The ones that produce slow, expensive, inflexible, or unsatisfactory results should be progressively replaced.

USE OF OTHER FRONT-END METHODOLOGIES
The HOS software can be made more acceptable and easy to use by linking it to familiar, powerful, or user-friendly front-end methodologies. *The extent to which the HOS software encompasses such methodologies is likely to determine its level of success.*

Figure 18.7 shows various ways of linking HOS techniques to other front-end techniques. In diagram **1** of Fig. 18.7 the HOS technique is used for creating specifications and the control maps are converted to a familiar representation. Chapter 15 shows examples of control maps being converted to data flow diagrams; for example, Fig. 15.9 is a direct translation of Fig. 15.8 and it may give some designers more insight into how the radar scheduler works than Fig. 15.8. Diagram **1** of Fig. 18.7 shows design feedback from the familiar representation to the HOS version. Software might be created for automatically transforming an HOS control chart into an alternative representation.

Diagram **2** of Fig. 18.7 shows a front-end representation being translated into an HOS representation with the aid of specially designed control structures and defined operations. Chapter 14, for example, shows data-base navigation diagrams, and their corresponding data-base action diagrams being translated into HOS control maps with the aid of the FOR ALL control structure that was designed for this purpose. Chapter 6 shows a data model, possibly created with a tool like DATA DESIGNER [1], being automatically converted in HOS data representation.

Various different methodologies are powerful for the overall planning or design of computer systems. It is often desirable to retain these and enhance them. This is easy to do by building special HOS control structures for them, and occasionally creating software to convert the output of design tools into HOS notation.

Although powerful front-end methodologies exist which can enhance the conceptual clarity of systems design or create overview designs for corporate data processing, many of these methodologies are not rigorous. The specifications they create (contrary to the sales claims) are inconsistent, incomplete, redundant, and ambiguous. HOS reveals these deficiencies, so the step of translating their designs into HOS is very valuable. It allows problems to be found at the front end, where they are easily correctable, rather than at the back end, where they are disastrous. Diagram **2** shows design feedback from the HOS representation to the front-end representation.

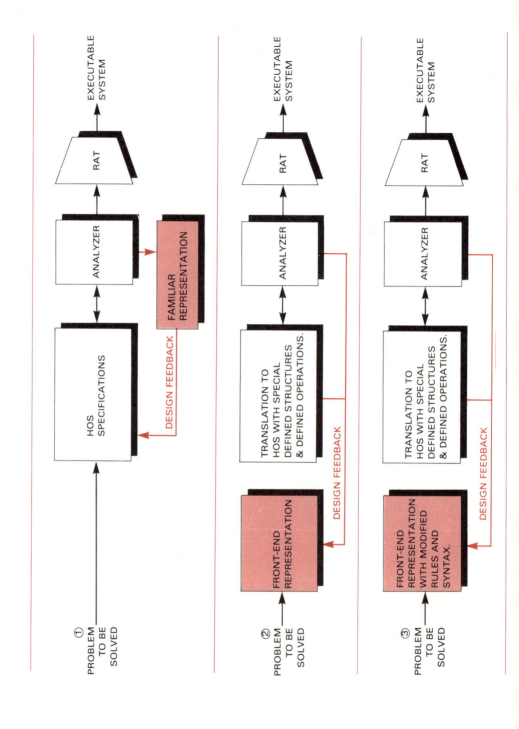

312

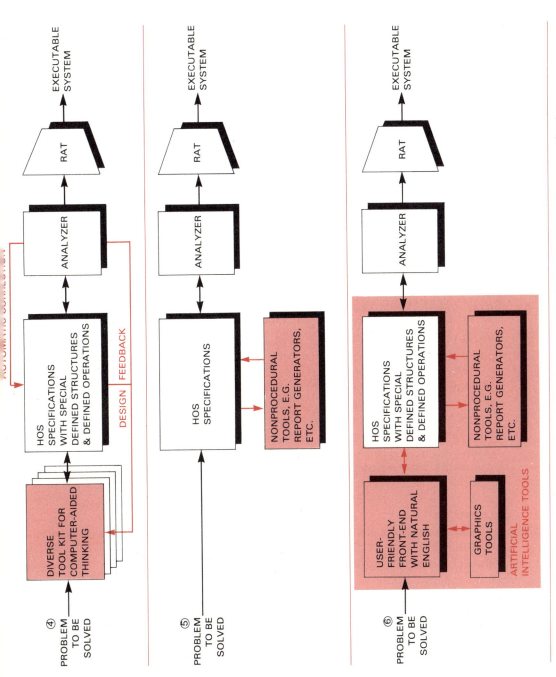

Figure 18.7 Various ways of combining the use of HOS with familiar or easy-to-use specification tools and techniques. Chart 4 or 5 may be combined with 1, 2, or 3.

313

In one case a module that was part of a battlefield intelligence system [2] was documented with a mixture of English, equations, and the SREM specification language [3]. Translation of this into HOS revealed and removed multiple design inconsistencies [2].

The improvement in rigor of the specification methodology may be made more directly than with the off-line feedback of Diagram **2**. The front-end methodology may itself be analyzed with the HOS technique and consequently enhanced to make it computable, or directly convertible into HOS control maps (Diagram **3**).

IDEF-O [4] is a specification technique for the design of ICAM systems for computer-aided manufacturing [5]. It uses a type of diagram which represents complex flows and relationships and is easy to use and understand. It is not completely rigorous from a computability point of view. HOS was used to create a computable version of IDEF so that this valuable technique becomes rigorous [6]. A graphics tool was specified which might be described as an IDEF-O typewriter [7]. A single keystroke can produce a box, an arrow path, an arrow end, a shift to the next location, and so on. The arrows fall along uniform and predictable paths. This chart becomes part of a computable specification, linked directly to HOS control maps which can be ANALYZEd and from which correct code can be generated. Tight coupling to powerful front-end methodologies allows the benefits of these methodologies to be retained and allows their users to "speak their own language."

Different types of graphics tools are useful for different types of problems. For example, decision trees and tables are valuable for certain types of logic. Finite state machine notation is valuable for other types of logic [8]. The diagramming techniques we use are really a form of language, and the language we use for thinking about a problem determines how easily we can solve the problem. Action diagrams, data navigation diagrams, dependency diagrams, and other forms of diagrams are useful for conceptualizing different problems [8], and *can automatically be converted into HOS control maps*. Some types of problems are best thought about mathematically, and the mathematics can be converted directly into AXES code.

The systems analyst of the future will have a diverse set of tools for approaching different situations. Most of these tools will operate on a personal computer. Diagram **4** of Fig. 18.7 shows such a tool kit acting as a front-end to the HOS tool.

INCORPORATION OF NONPROCEDURAL LANGUAGES

Diagram **5** of Fig. 18.7 shows a different type of linkage. The front-end specification is done with the HOS techniques, but certain leaf nodes of the control map refer to the use of other nonprocedural languages. A node might represent an operation done with a report generator, for example, or with a screen painter, decision tree, or data-base query/ update language.

This other nonprocedural language might be used separately from the code generated by the HOS RAT. End users, for example, might employ an end-user language as one facility in the design of a complex system.

Alternatively, the intermediate use of a lower-level nonprocedural language might be translated into the HOS notation. It is then analyzed together with the rest of the system and jointly RATted. The control map created by the nonprocedural language becomes a defined operation [OP] in the library. This is an important way of enhancing the power of the HOS tool.

Combinations of the diagrams in Fig. 18.7 are likely to be used. The linkage to nonprocedural languages in Diagrams **5** and **6** may be used in conjunction with the approaches in Diagrams **1** to **4**.

The techniques of artificial intelligence are having two important effects on our interaction with computers. First, they permit certain types of communication to take place in natural, free-form English, as with the query language INTELLECT [9]. Second, they have facilitated the building of expert systems in which complex expertise is communicated to a computer by means of rules. These two types of person-machine communication can be enhanced by combining them with suitable diagramming techniques [10].

The combination of natural English, graphics tools, expert system tools, nonprocedural tools, and HOS, as indicated in Diagram **6** of Fig. 18.7 would constitute an extremely powerful tool kit for an analyst.

DATA MODELING AND THE LIFE CYCLE

The DP development life cycle of the 1970s usually encompassed the design of the data. It became realized that data need to be planned on a corporate-wide basis, and that this is practical because the data entities do not change much, even though the ways in which data are used change greatly. Efficient data administration, then, began to separate the planning and modeling of data from the life cycle of individual projects [11]. As we saw in Chapter 12, data modeling expresses the inherent associations in data which are largely independent of any one application of those data.

Once canonical data models exist, the design of applications becomes easier and quicker, and another class of errors is removed. Well-executed data administration shortens the front end of projects' life cycles. Code generators shorten the back end. Where the code generators are very easy to use, the life cycle, in the normal sense of the term, disappears for some projects. We find applications being generated from a previously existing data base in days, and reports being generated in hours.

A CONTINUUM OF INFORMATION RESOURCE BUILDING

Rather than thinking of a succession of projects each with a discrete life cycle, an enterprise should think of an ongoing continuum of information resource building. There will be some big projects with a lengthy life cycle, but many of the new needs of users will be

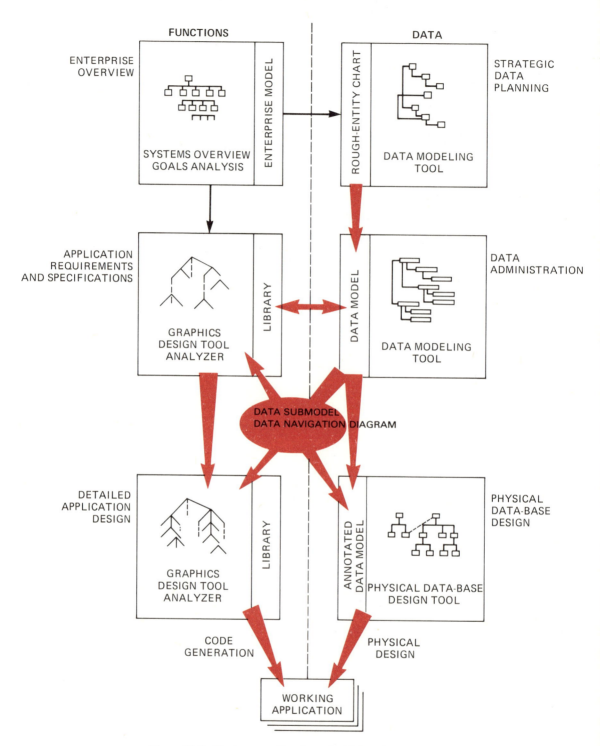

Figure 18.8 Design extending from the highest-level strategic planning down to working applications. The red arrows show automatable links.

met with nonprocedural languages employing previously existing data bases. Often data are extracted from existing files or data bases, restructured with relational data management systems, and manipulated with powerful nonprocedural languages. Some of the languages are sufficiently easy to use that end users can employ them, with help from information center staff. Some applications are too complex for the users in question to build but can be quickly protyped by DP staff.

Figure 18.8 illustrates the continuum of planning and design that is needed, extending from higher management strategic planning down to application building. The left side of Fig. 18.8 relates to functions and the right relates to data. The top relates to top-level planning. On the left an overview of the entire enterprise is created with strategic planning of what information systems are needed. On the right strategic data planning is done and a chart is produced of the data entities in the enterprise [11].

The entity chart at the top right of Fig. 18.8 is expanded into detail in the middle right-hand block. This is the task of the data administrator—to build stable canonical data models, obtain agreements about the definitions of data, and represent these in a data dictionary.

The middle left-hand block relates to the requirements planning of applications and the creation of specifications. The specifications are decomposed into detail until an application can be generated. The lower left block shows the application design.

Applications are designed using the data model. A submodel of the data for that particular application is extracted from the overall model, and a data navigation chart is drawn showing the access paths through the data, as discussed in Chapter 14. If HOS software is used, the data model and the control maps for the applications reside in the library.

The collection of data navigation charts for one hardware system form the basis for *physical* design and layout of the data base, indicated in the bottom right block of Fig. 18.8. Annotations on the data model, such as cardinality (on a one-to-many association, *how* many of one record are associated with another), assist in the physical design.

In some uses of data the middle left block of Fig. 18.8 is bypassed. Reports are generated, information is extracted and manipulated, or decision-support aids are created, directly from the data bases with easy-to-use languages without the need for detailed specification or design.

The red arrows in Fig. 18.8 represent automatable links. A compatible family of tools is needed for strategic data planning, data modeling, data dictionary representation, extraction of submodels and data navigation charts, representation of requirements, specifications, and application design, design verification, generation of provably correct code, and physical design. This family of tools, all using interactive graphics, will constitute the systems engineer's workbench of the future and will provide a quantum leap in the efficiency of system building.

REFERENCES

1. Data Designer, a tool that creates a stable data model from multiple separately entered representations of data, from DDI, Ann Arbor, MI.

2. R. Hackler, *An HOS View of ASAS*, Technical Report 32, Higher Order Software, Inc., Cambridge, MA, December 1981.

3. M. Alford, ''A Requirements Engineering Methodology for Real-Time Processing Requirements,'' *IEEE Transactions on Software Engineering*, January 1977.

4. SofTech, Inc., *Architect's Manual: ICAM Definition Method*, IDEF, Version 0, 1978; Version 1, 1979, Waltham, MA.

5. SofTech, Inc., *Integrated Computer Aided Manufacturing*, (ICAM), Waltham, MA, June 1978.

6. *Computable IDEF*, A series of reports prepared for the Air Force Systems Command, Wright-Patterson Air Force Base, Ohio, by Higher Order Software, Inc., Cambridge, MA, 1978–1982.

7. *Computable IDEF Preliminary Design*, Higher Order Software, Inc., Cambridge, MA, 1982.

8. James Martin and Carma McClure, *Diagramming Techniques for Analysts and Programmers*, Prentice-Hall Inc., Englewood Cliffs, NJ, 1985.

9. INTELLECT is a data base query language created by the Artificial Intelligence Corporation of Boston, and marketed by IBM and others.

10. James Martin, *Fourth Generation Languages*, Chapter 11, Prentice-Hall Inc., Englewood Cliffs, NJ, 1985.

11. James Martin, *Strategic Data-Planning Methodologies*, Prentice-Hall, Inc., Englewood Cliffs, NJ, 1982.

19 FUTURE

Norbert Wiener, the great pioneer of computers, wrote a book the title of which will long be remembered: *The Human Use of Human Beings* [1]. His view was that jobs which are inhuman because of drudgery should be done by machines, not people. Among these jobs he did not include that of the programmer! In a sense the programmer's job is inhuman because we require him to write a large amount of complex code without errors. Error-free coding is not natural for our animal-like brain. We cannot handle the meticulous detail and the vast numbers of combinatorial paths. Furthermore, if we want a thousand lines of code produced per day, not ten, then the job is even more inhuman. It is a job for machines, not people. Only recently have we understood how to make machines do it.

Once we have the capability to make machines create error-free code, the whole evolution of computers must change. The era of ad hoc hand coding is a temporary aberration in the history of computing.

Whether or not the design method described in this book will be the one that changes a multibillion-dollar industry is too early to know. There may be better ways. Certainly there will be many different ways. Today we have a variety of types of code generators which need to be integrated to form a powerful tool kit.

The automation of automation is the beginning of a chain reaction. This book has described how high-level *control structures* can be built out of primitive control structures. Still higher-level ones can be built out of these, and so on. High-level operations are similarly built out of primitive operations, and higher-level ones built out of these, until highly powerful operations and control structures exist for various different application areas and system types. Essential in this is the rigor of the mechanism that enforces correct interfacing among the modules. It is this rigor that allows pyramiding of modules and control structures.

As the pyramids build we will reach very high level constructs. High-level design languages will allow fast, very complex design. Millions of computers on worldwide data networks will interchange libraries and data bases. Knowledge-based systems will acquire ever larger numbers of rules and become self-feeding. Intelligent network directories will allow machines and users to find the resources they need.

As the pyramiding takes us to higher-level semantics we will have higher-level problems with semantics—external semantics which the internal correctness-proofs will not cover. We will have higher-level forms of garbage-in-garbage-out, so that higher-level controls will need to be devised for protection. Knowledge-based systems, for example, could be filled by human beings with some incorrect knowledge or assertions. Artificial intelligence systems may become very difficult to debug. Self-feeding knowledge bases may constitute a chain reaction that quickly passes beyond our ability to maintain accuracy controls. A problem for the future.

USER-FRIENDLY POWER

Once the mathematical basis for programming and system design exists and the rigorous foundations are built, the objective of software evolution should be to make it as user-friendly and powerful as possible. Powerful user-friendly constructs are needed at both the front end and the back end of systems design. At the front end we need high-level specification languages and design methodologies. We have shown how these can be translated into HOS and made rigorous. Easy-to-use control structures can be created for different design methodologies. The FOR ALL of Fig. 14.10 or the MAIN FILE LOOP of Fig. 7.8 are examples. More powerful ones than these are needed for different front-end methodologies.

At the back end or detailed level, the control maps need simple representation of formulas, report generation blocks, data-base accessing, relational operations, terminal dialogue design, decision tables, graphic representation, and so on. The extent to which these constructs are made powerful and easy to use will determine the acceptance and value of the software. The human talent needed to make it user-friendly is quite different from and even alien to the human talent needed to make it mathematically rigorous. New and different software houses may succeed by employing HOS as their foundation and building powerful tools with it.

Libraries of constructs need to be built in the HOS world for different classes of applications. Some examples of application classes which need their own libraries of operations and control structures are:

- Commercial procedures
- Financial applications
- Design of operating systems
- Automatic data-base navigation
- Query languages

- Design of circuits with NOR, NAND gates, etc.
- Control of robots
- Cryptanalysis
- Missile control
- Building architecture
- Design graphics
- Network design
- Avionics
- CAD/CAM
- Production control
- Project management
- Decision support graphics

The list is endless.

A WAY TO THINK ABOUT SYSTEMS   HOS is really *a way to think about systems* which leads to higher precision specification and design. As such, it ought to be taught in business schools and management training courses, as well as computer science schools and systems analysts' courses. At its different levels it can be understood by both business persons and users, and by computer professionals. It provides a way to bridge the gap.

The concepts of accountants and double-entry bookkeeping can be mapped into HOS charts. The ideas of planning business resources, or scheduling production, or controlling projects can be drawn as HOS charts. Other types of charts that help human communication are also desirable, but if they are to become the basis of system specifications, enough rigor ought to be imposed on them for them to be convertible into HOS control maps.

STANDARDS   The author was recently in communication with a standards committee concerned with the rapidly evolving standards for data networks. The committee produced a document of several hundred pages specifiying the draft standard in fine detail. Its object was "to ensure compatibility between equipment made by different manufacturers." To accomplish this it provided specifications "which establish common interfaces and protocols." Like all such standards it was not designed from provably correct constructs, and it almost certainly contained internal errors that HOS would have caught. Among other notations it contained state diagrams which could easily be transformed into the rigorous notation of HOS. Once in that notation these could be manipulated by the graphics editor, and code automatically generated, and tested.

Computer standards committees everywhere should be upgrading their notation to use provably correct constructs. Now that we know that it is possible, future standards, future network interfaces, future operating systems, future database management systems, and so on, all ought to be built with rigorous provable design which helps eliminate redundancies and enforces rigorously correct interfaces between modules. Software of all types ought to have a certification stamped on it saying whether it was built with a rigorous mathematical foundation.

MACHINE LANGUAGE

The software described in Chapter 8 generates code in FORTRAN, COBOL, Pascal, and C. DP staff should never modify this code directly because then it would lose its provably correct characteristic. It would be more efficient for the RAT to generate machine language. There is not then the added inefficiency of a further compilation. The generation of FORTRAN, COBOL or even ADA seems to result from a somewhat irrational desire to hang on desperately to something familiar, even if one is now forbidden to tinker with it. If one wants Department of Defense contracts, FORTRAN or ADA adds to DOD's comfort level. It could be argued that it makes the code portable, but it would be more efficient to achieve portability by regeneration for different machines.

AN HOS MACHINE

Still more efficient would be a change in hardware. All HOS code is based on the three primitives, JOIN, INCLUDE, and OR. A machine could be built to execute these three primitives. It would thus have a much narrower instruction set than today's computers. Speed would be gained in two ways. First, the code generated would relate directly to the machine. The substantial waste of mismatched machine instructions would be avoided. Second, because the machine has a narrow instruction set it could be made much faster.

Processor chips of the future will be much faster than those in today's machines. The military VHSIC (Very High Speed Integration Chips) program aims to produce processors of much higher speed. If this technology were used to produce processors that executed JOINs, INCLUDEs and ORs, these could be made to execute more than 10 million instructions per second.

PARALLELISM

Processor chips of the future will be mass produced in vast quantities. When many millions of one processor chip are made, that processor can be very low in cost. It will be highly desirable in the future for powerful computers to be built out of many small computers which yield to the economics of mass production. Examples of highly parallel machines have existed for some time. The problem with them is that it has been extremely difficult to design software for normal applications which runs efficiently on them.

The search for how to introduce a high degree of parallelism into computing is an important one. A million-dollar computer should not be doing one thing at a time; it should be doing a thousand things at a time.

The HOS technique breaks high-level operations into the three primitives. The INCLUDE primitive allows two operations to proceed in parallel, independently. The JOIN primitive shows that two operations could execute sequentially, possibly on separate processors if the output of the right-hand operation is passed from one processor to the other where it becomes the input to the left-hand operation.

The HOS decomposition thus clearly states what can take place in parallel, and what can take place sequentially on separate processors. The possibility thus arises of a highly parallel machine built of many fast mass-produced processors each designed to execute the HOS primitives. This is referred to as a Higher Order Machine (HOM), a machine designed specifically for Higher Order Software. If such a machine comes into existence (whether with HOS techniques or any equivalently rigorous technique) the operating system and data-base management system should not be separate facilities independent of the hardware architecture. The hardware and controlling software should be one integrated design, built together with control maps which represent both hardware and software design and allow trade-offs between them to be explored.

The language OCCAM is designed for parallel computing and has been used for programming configurations of transputers—chips specially designed for parallel processing. The three highest-level constructs of OCCAM are SEQ, ALT and PAR, which correspond in their structure to HOS's JOIN, OR, and INCLUDE. It would seem natural for HOS to generate OCCAM code and allocate transputer resources for efficient parallel processing.

CHANGING COMPUTER INDUSTRY

Conversion of the computer industry to rigorous design will obviously not happen overnight. The investment tied up in existing hardware, software, and techniques is gigantic. The insularity of the major computer corporations is immense and so is their resistance to methods that do not originate internally. Techniques like HOS need to have their worth proven on very large projects before they will penetrate much of the computer industry. Some software houses and other organizations have embarked on large HOS projects, believing that it gives them a major competitive edge.

The Japanese have heralded their *fifth generation* of computers as *the dawn of the second computer age*. They talk of mainframes built with 10,000 mass-produced processors operating in parallel, giving an overall instruction rate of 10 billion instructions per second. They talk of personal computers with 32 processors, giving 10 million instructions per second.

Let us hope that the software for this dramatic hardware will not again be the undebuggable mess that has characterized large-computer operating systems in the past. C. A. R. Hoare described manufacturers' software as "the worst engineered products of the computer age" of unnecessary and still increasing complexity "which totally beggars the comprehension of both user and designer" [2].

Much Japanese software had been atrocious and this failing of the Japanese has to some extent protected the West from an onslaught of Japanese computers. If the Japanese started using HOS to develop their software, the West might have cause for concern.

Software for highly parallel machines will necessarily be intricate and tricky. When the software development has problems they will not be solved by rounding up hoards of coders across the country and putting them on trains to Poughkeepsie or Tokyo. The design needs to have a rigorous basis from the start. The hardware and software are really parts of the same design, and the same mathematical approach needs to apply to both. Some of the current papers describing highly parallel architectures do not have the rigor of the HOS technique.

The challenge of the computer industry today is indeed to have a new dawn, in which highly complex mass-produced microelectronic wafers and software are designed with an integrated technique that is rigorously based. Vast new libraries of operations will grow which can be interlinked without interface problems. The teams of hand programmers with their ad hoc designs will become a romantic part of computer history, like the weavers in their cottages when the industrial revolution began.

REFERENCES

1. N. Wiener, *The Human Use of Human Beings*, The MIT Press, Cambridge, MA.

2. C. A. R. Hoare, "The Engineering of Software: A Startling Contradiction," *Computer Bulletin* (British Computer Society), December 1975.

AXIOMS AND PRIMITIVES

The mathematical provability of the constructs in complex applications such as those in Chapter 9 depends on the fact that they were built out of primitives to which mathematical proofs of correctness apply. If an ordinary user had to build an application out of these primitives, such a methodology would be extremely painful and time consuming. The usability of the methodology depends on having useful control structures and defined operations, which are built out of the primitives. The user employs these, like he uses his car, without knowing the details of their construction. In this appendix we discuss the primitives further.

SIX AXIOMS   The control structures are founded on six basic axioms. The three primitive control structures, JOIN, IN-CLUDE, and OR, obey these axioms. It then follows that any nonprimitive mechanisms built from the primitives will also have the correct properties. Box I.1 summarizes the six axioms.

Axiom 1 is concerned with *invocation*. A parent node can invoke only its immediate offsprings. It cannot invoke itself. It cannot invoke descendents which are lower than its immediate offsprings.

Axiom 2 says that the job of a parent node is to perform a function and that, while the node can get help from its offspring in the performance of this function, it cannot delegate this responsibility. For a given input only the parent node can ensure the delivery of the corresponding output. The parent is *responsible* for producing the output data types with correct values.

Axiom 3 is concerned with where the required output value is delivered. It is clearly undesirable for a function to obtain or alter any value in the system. The ability to alter the values of variables is called *access rights*. Axiom 3 states that the parent node can assign to its offspring the right to alter the values of the output variables of the parent. Each output variable of the parent node must appear as an output variable of at least one of its offsprings.

BOX I.1   Axioms of HOS

DEFINITION: *Invocation* provides for the ability to perform a function.

AXIOM 1:   A given module controls the invocation of the set of functions on its immediate, and only its immediate, lower level.

DEFINITION: *Responsibility* provides for the ability of a module to produce correct output values.

AXIOM 2:   A given module controls the responsibility for elements of only its own output space.

DEFINITION: An *output access right* provides for the ability to locate a variable, and once located, the ability to place a value in the located variable.

AXIOM 3:   A given module controls the output access rights to each set of variables whose values define the elements of the output space for each immediate, and only each immediate, lower-level function.

DEFINITION: An *input access right* provides for the ability to locate a variable, and once located, the ability to reference the value of that variable.

AXIOM 4:   A given module controls the input access rights to each set of variables whose values define the elements of the input space for each immediate, and only each immediate, lower-level function.

DEFINITION: *Rejection* provides for the ability to recognize the improper input element in that if a given input element is not acceptable, null output is produced.

AXIOM 5:   A given module controls the rejection of invalid elements of its own, and only its own, input set.

(Continued)

BOX I.1   *(Continued)*

> DEFINITION: *Ordering* provides for the ability to establish a relation in a set of functions so that any two function elements are comparable in that one of said elements precedes the other said element.
>
> AXIOM 6:   A given module controls the ordering of each tree for the immediate, and only the immediate, lower level.

Axiom 4 is concerned with the way the parent node controls access to its input variables. The parent node can grant its offsprings the right to access its input elements. The offsprings cannot change them. Every input variable of the parent must appear as an input variable of at least one of its offsprings.

Axiom 5 requires that the parent node must *reject* inputs received which are not in the input of the parent. If improper inputs are received, a *null* output is produced.

Axiom 6 is concerned with ordering. It requires the parent node to control the *order* of invocation of its offsprings.

These six axioms are discussed mathematically in Appendix II.

THREE PRIMITIVE STRUCTURES

These six axioms are satisfied by the three primitive binary control structures giving sequential, parallel, and branching control, respectively. These are HOS's JOIN, INCLUDE, and OR structures. With these, any system structure can be described.

Four rules apply to the variables of any function in these structures:

1. All functions must have inputs.
2. All functions must have outputs.
3. Inputs and outputs of a function must be disjoint.
4. There must be no repetition of variables in inputs or outputs for a function.

The rules for the JOIN, INCLUDE, and OR control structures were given in Box 4.1. They are simple and confining, so that the mathematical guarantees of correctness apply. They permit no repetition of variables, for example. Sometimes two copies of the same variable are needed: for example, if we have to evaluate $a(a + b)$. To achieve this a second copy of a must be created with a primitive operation CLONE. CLONE1 creates one identical copy. CLONE2 creates two identical copies. Thus

$$a' = \text{CLONE1}(a)$$
$$a', a'' = \text{CLONE2}(a)$$

Using this we can evaluate $a(a + b)$ with a control map of the three primitive structures:

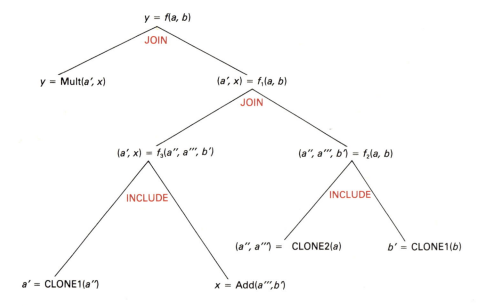

This is tediously explicit, but guaranteed correct because the three primitive control structures obey the mathematical rules.

With a COJOIN structure it becomes much simpler:

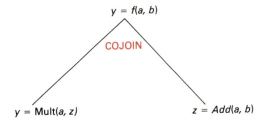

DERIVING CO-CONTROL STRUCTURES

In order for the COJOIN to produce mathematically guaranteed results, the COJOIN structure must be derivable from the three primitive control structures. The following diagram shows the use of a COJOIN and turns it into primitives:

USE OF A
COJOIN STUCTURE

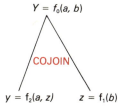

$Y = f_0(a, b)$

COJOIN

$y = f_2(a, z)$ $z = f_1(b)$

EXPANSION INTO PRIMITIVES

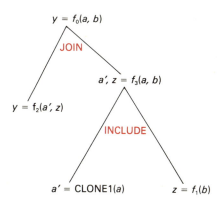

$y = f_0(a, b)$

JOIN

$a', z = f_3(a, b)$

$y = f_2(a', z)$

INCLUDE

$a' = CLONE1(a)$ $z = f_1(b)$

Similarly, the use of a COINCLUDE structure can be split into primitives:

USE OF A
COINCLUDE STRUCTURE

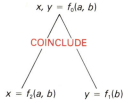

$x, y = f_0(a, b)$

COINCLUDE

$x = f_2(a, b)$ $y = f_1(b)$

EXPANSION INTO PRIMITIVES

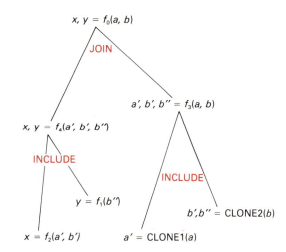

$x, y = f_0(a, b)$

JOIN

$a', b', b'' = f_3(a, b)$

$x, y = f_4(a', b', b'')$

INCLUDE

$y = f_1(b'')$

INCLUDE

$b', b'' = CLONE2(b)$

$x = f_2(a', b')$ $a' = CLONE1(a)$

and a COOR structure can be split into primitives (where B is the Boolean):

USE OF A
COOR STRUCTURE   EXPANSION INTO PRIMITIVES

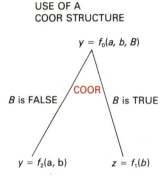

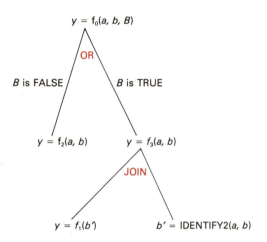

Here IDENTIFYi is a primitive function which picks out the *i*th element of a list of elements. Thus IDENTIFY2 picks out *b* from (a, b).

In this way, the various different co-control structures can be decomposed into primitive structures and hence are mathematically guaranteed to be correct. A user or designer of a language based on HOS could create nonprimitive control structures of his own.

PRIMITIVE OPERATIONS

The examples above contain certain primitive operations, for example:

$$x' = \text{CLONE1}(x)$$
$$(x', x'') = \text{CLONE2}(x)$$
$$y' = \text{IDENTIFY2}(x, y, z)$$

A constant is also derived with a primitive operator, thus:

$$y = \text{K6}(x)$$

Here *y* has the value "6" regardless of what *x* is.

MATHEMATICAL FORMULATION

The mathematics which is the basis of the HOS methodology originally appeared in a paper by M. Hamilton and S. Zeldin in 1976. Here we reproduce, with permission, the appendices of that paper, which give the mathematics.

APPENDIX I: FORMULATION*

Let us describe a control system in which all logical possibilities of control can be represented as a tree structure.

Each node (any point at which two or more branches intersect) of the tree represents a unique point of execution of a function. Each node and all its dependents represent the unique tree structure T.

A *function*, F: $Q \rightarrow P$ or $P = F(Q)$, is a mapping from the input set Q to the output set P. Each element of the input set is expressed as a unique element of the output set.

We define an A-dimensional input space by the values of the A variables $(x_1, x_2 \ldots x_A)$. And we define a B-dimensional output space by the values of the B variables $(y_1, y_2 \ldots y_B)$. An element of the input set $q \in Q$ is a particular point for $(x_1, x_2 \ldots x_A)$. An element of the output set $p \in P$ is a particular point for $(y_1, y_2 \ldots y_B)$.

In order to execute a function, we must define a controller, the *module*. The module exists at the node just immediately higher on the tree relative to the functions it controls.

A module has the responsibility to perform a function. For that purpose, the module controls functions only on the immediate lower level. For implementation this is done by invocation (e.g., **call**[20] or **schedule**), by assignment of access rights (e.g., parameter passing or restricted use of global variables), and by the determination of the ordering

---

[20]A **call** can be explicit or implicit, e.g., $y = z^2 + 3$ is an implicit **call**.

---

* Reprinted, with permission, from ''Higher Order Software—A Methodology for Defining Software'' by M. Hamilton and S. Zeldin, appearing in *IEEE Transactions on Software Engineering*, Vol. SE.2, No. 1, pp. 25–32, March 1976, Copyright © 1976 IEEE.

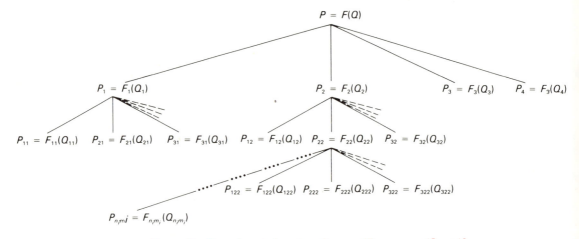

Figure 15   Formal control system: $S_{n_i m_i} = [P_{n_i m_i} = Fn_i m_i (Q_i m_i)]$.

of the functions on that level (e.g., priority assignments). Every function receives input from and produces outputs for its controller either directly or indirectly. Every node is a module with respect to its immediate lower level functions. With respect to control relationships, the elements of the lowest level of any tree are referred to only as functions; the highest node of the entire tree structure is referred to only as a module.

The following symbols are used in the discussion below:

∀	for every
∧	logical "and"
∨	logical "or"
∈	element of
⊂	subset of
∪	union of
○	controls
Ø	does not control
ȯ	interrupts
ø̇	does not interrupt
∃!	there exists a unique
$a \rightarrow b$	logical "*if a then b*"
{ }	set of

Definition: The formal control system (Fig. 15) is one in which each module S has a unique identification

$$S_{n_i m_i} \equiv [P_{n_i m_i} = F_{n_i m_i}(Q_{n_i m_i})].$$

$n_i m_i$ defines a particular level of control in which i is the nested level of the module. $i = 1$ implies the level directly below the top level. n_i is the node position (from the left) relative to its most immediate higher node, m_i. At each level there is a set, N_i, of node positions, i.e., $n_i \in N_i$. m_i is the recursive relationship $m_i = n_{i-1} m_{i-1}$ defined for $i > 2$. If $i = 2$, $m_i = n_{i-1}$. If $i = 1$, $n_i m_i = n_i$.

Axiom 1:   The module $Sn_i m_i$ controls the invocation of the set of valid functions on its immediate, and only its immediate, lower level, $\{F_{n_{i+1}n_i m_i}\}$. That is,

$$\forall j\, \forall\, n_{i+1} \in N_{i+1}\; \exists!\, S_{n_i m_i},\; [(S_{n_i m_i} \circ F_{n_i m_i}) \wedge ((n_j m_j \neq n_{i+1} n_i m_i) \rightarrow S_{n_i m_i} \not\!\!\varnothing\, F_{n_i m_i})]. \quad (1)$$

Thus, the module $S_{n_i m_i}$ cannot control the invocation of functions on its own level.

It also follows that the module $S_{n_i m_i}$ cannot control the invocation of its own function.

In addition, the "no **goto**" concept of structured programming is therefore consistent with the control system. For example,

If "*C* **goto** *D*" exists, *C* loses control. e.g., *C* can control itself to terminate. In addition, if "*D* **goto** *C*" exists, *D* is controlling *C* and, in effect, is controlling itself.

Theorem 1.1:   a module *C* cannot invoke function *D*, which, as a module, invokes function *C*, for then *C* would be controlling itself.

$$C \not\!\!\varnothing\, (D \circ C).$$

Corollary 1.1.1:   A logical antecedent cannot be assigned by its consequent.

e.g., If function *C* is comprised of "if *G* **then** *D*," *G* cannot be assigned by *D*.

Theorem 1.2:   If a function from $level_{i+1}$ is removed and the controller module at $level_i$ still maintains its same mapping, the function at $level_{i+1}$, $F_{n_{i+1}n_i m_i}$, is extraneous. The extraneous function is a direct violation of Axiom 1, for if the function is not removed, $S_{n_i m_i} \not\!\!\varnothing\, F_{n_{i+1}n_i m_i}$.

Note: Violation of Theorem 1.2, in common practice, manifests itself in modules with many user options. With respect to the entire system, the use of extraneous functions proliferates test cases and complicates interfaces.

Corollary 1.2.1:   Consequents of a decision do not interrogate the antecedent for this would result in an extraneous function.

e.g., "*if G then D*" where D implies "*if G then E*" must be reduced to "*if G then E*."

Theorem 1.3:   Assignment to a variable is restricted to one process when more than one process is concurrent. This is true because modules may only invoke valid functions, and a valid function has only one output value for a particular input value.

Axiom 2:   The module $Sn_i m_i$ controls the responsibility for elements of the output space, of only $Pn_i m_i$, such that the mapping $F_{n_i m_i}(Q_{n_i m_i})$ is $P_{n_i m_i}$. That is,

$$\forall j\, \forall\, n_i m_i\; \exists!\, S_{n_i m_i},\; [(S_{n_i m_i} \circ P_{n_i m_i}) \wedge ((n_j m_j \neq n_i m_i) \rightarrow S_{n_i m_i} \not\!\!\varnothing\, P_{n_j m_j})]. \quad (2)$$

Thus, there must not exist any member of the input space for which no member of the output space is assigned. For, if this were not the case, we would have an invalid function.

Theorem 2.1:   There may be more than one formulation for a particular function. It is only necessary that the mapping be identical. Equivalent computer functions may require a different formulation due to timing restrictions, etc.

Axiom 3:   The module $S_{n_i m_i}$ controls the access rights to each set of variables $\{Y_{n_{i+1}n_i m_i}\}$ whose values define the elements of the output space for each immediate, and only each immediate, lower level function.

$$\forall j \forall n_{i+1} \in N_{i+1} \; \exists! \; S_{n_i m_i}, \; [(S_{n_i m_i} \circ Y_{n_{i+1} n_i m_i}) \wedge ((n_j m_j \neq n_{i+1} n_i m_i) \rightarrow S_{n_i m_i} \varnothing Y_{n_j m_j})] \quad (3)$$

Note: If any two modules, $S_{n_i m_i}$ and $S_{n_j m_j}$, require the same function formulation, the same set of computer residing instructions can be used for the functions as long as the access rights of the variables are controlled via Axiom 3.

Theorem 3.1: The variables whose values define the elements of the output space at $level_i$ are a subset of the variables whose values define the elements of the output space at $level_{i+1}$, that is,

$$Y_{n_i m_i} \subset \{Y_{n_{i+1} n_i m_i}\}.$$

Axiom 4: The module $S_{n_i m_i}$ controls the access rights to each set of variables $\{X_{n_{i+1} n_i m_i}\}$ whose values define the elements of the input space for each immediate, and only each immediate, lower level function.

$$\forall j \forall n_{i+1} \in N_{i+1} \; \exists! \; S_{n_i m_i}, \; [(S_{n_i m_i} \circ X_{n_{i+1} n_i m_i}) \wedge ((n_j m_j \neq n_{i+1} n_i m_i) \rightarrow S_{n_i m_i} \varnothing X_{n_j m_j})]. \quad (4)$$

Thus, the module $S_{n_i m_i}$ cannot alter the members of its own input set, i.e., the access to the elements of the input set of $S_{n_i m_i}$ cannot be controlled by $S_{n_i m_i}$.

Theorem 3.4.1: The variables of the output set of a function cannot be the variables of the input set of that same function. If $y = f(y,x)$ could exist, access to y would not be controlled by the next immediate higher level.

Note: Adherence to Theorem 3.4.1 simplifies error recovery techniques associated with parameter passing and functionally dependent iterative processes.

Theorem 3.4.2: The variables of the output set of one function can be the variables of the input set of another function only if the variables associated with the output set of the first function and the variables associated with the input set of the second function are variables of functions that exist on the same level and are controlled by the same immediate higher node. If $y = f_1(x)$ and $g = f_2(y)$, both functions exist at the same level. If $g = f_2(y)$ is at a lower level, access rights to the input set y imply y is determined before y exists. $y = f_1(x)$ at a lower level implies an alteration to the input set of $g = f_2(y)$.

Theorem 3.4.3: Each member of the set of variables whose values define the elements of the output space of a function is either a variable of the output space of the controller or is a variable of the input space for any of the functions on the same level excluding the variables of its own function.

$$\forall y_{n_i m_i} \in Y_{n_i m_i}, y_{n_i m_i} \in \{Y_{m_i} \cup \{\{X_{n_i m_i}\} - X_{n_i m_i}\}\}.$$

Note: Violation of Theorem 3.4.3 in common practice, manifests itself in modules that calculate by-product results for anticipated users: e.g., a Shuttle module that calculates the position vector of a vehicle might also calculate altitude, apogee, and perigee, instead of creating separate modules to perform the separate functions.

Theorem 3.4.4: Each member of the set of variables whose values define the elements of the input space of a function is either a variable of the input space of the controller or is a variable of the output space for any of the functions on the same level excluding those variables of its own function.

$$\forall x_{n_i m_i} \in X_{n_i m_i}, x_{n_i m_i} \in \{X_{m_i} \cup \{\{Y_{n_j m_j}\} - Y_{n_i m_i}\}\}.$$

Axiom 5: The module $S_{n_i m_i}$ controls the rejection of invalid elements of its own, and only its own, inputs set $Q_{n_i m_i}$, that is,

$$\forall j \, \forall n_i m_i \, \exists! \, S_{n_i m_i}, \, [(S_{n_i m_i} \circ Q_{n_i m_i}) \land ((n_j m_j \neq n_i m_i) \to S_{n_i m_i} \, \mathcal{D} \, Q_{n_j m_j})]. \quad (5)$$

Axiom 6: The module $S_{n_i m_i}$ controls the ordering of each tree $\{T_{n_{i+1} n_i m_i}\}$ for the immediate, and only the immediate, lower level.

$$\forall j \, \forall \, n_{i+1} \in N_{i+1} \, \exists! \, S_{n_i m_i}, \, [(S_{n_i m_i} \circ T_{n_{i+1} n_i m_i}) \land ((n_j m_j \neq n_{i+1} n_i m_i) \to S_{n_i m_i} \, \mathcal{D} \, T_{n_j m_j})]. \quad (6)$$

Thus, the module $S_{n_i m_i}$ controls the ordering of the functions, the input set, and the output set for each node of $\{T_{n_{i+1} n_i m_i}\}$. A process ℓ is a function scheduled to occur in real time.

Note: If two processes are scheduled to execute concurrently, the priority of a process, ℓ determines precedence at the time of execution.

If one process has a higher priority than another process, the higher priority process can interrupt the lower priority process. The lower priority process is resumed when the higher priority process is either terminated or is in its wait state.

Theorem 6.1: The priority of a process is higher than the priority of any process on its most immediate lower level.

Theorem 6.2: If two processes have the same controller such that the first has a lower priority than the second, then all processes in the control tree of the first are of lower priority than the processes in the control tree of the second.

Theorem 6.3: The ordering between members of any given process tree cannot be altered by an interrupt. For, if process A is of higher priority than process B, process A interrupts all of B, i.e., the priorities of the dependent processes of B are less than the priority of B.

Theorem 6.4: A module $S_{n_i m_i}$ controls the priority relationships of those processes on the immediate, and only the immediate, lower level.

$$\forall j \, \forall k \, \forall \, n_{i+1}, w_{i+1} \in N_{i+1} \, \exists! \, S_{n_i m_i}, [n_{i+1} \neq w_{i+1} \to (S_{n_i m_i} \circ (\ell_{n_{i+1} n_i m_i} \, \dot{\ell} \, \ell_{w_{i+1} n_i m_i})$$
$$\land ((n_j m_j \neq n_{i+1} n_i m_i) \to (S_{n_i m_i} \, \mathcal{D} \, (\ell_{n_j m_j} \, \dot{\ell} \, \ell_{n_k m_k}))].$$

Corollary 6.4.1: An explicit priority relationship exists among each pair of processes at the same level which branch from the same most immediate higher level node.

Note: If the priority of process $\ell_{a_i m_i}$ is greater than the priority of $\ell_{b_i m_i}$, and the priority of $\ell_{b_i m_i}$ is less than the priority of $\ell_{c_i m_i}$, the controller at node m_i does not control the priority relationships of $\ell_{a_i m_i}$ and $\ell_{c_i m_i}$. To avoid a violation of Theorem 6.4, the priority relationship of $\ell_{a_i m_i}$ and $\ell_{c_i m_i}$ must also be stated explicity.

Corollary 6.4.2: If a process $\ell_{n_i m_i}$ can interrupt another process $\ell_{w_i m_i}$ the control tree of $\ell_{n_i m_i}$ can interrupt $\ell_{w_i m_i}$ and each member of the control tree of $\ell_{w_i m_i}$.

Corollary 6.4.3: Since $S_{n_i m_i}$ controls the priority relationships of the set of processes $\{\ell_{n_{i+1} n_i m_i}\}$, then it itself cannot interrupt any member of the processes of the control tree $\{T_{n_{i+1} n_i m_i}\}$.

Corollary 6.4.4: A process cannot interrupt itself.

Lemma 6.4.4.1: The multiprogram statement **wait** is an implicit decision of a process to interrupt itself at a future time, and therefore is not consistent with the control system.

Corollary 6.4.5:   A process cannot interrupt its controller.

Corollary 6.4.6:   A process $\varrho_{n_im_i}$ that can interrupt another process $\varrho_{n_jm_j}$ affects the absolute time loss for $\varrho_{n_jm_j}$.

Theorem 6.5:   If the antecedent of a decision within a module is a time relationship, the relationship is extraneous. For, only if the relationship is removed, could the ordering be controlled by the next higher level.

> e.g., ''(time $= t_1) \rightarrow A$'' can be replaced by A where the controller schedules A at time t_1.

Theorem 6.6:   If a function is invoked by a **call** or **schedule**, the corresponding module of said function can invoke another function by a call.

Theorem 6.7:   A **schedule** of two processes may be commutative, but a **call** of two functions is not commutative.

Theorem 6.8:   If a function $F_{n_im_i}$ is invoked by a **call**, the module corresponding to the function $S_{n_im_i}$ cannot invoke a process. If the module schedules a process and the set of operations of the function $F_{n_im_i}$ is performed before the process is executed, the module does not control the scheduled process.

Theorem 6.9:   A **schedule** must always cause the processes invoked to be dependent so that the higher level maintains control at all times.

Theorem 6.10:   The maximum time for a cycle of a process to be completed or delayed can be determined. Consider a particular level which has N processes. The nth process has a frequency, f_n cycles per second, such that the period t_n for the nth process is $1/f_n$, and the total maximum execution time for that process is Δt_n. The jth process has a maximum number of cycles $t_n f_i$ during time t_n. Then, $t_n f_j \Delta t_j$ is the maximum time a process could consume during t_n.

From Corollary 6.4.1, there exists priority relationships for N processes such that

$$\bar{\varrho}_{1m_i} > \bar{\varrho}_{2m_i} > \ldots \bar{\varrho}_{n_im_i} > \ldots \bar{\varrho}_{N_im_i}.$$

Therefore, process n can be completed within time t_n if its maximum completion time t_c is less than t_n where

$$t_c = \sum_{j=1}^{J} t_n f_j \Delta t_j + \Delta t_n,$$

and J equals the total number of processes of higher priority than process n on the control level of n. Also, the maximum delay time for process n is the maximum completion time for the process of the nearest higher priority on its own level.

Theorem: It is possible to control all functions of any given software problem such that one controller controls all functions.

If we have only one level of control, every function can be performed, all access rights can be allocated, and the ordering between functions can be controlled.

Thus, it is always possible to perform every required function of any software system by adhering to the six axioms of the control system.

A Real-Time Control Problem

The design of any system which does not have the potential to assign the same variables concurrently is deterministic. In this type of system, functions can either be functionally independent, functionally dependent, or mutually dependent.

An independent function is one in which the output set is not the input set of another function. A dependent function is one in which the output set is an input set of another function. Two functions are mutually dependent if the output set of the first is the input set of the second, and the output set of the second is the input set of the first.

The design of any system which has the potential to assign the same variables concurrently is nondeterministic.

A system is able to provide for mutually dependent functions to be executed concurrently if the HOS axioms are applied in real time. With such a system, the operator need not memorize permutations of proper operational sequences. In addition, the software system is able to handle error detection and recovery for all operator-selected processes by simple algorithms rather than by special algorithms for each operator selection or by complicated table look-up algorithm schemes.

Consider a typical Shuttle example of a nondeterministic system where the modules M_1 and M_2 are mission phases. M_1 and M_2, if executed in parallel, could both perform the same function of **guidance**, **navigation**, and **vehicle control**. In this case, a mechanism is needed to prevent the M_1 and M_2 processes from conflicting with each other.

Let us now consider a dynamic scheduling algorithm (or structuring executive). The scheduler (1) controls the ordering of those modules which can vary in real time dependent on operator selection; (2) assigns priorities to processes based on the relative priority relationships, according to Axiom 6, for each control level; (3) prevents a violation of the HOS axioms so that no two processes can conflict with each other; and (4) determines when the total resources of the computer are approached. Such a dynamic scheduler would assume the following tools: process locks, data locks, and a scheduling algorithm which provides relative and variable priorities. The process lock for each process locks out lower priority processes other than those on its own tree from assigning data for as long as the process is active (i.e., executing or in the wait state). Data locks within a process temporarily lock out all other processes from reading elements of a data block when that block is being updated. The controller for a process is a real-time scheduler. The scheduler invokes a process, via the schedule statement, to automatically set a process lock, assign a priority, and set up data locks for the process invoked.

Each scheduled process is dynamically assigned a unique priority set which bounds unique priority sets of its dependent processes. The priority of a process is determined by its (1) level of control; (2) order of selection by the operator; and (3) predetermined priority relationships. The highest priority process is, by definition, the highest level controller. Each controller has a higher priority than the processes it controls. In order to compare the priorities of two processes, a process chain up the tree for each process is made until one level before the branches intersect. The priorities of the parent processes at that level determine the priority of the two processes in question, i.e., the process with the highest priority parent has the higher priority. Thus, we have a system where a process and all its dependent processes are either *all* higher or *all* lower than another nondependent process, and all of its dependents. Consider Fig. 1 to be a subset of the Shuttle system S.

S_1, S_2, S_3, S_4	Ascent mission phase, atmospheric entry mission phase, astronaut display, and abort mission phase, respectively
S_{11}, S_{21}, S_{31}	Ascent guidance (G_A), ascent navigation (N_A), and ascent vehicle control (C_A), respectively
S_{12}, S_{22}, S_{32}	Entry Guidance G_E, entry navigation N_E, and entry vehicle control C_E, respectively
S_{121}, S_{211}	Navigation state extrapolation and measurement incorporation, respectively

Thus, for example, in Fig. 15 the relative priorities of ascent guidance S_{11}, and measurement incorporation S_{22}, are determined by comparing the priorities of the parent mission phases S_1 and S_2.

Each module defines priority relationships for each function it controls. For example, S controlling $\{S_1\}$ might have the priority relational information: $((\bar{S}_1, \bar{S}_2) < (\bar{S}_4))$. S_3 is a function invoked by a *call* and, therefore, has the same priority as the scheduler S. The priorities S_1 and S_2 are initially equal, but their priorities (and thus, priority sets) are decided by the ordering of schedule invocation. Yet, S_1 and S_2 are always of lower priority than S_4. A typical Shuttle relationship is $(\bar{C}_E > \bar{G}_E > \bar{N}_E)$, where the dependent relationships between **vehicle control**, **guidance**, and **navigation** are maintained on a fixed relative priority basis. In the latter example, C_E can interrupt N_E. C_E is functionally dependent on G_E, i.e., C_E uses the output set of G_E as its own input set. In addition, a mission phase schedules N_E at a higher frequency than G_E. At all times the priority relationships of C_E, G_E, and N_E remain fixed.

If S_1 is selected first, S_2 cannot interrupt S_1 as long as S_1 or any of its dependent processes are being executed. When S_1 is in a wait state, S_2 can execute, but only if S_1 is not ready to execute. When S_1 is ready, process set S_1 interrupts process set S_2. If the S_2 set attempts to assign data process locked in the S_1 set, S_2 and its dependents are terminated by the scheduler. At this point the last display is regenerated by the scheduler of the terminated process, thus giving the astronaut complete visibility. If however, S_1, when it becomes active, attempts to assign data which are process locked by S_2, S_2 is terminated since S_1 has a higher priority lock than S_2. If S_2 attempts to read data process locked by S_1, and these data are presently being assigned by the other set, the S_2 process waits for the S_1 block of data to be updated. Likewise, S_1 must wait to read data presently being assigned by S_2.

The operational levels of a system are, by definition, those levels where the operator has at least one option. Each level has the potential to be an operational level. Consider the Shuttle example. The operational level S allows the astronaut to select, reselect, proceed from, or terminate S_1, S_2, or S_4 via S_3. Operator errors at each operational level are prevented via the process lock mechanism. Due to HOS axioms, at a nonoperational level (i.e., one where a conflicting process is not initiated by the operator) an error of this type would not occur. Without a static analyzer, however, the process lock mechanism of the scheduler would discover the error dynamically. Of course, the analyzer avoids an expensive way to find a software error.

Alternatives for reselecting or terminating an existing process depend, to a large extent, on desired operational procedures. The scheduler could display a "select" or "terminate" option for each operational process. Or, the operator could request the highest level scheduler which has the highest priority to terminate a specific process. If S_1 is selected when S_1 is in the queue, either the first S_1, or the second, is terminated.

Consider two processes S_1 and S_2, where S_1 has a higher priority than S_2. Scheduler S_{11} schedules S_{111}. S_{111} could have a very low or a very high priority relative to but less than S_1: but relative to S_2, S_1, and all its dependent processes have higher priorities. Thus, if S_{111} is controlled by a **do while** instead of a cyclic schedule, S_2 and its dependent processes are locked out for the duration of the **do while**. However, if S_{111} is scheduled cyclically, S_2 can be processed when S_1 and its dependents are in the wait state. In conventional priority schemes, this would not be the case, since S_2 could be arbitrarily assigned a priority less than S_1 but greater than S_{111}. Thus, the use of a **do while** construct as a substitute for a cyclic process is discouraged. It is interesting to note that a **do while** within a nonmultiprogrammed function can never be terminated by an outside controller. Thus, in this case, one would be advised to use a **do for while** instead.

APPENDIX II

Theorems directly stated in the text are presented here, with corresponding proofs.

Immediate Self-Control Theorem: Two functions cannot exist such that each is defined by the same sets of variables and one of said functions is a subfunction of the other. For if this were the case, we can show the controller function is controlling itself.

Proof: If the sets of the input variables of two functions are equal and the sets of the output variables of the same two functions are equal, the mappings are either the same or different. If the mappings are different, then the specification must be incorrect, for the controlled function must produce the result for its controller. If the mappings are equal, the two functions are equal.

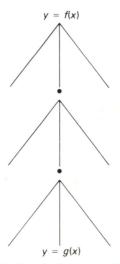

$y = f(x)$

$y = g(x)$

Figure 16   Proof of indirect self-control.

Indirect Self-Control Theorem: If a function is defined, a node defined within the tree of said function cannot be defined so that the sets of input variables are equal and the sets of output variables are equal. Again, we can show that if this condition were to exist, the controller function is controlling itself.

Proof: Consider Fig. 16. The lower level function must perform for its controller since y is not local. Each subsequent higher node must likewise perform for its controller since y is not local to any node below the highest node in which it is a member of the set of output variables (cf. Theorem 3.4.4 [1]). The lower level must be able to perform for each value of its input set. But the set of input variables is equal to the highest set of input variables. Therefore, the mapping must be the same or there would exist at least one value for y which would be incorrect. Thus, function f must be identical to function g. If we assign a value for y for each element of x, then we have performed the total function for the immediate controller.

Any other subfunction at that lower level is extraneous (cf. Theorem 1.2 [1], because every value of y can be obtained via that one subfunction. Thus, the most immediate controller and its subfunction are equal. We can either eliminate the lowest subfunction as redundant or recognize that a formulation of the type has not decomposed the controller and redesign. If we eliminate the lowest subfunction, we again continue to apply the same argument until we reach the highest node at which the equal function exists. At this point there is no recourse other than to admit the function is controlling an equal function.

Uniqueness Theorem: Each node of an HOS hierarchy is unique, i.e., two functions cannot exist within the same hierarchy such that the same relationship exists between input and output elements and the same sets of input variables and output variables are defined for each function.

Proof: Suppose the function $y = f(x)$ existed within a system at two different nodes. The two nodes could exist at the same level [Fig. 17(a)]. In this case, one of the nodes could be removed and, since the functions are equal, the controller could still perform its same mapping. Thus, all but one of the equal functions on the same level are extraneous and invalid via Theorem 1.2[1].

If $y = f(x)$ appeared as a node inner to its own tree [Fig. 17(b)] the module would be controlling its own function and is invalid via the proof of immediate self-control (cf. Section III). Likewise, any node that can be traced up the tree or down the tree from $y = f(x)$ must be of the form $y = f(x)$ [Fig. 17(c)], via the proof of indirect self-control (cf. Section III).

Consider $y = f(x)$ at one node. Variable y must communicate on its own level or perform an output element for its controller (Theorem 3,4.3 [1]). If y were a local variable [Fig. 17(d)], y could not communicate to any higher level because the controller of $y = f(x)$ could not perform an output element for y. Thus, $y = f(x)$ could not exist outer to the level at which y were a local variable. Suppose, on the other hand, that $y = f(x)$ was invoked by its controller to perform an output element for the controller. If $y = f(x)$ appeared as a node inner to any tree on the same level in which it is local [Fig. 17(e)], it would also be invalid because y could only communicate as an input variable, in this case, by Theorem 3.4.2[1].

Suppose y does not communicate on its own level. The controller of $y = f(x)$ must be a selector in which case y could be assigned by another node at the level of $y = f(x)$

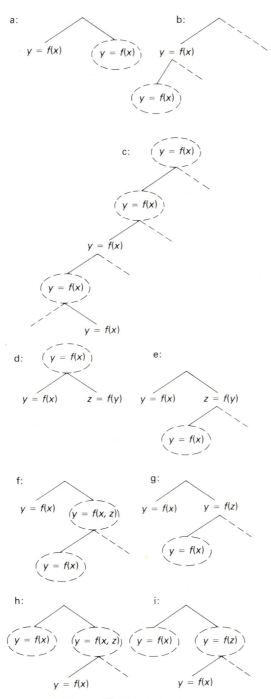

Figure 17   Proof of uniqueness.

or y is not known to another node at the level of $y = f(x)$. In the case where y is not known to a node which exists at the same level as $y = f(x)$, $y = f(x)$ could never exist inner to that node (Theorem 3.1 [1]).

In order for $y = f(x)$ to be considered as a node inner to any tree on that same level at which another $y = f(x)$ node is known to exist, the node at the same level as $y = f(x)$ can be of the form $y = f(x, z)$ or $y = f(z)$. If that function were of the form $y = f(x, z)$ [Fig. 17(f)], then the controller of $y = f(x, z)$ and $y = f(x)$ is an invalid function because it is possible that for a given element of x, more than one value of y can exist. This will be the case if we assume a selection mechanism (i.e., we have an invalid partition) or if we try to perform both functions (i.e., concurrent assignment or invalid composition). If that function were of the form $y = f(z)$ [Fig. 17(g)], the function $y = f(x)$ could not exist at any node inner to the node $y = f(z)$ because the variable is not known inner to $y = f(z)$. Thus, if $y = f(x)$ exists, another node of this form, $y = f(x)$, cannot exist at the same level or at an inner node to any other node at said level.

If y performs a direct output value for its controller, the form of the controller must be $y = f(x, z)$ [Fig. 17 (h)] or $y = f(z)$ [Fig. 17 (i)].

If the controller is of the form $y = f(z)$, x is internal to $y = f(z)$ and can never exist outer to $y = f(z)$ (Theorem 3,4.4[1]). Thus, in this case $y = f(x)$ could not exist outer to $y = f(z)$.

If the controller is of the form $y = f(x, z)$, it is not possible to have a node of the form $y = f(x)$ at the same level as $y = f(x, z)$ for the same reasons presented above (i.e., invalid function formulation of the controller). In order for $y = f(x)$ to exist at any higher level, we must perform a value for y by attempting a higher controller of the form $y = f(x, z)$. Each time, the higher controller becomes an invalid function. Thus, we have shown that $y = f(x)$ must be a unique node of a system.

ACKNOWLEDGMENT   The authors would like to express appreciation to L. Robinson of Stanford Research Institute for a most helpful and critical review of this paper. The authors would also like to thank A. Volta for technical editing assistance, and G. Lopes for the preparation of the manuscript.

REFERENCES

1. M. Hamilton and S. Zeldin, "Higher order software techniques applied to a space shuttle prototype program," in *Lecture Notes in Computer Science*, vol. 19, G. Goos and J. Hartmanis, Eds. New York: Springer-Verlag, pp. 17–31, presented at Program. Symp. Proc., Colloque sur la Programmation, Paris, France, April 9–11, 1974.

2. M. Hamilton, "Design of the GN&C flight software specification," Charles Stark Draper Lab., Cambridge, MA, Doc. C-3899, Feb. 1973.

3. R. Millard, internal Charles Stark Draper Lab. study of APOLLO, Cambridge, MA, 1969–1972.

4. L. Fair et al., *Planning Guide for Computer Program Development,* System Development Corp., Santa Monica, CA, Tech. Memo. TM-2314/000/00A, May, 1965, p. 57.

5. B. W. Boehm, "Some information processing implications of air force space missions: 1970–1980," Rand Corp., Santa Monica, CA, Tech. Memo. RM-1213-PR, Jan. 1970.

6. A. M. Turing, "On computable numbers with an application to the entscheidungs problem," in *Proc. London Math. Soc.*, ser. 2, vol. 42, 1936.

7. D. Parnas, "On a 'buzzword': Hierarchical structure," in *1971 Fall Joint Comput. Conf., IFIPS Conf. Proc.*, vol. 39. Montvale, NJ: AFIPS Press, 1971.

8. D. D. Chamberlin, "The single-assignment approach to parallel processing," in *AFIPS Proc.* New York: Elsevier, 1974.

9. W. A. Wulf et al., "Bliss: A language for systems programming," *Commun. Ass. Comput. Mach.*, vol. 12, Dec. 1973.

10. B. Randell, "Research on computing system reliability at the University of Newcastle upon Tyne, 1972–1973," Comput. Lab., Univ. Newcastle upon Tyne, Newcastle upon Tyne, Scotland, Tech. Rep. Ser. 57, Jan. 1974.

11. J. Miller et al., CS-4 *Language Reference Manual,* Intermetrics, Inc., Cambridge, MA.

12. J. Schwartz, *On Programming. An Interim Report on the SETL Project,* Dept. Comput. Sci., Courant Inst. Math. Sci., New York University, New York. "Installment 1: Generalities," 1973; "Installment 2: The SETL Language and Examples of Its Use, 1973.

13. O. J. Dahl, E. W. Dijkstra, and C. A. R. Hoare, *Structured Programming,* C. A. R. Hoare, Gen. Ed. New York: Academic, 1972.

14. M. Hamilton, "Management of APOLLO programming and its application to the shuttle," Charles Stark Draper Lab., Cambridge, MA, Software Shuttle Memo. 29, May 1971.

15. M. Hamilton and S. Zeldin, "MERCURY statistical analysis," Charles Stark Draper Lab., Cambridge, MA, MERCURY Memo. 34, Nov. 1973.

16. N. Brodeur, "MERCURY statistical analysis report revisited," Charles Stark Draper Lab., Cambridge, MA, MERCURY Memo. 34, Nov. 1973.

17. M. Hamilton, "First draft of a report on the analysis of APOLLO system problems during flight," Charles Stark Draper Lab., Cambridge, MA, Shuttle Management Note 14, Oct. 1972.

18. _____, "The AGC executive and its influence on software management," Charles Stark Draper Lab., Cambridge, MA, Shuttle Management Note 2, Feb. 1972.

19. H. Laning, AGC Program Sundisk, Charles Stark Draper Lab., Cambridge, MA, Executive Rev. 267, NASA 2021108-011, Nov. 1967.

20. M. Hamilton, AGC Program Sundisk, Charles Stark Draper Lab., Cambridge, MA, Display Interface Rev. 267, NASA 2021108-011, Nov. 1967.

21. D. Lickly, AGC Program Sundisk, Charles Stark Draper Lab., Cambridge, MA, Restarts Rev. 267, NASA 2021108-011, Nov. 1967.

22. C. Muntz, "Users guide to the block II AGC/LGC interpreter," Draper/M.I.T. Doc. R-489, Apr. 1965.

23. D. L. Parnas, "On the criteria to be used in decomposing systems into modules," *Commun. Ass. Comput. Mach.*, vol. 15, Dec. 1972, pp. 1053–1058.

24. _____, "A technique for software module specification with examples," *Commun. Ass. Comput. Mach.*, vol. 15, May 1972, pp. 330–336.

25. M. Hamilton and S. Zeldin, "Higher order software requirements," Charles Stark Draper Lab., Cambridge, MA, Doc. E-2793, Aug. 1973.

26. _____, "Top-down/bottom-up, structured programming and program structuring," Charles Stark Draper Lab., Cambridge, MA, Rev. 1, Doc. E-2728, Dec. 1972.

27. W. Daly, "Automatic flowcharts," Charles Stark Draper Lab., Cambridge, MA, MERCURY Memo. 53, Mar. 1974.

28. IBM, "Chief programmer teams principles and procedures," IBM Fed. Syst. Div., Gaithersburg, MD, Rep. FSC-71-5108, June 1971.

29. G. M. Weinberg, *Psychology of Computer Programming*. New York: Van Nostrand Reinhold, 1971.

30. J. R. White and L. Presser, "A tool for enforcing system structure," in *Proc. Ass. Comput. Mach.*, 1973.

31. M. Hamilton, "A discussion of higher order software concepts as they apply to functional requirements and specifications," Charles Stark Draper Lab., Cambridge, MA, Doc. P-019, Dec. 1973.

32. B. McCoy, "DAIS avionic software development techniques," presented at the Amer. Inst. Aeronaut. and Astronaut. Digital Avionics Syst. Conf., Boston, MA, Apr. 2–4, 1975.

33. G. Boetje, "Managing software development: A new approach," presented at the IEEE Nat. Aerospace Electron. Conf. (NAECON), Dayton, OH, June 10–12, 1975; Charles Stark Draper Lab., Cambridge, MA, Doc. P-165.

34. D. DeVorkin, "The DAIS executive system," to be published.

35. The Charles Stark Draper Lab., Inc., "Submittal of structured flowcharts of the approach and landing test (ALT) GN&C design for the space shuttle orbiter GN&C integration task," Charles Stark Draper Lab., Cambridge, MA, Jan. 1975.

36. Rockwell Int. Corp., "Space shuttle orbiter approach and landing test, level C, functional subsystem software requirements document guidance, navigation and control, part A, guidance," append. A, Nov. 1974; also as above, "Part B, flight control," Downey, CA.

37. Honeywell, Inc., "Horizontal flight digital autopilot requirement definition," Honeywell, Sarasota, FL, ED 21532, PRD UA17, July 1974, vol. II, sect. 5–7.

38. IBM, "Space shuttle orbiter avionics software," vol. III, "Applications software, part 1-GN&C," "Approach and landing test (ALT) functional design specification," 75-SS-0473, Fed. Syst. Division, Houston, TX, Feb. 1975.

39. D. J. Lickly et al., *HAL/S Language Specification*, Intermetrics, Inc., Cambridge, MA.

40. G. Goddard, "Control map development," Charles Stark Draper Lab., Cambridge, MA, Software Control System Analyzer Memo. 4, Jan. 1975.

Margaret Hamilton received the A.B. degree in mathematics from Earlham College, Richmond, IN, in 1958.

Since 1965 she has been with The Charles Stark Draper Laboratory, Cambridge, MA, where she is currently Division Leader of the Computer Science Division. She heads a group of software engineers, the members of which are engaged in both research and application in the areas of systems flight software for: Space Shuttle, C4, DAIS and F8. In addition, her group has been involved in software design and implementation for automatic aircraft control, production control systems, computer graphics, biomedical research, transportation, consumer durables, data management, helicopter navigation and control, and instrumentation redundancy studies. She is presently engaged in designing software techniques covering subjects of software reliability and management. As head of a 100 plus member programming group, she was responsible for the design, development, verification, and documentation of all command and lunar module on-board software for the Apollo and Skylab programs. She has personally contributed to such software activities as command module flight software design and programming, quality assurance, test engineering, systems analysis, real-time software systems integration, multiprogramming, task management, error detection and recovery, and man/machine interface design.

Saydean Zeldin received the A.B. degree in physics from Temple University, Philadelphia, PA, in 1961.

Since 1966 she has been with The Charles Stark Draper Laboratory, Cambridge, MA, where she is currently Section Chief of the Computer Science Division. She leads a group of software engineers presently engaged in the design of software techniques which include such areas as software reliability, management, design techniques, verification methods, and real-time multiprogrammed systems. Her interest in the reliability of large-scale software systems stems from her experience in the design, development, and verification of the Apollo on-board software. These software activities included: command and lunar module flight software design and programming, test engineering, systems analysis, and real-time software systems integration. As a Principal Engineer at The Charles Stark Draper Laboratory she personally contributed to Apollo programs involving orbital maneuvers, atmospheric entry, and mission sequences that interfaced with the astronaut and various hardware systems.

ALGEBRAIC SPECIFICATION OF SIX
INTRINSIC DATA TYPES USED IN AXES*

Although AXES provides the means for algebraically specifying any desired abstract data type, there are a few types that are of sufficiently general usefulness in a wide variety of systems that we include them in AXES as intrinsic types. These types are specified algebraically in this Appendix.

In all we provide six intrinsic data types in AXES: Booleans, properties, sets, natural numbers, integers, and rational numbers. The Boolean data type automatically solves the "boot-strap" problem for abstract data types, because it can be characterized as a homogeneous algebra, i.e., entirely in terms of itself. All our other intrinsic types presuppose the prior characterization of type **Boolean** and so must be characterized as heterogeneous algebras. Type **Property** presupposes only type **Boolean**, while type **Set** and type **Natural** all presuppose type **Property**. Type **Integer** presupposes type **Natural**, and type **Rational** presupposes type **Integer**. Our reasons for not providing the real numbers as an intrinsic data type will be discussed in connection with our algebraic specification of the rationals. All our intrinsic types will be specified in AXES syntax, rather than in the strictly mathematical format used in Appendix III. In this Appendix, AXES statements are often numbered for purposes of discussion (these numbers are not intended to be included as part of the AXES syntax).

Type **Boolean** is particularly easy to characterize, because it contains only two values, true and false (truth and falsity). Since Σ contains only one set and that set is finite, we could identify that set explicitly by simply listing its members. This frees us from the need to characterize the equality relation on type **Boolean**, which we could not do without a prior characterization of type **Property**. Since there are only two distinct Booleans, which we explicitly list in the category specification, we can always tell which one we are dealing with simply by looking at it:

DATA TYPE: BOOLEAN;
PRIMITIVE OPERATIONS:

$boolean_3$ = And($boolean_1$,$boolean_2$);   1.
$boolean_2$ = Not($boolean_1$);   2.

*From Higher Order Software, Inc., Technical Report TR-4. *Axes Syntax Description* by M. Hamilton and S. Zeldin, with this appendix written by S. Cushing, December 1976.

AXIOMS:
 WHERE True IS A CONSTANT BOOLEAN:
 WHERE False IS A CONSTANT BOOLEAN;

And(True,True) = True;	1.
And(True,False) = False;	2.
And(False,True) = False;	3.
And(False,False) = False;	4.
Not(True) = False;	5.
Not(False) = True;	6.

END BOOLEAN;

In this algebra we specify that Σ's single member contains exactly two elements, true and false, and that ω contains exactly two primitive operations, And and Not. And is characterized as behaving exactly like the conjunction operator of propositional logic and Not is characterized as behaving like the negation operator. These two elements and these two operations, as axiomatized, are all we need to characterize the type **Boolean** as an abstract data type.

Once we have characterized an abstract data type in terms of its categories and its primitive operations, defined collectively and implicitly through its axioms, we will often find it useful to define other operations on that type. Note that the categories of the type algebra **Boolean** other than Boolean itself were not listed explicitly in the AXES specification above, but only implicitly through their appearance in the PRIMITIVE OPERATION specification.

We are free to define any operation we want on an already-defined type as long as the operation definition is consistent with the axioms of the type. New operations can be characterized either as operations (cf. HAM76, Section 8) or as derived operations (cf. HAM76, Section 16). An operation is specified in AXES explicitly in a form that is directly translatable to a control map. A derived operation is specified implicitly by means of assertions that describe the behavior of the operation with respect to other already-defined operations. Either kind of operation *could* be written as a control map, if desired. They differ in how they are specified, not in what they are. What distinguishes both of these kinds of operations from primitive operations on their data type is that their existence is provable mathematically from the existence of the primitive operations and the axioms of the type. If an operation's existence is not so provable, then adding it to the type produces a new type, of which the new operation is a primitive.

In the case of type **Boolean**, for example, we will often find it useful, as in logic, to have available the notions of disjunction, entailment, and sameness of truth-value. We can introduce these notions as operations on type **Boolean** by means of the following definitions:

OPERATION: b_3 = Or(b_1,b_2);
WHERE b_1,b_2,b_3 ARE BOOLEANS;
WHEREBY b_3 = Not(And(Not(b_1),Not(b_2)));
END Or;

OPERATION: b_3 = Entails(b_1,b_2);
WHERE b_1,b_2,b_3 ARE BOOLEANS;
WHEREBY b_3 = Or(Not(b_1),b_2);
END Entails;

OPERATION: b$_3$ = Same(b$_1$,b$_2$)
WHERE b$_1$,b$_2$,b$_3$ ARE BOOLEANS;
WHEREBY b$_3$ = Or(And(b$_1$,b$_3$),And(Not(b$_1$),Not(b$_2$)));
End Same;

The first definition defines Or in terms of And and Not in a way that is familiar from propositional logic. We could have introduced it as a primitive operation by including the axioms:

Or (True,True)   = True;
Or (True,False) = True;
Or (False,True) = True;
Or (False,False) = False;

in our axiomatic specification of type **Boolean**, but this would have complicated our algebra unnecessarily. We simply do not *need* Or to *characterize* the Booleans as a *data type*. Similarly, we could have included Entails and Same as primitive operations, but there was no point in doing so as long as we can define them as operations. The point is that And and Not are all we *need* to *characterize* the Booleans, even though there are other operations that we find useful, and that we therefore introduce for other purposes.

It should be noted that Same is an equivalence relation on type **Boolean**. This relation coincides with equality, because we already know when two Booleans are the same or distinct, as a result, as noted above, of the finiteness of the single set in Σ. If this were not the case, in fact, that is, if equality were not automatically given to us, then it would be impossible to write axioms for type **Boolean**, because the "=" sign would be meaningless. For convenience and clarity, we will sometimes use "=", and a few other symbols like "<", in the conventional way, rather than in strictly functional notation, once we have already defined them functionally. For example, it may be simpler to write "$i_1 < i_2$" in an axiom for type **Rational**, rather than "$I<(i_1,i_2)$." This is permissible, because we will already have characterized I< (i.e., "integer-less than") in our specification of type **Integer** (cf. HAM76, Section 11).

The second intrinsic data type that AXES provides is that of properties. We will need properties in characterizing the sets as a data type. Properties are basically things that map other things onto truth-values, i.e., Booleans. The property "prime", for example, maps the integer 2 onto true, 3 onto true, and 4 onto false, because 2 is prime and 3 is prime, but 4 is not prime. In characterizing properties algebraically, we will have to state what kinds of things the properties are properties of. We can do this by including a type parameter "T" in our category specification and treating our algebraic specification as a function of T. It follows that our algebra for type **Property** is really an algebra schema depending on the type parameter T and that there is, therefore, a distinct type **Property of (T)** for every type **T**.

We can express the fact that properties map other things (i.e., t's) onto Booleans by introducing a function that maps properties and t's onto Booleans. If we call this function "Has", so that "Has(P,t)" is true, when t has the property P, then we must specify that Has maps properties and t's onto Booleans in a way that preserves conjunctions and negations. This can be stated very simply in terms of axioms. To define equality or identity of properties, we will also have to introduce two quantifier operations Forall and Exists (CUS76a). Properties can be mapped onto Booleans by combining them with t's via the Has function, but they can also be mapped onto Booleans directly via these quantifier functions. Has maps P *and t* onto true, if *t* has the property P. Forall maps P *itself* onto true, *if every t* has the property P. Exists, similarly, maps P onto true, if *there is some* t that has P, regardless of which particular t that is. Once we have Forall available to us, it will be a simple matter to specify when two properties are equal (identical).

As well as characterizing the relationship, which we have just discussed, between type **Property (of T)** and type **Boolean**, we must also characterize the internal structure of type **Property (of T)**. Properties constitute a Boolean lattice (FUN74), so we must include the axioms for a Boolean lattice in their algebraic specification as a data type. The Booleans also constitute a Boolean lattice, but since there are only two Booleans, enabling us to list the values of their primitive operations explicitly, we can prove the axioms for a Boolean lattice from that explicit list of values. For properties, however, we must include the axioms for a Boolean lattice as axioms of algebra, because there is nothing else that we can prove them from.

The foregoing discussion is summarized (and elaborated) in the following AXES specification:

```
DATA TYPE: PROPERTY(OF T);
PRIMITIVE OPERATIONS:
```

$property_3$ = Pand($property_1$,$property_2$);	1.
$property_3$ = Por($property_1$,$property_2$);	2.
$property_2$ = Pnot($property_1$);	3.
$property_3$ = Pentails($property_1$,$property_2$);	4.
boolean = Has(property,t);	5.
boolean = Forall(property);	6.
boolean = Exists(property);	7.
boolean = Ident($property_1$,$property_2$);	8.

```
AXIOMS:
        WHERE T IS SOME TYPE;
        WHERE P₁,P₂,P₃ ARE PROPERTIES;
        WHERE t is a T;
        WHERE Nec is a constant property;
        WHERE Contra IS A CONSTANT PROPERTY;
```

$Pand(P_1,P_2) = Pand(P_2,P_1)$;	1.
$Por(P_1,P_2) = Por(P_2,P_1)$;	2.
$Pand(P_1,Pand(P_2,P_3)) = Pand(Pand(P_1,P_2),P_3)$;	3.
$Por(P_1,Por(P_2,P_3)) = Por(Por(P_1,P_2),P_3)$;	4.
$Pand(P_1,Por(P_1,P_2)) = P_1$;	5.
$Por(P_1,Pand(P_1,P_2)) = P_1$;	6.
$Pand(P_1,Por(P_2,P_3)) = Por(Pand(P_1,P_2), Pand(P_1,P_3))$;	7.
$Por(P_1,Pand(P_2,P_3)) = Pand(Por(P_1,P_2), Por(P_1,P_3))$;	8.
$Pand(P,Pnot(P)) = Contra$;	9.
$Por(P,Pnot(P)) = Nec$;	10.
$Has(Nec,t) = True$;	11.
$Has(Contra,t) = False$;	12.
$Has(Pand(P_1,P_2),t) = And(Has(P_1,t), Has(P_2,t))$;	13.
$Has(Por(P_1,P_2),t) = Or(Has(P_1,t),Has(P_2,t))$;	14.
$Has(Pnot(P),t) = Not(Has(P,t))$;	15.
$Forall(Nec) = True$;	16.
$Exists(Contra) = False$;	17.
$Forall(P) = Not(Exists(Pnot(P)))$;	18.

Exists(P) = Not(Forall(Pnot(P)));   19.
Entails(Forall(P), Same(Has(P,t),True)) = True;   20.
Entails(Same(Has(P,t),True), Exists(P)) = True;   21.
Ident(P_1,P_2) = And(Forall(Pentails(P_1,P_2)),
                    Forall(Pentails(P_2,P_1)));   22.
END PROPERTY(OF T)
OPERATION: P_3 = Pentails(P_1,P_2);
WHERE P_1,P_2,P_3 ARE PROPERTIES;
WHEREBY P_3 = Por(Pnot(P_1),P_2);
END Pentails;

Axioms 1–10 in this specification characterize type **Property (of T)** as a Boolean lattice, and together with Axiom 22, give us the internal structure of the type. Axiom 22 is essential to the internal structure, because it tells us when two properties are the same and when they are distinct. The value Nec is the necessary property, which every t has, and serves as the unit element of the lattice, while the value Contra is the contradictory property, which no t has, and serves as the zero element of the lattice. Axioms 18 and 19 tell us that Forall and Exists are related by dual negation, which is definable for any quantifier (CUS76a, CUS76b). Axioms 11–21 characterize the interface of type **Property (of T)** with type **Boolean**, but they also provide the prerequisite for the meaningfulness of Axiom 22. We thus see the sort of mutual dependence among the various aspects of specification, in this case between the internal structure and the external interface, that is characteristic of algebraic specification. One might think that Ident could be defined as an operation, since Axiom 22 defines it explicitly in terms of already defined operations. This would be wrong however, because a notion of identity (equality) is essential to characterizing the internal structure of the type. Without Axiom 22, Axioms 1–10 would literally be meaningless, because we would have no clearly specified interpretation of the " = " signs that occur in them.

We have stated (in Axiom 22) that two properties are identical if they are mutually entailing for every member of the type whose members they are properties of, that is, if they hold for exactly the same members of that type. Ultimately, such a definition is inadequate, because it treats certain properties as identical which, for some purposes, should not be considered identical. The two conjunctive properties, "both less than and greater than 2" and "both less than and greater than 100", for example, are distinct properties, in the general sense, because they "say different things" about the objects they are supposed to hold for. By our definition, however, these two properties are identical and, in fact, are both identical to Contra, because they hold for exactly the same objects, namely none. Since we are interested in properties primarily as a way of specifying set partitions in system specifications, our definition of identity nevertheless suffices for our purposes.

Given the way we have characterized properties as an abstract data type, it is a simple matter to do the same for sets. Because of the way we have defined identity for properties, the type **Property (of T)**, as we have specified it, will be isomorphic to the type **Set (of T)**. For every property there is a set, called the *extension* of that property, which consists of exactly the objects that have that property. Given our definition of property identity, this mapping from properties to sets is one-to-one. It follows that we can characterize type **Set (of T)** isomorphically to type **Property (of T)** in terms of this extension mapping, if we guarantee that the mapping and its inverse preserve the primitive operations of the two types. This is done in the following specification:

```
DATA TYPE: SET(OF T);
PRIMITIVE OPERATIONS:
set₃ = Inters(set₁,set₂);                                          1.
set₃ = Union(set₁,set₂);                                           2.
set₂ = Comp(set₁);                                                 3.
set = Extension(property);                                         4.
property = Prop(set);                                              5.
boolean = Element(t,set);                                          6.
boolean = Subset(set₁,set₂);                                       7.
boolean = Equal(set₁,set₂);                                        8.

AXIOMS:
        WHERE s₁,s₂,s₃ ARE SETS;
        WHERE P IS A PROPERTY;
        WHERE Null IS A CONSTANT SET;
        WHERE T IS SOME TYPE;
Inters(s₁,s₂) = Inters(s₂,s₁);                                     1.
Union(s₁,s₂) = Union(s₂,s₁);                                       2.
Inters(s₁,Inters(s₂,s₃)) = Inters(Inters(s₁,s₂),s₃);               3.
Union(s₁,Union(s₂,s₃)) = Union(Union(s₁,s₂),s₃);                   4.
Inters(s₁,Union(s₁,s₂)) = s₁;                                      5.
Union(s₁,Inters(s₁,s₂)) = s₁;                                      6.
Inters(s₁,Union(s₂,s₃)) = Union(Inters(s₁,s₂),
                                Inters(s₁,s₃));                    7.
Union(s₁,Inters(s₂,s₃)) = Inters(Union(s₁,s₂),
                                Union(s₁,s₃));                     8.
Inters(s,Comp(s)) = Null;                                          9.
Union(s,Comp(s)) = T;                                             10.
Extension(Prop(s)) = s;                                           11.
Prop(Extension(P)) = P;                                           12.
Prop(T) = Nec;                                                    13.
Prop(Null) = Contra;                                             14.
Prop(Inters(s₁,s₂)) = Pand(Prop(s₁), Prop(s₂));                  15.
Prop(Union(s₁,s₂)) = Por(Prop(s₁), Prop(s₂));                    16.
Prop(Comp(s)) = Pnot(Prop(s));                                   17.
Element(t,s) = Has(Prop(s),t);                                   18.
Subset(s₁,s₂) = Forall(Pentails(Prop(s₁), Prop(s₂)));            19.
Equal(s₁,s₂) = And(Subset(s₁,s₂), Subset(s₂,s₁));                20.
END SET(OF T);
```

Axioms 1–10 in this specification characterize type *Set of (T)* as a Boolean lattice, with the null set Null as the zero element and the universal set T as the unit element. Axioms 11–17 define the isomorphism mapping between type *Set (of T)* and type *Property (of T)*. The function Extension maps a property onto the set of elements that have that property, and the function Prop, meaning ''property'', maps a set onto the property of being in that set. This automatically accounts for all properties because of our definition of property identity, as noted above. Axioms 18 and 19 define the usual notions of element and subset, and Axiom 20 defines equality as mutual subset. Something is in a set if it has the property that corresponds to the set and one set is a subset of a second if everything that has the property of the first has the property of the second. Two sets are equal if each is a subset of the other. Upon reflection, we realize that the *set* Set (of T), i.e., the member of Σ, as opposed to the algebra, turns out to be just the power set of T itself.

Now that we have sets and properties available to us, we can construct an adequate specification of the natural numbers as an abstract data type. As we noted in Appendix III, Guttag's specification of the type **Natural Number** is inadequate, because it leaves out the crucial axiom of induction. This axiom can be formulated as follows (FUN74, p. 72):

If a property P of the natural numbers satisfies the following two conditions, then P holds for every natural number:

1. P holds for 0.
2. For every natural number n, if P holds for n, then P holds for n^1.

where n^1 is the successor of n. This axiom tells us that we can be sure *every* natural number has a given property, if we know that 0 has that property and that $n + 1$'s having it follows from n's having it, for every n. If we begin at 0, in other words, and go successively from each natural number to the next, then we eventually get to every natural number. This is a crucial characteristic of the natural numbers and cannot be omitted if our intent is to characterize their data type as fully as possible.

Since we now have the facility for dealing with properties, we could formalize the axiom of induction as an axiom of type **Natural Number** in terms of the members of type **Property (of Natural Number)**, by taking $T =$ **Natural Number**, in other words, in our type **Property (of T)**. It turns out, however, that the actual formulation of this axiom in our framework is very complicated and somewhat unintuitive, so we are led to look for an alternative axiom that would have the same effect as the axiom of induction. Fortunately, this purpose can be served by a characteristic of the natural numbers called the "well-ordering principle", which states that every non-empty set of natural numbers contains a least element. The axiom of induction and the well-ordering principle are logically equivalent, in the sense that each can be derived from the other within the context of the other axioms for the natural numbers (LAN67), so we are free to take either one as one of our axioms. The well-ordering principle can be formulated very simply in our framework, in contrast to the complexity and unintuitive character of the axiom of induction, so we will adopt it to complete our specification of type **Natural Number**.

This gives us the following AXES specification:

```
DATA TYPE: NATURAL;
PRIMITIVE OPERATIONS:
natural₂ = Succ(natural₁);                              1.
boolean = ?Zero?(natural);                              2.
boolean = ?Equal?(natural₁,natural₂);                   3.
boolean = ?>?(natural₁,natural₂);                       4.
natural = Smin(set(of naturals)₁);                      5.

AXIOMS:
     WHERE n, n₁ ARE NATURALS;
     WHERE s IS A SET(OF NATURALS);
     WHERE Zero IS A CONSTANT NATURAL;
```

?Zero?(Zero) = True;	1.
?Zero?(Succ(n)) = False;	2.
?Equal?(Zero,Zero) = True;	3.
?Equal?(Succ(n),Zero) = False;	4.
?Equal?(Zero,Succ(n)) = False;	5.
?Equal?(Succ(n),Succ(n_1)) = ?Equal?(n,n_1);	6.
?>?(Zero,Zero) = False;	7.
?>?(Succ(n),Zero) = True;	8.
?>?(Zero,Succ(n)) = False;	9.
?>?(Succ(n),Succ(n_1)) = ?>(n,n_1);	10.
Element(Smin(s),s) = True;	11.
Entails(Element(n,s), ?>?(n,Smin(s))) = True;	12.
END NATURAL;	

This specification is identical to Guttag's specification of type **Natural Number**, which we saw in Appendix III, except for the new operation Smin and the two new Axioms 11 and 12. Axioms 11 and 12, along with the presence of Smin in ω, provide us with the effect of the well-ordering principle. The fact that the Smin is in ω tells us that every set s of natural numbers is associated with a natural number Smin(s). Axiom 11 tells us that the natural Smin(s) is an element of s and Axiom 12 tells us that Smin(s) is, in fact, the minimum element of s. This specification, then, completely specifies type **Natural Number** as the type of what we usually think of as the natural numbers.

Now that we have a full specification of the natural numbers, we can define operations on their data type. Since we have already characterized equality of natural numbers as a primitive operation of our data type, we are free to interpret the " = " sign in our definitions as referring to that equality. We will also use other operations such as "And" in the customary way, rather than the more complicated functional notations, as long as these operations have been fully characterized (cf. Section 10). Some of the following operations, such as Sum and Prod, meaning sum and product, respectively, are included because of their general usefulness; others are included because they will be useful in specifying later data types:

DERIVED OPERATION: n_3 = Sum(n_1,n_2);	
WHERE n_1,n_2,n_3 ARE NATURALS;	
Sum(Zero,n_2) = n_2;	1.
Sum(n_1,Zero) = n_1;	2.
Sum(n_1,Succ(n_2)) = Succ(Sum(n_1,n_2));	3.
Sum(Succ(n_1),n_2) = Succ(Sum(n_1,n_2));	4.
END Sum;	
DERIVED OPERATION: n_3 = Prod(n_1,n_2);	
WHEREn_1,n_2,n_3 ARE NATURALS;	
Prod(Zero,n_2) = Zero;	1.
Prod(n_1,Zero) = Zero	2.
Prod(n_1,Succ(n_2)) = Sum(Prod(n_1,n_2),n_1);	3.
Prod(Succ(n_1),n_2) = Sum(Prod(n_1,n_2),n_2);	4.
END Prod;	
DERIVED OPERATION: n_3 = Ndiff(n_1,n_2);	
WHERE n_1,n_2,n_3 ARE NATURALS;	
Sum(n_1,Ndiff($^1n_1$,n_2)) = n_2;	1.
Ndiff(^{2}(n_1,n_2)) = REJECT;	2.

PARTITION OF (n_1,n_2) IS
 $^1(n_1,n_2)|n_1>n_2,$
 $^2(n_1,n_2)|n_2>n_1;$
END Ndiff;

DERIVED OPERATION: $n_3 = Max(n_1,n_2);$
WHERE n_1,n_2,n_3 ARE NATURALS;
$Max^1(n_1,n_2) = n_1;$ 1.
$Max\ ^2(n_1,n_2) = n_2;$ 2.
PARTITION OF (n_1,n_2) IS
 $^1(n_1,n_2)|n_2\leq n_1,$
 $^2(n_1,n_2)|n_1\leq n_2;$
END Max;

DERIVED OPERATION: $n_3 = Min(n_1,n_2);$
WHERE n_1,n_2,n_3 ARE NATURALS;
$Min(^1(n_1,n_2)) = {}^1n_2;$ 1.
$Min(^2(n_1,n_2)) = {}^2n_1;$ 2.
PARTITION OF (n_1,n_2) IS
 $^1(n_1,n_2)|n_2\leq n_1,$
 $^2(n_1,n_2)|n_1\leq n_2;$
END Min;

DERIVED OPERATION: $n_3 = Quot(n_1,n_2);$
WHERE n_1,n_2,n_3 ARE NATURALS;
$Quot\ ^1(n_1,n_2) = REJECT;$ 1.
$Sum(Prod(Quot\ ^2(n_1,n_2), Rem\ ^2(n_1,n_2)))=n_1;$ 2.
PARTITION OF (n_1,n_2) IS
 $^1(n_1,n_2)|n_2 = 0$
 $^2(n_1,n_2)|n_2 = 0;$
END Quot;

DERIVED OPERATION: $n_3 = GCD(n_1,n_2);$
WHERE n_1,n_2,n_3 ARE NATURALS;
$Factor(GCD(n_1,n_2),n_1) = True;$ 1.
$Factor(GCD(n_1,n_2),n_2) = True;$ 2.
$Entails(And(And(Factor(n_1,n_2),Factor(n_1,n_3)),Not(?Equal?(n_1,Zero))),$
$Factor(n_1,GCD(n_2,n_3))) = True;$ 3.
END GCD;

OPERATION: $n_3 = Rem(n_1,n_2);$
WHERE n_1,n_2,n_3 ARE NATURALS;
EITHER $n_3 = K_{REJECT}(^1n_1,{}^1n_2)$ OTHERWISE
EITHER $n_3 = IDENTIFY\ (^2n_1,{}^2n_2)$ OTHERWISE
WHEREBY $n_3 = Rem(Ndiff\ ^3(n_1,n_2),{}^3n_2;$
PARTITION OF (n_1,n_2) IS
 $^1(n_1,n_2)|n_2 = 0,$
 $^2(n_1,n_2)|n_2\quad 0\ AND\ n_1 < n_2,$
 $^3(n_1,n_2)|n_2\quad 0\ AND\ n_2 \leq n_1;$
END Rem;

OPERATION: $b = Factor\ (n_1,n_2);$
WHERE n_1,n_2 ARE NATURALS;
WHERE b IS A BOOLEAN;
WHEREBY $b = ?Equal?(Rem(n_2,n_1),Zero);$
END Factor;

Derived operations Sum and Prod give us addition and multiplication, respectively. Derived operation Ndiff gives us the subtraction of smaller naturals from larger ones. Derived operation Max gives us the larger of two naturals, derived operation Rem gives us division (quotient) with remainder, and operation Factor tells us when one natural is a factor of another. Derived operation GCD gives us the greatest common divisor of two naturals and will be needed in the specification of the rationals.

The Integers can be characterized as a data type in terms of the natural numbers by recognizing that an integer is just a natural number with a sign. Since we need two distinct signs, we can take our signs to be the Booleans, with True interpreted as plus and False interpreted as minus. This gives us the following specifications:

```
DATA TYPE: INTEGER;
PRIMITIVE OPERATIONS:
boolean = ?Iequal?(integer₁,integer₂);                          1.
boolean = ?I>?(integer₁,integer₂);                              2.
natural = Abs(integer);                                         3.
boolean = Sign(integer);                                        4.
integer₃ = Isum(integer₁,integer₂);                             5.
integer₃ = Iprod(integer₁,integer₂);                            6.
integer₃ = Iquot(integer₁,integer₂);                            7.

AXIOMS:
        WHERE i₁,i₂ ARE NATURALS;
        WHERE Izero IS A CONSTANT INTEGER;
        WHERE Ione IS A CONSTANT INTEGER;
?Iequal?(i₁,i₂) = Or(And(?Equal?(Abs(i₁),Zero),
                         ?Equal?(Abs(i₂),Zero)),
                     And(?Equal?(Abs(i₁),Abs(i₂)),
                         Same(Sign(i₁),Sign(i₂))));            1.
?I?(i₁,i₂) = (Same(Sign(i₁),True) & Same(Sign(i₂),True)
                 &>?(Abs(i₁),Abs(i₂)))
             !(Same(Sign(i₁),False) & Same(Sign(i₁),False)
                 &>?(Abs(i₂),Abs(i₁)))
             !(Same(Sign(i₁),True) & Same(Sign(i₂),False));   2.
Abs(Isum(i₁,i₂)) = Sum(Abs(¹i₁),Abs(¹i₂)) AND
                   (Ndiff(Max(Abs(²i₁), Abs(²i₂)),
                         Min(Abs(²i₁),Abs(²i₂)));             3.
PARTITION OF (i₁,i₂) IS
        ¹(i₁,i₂)|Sign(i₁) = Sign(i₂),
        ²(i₁,i₂)|Sign(i₁)      Sign(i₁);
Sign(Isum(i₁,i₂)) = Sign(¹i₁) AND Sign(²i₁) AND Sign(³i₂);    4.
PARTITION OF (i₁,i₂) IS
        ¹(i₁,i₂)|Sign(i₁) = Sign (i₂),
        ²(i₁,i₂)|Sign(i₁) = Sign(i₂) AND Abs(i₂) ≤ Abs(i₁),
        ³(i₁,i₂)|Sign(i₁) = Sign(i₂) AND Abs(i₁) ≤ Abs(i₂);
Abs(Iprod(i₁,i₂)) = Prod(Abs(i₁),Abs(i₂));                    5.
Sign(Iprod(i₁,i₂)) = Same(Sign(i₁),Sign(i₂));                 6.
Abs(Izero) = Zero;                                            7.
Sign(Izero) = True;                                           8.
Abs(Ione) = Succ(Zero);                                       9.
Sign(Ione) = True;                                           10.
```

Abs(Iquot(i_1,i_2)) = Quot(As(i_1),Abs(i_2));   11.
Sign(Iquot(i_1,i_2)) = Same(Sign(i_1),Sign(i_2));   12.
END INTEGER;

DERIVED OPERATION: $integer_2$ = Iopp($integer_1$);
WHERE i IS AN INTEGER;
Sum(i,Iopp(i)) = Izero;
END Iopp;

OPERATION: i_3 = Idiff(i_1,i_2);
WHERE i_1,i_2,i_3 ARE INTEGERS;
WHEREBY i_3 = Sum(i_1,Iopp(i_2));
END Idiff;

DERIVED OPERATION: $integer_3$ = IGCD($integer_1,integer_2$);
WHERE i_1,i_2 ARE INTEGERS;
Abs(IGCD(i_1,i_2)) = GCD(Abs(i_1),Abs(i_2));   1.
Sign(IGCD(i_1,i_2)) = True;   2.
END IGCD;

Axiom 1 is complicated by the fact that zero can have either a plus (true) or minus (false) sign. We want Sign to be a mapping, however, (i.e., a *function* in the mathematical, not AXES, sense, cf. HAM76, Section 8.0) so we assume from the start that plus zero and minus zero are the same entity. In Axiom 8 we say zero has a plus sign, but Axiom 1 tells us that if a minus zero occurs, it is really the same integer as plus zero. Two integers are equal if they have the same absolute value and the same sign, unless their absolute values are both zero. In that case, they are equal regardless of their signs.

The rational numbers can be characterized, as in modern arithmetic theory, as ordered pairs of integers that have no common factors. Adopting this approach we get the following specification:

DATA TYPE: RATIONAL;
PRIMITIVE OPERATION:
boolean = ?Requal?($rational_1,rational_2$);   1.
boolean = ?R>?($rational_1,rational_2$);   2.
integer = Num(rational);   3.
integer = Denom(rational);   4.
rational = Rsum($rational_1,rational_2$);   5.
rational = Rprod($rational_1,rational_2$);   6.
boolean = Pos(rational);   7.
AXIOMS:
          WHERE r,r_1,r_2 ARE RATIONALS;
          WHERE Rzero IS A CONSTANT RATIONAL;
          WHERE Rone IS A CONSTANT RATIONAL;
?Iequal?(Denom(r),Izero) = False;   1.
IGCD(Abs(Num(r),Abs(Denom(r)))) = Ione;   2.
Rprod(r,Denom(r)) = Num(r);   3.
?Requal?(r_1,r_2) = ?Iequal?(Iprod(Num(r_1),Denom(r_2)),
                    Iprod(Denom(r_1),Num(r_2)));   4.
Num(Rsum(r_1,r_2)) = Iquot(Cross(r_1,r_2),IGCD(Abs(Cross(r_1,r_2)),
                    Abs(Dprod(r_1,r_2)))));   5.
Denom(Rsum(r_1,r_2)) = Iquot(Dprod(r_1,r_2), IGCD(Abs(Cross(r_1,r_2)),
                    Abs(Dprod(r_1,r_2)))));   6.

$NUM(Rprod(r_1,r_2)) = Iquot(Nprod(r_1,r_2), IGCD(Abs(Nprod(r_1,r_2)),$
$\qquad\qquad Abs(Dprod(r_1,r_2))));$ 7.

$Denom(Rprod(r_1,r_2)) = Iquot(Dprod(r_1,r_2), IGCD(Abs(Nprod(r_1,r_2)),$
$\qquad\qquad Abs(Dprod(r_1,r_2))));$ 8.

$Num(Rzero) = Izero;$ 9.

$Denom(Rzero) = Ione;$ 10.

$Pos(r) = And(Not(Equal(r,Rzero)),Same(Sign(Num(r)),$
$\qquad\qquad Sign(Denom(r))));$ 11.

$?R>?(r_1,r_2) = Pos(Rdiff(r_1,r_2));$ 12.

END RATIONAL;

OPERATION: $r_3 = Cross(r_1,r_2);$
WHERE r_1,r_2,r_3 ARE INTEGERS;
WHEREBY $r_3 = Isum(Iprod(Num(r_1),Denom(r_2)),$
$\qquad\qquad Iprod(Denom(r_1),Num(r_2)));$
END Cross;

OPERATION: $r_3 = Nprod(r_1,r_2);$
WHERE r_1,r_2,r_3 ARE INTEGERS;
WHEREBY $r_3 = Iprod(Num(r_1),Num(r_2));$
END Nprod;

OPERATION: $r_3 = Dprod(r_1,r_2);$
WHERE r_1,r_2,r_3 ARE INTEGERS;
WHEREBY $r_3 = Iprod(Denom(r_1),Denom(r_2));$
END Dprod;

The functions Num and Denom give the numerator and denominator of a "fraction" in the "lowest terms". The operations Iquot and GCD are used throughout the axioms to guarantee that sums and products of rationals are always expressed in such "lowest terms". The operations Cross, Nprod, and Dprod are just useful abbreviations that greatly simplify the definitions of addition and multiplication.

DERIVED OPERATION: $rational_2 = Ropp(rational_1);$
WHERE r IS A RATIONAL;
$Rsum(r,Ropp(r)) = Rzero;$
END Ropp;

OPERATION: $r_3 = Rdiff(r_1,r_2);$
WHERE r_1,r_2,r_3 ARE RATIONALS;
WHEREBY $r_3 = Rsum(r_1,Ropp(r_2));$
END Rdiff;

DERIVED OPERATION: $rational_2 = Rinv(rational_1);$
WHERE r,r_1,r_2 ARE RATIONALS;
$Rinv(Rzero) = REJECT;$
EITHER $Num(Rprod(r_1),Rinv(r_2)) = K_{REJECT}(^1r)$
OTHERWISE $Num(Rprod(r_1),Rinv(r_2)) = K_{Ione}(^2r);$
EITHER $Denom(Rprod(r,Rinv(r_2))) = K_{reject}(^1r)$
OTHERWISE $Denom(Rprod(r,Rinv(r_2))) = K_{Ione}(^2r);$
PARTITION OF r IS
$\qquad ^1r|r = 0,$
$\qquad ^2r|r = 0;$
END Rinv;

OPERATION: r_3 = Rdiv(r_1,r_2);
WHERE r_1,r_2,r_3 ARE RATIONALS;
WHEREBY r_3 = Rprod(r_1,Rinv(r_2));
ENDRdiv;

These are the usual opposite, difference, inverse, and division for the rational numbers.

The problem of specifying the real numbers presents a serious problem for the algebraic specification techniques introduced by Guttag and expanded here. We have already seen how Guttag's approach must be expanded to give an adequate specification of the natural numbers. A complete account of the the natural numbers requires an axiom equivalent to the axiom of induction and well-ordering principle and such an axiom cannot be formulated without a specification of properties or sets as abstract data types, or some equivalent modification of Guttag's approach. In the case of the reals we encounter a similar situation. The principal reason for introducing the real numbers in mathematics is to fill in the "holes", so to speak, in the set of rationals visualized as a "line". Speaking somewhat more formally, there exist sequences of rationals that seem for all the world as if they "ought" to converge, but for which there is no rational to which they do converge. The reals are introduced to provide limits for these otherwise non-convergent sequences. Speaking still more formally, we introduce the following definitions, where K is the set of rationals (actually, any ordered field) (LAN67, pp. 123–4):

A sequence $\{x_n\}$ in K is said to be a *Cauchy sequence* if given an element $\epsilon > 0$ in K, there exists a positive integer N such that for all integers m, n $\geq$ N we have

$$| x_n - X_m | \leq \epsilon |$$

An ordered field in which every Cauchy sequence converges is said to be *complete*.

The principal formal difference between the rationals and the reals is that, while the rationals constitute an ordered field, the reals constitute a complete ordered field. The obstacle we face in trying to axiomatize the reals in our modified Guttag framework is that there seems at this time to be no clearly satisfactory way to formulate this notion of completeness within that framework.

In retrospect, although we may eventually find a way to formulate completeness within our framework, it may be that our present inability to do so is really a virtue, rather than a defect of our framework. The real numbers have always been really a convenient myth with respect to computer-based systems. Although we often talk in terms of real numbers, the finite character of our machines (and of ourselves) always forces us, in the end, to "round-off" our real numbers and approximate them by rationals. The problems that arise as a result of this situation are widely known (e.g., see (ZEL73)). This suggests that our present inability to formulate completeness (and thus the reals) in the framework of type algebra may, in fact, be a strength of that framework, rather than a weakness, reflecting its correctness as a model of what computer-based systems are really capable of.

IV THIRD NORMAL FORM

The definitive paper on third normal form was first published by Ted Codd in 1972, and is included here for the convenience of the reader.

FURTHER NORMALIZATION OF THE DATA BASE RELATIONAL MODEL*

1 INTRODUCTION

1.1 Objectives of Normalization

In an earlier paper [1] the author proposed a relational model of data as a basis for protecting users of formatted data systems from the potentially disruptive changes in data representation caused by growth in the variety of data types in the data base and by statistical changes in the transaction or request traffic. Using this model, both the application programmer and the interactive user view the data base as a time-varying collection of normalized relations of assorted degrees. Definitions of these terms and of the basic relational operations of projection and natural join are given in the Appendix.

The possibility of further normalization of the data base relational model was mentioned in [1]. The objectives of this further normalization are:

1. To free the collection of relations from undesirable insertion, update and deletion dependencies
2. To reduce the need for restructuring the collection of relations as new types of data are introduced, and thus increase the life span of application programs
3. To make the relational model more informative to users

*E. F. Codd, "Further Normalization of the Data Base Relational Model," in *Data Base Systems*, Randall Rustin ed., © 1972, pp. 65–98. Reprinted by permission of Prentice-Hall, Inc., Englewood Cliffs, New Jersey.

4. To make the collection of relations neutral to the query statistics, where these statistics are liable to change as time goes by

The rules or conventions upon which the second and third normal forms are based can be interpreted as guidelines for the data base designer. They are also of concern in the design of general purpose, relational data base systems.

1.2 Functional Dependence

When setting up a relational data base, the designer is confronted with many possibilities in selecting the relational schema itself, let alone its representation in storage. A fundamental consideration is that of identifying which attributes are functionally dependent on others (see Appendix for definition of "attribute"). Attribute B of relation R is *functionally dependent* on attribute A of R if, at every instant of time, each value in A has no more than one value in B associated with it under R. In other words, the projection $\Pi_{A,B}(R)$ is at every instant of time a function from $\Pi_A(R)$ to $\Pi_B(R)$ (this function can be, and usually will be, time-varying). We write $R.A \rightarrow R.B$ if B is functionally dependent on A in R, and $R.A \nrightarrow R.B$ if B is not functionally dependent on A in R. If both $R.A \rightarrow R.B$ and $R.B \rightarrow R.A$ hold, then at all times R.A and R.B are in one-to-one correspondence, and we write $R.A \longleftrightarrow R.B$.

The definition given above can be extended to collections of attributes. Thus, if D,E are distinct collections of attributes of R, E is functionally dependent on D if, at every instant of time, each D-value has no more than one E-value associated with it under R. The notation $\rightarrow$, $\nrightarrow$ introduced for individual attributes is applied similarly to collections of attributes. A functional dependence of the form $R.D \rightarrow R.E$ where E is a subset of D will be called a *trivial dependence*.

As an example to illustrate functional dependence (both trivial and non-trivial), consider the relation

$$U(E\#, D\#, V\#)$$

where E# = employee serial number; D# = serial number of department to which employee belongs; and V# = serial number of division to which employee belongs.

Suppose that an employee never belongs to more than one department, that a department never belongs to more than one division, and an employee belongs to the division to which his department belongs. Then, we observe that

$$U.E\# \rightarrow U.D\# \tag{1}$$
$$U.D\# \rightarrow U.V\# \tag{2}$$
$$U.E\# \rightarrow U.V\# \tag{3}$$
$$U.(E\#, D\#) \rightarrow U.V\# \tag{4}$$

where (4) is a consequence of (3)
       (3) is a consequence of (1) and (2) together.

Suppose we are also given the following additional facts: normally, there are many employees belonging to a given department and many departments belonging to a given division. Then, we may observe that

$$U.D\# \nrightarrow U.E\#$$

and

$$U.V\# \nrightarrow U.D\#$$

An example of a trivial dependence is:

$$U.(E\#,D\#) \rightarrow U.E\#$$

since E# is included in (E#,D#).

1.3 Candidate Keys

Each *candidate key* K of relation R is, by definition, a combination of attributes (possibly a single attribute) of R with properties P_1 and P_2:

   P_1: *(Unique Identification)* In each tuple of R the value of K uniquely identifies that tuple; i.e., $R.K \rightarrow R.\Omega$ where Ω denotes the collection of all attributes of the specified relation.

   P_2: *(Non-redundancy)* No attribute in K can be discarded without destroying property P_1.

Obviously, there always exists at least one candidate key, because the combination of *all* attributes of R possesses property P_1. It is then a matter of looking for a subset with property P_2.

Two properties of candidate keys can be deduced from P_1 and P_2:

   P_3: Each attribute of R is functionally dependent on each candidate key of R.

   P_4: The collection of attributes of R in a candidate key K is a maximal functionally independent set (i.e., every proper subset of the attributes of K is functionally independent of every other proper subset of attributes of K, and no other attributes of R can be added without destroying this functional independence).

It is left to the reader to show that

1. P_1 is logically equivalent to P_3.
2. $P_1 \hat{\ } P_2$ implies P_4.
3. A maximal functionally independent set of attributes is not necessarily a candidate key.

For each relation R in a data base, one of its candidate keys is arbitrarily designated as the *primary key* of R. The usual operational distinction between the primary key and other candidate keys (if any) is that no tuple is allowed to have an undefined value for any of the primary key components, whereas any other components may have an undefined value. This restriction is imposed because of the vital role played by primary keys in search algorithms. The statement "B functionally depends on A in R" may be expressed in the alternative form "A identifies B in R", since in this case A satisfies condition P_1 for $\Pi_{A,B}(R)$.

2 THE SECOND NORMAL FORM

2.1 Introductory Example

The basic ideas underlying the second and third normal forms are simple, but they have many subtle ramifications. The author has found that numerous examples are needed to explain and motivate the precise definitions of these normal forms. Accordingly, we begin with the simplest case of a relation in first normal form but not in second (i.e., a relation of degree 3):

$$T(\underline{S\#,P\#},SC)$$

where   S# = supplier number
        P# = part number
        SC = supplier city

A triple (x,y,z) belongs to T if the supplier with serial number x supplies the part with serial number y, and supplier x has his base of operations in city z. A given part may be supplied by many suppliers, and a given supplier may supply many parts. Thus, the following time-independent conditions hold:

$$T.S\# \not\rightarrow T.P\#$$
$$T.P\# \not\rightarrow T.S\#$$

In other words, although the attributes S#, P# are related under T, they are functionally independent of one another under T. Now, each supplier has (in this example) only one base of operations and therefore only one city. Thus,

$$T.S\# \rightarrow T.SC$$

Intuitively, we can see that the only choice for the primary key of T is the attribute combination (S#,P#).

Looking at a sample instantaneous tabulation of T (Figure 1), the undesirable properties of the T schema become immediately apparent. We observe for example that, if supplier u relocates his base of operations from Poole to Tolpuddle, more than one tuple has to be updated. Worse still, the number of tuples to be updated can, and usually will, change with time. It just happens to be three tuples at this instant.

Now suppose supplier v ceases to supply parts 1 and 3, but may in the near future supply some other parts. Accordingly, we wish to retain the information that supplier v is located in Feistritz. Deletion of one of the two tuples does not cause the complete disappearance of the association of v with Feistritz, but deletion of both tuples does. This is an example of a deletion dependency which is a consequence of the relational schema itself. It is left to the reader to illustrate a corresponding insertion dependency using this example.

T(<u>S#, P#</u>, SC)

u   1   'POOLE'

u   2   'POOLE'

u   3   'POOLE'

v   1   'FEISTRITZ'

v   3   'FEISTRITZ'

Figure 1   A relation not in second normal form

$$T_1(\underline{S\#},\ P\#) \qquad T_2(\underline{S\#},\ SC)$$

u	1	u	'POOLE'
u	2	v	'FEISTRITZ'
u	3		
v	1		
v	3		

Figure 2   Relations in second normal form

Conversion of T to second normal form consists of replacing T by two of its projections:

$$T_1 = \Pi_{S\#,P\#}(T)$$
$$T_2 = \Pi_{S\#,SC}(T)$$

We thus obtain the relations tabulated in Figure 2.

Note how the undesirable insertion, update and deletion dependencies have disappeared. No essential information has been lost, since at any time the original relation T may be recovered by taking the natural join (see page 64) of T_1 and T_2 on S#.

2.2 More Probing Examples

Unfortunately, the simple example above does not illustrate all of the complexities which can arise. For expository purposes we now consider five possible relations in a data base concerning suppliers, parts, and projects. In a crude sense these relations represent five alternative possibilities—it is not intended that they coexist in a single data base. Note, however, that some contain more information (in the form of additional attributes) than others. In each case the primary key is underlined.

$R_1(\underline{S\#,P\#,J\#})$
$R_2(\underline{X\#},S\#,P\#,J\#)$
$R_3(\underline{X\#},S\#,P\#,J\#,Q)$
$R_4(\underline{X\#},S\#,P\#,J\#,Q,SC)$
$R_5(\underline{S\#,P\#,J\#},Q,SC)$

where   S# = supplier number
        P# = part number
        J# = project number
        X# = serial number
         Q = quantity supplied
        SC = supplier city

A triple (x,y,z) belongs to R_1 if supplier x supplies part y to project z. The same interpretation holds for $\Pi_{S\#,P\#,J\#}(R_i)$ for i = 2,3,4,5. In each of the five relations, a given combination of supplier and part may be associated with more than one project, a given combination of part and project may be associated with more than one supplier, and a given combination of project and supplier may be associated with more than one part. Thus, for all i

$$R_i \cdot (S\#,P\#) \twoheadrightarrow R_i \cdot (J\#)$$
$$R_i \cdot (P\#,J\#) \twoheadrightarrow R_i \cdot (S\#)$$
$$R_i \cdot (J\#,S\#) \twoheadrightarrow R_i \cdot (P\#)$$

In each of the relations that have the attribute Q, there is only one value of Q for a given value of the attribute combination (S#,P#,J#). Thus,

$$R_i \cdot (S\#,P\#,J\#) \rightarrow R_i \cdot Q \text{ for } i = 3,4,5$$

However, the value of Q is not uniquely determined by any proper subset of these attributes. Thus, for i = 3,4,5

$$R_i \cdot (S\#,P\#) \twoheadrightarrow R_i \cdot Q$$
$$R_i \cdot (P\#,J\#) \twoheadrightarrow R_i \cdot Q$$
$$R_i \cdot (J\#,S\#) \twoheadrightarrow R_i \cdot Q$$

In each of the relations that have the attribute SC, there is only one value of SC for a given value of S#. Thus, for i = 4,5

$$R_i \cdot S\# \rightarrow R_i \cdot SC$$

In three of the relations a serial number key X# has been introduced and selected as the primary key, even though there is already an attribute combination (S#,P#,J#) capable of acting as the primary key. Thus, for i = 2,3,4

$$R_i \cdot X\# \leftrightarrow R_i \cdot (S\#,P\#,J\#)$$

This is not at all unusual in practice (consider a purchase order number, for instance).

In what follows, we shall suppose that in the given relations there are no functional dependencies other than those itemized above together with those that can be formally deduced from them. Figure 3 summarizes the non-trivial dependencies (but not the non-dependencies) in a parent relation R from which R_1,R_2,R_3,R_4,R_5 can be derived by projection.

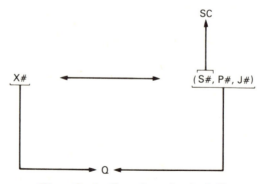

Figure 3   Attribute dependencies in R

In all five sample relations above, (S#,P#,J#) is a candidate key. In R_1 and R_5 it is the primary key also. X# is both a candidate key and the primary key in relations R_2, R_3, R_4.

2.3 Prime Attributes

We have observed that in a given relation there may be several distinct candidate keys (although distinct, they need not be disjoint) and, in this case, one is arbitrarily designated as the primary key. Let us call any attribute of R which participates in at least one candidate key of R a *prime attribute* of R. All other attributes of R are called *non-prime*. In sample relations R_1,R_2 all attributes are prime. In R_3 the only non-prime attribute is Q, while in R_4,R_5 both Q and SC are non-prime.

2.4 Full Functional Dependence

Suppose D,E are two distinct subcollections of the attributes of a relation R and

$$R.D \rightarrow R.E$$

If, in addition, E is not functionally dependent on any subset of D (other than D itself) then E is said to be *fully dependent* on D in R. Intuitively, E is functionally dependent on the whole of D, but not on any part of it. An example of full dependence is:

$$R_3 \cdot (S\#,P\#,J\#) \rightarrow R_3 \cdot Q$$

2.5 Definition of Second Normal Form

A relation R is in *second normal form* if it is in first normal form and every non-prime attribute of R is fully dependent on each candidate key of R. Although each prime attribute is dependent on each candidate key *of which it is a component*, it is possible for a prime attribute to be non-fully dependent on a candidate key of which it is not a component. Thus, this definition is changed in meaning if the term "non-prime" is dropped. An example which illustrates this distinction is R(A,B,C,D,E,F) where

$$R.(A,B,C) \longleftrightarrow R.(D,E) \rightarrow R.F$$
$$R.(A,B) \rightarrow R.D$$
$$R.E \rightarrow R.C$$

Prime attribute C is not fully dependent on candidate key (D,E); neither is D on (A,B,C). This definition rules out both kinds of undesirable dependence of the attribute SC in the example above.

1. The obvious functional dependence of SC in R_5 on a portion S# of the primary key
2. The less obvious functional dependence of SC in R_4 on a portion S# of a candidate key that is not the primary key

Thus, R_4 and R_5 are not in second normal form.

Two special cases of the definition are worth noting. Suppose R is in first normal form and one or both of the following conditions hold:

> C1:   R has no non-prime attribute;
>
> C2:   Every candidate key of R consists of just a single attribute.

Then, without further investigation, we can say that R is in second normal form. Observe that both R_1 and R_2 are in second normal form, because special case C1 applies. Relation R_3 is an example of a relation in second normal form, but not as a result of the special conditions C1,C2 above.

2.6   Optimal Second Normal Form

In section 1 of this chapter, a simple example of conversion from first to second normal form was discussed. The operation of projection, employed twice in that example, is adequate for the general case. However, to keep the user from being confused by unnecessary relation names (and to keep the system catalog from getting clogged by such names), projection should be applied sparingly when normalizing.

Consider the relation $T(S\#,P\#,SN,SC)$, where

$$S\# \to SN \text{ (supplier name)}$$
$$S\# \to SC \text{ (supplier city)}$$

If we apply projection sparingly in converting to second normal form, we obtain collection C_1, say:

$$\Pi_{S\#,P\#}(T), \Pi_{S\#,SN,SC}(T)$$

On the other hand, we could apply projection liberally and obtain collection C_2, say:

$$\Pi_{S\#,P\#}(T), \Pi_{S\#,SN}(T), \Pi_{S\#,SC}(T)$$

Both C_1 and C_2 are in second normal form and both retain all the essential information in the original relation T. However, collection C_1 contains the fewest possible relations, and is accordingly said to be in *optimal second normal form*. C_2 is in non-optimal second normal form.

3   THIRD NORMAL FORM

3.1   Transitive Dependence

Suppose that A,B,C are three distinct collections of attributes of a relation R (hence R is of degree 3 or more). Suppose that all three of the following time-independent conditions hold:

$$R.A \to R.B, \qquad\qquad R.B \nrightarrow R.A,$$

$$R.B \to R.C$$

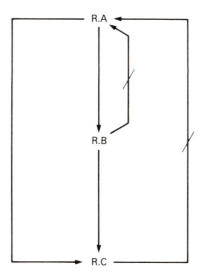

Figure 4   Transitive dependence of C on A under R

From this we may conclude that two other conditions must hold:

$$R.A \rightarrow R.C \qquad R.C \nrightarrow R.A$$

and we may represent the entire set of conditions on A,B,C as shown in Figure 4. Note that R.C $\rightarrow$ R.B is neither prohibited nor required.

In such a case we say that C is *transitively dependent* on A under R. In the special case where R.C $\rightarrow$ R.B also, both B and C are transitively dependent on A under R.

To illustrate transitive dependence, consider a relation W concerning employees and their departments:

$$W(E\#,JC,D\#,M\#,CT)$$

where	E# = employee serial number
	JC = employee jobcode
	D# = department number of employee
	M# = serial number of department manager
	CT = contract type (government or non-government)

Suppose that each employee is given only one jobcode and is assigned to only one department. Each department has its own manager and is involved in work on either government or non-government contracts, not both. The non-trivial functional dependencies in W are as shown in Figure 5 (the non-dependencies are implied). If M# were not present, the only transitive dependence would be that of CT on E#. With M# present, there are two additional transitive dependencies: both D# and M# are transitively dependent on E#. Note, however, that CT is not transitively dependent on either D# or M#.

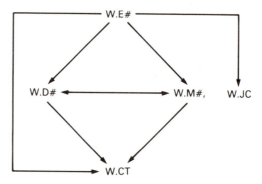

Figure 5 Example of several transitive dependencies

Looking at a sample instantaneous tabulation of W (Figure 6) the undesirble properties of the W schema become immediately apparent. We observe, for example, that, if the manager of department y should change, more than one tuple has to be updated. The actual number of tuples to be updated can, and usually will, change with time. A similar remark applies if department x is switched from government work (contract type g) to non-government work (contract type n).

Deletion of the tuple for an employee has two possible consequences: deletion of the corresponding department information if his tuple is the sole one remaining just prior to deletion, and non-deletion of the department information otherwise. If the data base system does not permit any primary key to have an undefined value, then D# and CT information for a new department cannot be established in relation W before people are assigned to that department. If, on the other hand, the primary key E# could have an undefined value, and if a tuple were introduced with such a value for E# together with defined values for D# (a new department) and CT, then insertion of E# and JC values for the first employee in that department involves no new tuple, whereas each subsequent assignment of an employee to that department does require a new tuple to be inserted.

Conversion of W to third normal form consists of replacing W by two of its projections:

$$W_1 = \Pi_{E\#,JC,D\#}(W)$$
$$W_2 = \Pi_{D\#,M\#,CT}(W)$$

We thus obtain the relations tabulated in Figure 7. Note how the undesirable insertion update and deletion dependencies have disappeared with the removal of the transitive

W(E#,	JC,	D#,	H#,	CT)
1	a	x	11	g
2	c	x	11	g
3	a	y	12	n
4	b	x	11	g
5	b	y	12	n
6	c	y	12	n
7	a	z	13	n
8	c	z	13	n

Figure 6 A relation not in third normal form

```
W₁(E#,  JC,  D#)  W₂(D#,  M#,  CT)
   1     a    x       x     11    g
   2     c    x       y     12    n
   3     a    y       z     13    n
   4     b    x
   5     b    y
   6     c    y
   7     a    z
   8     c    z
```

Figure 7   Relations in third normal form

dependencies. No essential information has been lost, since at any time the original relation W may be recovered by taking the natural join of W_1 and W_2 on D#.

3.2 Keybreaking Transitive Dependence

It is not always possible to remove all transitive dependencies without breaking a key or losing information. This is illustrated by a relation R(A,B,C) in which

$$R.(A,B) \rightarrow R.C, \ R.C. \nrightarrow R.(A,B)$$
$$R.C \rightarrow R.B$$

Thus, B is transitively dependent on the primary key (A,B).

3.3 Definition of Third Normal Form

A relation R is in *third normal form* if it is in second normal form and every non-prime attribute of R is non-transitively dependent on each candidate key of R. Relations T_1, T_2, R_1, R_2, R_3 of section 2.1 are in third normal form. Relations R_4, R_5 are not in third normal form, because they are not even in second. Relation U of section 1.2 is in second normal form, but not in third, because of the transitive dependence of V# on E#.

Any relation R in third normal form has the following property:

P_5: Every non-prime attribute of R is both fully dependent and non-transitively dependent on each candidate key of R.

This property is an immediate consequence of the definition given above. Note that the definition has been so formulated that it does not prohibit transitive dependence of a prime attribute on a candidate key of R, as in section 3.2.

3.4 Optimal Third Normal Form

Suppose C_2 is a collection of relations in optimal second normal form and projection is applied to convert to third normal form. The resulting collection of relations C_3 is in optimal third normal form relative to C_2 if both of the following conditions hold:

1. C_3 must contain the fewest possible relations (as in the case of the optimal second normal form) each in third normal form.

2. Each relation in C_3 must not have any pair of attributes such that one member of the pair is strictly transitively dependent on the other in some relation of C_2 (this condition forces attributes

which are "remotely related" to be separated from one another in the normalized collection of relations).

(*Note:* Attribute C is *strictly transitively dependent* on attribute A under R if there is an attribute B such that

$$R.A \rightarrow R.B \qquad R.B \nrightarrow R.A$$
$$R.B \rightarrow R.C \qquad R.C \nrightarrow R.B$$

This is a special case of transitive dependence.)

Application of these conditions is illustrated in Figure 8a, 8b using the relation W of section 3.1. Figure 8a treats the normalization of W_o (obtained from W by dropping manager number M#). Figure 8b treats the normalization of W itself, and shows how one-to-one correspondences are forced to occur between candidate keys of the projections (instead of between non-prime attributes). Note also the non-uniqueness of the optimal third normal form in Figure 8b.

4 ADMISSIBLE STATES

When converting a time-varying data base from first normal form to second, or from second to third, certain new insertion and deletion possibilities are introduced. Let us look at the example in section 2.1 again.

In first normal form the data base B_1 consists of the single time-varying relation denoted by the schema

$$T(\underline{S\#,P\#},SC)$$

In second normal form the corresponding data base B_2 consists of two relations denoted by the schema

$$T_1(\underline{S\#,P\#}) \qquad T_2(\underline{S\#},SC)$$

where, for any time

1. $T_1 = \Pi_{S\#,P\#}(T)$
2. $T_2 = \Pi_{S\#,SC}(T)$

As usual, the primary keys are underlined.

A data base state (i.e., instantaneous snapshot) is *admissible* relative to a given schema if

1. Each relation named in the schema has tuples whose components belong to the specified domains.

2. All tuples of a relation named in the schema are distinct.

3. No tuple has an undefined value for its primary key (and thus no *component* of the primary key may have an undefined value).

The last condition makes an operational distinction between that candidate key selected to act as the primary key of a relation and all other candidate keys of that relation.

Given any admissible state for B_1, we can produce a corresponding admissible state for B_2 by applying the operation of projection as in the example above. The original B_1 state can be recovered by taking the natural join (see Appendix for definition) of T_1 and T_2 on S#.

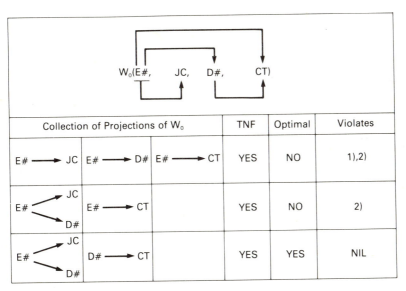

Collection of Projections of W_0			TNF	Optimal	Violates
E# ⟶ JC	E# ⟶ D#	E# ⟶ CT	YES	NO	1),2)
E# ⟨ JC / D#	E# ⟶ CT		YES	NO	2)
E# ⟨ JC / D#	D# ⟶ CT		YES	YES	NIL

Figure 8a   Conversion of W_0 to third normal form

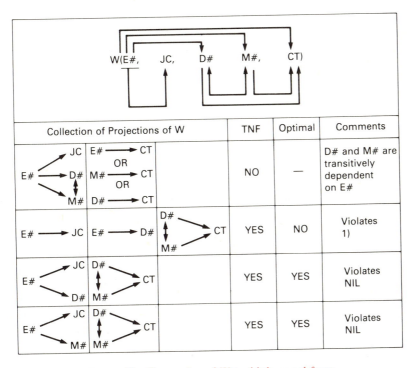

Collection of Projections of W			TNF	Optimal	Comments
E# → JC, D#, M#	E# ⟶ CT OR M# ⟶ CT OR D# ⟶ CT		NO	—	D# and M# are transitively dependent on E#
E# ⟶ JC	E# ⟶ D#	D# ⇕ M# → CT	YES	NO	Violates 1)
E# ⟨ JC / D#	D# ⇕ M# → CT		YES	YES	Violates NIL
E# ⟨ JC / M#	D# → M# ⇕ → CT		YES	YES	Violates NIL

Figure 8b   Conversion of W to third normal form

We now observe that the schema for B_2 has more admissible states than that for B_1. Thus, in B_2 it is perfectly admissible to have a S# value appearing in T_2 which does not appear at all in T_1, or vice versa, as in the B_2-state exhibited in Figure 9.

```
T₁(S#, P#)              T₂(S#, SC)
  u    1           u    'POOLE'
  u    2           v    'FEISTRITZ'
  v    1           w    'SWANAGE'
  z    3
```

Figure 9   An admissible state for B_2

If we now take the natural join of T_1 and T_2 on S#, we obtain the state (or tabulation) of T exhibited in Figure 10. Although this state is admissible for B_1, essential information has been lost.

```
T (S#, P#, SC)
  u   1   'POOLE'
  u   2   'POOLE'
  v   1   'FEISTRITZ'
```

Figure 10   The natural join of relations in Figure 9

An obvious property of the class of admissible states for a given data base schema is that by means of the operations of tuple insertion and tuple deletion all the admissible states are reachable from any given admissible state. Clearly, the schema for B_2 permits insertions and deletions not permitted by the schema for B_1. It is accordingly reasonable to say that these schemata are not *insertion-deletion equivalent*.

5   QUERY EQUIVALENCE

A useful notion of *query equivalence* of data base states can be based on the algebraic view of queries. In this view retrieval of data is treated as the formation of a new relation from the data base relations by some operation of a relational algebra (see [2]).

If θ is a relational algebra, B is a collection of relations and R is a relation which is derivable from B using operations of the algebra θ only, then we say (as in [1]) that R is θ-*derivable* from B. Suppose now that we have two data bases A,B which at time t are in states A_t, B_t respectively. We say that the data base states A_t, B_t are *query-equivalent* providing they are each θ-derivable from the other and θ is a relationally complete algebra (see [2]). The reasonableness of this definition stems from the fact that, if each of the data-base states A_t, B_t is θ-derivable from the other, then any relation R which is θ-derivable from one must be θ-derivable from the other.

Figure 11 summarizes the observations made in section 4 on admissible states. It also illustrates the fact that the set S of all admissible states for a data base cast in first normal form is query-equivalent to a subset T_1 of all admissible states when this data base is cast in second normal form. Similarly, the set $T_1 \mu T_2$ of all admissible states for this data base cast in second normal form is query-equivalent to a subset U_1 of all admissible states when the same data base is cast in third normal form.

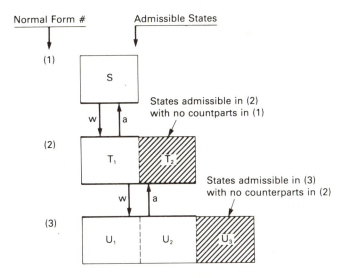

Normal Form #   Admissible States

(1)

S

States admissible in (2)
with no countparts in (1)

w   a

(2)

T_1 T_2

States admissible in (3)
with no counterparts in (2)

w   a

(3)

U_1 U_2 U_3

Figure 11   Admissible states for a data base cast in normal forms # 1, 2, 3

6 GROWTH AND RESTRUCTURING

One of the principal reasons for making application programs interact with an abstract collection of relations instead of their storage representations is to keep these programs from being logically impaired when the storage representations change. Now we wish to consider (but only briefly) what happens to the application programs when the collection of relations is itself changed to conform to a new schema. Simple additions of new data base domains and new relations have no effect. Outright removal of a relation R obviously cripples those programs that previously made use of R. Replacement of a relation by *one* of its projections will cripple those programs that previously made use of the attributes now dropped.

The really interesting type of change is replacement of a relation R by two or more of its projections such that R may be recovered by taking the natural join of these projections. We discussed this type of change in sections 2 and 3 in the context of conversion to second and third normal forms respectively. In the present context of data base growth we call this phenomenon *attribute migration*.

Some of the reasons why attribute migration may accompany data base growth are as follows:

1. Through continued acquisition of additional attributes a relation has become too cumbersome in size and fuzzy in meaning.

2. New controls (e.g., ownership of data, access authorization, recovery, etc.) are being introduced.

3. There has been a change in that part of the real world which the data base reflects or models.

To illustrate the effect of attribute migration on application programs, consider the splitting of data base relation U(E#,JC,D#,M#,CT) into the two projections:

$$U1 = II_{E\#,JC,D\#}(U)$$
$$U2 = II_{D\#,M\#,CT}(U)$$

(see section 3.1 for the interpretation of U and its attributes).

We first examine a query and then an insertion. Each is expressed in the data base sublanguage ALPHA [3].

> Find the contract type (CT) for the employee whose serial number (E#) is 1588. Place result in workspace W.

<u>GET</u>   W   U.CT:(U.E# = 1588)

When U is replaced by the two projections U1, U2, queries on U must undergo a transformation to make them work as before. If the data base system were supplied with a suitable set of substitutions it could make this transformation automatically. We do not propose to go into the details here, but merely state that the resulting transformed query would be:

<u>GET</u>   W   U2.CT: 3U1((U1.D# = U2.D#)ˆ(U1.E# = 1588))

The real difficulty arises with insertion and deletion.

> Insert from workspace W into the data base relation U a tuple for a new employee with serial number 1492 and contract type non-government (n). Values for his jobcode, department number, and manager number are not yet available.

<u>PUT</u>   W   U

When data base relation U is replaced by U1, U2 and we attempt to transform this insertion to make it work on these projections, we find that the insertion of two new tuples is necessary: one into U1, and one into U2. The insertion into U1 presents no problem, because we have a value (1492) for its primary key component (E#). In the case of U2, however, we do not have a value for its primary key component (D#). To cope with this difficulty, the system could temporarily insert a fictitious (but defined) value to represent a department (as yet undetermined) which is assigned to non-government work. Unfortunately, when the total data base is considered together with all the possible partially defined associations which may have to be temporarily remembered, the system may require a very large pool of fictitious values to call upon.

We have seen that attribute migration can logically impair an application program. Further, it may be feasible to systematically re-interpret the data base requests made by a program P so as to make P work correctly again. This problem is simpler for those programs that avoid insertion and deletion on the relations affected by attribute migration. Whether or not this special case holds, the re-interpretation is likely to cause significant system overhead. Avoidance of attribute migration is accordingly desirable. It is this author's thesis that, by casting the data base in third normal form at the earliest possible time and by keeping it that way, an installation will reduce the incidence of attribute migration to a minimum, and consequently have less trouble keeping its application programs in a viable state.

7 CONCLUSION

In section 1 we introduced the notion of functional dependence within a relation—a notion that is fundamental in formatted data base design. Using this notion, two new normal forms were defined.

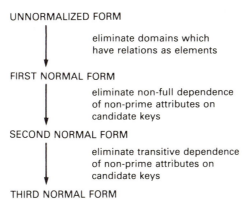

UNNORMALIZED FORM

　　　　　　eliminate domains which
　　　　　　have relations as elements

FIRST NORMAL FORM

　　　　　　eliminate non-full dependence
　　　　　　of non-prime attributes on
　　　　　　candidate keys

SECOND NORMAL FORM

　　　　　　eliminate transitive dependence
　　　　　　of non-prime attributes on
　　　　　　candidate keys

THIRD NORMAL FORM

Figure 12　　Three normal forms

Figure 12 summarizes the relationship between the three normal forms introduced by this author. Notice that as a collection of relations is translated from first normal form to second, and then to third, the conditions applied are progressively more stringent.

In the past, design of records (computerized or not) for commercial, industrial and government institutions has been oriented in an ad hoc way to the needs of particular applications. For the large integrated data bases of the future, application-independent guidelines for logical record design are sorely needed. This paper is intended to provide such guidelines.

It is also conjectured that physical records in optimal third normal form will prove to be highly economical in space consumed. In some cases a further saving in space can be obtained by factoring (see [2]) relations in third normal form.

Although the three normal forms are query-equivalent in the sense that the set of queries answerable by a collection C in first normal form is transformable into queries yielding the same information from the second and third normal forms of C, there is a difference in information content of the three forms. The second is more informative than the first, and the third is more informative than the second. The increased information lies in the data description (rather than in the data described) as a consequence of the underlying conventions. Like the declarations of redundancies and combinational possibilities within the relational model (see [1]), the normal forms described above tend to capture some aspects of the semantics (minor, of course). Thus, a relational model in second normal form, and more especially, one in third normal form is likely to be more readily understood by people who are not everyday users of the data. It is also likely to be better tuned to the authorization requirements of installations.

Compared with first normal form, the second and third do carry with them the penalty of extra names. In the many data bases that have relations of high degree, this name penalty will not be nearly as severe as that associated with a complete conversion to nested binary relations.

Some queries will also need to employ more join terms for cross-referencing between relations than might otherwise be the case. This potential burden on the user can be eased by user-declared (and possibly pooled) cross-referencing for heavily used types of queries.

ACKNOWLEDGMENTS   The author is indebted to Claude Delobel of the Conservatoire National des Arts et Métiers, Paris, for indicating an inadequacy in the treatment of one-to-one correspondences in an early draft of this paper. Working from this draft, C. J. Date, I. J. Heath and P. Hopewell of the IBM Development Laboratory in Hursley, England have developed some theoretical and practical applications of the third normal form, which will be published soon [4,5]. Their interest in and enthusiasm for the third normal form encouraged the author to produce a more detailed paper than the original version. Thanks are also due to F. P. Palermo and J. J. Rissanen of IBM Research, San Jose, for suggesting changes which improved the clarity.

REFERENCES

1. E. F. Codd, "A Relational Model of Data for Large Shared Data Banks," *CACM 13, 6,* June 1970, 377–387.

2. _____, "Relational Completeness of Data Base Sublanguages," *this volume.*

3. _____, "A Data Base Sublanguage Founded on the Relational Calculus," *IBM Research Report RJ893*, July 1971.

4. I. J. Heath, "Unacceptable File Operations in a Relational Data Base," Proc. 1971 ACM-SIGFIDET Workshop on Data Description, Access and Control, to be available from ACM HQ, 1972.

5. C. J. Date, and P. Hopewell, "File Definition and Logical Data Independence," Proc. 1971 ACM-SIGFIDET Workshop on Data Description, Access and Control, to be available from ACM HQ, 1972.

APPENDIX

A1 Basic Definitions

Given sets $D_1, D_2, \ldots, D_n$ (not necessarily distinct), R is a *relation* on these n sets if it is a set of elements of the form $(d_1, d_2, \ldots, d_n)$ where $d_j \epsilon D_j$ for each $j = 1, 2, \ldots, n$. More concisely, R is a subset of the Cartesian product $D_1 x D_2 x \ldots x D_n$. We refer to D_j as the jth *domain* of R. The elements of a relation of degree n are called *n-tuples* or *tuples*. A relation is in *first normal form* if it has the property that none of its domains has elements which are themselves sets. An *unnormalized relation* is one which is not in first normal form.

A data base B is a finite collection of time-varying relations defined on a finite collection of domains, say $D_1, D_2, \ldots, D_p$. Suppose relation R is one of the relations in B, and is of degree n. To declare R to a data base system we need to cite n of the p data base domains as those on which R is defined.

Now, not all these n cited domains need be distinct. Instead of using an ordering to distinguish these n citations from one another (as is common in mathematics), we use a distinct name for each citation and call this the *attribute name* for that particular use of a data base domain. Each distinct use (or citation) of a data base domain in defining R is accordingly called an *attribute* of R. For example, a relation R of degree 3 might have attributes (A_1, A_2, A_3) while the corresponding data base domains are (D_5, D_7, D_5). Attribute names provide an effective means of protecting the user from having to know domain positions.

A2 Projection

Suppose r is a tuple of relation R and A is an attribute of R. We adopt the notation r.A to designate the A-component of r. Now suppose A is instead a list $(A_1, A_2, \ldots, A_k)$ of attributes of R. We extend the notation r.A so that, in this case:

$$r.A = (r.A_1, R.A_2, \ldots, r.A_k)$$

When the list A is empty, r.A = r.

Let $C = (C_1, C_2, \ldots, C_n)$ be a list of all the attributes of R. Let A be a sublist (length k) of C and r a tuple of R. Then, we adopt the notation $r.\bar{A}$ to designate the (n-k)-tuple r.B where B is the complementary list of attributes obtained by deleting from C those listed in A.

The *projection* of R on the attribute list A is defined by

$$\Pi_A(R) = (r.A: r\epsilon R)$$

A more informal definition is given in [1].

A3 Natural Join

Suppose R,S are two relations and

$$A = (A_1, \ldots, A_k) \quad B = (B_1, \ldots, B_k)$$

are equal-length lists of the attributes of R,S respectively. Suppose that for $i = 1, 2, \ldots, k$ attributes A_i, B_i are comparable: that is, for every $r\epsilon R$, $s\epsilon S$

$$r.A_i = s.B_i$$

is either true or false (not undefined). We say that

$$r.A = s.B$$

if $(r.A_1 = s.B_1)\hat{} \ldots \hat{}(r.A_k = s.B_k)$

Then, the *natural join* of R on A with S on B is defined by:

$$R*S = \{(r, s.\bar{B}): r\epsilon R \hat{} \ s\epsilon S \hat{} \ (r.A = s.B)\}$$

This definition is the same as that given in [1] except that there is no requirement that

$$\Pi_A(R) = \Pi_B(S)$$

for relations R,S to be joinable. This condition was imposed in [1] solely for the purposes of treating redundancy and consistency.

INDEX

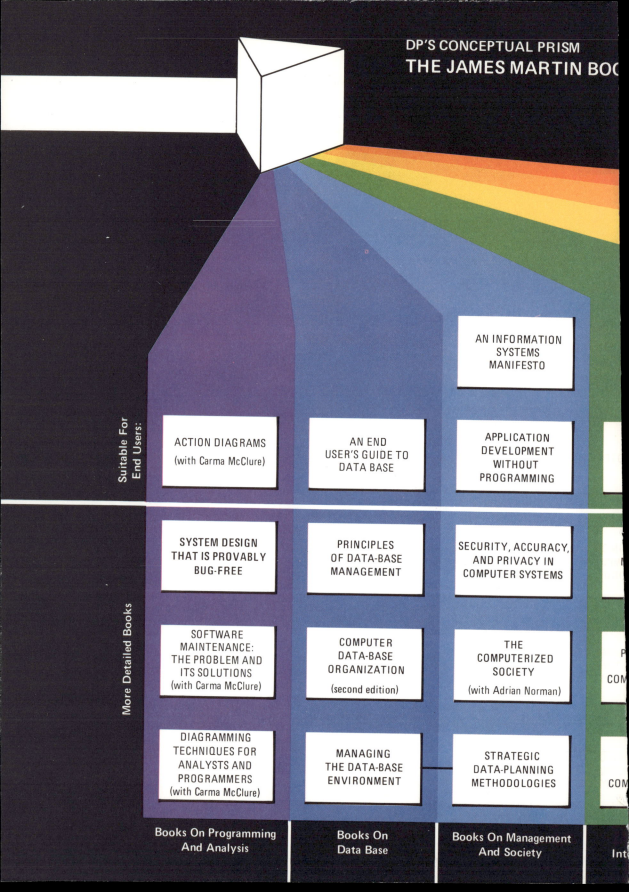

DP'S CONCEPTUAL PRISM
THE JAMES MARTIN BOO

Suitable For End Users:

		AN INFORMATION SYSTEMS MANIFESTO
ACTION DIAGRAMS (with Carma McClure)	AN END USER'S GUIDE TO DATA BASE	APPLICATION DEVELOPMENT WITHOUT PROGRAMMING

More Detailed Books

SYSTEM DESIGN THAT IS PROVABLY BUG-FREE	PRINCIPLES OF DATA-BASE MANAGEMENT	SECURITY, ACCURACY, AND PRIVACY IN COMPUTER SYSTEMS
SOFTWARE MAINTENANCE: THE PROBLEM AND ITS SOLUTIONS (with Carma McClure)	COMPUTER DATA-BASE ORGANIZATION (second edition)	THE COMPUTERIZED SOCIETY (with Adrian Norman)
DIAGRAMMING TECHNIQUES FOR ANALYSTS AND PROGRAMMERS (with Carma McClure)	MANAGING THE DATA-BASE ENVIRONMENT	STRATEGIC DATA-PLANNING METHODOLOGIES

Books On Programming And Analysis

Books On Data Base

Books On Management And Society